1000
7N

On Human
Communication

STUDIES IN COMMUNICATION

Signification and Significance :
A Study of the Relations of Signs and Values
By Charles Morris

Thought and Language
By L. S. Vygotsky

Word and Object
By Willard Van Orman Quine

On Human Communication : A Review, a Survey, and a Criticism
By Colin Cherry

On Human
Communication

A REVIEW, A SURVEY, AND A CRITICISM

Second Edition

Colin Cherry

Henry Mark Pease Professor of Telecommunication,
Imperial College, University of London

THE M.I.T. PRESS

Massachusetts Institute of Technology

Cambridge, Massachusetts, and London, England

Library of Congress Catalog Card Number: 56–9820

To my dog, Pym

Dedication of the Second Edition:

To all those human beings who have enquired so kindly after my dog Pym

Preface to the First Edition

I have written this book at the invitation of the editors of the series "Studies in Communication," to serve as an introduction to that series of volumes which will appear during the next few years. It is intended as a review, a survey, and a criticism—nothing more.

In this work I have attempted to unite the material of numerous lectures which I have had the pleasure of giving in Britain, America, and several European countries during the past five years. This experience has convinced me of the widespread interest today in the whole field of "human communication"—an interest which has been fertilized greatly (and often mistakenly) by the development of "communication theory" and, at the same time, has shown me the difficulties of many newcomers to the field, who find themselves baffled by the speciality and scattered nature of the literature. It is my opinion that there is need for a simple book, such as this, to introduce these apprentices to their masters.

The book is, then, not for experts. It consists of a series of simple essays, written in the simplest language that I am able to command. I am aware that in places it is naive. But if it gives some notion of the relations between the diverse studies of communication, of the causes and the growth of this modern interest, together with some idea of the unification which exists (and even more important, the differences of opinion, controversies, and lack of unification), then this book will have achieved its object.

COLIN CHERRY

"Tillingbrook," Rectory Lane, Shere, Surrey, England
October, 1956

I am indebted to Professor Sir Ronald A. Fisher, Cambridge, and to Messrs. Oliver & Boyd, Ltd., Edinburgh, for permission to reprint the sentence: "inductive inference is the only process . . . by which new knowledge comes into the world," from their book *Design of Experiments*.

Preface to the Second Edition

Surely it must always be a pleasure for an author to write the Preface to the second edition of his book? The fate of this new issue may be quite unknown, but its appearance at least gives evidence that the first edition has sold out. Whether that sale has in any way whatever benefited the human race, apart from the publisher and author, is another matter, of course, but one which may be judged to some extent by the author, from the abuse or praise received. I can only say that the English speaking people of the race seem to have suffered no direct harm, and appearance of German and Japanese translations suggests that these people too have been willing to take the risk.

In preparation of the current volume, I have examined the original carefully and have decided not to withdraw from anything said there, but merely to add some comments, to update some figures, and to extend the bibliography. The latter task has presented a great problem, since, during the past 10 years, the development of world communication techniques has proceeded at a rate commonly called "explosive." In that decade, words like *automation, satellites, space, computer* have come into everyday chatter and newspaper talk; they are used by the innocent as the jargon of a cult. This explosive growth of the "technology of information" has created thousands of publications in the journals and hundreds of books. Since detailed reference is impossible, I have decided to restrict the new Bibliography to useful sources of reference, a few of the more significant technical and historical works, and a few items which were omitted from the first edition.

COLIN CHERRY

"Tillingbrook," Rectory Lane, Shere, Surrey, England
June, 1965

Acknowledgments

It is with a sense of deepest gratitude that I acknowledge the assistance which has been afforded me so kindly by numerous friends on both shores of the Atlantic.   Particularly would I mention Professor Roman Jakobson and Professor A. S. C. Ross for discussion of linguistic matters, Professor Yehoshua Bar-Hillel of Jerusalem for help with semantic and philosophic aspects, Professor R. C. Oldfield and my colleague Dennis Gabor for endless debate.

Financial worry was removed at commencement by the great generosity of the Center for International Studies (M.I.T.) which has covered the whole of the expenses of preparation, and enabled me to travel extensively in order to visit and discuss personally with many experts, whose work I have attempted to survey.

It is only this direct acquaintance, and personal friendship, with those principally active in the field that has made my work possible.

C. C.

Contents

xi

Communication and Organization— an Essay

> *And the Lord said, "Behold the people is one, and they have all one language; and this they begin to do: and now nothing will be restrained from them, which they have imagined to do. Go to, let us go down and there confound their language, that they may not understand one another's speech." So the Lord scattered them abroad from thence upon the face of all the earth: and they left off to build the city. Therefore is the name of it called Babel....*
>
> *Genesis,* Ch. 11.

Leibnitz, it has sometime been said, was the last man to know everything. Though this is most certainly a gross exaggeration, it is an epigram with considerable point. For it is true that up to the last years of the eighteenth century our greatest mentors were able not only to compass the whole science of their day, perhaps together with mastery of several languages, but to absorb a broad culture as well. But as the fruits of scientific labor have increasingly been applied to our material betterment, fields of specialized interest have come to be cultivated and the activities of an ever-increasing body of scientific workers have diverged. Today we are most of us content to carry out an intense cultivation of our own little scientific gardens (to continue the metaphor), deriving occasional pleasure from a chat with our neighbors over the fence, while with them we discuss, criticize, and exhibit our produce.

1

Too many of us today are scientifically lonely; we tire of talking continually to ourselves, and seek companionship. We attend Symposia and Congresses, perhaps too many! From time to time since the growth of specialization, broad movements have arisen in reaction to this trend, seeking unity and attempting integration. Some have lived and prospered; others were stillborn.

There are signs of such a movement today; an awareness of a certain unity of a group of studies is growing, originally diverse and disconnected, but all related to our *communicative* activities. The movement is rapidly becoming "popular," so great is the desire for unification, and this popularity carries with it a certain danger. By all means let us encourage any tendency toward unity, any attempts to make common ground, but we must continually be critical. The concept of "communication" certainly arises in a number of disciplines; in sociology, linguistics, psychology, economics; in physiology of the nervous system, in the theory of signs, in communication engineering. Awareness of the universal nature of "communication" has existed for a very long time, in a somewhat vague and empirical way, but recently the mathematical developments which come under the heading of the "Theory of Communication" have brought matters to a head, and many there are who regard this work as a panacea. True, it has very considerable relevance to these different disciplines, which we shall try to explain in these pages; but it is not a cure-all. Perhaps, since we shall be discussing this relevance, we had better state a point of view right at the start, and write it in italics: *At the time of writing, the various aspects of communication, as they are studied under the different disciplines, by no means form a unified study; there is a certain common ground which shows promise of fertility, nothing more.* In this little book, as our subtitle claims, we shall attempt a review, a survey, and a criticism of the study as it is being developed. The level will necessarily be elementary. There is a wide sea of literature which we shall try to chart for the novice, and there are a few classic islands where we shall land and explore in some detail. And in this little ship, our book, we shall be taking no experts amongst the passengers. It is a cruise for novices only, but they will be introduced to the professional crew.

1. THE SCHEME OF THIS BOOK

It should be emphasized at the outset that this book is in no sense an exposition of the mathematical theory of communication, though we shall be making some reference to this subject, and Chapter 5 attempts a survey of its principal concepts and theorems. This book is intended to take its place as one of a series of texts on communication, to be prepared by different authors, the others of the series being more specific and detailed studies.* This one is introductory—no more.

The various chapters are written, so far as possible, as self-contained essays, and the chapter headings should give some guide. None of the chapters is written for the experts. Thus, linguists are asked to be lenient in reading Chapter 3, and psychologists may regard Chapter 7 as superficial to the extreme. Again, if any mathematicians or logicians come to Chapters 5 and 6—pass on, they are not for you! No; the book is written for that curious person, the "general reader." But you experts, if you read my little volume, please do comment, criticize, and correct. For that is the only way to progress.

One of the great difficulties of discussing a subject that lies in the borderland of a number of well-established fields of study is the choice of language and definitions. It may be true that concepts can be validly relevant in different fields, yet their expression in forms acceptable to students in these various specialities may not prove easy. In each field there may already be sets of definitions, and students may be loth to change, modify, or extend their customary definitions, framed for their specific purposes, to suit the interest of others. But a certain compromise is necessary if we are to find a common language of discussion; so in the Appendix a list of terms is given, together with explanations which in some cases may be dignified by the name of definition. This, it is hoped, forms a self-consistent terminology, and though the definitions given have no official backing, some have a degree of common usage among students of communication theory. The various chapters do not pretend to be expositions or even summaries (with the doubtful exception of Chapter 5) of different sciences—linguistics, phonetics, communication theory, semantics, psychology. Had this been the intention, the author would have been guilty of supreme conceit. Rather we are seeking to extract from these various sciences the common related concepts and ideas concerning communication, in such a way as to show the historical development and growth of this subject. At the same time we hope to stress in particular some of those snares and pitfalls which, though well known to the specialist, catch the unwary who chance to stray in from other fields.

2. WHAT IS "COMMUNICATION"?

Communication is essentially a social affair. Man has evolved a host of different systems of communication which render his social life possible— social life not in the sense of living in packs for hunting or for making war,

* For a complete list of the Series "Studies in Communication," published by The M.I.T. Press, see page facing title page.

but in a sense unknown to animals.   Most prominent among all these systems of communication is, of course, human speech and language. Human language is not to be equated with the sign systems of animals, for man is not restricted to calling his young, or suggesting mating, or shouting cries of danger; he can with his remarkable faculties of speech give utterance to almost any thought.   Like animals, we too have our inborn instinctive cries of alarm, pain, et cetera: we say *Oh!*, *Ah!*; we have smiles, groans, and tears; we blush, shiver, yawn, and frown.*   A hen can set her chicks scurrying up to her, by clucking—communication established by a releaser mechanism—*but human language is vastly more than a complicated system of clucking.*

The development of language reflects back upon thought; for with language thoughts may become organized, new thoughts evolved.   Self-awareness and the sense of social responsibility have arisen as a result of organized thoughts.   Systems of ethics and law have been built up.   Man has become self-conscious, responsible, a social creature.

Inasmuch as the words we use disclose the true nature of things, as truth is to each one of us, the various words relating to personal communication are most revealing.†   The very word "communicate" means "share," and inasmuch as you and I are communicating at this moment, we are one. Not so much a union as a unity.   Inasmuch as we agree, we say that we *are of one mind*, or, again, that we understand *one another*.   This one another is the unity.   A group of people, a society, a culture, I would define as "people in communication."   They may be thought of as "sharing rules" of language, custom, of habit; but who wrote these rules?   These have have evolved out of those people themselves—rules of conformity.   Inasmuch as that conformity is the greater or the less, so is the unity.   The degree of communication, the sharing, the conformity, is a measure of one-mindedness.   After all, what we share, we can not each have as our own possession, and no single person in this world has ever been born and bred in utter isolation.   "No man is an island, entire of itself."‡

Speech and writing are by no means our only systems of communication. Social intercourse is greatly strengthened by habits of gesture—little movements of the hands and face.   With nods, smiles, frowns, handshakes, kisses, fist shakes, and other gestures we can convey most subtle understanding.§   We also have economic systems for trafficking not in ideas but in material goods and services; the tokens of communication are coins,

* But such reflexes do not form part of true human language; like the cries of animals they cannot be said to be *right* or *wrong* though, as signs, they can be interpreted by our fellows into the emotions they express.

† See Sec. 6.1 for further comments.

‡ John Donne, the Sixteenth Devotion.

§ See reference 399 (Reusch and Kees) for many illustrations and examples of pictures, icons, motifs, gestures, manners, etc.

bonds, letters of credit, and so on. We have conventions of dress, rules of the road, social formalities, and good manners; we have rules of membership and function in businesses, institutions, and families. But life in the modern world is coming to depend more and more upon "technical" means of communication, telephone and telegraph, radio and printing. Without such technical aids the modern city-state could not exist one week, for it is only by means of them that trade and business can proceed; that goods and services can be distributed where needed; that railways can run on a schedule; that law and order are maintained; that education is possible. Communication renders true social life practicable, for communication means organization. Communications have enabled the social unit to grow, from the village to the town, to the modern city-state, until today we see organized systems of mutual dependence grown to cover whole hemispheres.[230,]* Communication engineers have altered the size and shape of the world.

The development of human language was a tremendous step in evolution; its power for organizing thoughts, and the resulting growth of social organizations of all kinds, has given man, wars or no wars, street accidents or no street accidents, vastly increased potential for survival.

As a start, let us now take a few of the concepts and notions to do with communication, and discuss them briefly, not in any formal scientific sense, but in the language of the market place. A few dictionary definitions may serve as a starting point for our discursive 'approach here; later we shall see that such definitions are not at variance with those more restricted definitions used in scientific analysis (Appendix). The following have been drawn from the *Concise Oxford English Dictionary*:†

Communication, n. Act of imparting (esp. news); information given; intercourse; . . . (Military, Pl.) connexion between base and front.
Message, n. Oral or written communication sent by one person to another.
Information, n. Informing, telling; thing told, knowledge, items of knowledge, news, (on, about); . . . .
Signal, n., v.t. & i. Preconcerted or intelligible sign conveying information . . . at a distance. . . .
Intelligence, n. . . . understanding, sagacity . . . information, news.
News, n. pl. Tidings, new information. . . .
Knowledge, n. . . . familiarity gained by experience, person's range of information. . . .
Belief, n. Trust or confidence (*in*); . . . acceptance as true or existing (of any fact, statement, etc.; . . .). . . .
Organism, n. Organised body with connected interdependent parts sharing common life, . . .; whole with interdependent parts compared to living being.
System, n. Complex whole, set of connected things or parts, organised body of material or immaterial things . . .; method, organisation, considered principles of procedure, (principle of) classification; . . . .

* These numbers refer to the references at the end of the book.
† With kind permission of the Clarendon Press, Oxford.

Such dictionary definitions are the "common usages" of words; scientific usage frequently needs to be more restricted but should not violate common sense—an accusation often mistakenly leveled against scientific words by the layman.

The most frequent use of the words listed above is in connection with *human* communication, as the dictionary suggests. The word "communication" calls to mind most readily the sending or receipt of a letter, or a conversation between two friends; some may think of newspapers issued daily from a central office to thousands of subscribers, or of radio broadcasting; others may think of telephones, linking one speaker and one listener. There are systems too which come to mind only to specialists; for instance, ornithologists and entomologists may think of flocking and swarming, or of the incredible precision with which flight maneuvers are made by certain birds, or the homing of pigeons—problems which have been extensively studied, yet are still so imperfectly understood. Again, physiologists may consider the communicative function of the nervous system, co-ordinating the actions of all the parts of an integrated animal. At the other end of the scale, the anthropologist and sociologist are greatly interested in the communication between large groups of people, societies and races, by virtue of their cultures, their economic and religious systems, their laws, languages, and ethical codes. Examples of "communication systems" are endless and varied.

When "members" or "elements" are in communication with one another, they are associating, co-operating, forming an "organization," or sometimes an "organism." Communication is a social function. That old cliché, "a whole is more than the sum of the parts," expresses a truth; the whole, the organization or organism, possesses a structure which is describable as a set of *rules*, and this structure, the rules, may remain unchanged as the individual members or elements are changed. By the possession of this structure the whole organization may be better adapted or better fitted for some goal-seeking activity. Communication means a *sharing* of elements of behavior, or modes of life, by the existence of sets of rules. This word *rule* will be discussed later.

It should be emphasized at this point that we shall make no attempt in this book to unify the host of different systems of communication which we see around us, and a few of which we have just instanced. We shall be discussing certain common aspects, nothing more. At the same time we hope to convince the reader of the extremely complex and difficult nature of certain concepts, which superficially seem so easy. And, in particular, we shall make reference to the mathematical theory of communication, but with no intention of applying this as a "unifying" theory. It has a right and proper place in the study of communication, which its originators thoroughly understood, and attempts to extend it outside the technical field in which it first arose will be fraught with pitfalls. Application of this theory to biological systems has scarcely begun, though some preliminary ground clearing has been done.

Perhaps we may be permitted to comment upon a definition of communication, as given by a leading psychologist:[313] *"Communication is the discriminatory response of an organism to a stimulus."** The same writer emphasizes that a definition broad enough to embrace all that the word "communication" means to different people may risk finding itself dissipated in generalities. We would agree; such definitions or descriptions serve as little more than foci for discussion. But there are two points we wish to make concerning this psychologist's definition. First, as we shall view it in our present context, communication is not the response itself but is essentially the *relationship* set up by the transmission of stimuli and the evocation of responses. Second, it will be well to expand somewhat upon the notion of a stimulus; we shall need to distinguish between human language and the communicative signs of animals, between languages, codes, and logical sign systems, at least.

The study of the signs used in communication, and of the rules operating upon them and upon their users, forms the core of the study of communication. There is no communication without a system of signs—but there are many kinds of "signs." Let us refer again to the *Oxford English Dictionary*:

Sign, n. . . . written mark conventionally used for word or phrase, symbol, thing used as representation of something . . . presumptive evidence or indication or suggestion or symptom *of* or *that*, distinctive mark, token, guarantee, password . . . portent . . .; natural or conventional motion or gesture used instead of words to convey information. . . .

Language, n. A vocabulary and way of using it. . . .

Code, n., and v.t. Systematic collection of statutes, body of laws so arranged as to avoid inconsistency and overlapping; . . . set of rules on any subject; prevalent morality of a society or class . . .; system of mil. or nav. signals. . . .

Symbol, n. . . . Thing regarded by general consent as naturally typifying or representing or recalling something by possession of analogous qualities or by association in fact or thought. . . .

In this book we shall use the word *sign* for any physical event used in communication—human, animal, or machine—avoiding the term *symbol*, which is best reserved for the Crown, the Cross, Uncle Sam, the olive branch, the Devil, Father Time, and others "naturally typifying or representing or recalling . . . by association in fact or thought," religious and cultural symbols interpretable only in specified historical contexts. The term *language* will be used in the sense of human language, "a

* With kind permission of the *Journal of the Acoustical Society of America*.

vocabulary [of signs] and way of using it"; as a set of signs and rules such as we use in everyday speech and conversation, in a highly flexible and mostly illogical way.   On the other hand, we shall refer to the strictly formalized systems of signs and rules, such as those of mathematics and logic, as *language systems* or *sign systems*.

The term *code* has a strictly technical usage which we shall adopt here. Messages can be coded *after* they are already expressed by.means of signs (e.g., letters of the English alphabet); then a code is an agreed transformation, usually one to one and reversible, by which messages may be converted from one set of signs to another.   Morse code, semaphore, and the deaf-and-dumb code represent typical examples.   In our terminology then, we distinguish sharply between *language*, which is developed organically over long periods of time, and *codes*, which are invented for some specific purpose and follow explicit rules.

Apart from our natural languages (English, French, Italian, etc.), we have many examples of *systems* of signs and rules, which are mostly of a very inflexible kind.   A pack of playing cards represents a set of signs, and the rules of the game ensure communication and patterned behavior among the players.   Every motorist in Britain is given a book of rules of the road called the *Highway Code*, and adherence to these signs and rules is supposed to produce concerted, patterned behavior on British roads. There are endless examples of such simple sign systems.   A society has a structure, definite sets of relationships between individuals, which is not formless and haphazard but organized.   Hierarchies may exist and be recognized, in a family, a business, an institution, a factory, or an army— functional relationships which decide to a great extent the patterned flow of communication.   The communication and the structure are subject to sets of rules, rules of conduct, authoritarian dictates, systems of law; and the structures may be highly complex and varied in form.   A "code" of ethics is more like a language, having developed organically; it is a set of guiding rules concerning "ought situations," generally accepted, whereby people in a society associate together and have social coherence. Such codes are different in the various societies of the world, though there is an overlap of varying degrees.   When the overlap is small a gulf of misunderstanding may open up.   Across such a gulf communication may fail; if it does, the organization breaks down.

The whole broad study of language and sign systems has been called, by Charles Morris, the theory of signs,[243,244] and owes much to the earlier philosophy of Charles Peirce.*   Morris distinguishes three types of rule

* Locke used the word "semeiotic" to denote the "doctrine of signs."   See reference 207.   For an appreciation and survey of Peirce's relevant work in digestible form, see reference 129.

operating upon signs, (*a*) *syntactic* rules (rules of syntax; relations between signs); (*b*) *semantic* rules (relations between signs and the things, actions, relationships, qualities—*designata*); (*c*) *pragmatic* rules (relations between signs and their users). We shall be making considerable reference later to the ideas of Peirce and Morris.

3. WHAT IS IT THAT WE COMMUNICATE?

The dictionary definition of communication, which was quoted before, includes the communication of goods and supplies. Certainly the transport of coal, oil, food, and people by the railways, or of parcels by the Post Office, or of raw materials from mine to factory, forms an essential social function; without such transport our society would collapse. But transport of goods is not communication in the sense we are adopting here, and does not raise the same subtle and difficult questions. What "goods" do we exchange when we send messages to one another?

Physically, we transmit signals or signs—audible, visual, tactual. But the mere transmission and reception of a physical signal does not constitute communication. A sign, if it is perceived by the recipient, has the potential for selecting responses in him. Physically, when we communicate, we make noises with our mouths, or gesticulate, or exhibit some token or icon, and these physical signals set up a response behavior.

The theory of communication is partly concerned with the measurement of *information content* of signals, as their essential property in the establishment of communication links. But the information content of signals is not to be regarded as a commodity; it is more a property or potential of the signals, and as a concept it is closely related to the idea of selection, or discrimination. This mathematical theory first arose in telegraphy and telephony, being developed for the purpose of measuring the information content of telecommunication signals. It concerned only the signals themselves, as transmitted along wires, or broadcast through the aether, and is quite abstracted from all questions of "meaning." Nor does it concern the importance, the value, or truth to any particular person. As a theory, it lies at the syntactic level of sign theory and is abstracted from the semantic and pragmatic levels. We shall outline this theory of "selective" information in Chapter 5 and shall argue there and in Chapter 6 that, though the theory does not directly involve biological elements, it is nevertheless quite basic to the study of human communication —basic but insufficient.

It may be helpful if, in this introductory essay, we first approach our problem descriptively, if only to illuminate some of its great difficulties before we enter into scientific discussion and become concerned with *measurement*.

It is always important to distinguish between a physical property (attribute, quality) and a measure, unit, or magnitude of that property. When talking of measurement, any statements we make should be scientific statements, but we may discuss properties, attributes, and qualities in a variety of ways. For example, "color" may be considered artistically, poetically, even musically—but we could not discuss it so in ångstrom units. Again, it is possible to discuss "length" emotionally ("There's a long, long trail a-winding . . ."), though we should not refer to 1000 meters with emotion. So with many other physical concepts, including communication, signals, information. Human communication can be discussed in the language of aesthetics, or of philology or history, for example, as well as in that of physical science. For physical science is not the only system of thinking; it is one particular way.

A complete group, society, or organism, as a preliminary study, or hors d'oeuvre, is too indigestible. It is quite sufficient to take an elementary link, say two people in conversation, to illustrate some of the difficult questions. A conversation is one of the commonest phenomena we encounter, yet it is one which raises very great scientific problems, many still unsolved. It is so often our commonest experiences, which we take for granted, that are most elusive of explanation and description.

Suppose we take an example of two friends, George and Harry, conversing. George wants to instill some idea into Harry—say the idea of drinking a scotch and soda. What does he do? He might, for instance, show him a glass, or go through the motions of drinking; that is, he might imitate the desired situation as closely as possible. But conversations limited by such means would be very meager! He does nothing of the kind, of course, but makes the sounds of speech, which we can represent in writing by the sentence: "Come and have a scotch, Harry, I'm thirsty" —and off they go to the nearest pub.

The suggestion that words are symbols for things, actions, qualities, relationships, et cetera, is naive, a gross simplification. Words are slippery customers. The full meaning of a word does not appear until it is placed in its context, and the context may serve an extremely subtle function— as with puns, or *double entendre*. And even then the "meaning" will depend upon the listener, upon the speaker, upon their entire experience of the language, upon their knowledge of one another, and upon the whole situation. Words do not "mean things" in a one-to-one relation like a code. Words, too, are empirical signs, not copies or models of anything; truly, onomatopoeia and gestures frequently seem to possess resemblance, but this resemblance does not bear too close examination.[254] A cockerel may seem to say *cook-a-doodle-do* to an Englishman, but a German thinks it says *kikeriki*, and a Japanese *kokke-kokkō*. Each can paint only with the phonetic sound of his own language.

Before George spoke, he had certain notions, ideas, or "desires" in his mind, a wish to set up some change in the situation. These ideas repressented a selection from his whole range, constituting some message he desired to communicate, and this message he framed into the sounds of speech, as an *utterance*. The particular utterance he made depended largely upon his environment, and upon his previous experiences of communicating with Harry. He did not necessarily "think out" exactly what words to speak, and how to order them according to rules in a way calculated to achieve his desired ends. His utterance was a stream of speech which the entire situation evoked. How do our ideas, our desired messages, set up utterances in such an effective goal-seeking way, as they do in real life?*

A further difficulty comes from the fact that we cannot say that George spoke "words." He did not; he made a physical utterance, noises made with his vocal organs. If the same words are spoken by a number of different people, their physical characteristics will be different, for no two people speak exactly alike. George's utterance was peculiar to George and, furthermore, *peculiar and unique to that one occasion*. An utterance is an event; a word is a class or universal, and it is essential to distinguish between *word-events* or *word-tokens* (utterances) and *word-types* ("words" as they are listed in dictionaries, a linguistic concept). Linguists are not commonly concerned with the utterances of any *one* particular speaker, but rather with description of the general characteristics, attributes, or invariants of large groups—those things which are broadly in common. They classify and are continually dividing groups into subgroups, as they wish to make finer and finer comparisons. Thus George might be classed as "Southern English speaking," or more precisely "South London"; perhaps Professor Higgins in *Pygmalion* might have tied him down to one street!

The utterance which George made falls upon the ears of Harry and sets him into response. He might reply: "O.K. George, let's go"; and off they go. A goal has been achieved. Before his friend spoke, Harry may have formed a number of hypotheses concerning George's "desired message," and the receipt of the utterance has placed weight upon one in particular. The utterance acts as no more than "evidence" which is weighed, in the light of the whole environment and past experience of the

---

* In animal communication too, the signs (movements, displays, calls, etc.) made by one may stimulate the other into activity which serves as a respondent sign, so that a "goal-seeking" behavior results (e.g., leading to mating). See references 209, 324.

hearer, though we must not regard such "weighing of evidence" and "making of decisions" as necessarily involving Harry in any logical deductions. He does not hear the utterances, identify the words, piece them together according to rules of grammar and semantics, and then calculate the relative likelihood of his various hypotheses being true. Far from it. He hears the utterance and responds immediately by replying; he may do little conscious "thinking out" at all. But we can perhaps describe what he appears to do in such terms, *for it is important to distinguish between the phenomenon itself* (the conversation on which we are eavesdropping) *and a description of that phenomenon.* To clarify this distinction, we shall refer to the observed conversation as being in *object-language* and the observer's description as being expressed in *meta-language.*

This very rough account of "a conversation" may illustrate a few of the uncertainties which surround any communicative event. We have first the physical, acoustic uncertainties of accent and articulation; then we have language uncertainty, of grammatical construction; for the "desired message" could be framed into an utterance in many varied ways. For example:

(1) "I'm tired out Harry—let's go and have a drink."
(2) "I've got a thirst I wouldn't sell—let's find a couple of scotches."
(3) "What about a drink, Harry—I'm thirsty?"

... and so on, with infinite variations on a theme. George and Harry have had different past communicative experiences, and there exists an uncertainty of communication for that very reason. Their languages are not identical; their habits of speech and habits of response differ. Further, there is a great range of uncertainty of theme, for George might have been going to speak about anything—the weather, the cricket results, his lumbago, anything—and Harry's "initial hypotheses" might also have had a similar spread. But in practice this is not so, because his range of expectation will be determined to a major degree by the earlier conversation; there is a "thread of discourse," or line directed toward a goal. An utterance stimulates the hearer into response with another utterance, back and forth. And the whole of this proceeds amid what we may call "environmental uncertainties"—street noises, other people's chatter, dogs barking. It is remarkable that human communication works at all, for so much seems to be against it; yet it does. The fact that it does depends principally upon the vast store of habits which we each one of us possess, the imprints of all our past experiences. With this, we can hear snatches of speech, see vague gestures and grimaces, and from such thin shreds of evidence we are able to make a continual series of inferences, guesses, with extraordinary effectiveness.

Let us return to an earlier point and look again at the essential property of signals which forges and maintains a communication link. We referred earlier to the "information content" of signals, and to the way in which this is measured in statistical communication theory (about which more is to be said in Chapter 5). "Information content" is not a commodity but rather a potential of the signals. To take a rough analogy, it is rather like the economist's concept of "labor." Labor is not a commodity, not a stuff—yet it is bought and sold; we cannot see it, but only its results. Labor is not the particular men performing it (the signals in our analogy), though its quantity depends upon the men and their trades or skills. A labor force represents a potential to produce goods; by analogy, signals possess a potential to communicate, and the information communicated will depend upon the choice of signals in any particular channel of communication with relation to the receiver's expectancies.

To continue in this descriptive, non-mathematical way—you and I are forming a communication link at this moment. I have put my thoughts, or "desired messages," into carefully selected words and these are printed in the book you are holding. How could this link be broken?

Suppose I had packed this chapter full of lies; would you continue to read it? You most probably would, perhaps to see how many errors you could detect, or for many reasons. Again, this chapter might be stuffed with utter nonsense (and I trust it is not), yet you might continue reading, in the hope that it will improve later, or to see just how bad it does become. After all, some very fascinating nonsense verse has been written and is widely read. So neither truth nor common sense seems strictly essential to the link.

If you had been told, beforehand, that this book was "utterly devoid of meaning," you might decide not to read it; the link would be broken. But how can all meaning be destroyed? What is "absolute nonsense"? It is questionable whether it is possible to write "absolutely meaninglessly," *so long as any of the rules whatever of the language are retained*, rules in common to the writer and reader. We might invent words not in the dictionary and string them haphazardly into texts—yet each one will play upon our experiences and call up images of some kind or other. They cannot be entirely void.[15] Lewis Carroll's nonsense verse comes close to this, yet is delightful reading.

> 'Twas brillig and the slithy toves
> Did gyre and gimble in the wabe. . . .

No; in writing, and in speaking, we may break some of the rules some of the time, but we cannot break them all. And to destroy communication completely, there must be no rules in common between transmitter and receiver —neither of alphabet nor of syntax. If from this point on I had written this book in Syriac, the chances are, dear reader, that you and I would part!

Even now, we are not quite out of the wood. For given time and patience you might be able to start deciphering, like a cryptographer; from assumptions about subject matter, and from your knowledge of other languages and cultures, you might make a series of prudent guesses and follow them up. Lost languages have been deciphered from the slightest of clues. You might, again, be attracted by the sheer beauty of calligraphy, and we might communicate aesthetically. Signs make a powerful social cement.

There is one particular way of weakening the bond, perhaps breaking it completely. Suppose that by a bookbinder's error all the pages of this book were identical, as a casual glance at the page numbers would tell you; then you might read the first page and no more. The book would form a cyclic or periodic signal, one cycle would communicate with you, the others you would know for *certain* beforehand. To set up communication, the signals must have at least some surprise value, some degree of unexpectedness, or it is a waste of time to transmit them.

Turning back to the list of dictionary definitions (page 5), perhaps the term "news" stands out, after our recent discussion. For news is "new information"; news suggests novelty. Can novelty be measured? Indeed it can, if the novelty of a signal is regarded as depending upon the relative number of times it has been received before, compared to all the possible alternatives. For this, the mathematical idea of probability as a *relative frequency* (or percentage) is applicable. The statistical theory of communication adopts this view, but with certain important restrictions, for it is not concerned with personal man-to-man conversations such as that between our George and Harry, but rather with the properties of telephones, telegraphs, and the like—with communication channels used by many people. The letters of the alphabet, or range of alternative signs (words, speech sounds, and so on), are initially specified and their relative frequencies assessed. It is not their probabilities as "appearing" to some one person that are considered, but their frequencies of use by a certain population, such as are observed in "newspaper English," "prose," "telephone speech," et cetera—the *average* or statistical properties of a *source*. And for this reason in particular, this mathematical work should be interpreted with the greatest care, in situations involving real people. In this mathematical sense, information is measured in terms of the *statistical rarity* of signs.*

---

* Of course, there are many examples of *value* assessments according to improbability, or rarity. Bernoulli assessed the value of money as proportional to the logarithm of the quantity you possess; Adam Smith observed that the "wages of labour in different employments vary according to the probability or improbability of success in them."

At our present descriptive level we may say that it is the most infrequent words, phrases, gestures, and other signs which arrest our attention; it is these that give strength to the links. The others we can predict very readily. The great majority of our everyday surroundings, the sights and sounds of home and street, we largely ignore from familiarity.

In Aesop's fable, the boy cried "Wolf!" too often.

4. SOME DIFFICULTIES OF DESCRIPTION OF HUMAN COMMUNICATION

In our introductory apologia to the description of a conversation between George and Harry, a distinction was drawn between qualitative and quantitative statements. This example—a conversation—was chosen partly to illustrate some of the difficulties which beset attempts to make quantitative, scientific description of a situation involving human individuals, and especially to warn the beginner against rushing in and "applying" the mathematical theory of communication.

There is first a difficulty in providing a *selective* basis to quantitative measurement of information conveyed by the signs, because the vocabularies used by the two individuals, George and Harry, are virtually impossible to define. What total range of sounds or words, or gestures, or phrases does each use? Added to this there is a further difficulty in defining sets of signs to be called their "vocabularies." In natural languages, spoken or written, the "signs" may be defined in many ways, depending upon the particular structural aspects of interest. Linguists break up languages into many different types of element. We are all so familiar with print and with dictionaries that we tend to accept the "word" as a kind of natural unit. But there are languages where the concept is far less evident. Again, it would be possible to compile, say, an English dictionary as a list, not of words but of syllables, though it might be inconvenient to use.[235]

Secondly, since no two individuals speak exactly alike, there are the great difficulties of defining, standardizing, and specifying utterances—the whole difficult field of phonetics and of signal analysis.

There is next the possibility of confusion between objective and subjective aspects of communication; between the personal sense impressions of an individual, private to him, and his overt behavior, which is observable and describable by an external observer. But a too rigid adherence to the strictly behavioral point of view can be cramping and may obscure many things of considerable interest. We shall be making particular reference to objective tests upon subjective phenomena later.

A man has remarkable powers of learning. Every communication, every perception, adds to his accumulation of experiences; he is continually becoming a different person, for his every experience is part of a continuing process. In a communication experiment he will show reactions to stimuli which may change as the experiment proceeds. These changes, of course, may be the phenomenon of interest, if his learning abilities are being studied; but in many experiments learning may provide a difficulty, and tests must be carefully designed to minimize or eliminate the consequences. In tests upon hearing or aural perception, for example, the listener may at first be unfamiliar with a speaker's accent but gradually improve his score as the tests proceed. In certain extreme cases, it may be impossible to use the same man twice for an experiment, because the second time he will know what is expected of him. Learning continually disturbs the *status quo* and may render the results of tests inconsistent or unreproducible.

Among the very simplest creatures, the absence of learning, or its restriction to elementary types, ensures fixed and common behavior patterns under similar conditions. Experiments are repeatable, and the results may to a great extent be generalized from one creature to his brothers. But as we proceed higher up the evolutionary scale, and learning faculties improve, behavior becomes far less regular and predictable. If a man is subjected to some experiment involving his responses to, say, spoken or visual signals, he may react in varied ways according to his personal experiences and habits, or his prejudices and anxieties—or he may deliberately cheat. His responses may even depend upon anticipation (of the consequences, or future test conditions, for example). But well-designed experiments may guard against such variables.

In conclusion, the human body is not to be thought of as a unit possessing a number of receptor organs, into which separate signals are received, like the wires entering a telephone exchange. .A man is an organism, and the various stimuli bring into action physiological functions which set the whole organism into adjustment. Response to a stimulus of one organ may be influenced by the states of others and by the whole environment.

5. CO-OPERATIVE AND NON-CO-OPERATIVE LINKS

In the preceding discussion we have rather presumed that a whole social field of communication may be broken down into simple links, as illustrated by a conversation between two friends. Such an isolation may be more or less valid. A telephone conversation, for example, represents a fairly close communication between two people, only loosely affected by external sources; yet the spoken language they use is a consequence of many different past contacts. A language grows from countless communications within a social group, and from mutual influence among different groups. In studies of crowd behavior we have another extreme, with individual links not forming a prominent characteristic.

A conversation forms a two-way communication link; there is a measure of symmetry between the parties, and messages pass to and fro. There is a continual stimulus-response, cyclic action; remarks call up other remarks, and the behavior of the two individuals becomes concerted, co-operative, and directed toward some goal.

The reading of a newspaper represents a unilateral, non-co-operative link (except that the reader can write letters to the editor!). The relation of a speaker in a broadcasting studio, speaking into a microphone, to his individual unseen listeners in the privacy of their homes is unilateral, whereas a speaker on a platform can see and hear the effects of his words upon the crowd; their facial expressions, their laughs and claps, and other signs reciprocate upon the speaker and affect the course of his speech.

An archaeologist deciphering a stone inscription forms a one-way communication link with his forebears. He receives no further help from them than the signs carved on the stone; he can make guesses and follow up to conclusions, but the dead cannot help or correct him.

The possibility of communication with a distant planet provides a currently popular example of communication that is initially one way. What can be assumed to exist in common between Earth and the planet that can serve as signs and rules, for a start, to build up a common language?[385,156] We have no knowledge, if living creatures exist there, of their intelligence level, their sense organs, their basic concepts. For the concepts we each of us possess, and for which we have signs, depend upon our individual experiences. The concepts held by people of one culture may differ from those of another culture, depending upon chance of history or geography. The system of description of nature we call "physics" has a certain form, constructed of concepts and laws, which has grown in a certain way from the accidents of our own history. Had history been different or had we different sense organs, physics might have become constructed otherwise. I see no reason to suppose, for example, that physics would be the same on Mars; nor need Martian mathematics have evolved along the same path. Perhaps the Martians share with us the concepts of day and night alternation, or of number, or of male and female, or of geometric figures—which we could represent not with empirical signs but with icon signs. Interesting, perhaps, to speculate about but rather a waste of time.

Man's life is a continuity of experience. It does not remain static but benefits from previous happenings; it advances now here, now there, and steadily grows in social scale. By contrast, animal life is relatively static, a here-now world, the animal living each moment as it comes. The very simplest creatures show little or no power of learning and benefiting from past experience. They do not have continued thoughts and do not readily form abstract concepts. They have no language in the sense that we have, and no system of organized thoughts, but use sign systems which are comparatively rigid and incapable of development.

Suzanne Langer has written,* "Between the clearest animal call of love or warning or anger and a man's least trivial word there lies a whole day of creation—or in modern phrase a whole chapter of evolution." She was referring specifically to our possession of language. With our language we share, we have relations, and we are involved. We are not animals in a herd nor insects in a swarm, for we can change these relations; we can have purpose and motives; we believe and adopt attitudes. We communicate in societies and we commune with ourselves. Our language canalizes our thoughts and permits us our particular way of looking at the world, not "as it is," but as we see it to be. A great bulk of our thoughts are word-thoughts, deep ruts of habit. Our own language is so structured as to set up in our minds the idea of the ever-flowing stream of time, that metaphysical background of our experience. There is only one "now," but we have created past, present, and future—the lesser creatures have not. It is as though these creatures use signs signifying immediacy; as though, to be anthropomorphic, they said "go," "friend," "come hither," "boss," and the like.

One of the most fascinating animal sign systems which has been studied is that of the bees, and this pioneer work of Karl von Frisch[118] illustrates the fixed nature of such systems compared to human language. You and I can have endless conversation about all sorts of subjects, but the bees mostly discuss one thing only—food and where to find it.† The bees make signs by peculiar forms of movement, a kind of "dancing" on the vertical combs in their hive. There are two distinct forms of dance. In the first, which is used to indicate that a source of food exists within a very short distance of the hive, the bee, carrying nectar and pollen from the flowers it has found, runs around in a small circle—one way and then the other—attracting the attention of the other bees, who smell and taste the pollen and nectar. The second dance is used to indicate food at greater distances, and is even more remarkable; in this, the bee walks in a figure

* See page 103 of reference 393.

† This may be too narrow, for they have other social behavior; they may change their hive to another place, for example, which may involve sign-usage.

eight, wagging its abdomen at a speed which depends upon the distance to the food.   Further than this, the center line of the figure lies in such a direction on the comb, relative to the vertical, that it indicates direction of the food relative to the sun.

Now this system of signs may seem to be "ingenious," though we would rather say it is simple but efficient, because we should not credit each bee with thinking out how to express its desires.   It follows these habits which remain unchanging through countless generations; its system of signs is not at all like human language, for it is not developable, flexible, and universal.   To catch the attention of its fellows, a bee can do nothing but continue its dance, repeating it over and over again.   J. B. S. Haldane has insisted that such signs are not to be considered as constituting a report, by the bee, of her recent excursion, but rather that they constitute *intention movements* which set other bees into imitative behavior until a major united action is achieved.   Very much the same is yawning, in humans; yawns are very infectious.   Many animal signs have similar consequences, setting up imitative behavior and leading to flocking and swarming.[209,324,*]   Animal signs can relate only to the *future*, but never, like human language, refer to the past.[139]   A man may change his method of expression, invoke new ideas; he can shift his line of argument, refer to past occasions, and hold out promise for the future.   He can co-operate with his companions by changing his language to suit their reactions, and so achieve his goal more readily.

Simple repetition of a signal is the most elementary way of introducing *redundancy*, an idea we shall discuss in Chapter 3.   Briefly, redundancy is a property of languages, codes, and sign systems which arises from a superfluity of rules, and which facilitates communication in spite of all the factors of uncertainty acting against it.   Human languages have grown to have an excess of rules, so that some can be broken without serious harm. The rules we call grammar and syntax are not inviolate, but the more we break them, the lower are our chances of successful communication.   The various rules supplement and duplicate one another, providing a great factor of safety.   We can break some of the rules, but we cannot break them all if we wish to remain within the social community.   In the Country of the Blind the one-eyed man is *not* a king—he is a gibbering idiot.

6. COMMUNICATION AND SOCIAL PATTERN

The title of this essay is "Communication and Organization."   So far we have confined our attention to communication; let us examine now something of the nature of organization in the sense of "social pattern."

* Much human social behavior is imitative, too (e.g., see reference 240).

6.1. Analysis and synthesis

During the mid-nineteenth century, the early theories of society as an institution set up by individuals, the better to serve and satisfy their needs and desires, became radically changed, to be replaced by the concept of social evolution—a process of natural selection leading not to a better serving of the individual's interests but to higher social efficiency and consequent survival of the society itself. This introduction of evolutionary concepts led to analogies and comparisons between the aggregate of individuals forming society and the living animal body; Herbert Spencer was perhaps the chief proponent of these analogies and discussed them in some detail: the veins and arteries compared to systems of transport; the brain as the seat of government, et cetera; all the specialized *functioning* of the various mutually dependent organs compared to the division of labor and the essential institutions of the State.[307]

But such comparisons are little more than metaphors. For analogies to serve a useful purpose in science, to be a genuine part of scientific method, they should at least suggest some form of analysis or type of experiment capable of being carried over from one scientific field to another. Mere superficial similarity carries nowhere.

In modern times, A. N. Whitehead has treated the concept of *organism* in a much broader and more purposeful sense, not for setting up analogies but as a doctrine, a guiding principle, in reaction to the predominance of analysis and abstraction in science which has existed since the time of Galileo. "The concrete enduring entities of the world are complete organisms, so that the structure of the whole influences the character of the parts."[346] He has argued that analysis has formed the greater part of natural science in the past, and that analysis essentially involves abstraction, with its consequent ignoring of the rest of nature and of experience. But "the synthetic method of approach to reality may be as valid as the analytic." Such reasons have led Whitehead to insist that a further stage of provisional realism is required, in which "the scientific scheme is recast and founded upon the ultimate concept of organism."[76,28] Today we see an increasing concern with the synthetic, as opposed to the analytic view; such a movement has arisen not as an alternative but as a vital supplement to analysis in physics, in physiology, in psychology, and in sociology; and indeed our whole attitude toward history has been affected (e.g., Toynbee's concepts[326]). The analysis and breaking down of social groups into individuals, or into elementary communication units, may leave untouched the main problems of sociology, which concern not the properties of the individual parts but their complex relationships, just as breaking down a man into atoms and electrons loses sight of the man. An army, a nation, an institution is not a mere crowd, not an amorphous collection of people, for all the members have certain dominant purposes; such "organisms" have continuity of existence and of form.[230]   We recognize in them certain characteristics of their integrated structure, "*esprit de corps*," "national self-consciousness," "popular will."   Again, although such characteristics suggest, by the terms used, extrapolations from the characters of individuals, comparison between the collective life of social groups and the life of an individual can so often become odious.   Toynbee warns us that there is no historical justification for analogies between nations and individuals;[326] we cannot carry over analogy to "birth and death of nations" or invoke "obscure principles of senility or decadence."[230]

This is not to say, however, that the mathematics and methods of biology have no application to social studies; they certainly have, of course, especially the statistical methods.   Biological evolution and social evolution have certain aspects in common; both represent a growth from simple beginnings, proceeding by trial and error to more complex structures, retaining advantageous changes and rejecting failures.   But the two evolutionary processes need not be assumed to follow identical or analogous laws.   Since man has evolved language and systems of organized thoughts, the evolution of social organizations can no longer be said to proceed by chance.   Today we see planned experiments; the social organizations we call businesses, industries, government, economics, and all the great interdependent systems which form our modern world have become so complex and costly, and their failure would represent disaster on such a scale, that planning, control, and social design are becoming ever more prominent.   This trend shows up as *logistics, operational research,*[245,299] *time and motion study*[298] and planned production in industry, *census* and *social survey* bureaus,[188,322] *planned economics* for full employment.   It is the political ideal of the Welfare State—group responsibility for the basic human standards of the individual person; it leads to a whole intensity of awareness of the urgent need for better understanding of social organizations of all kinds.   And for gaining this understanding, there has been a great search by sociologists for methods, a search which has led to the taking over of systems of analysis from other fields—not only physics, engineering, and chemistry, but also mathematical biology.

It is only too easy, in a discussion of this kind, to lapse into vague generalities; to use terms like *element, entity, relationship, structure, pattern,* with which we can write so much and say so little.   It is precision, above all, that is desired in social studies; we need to know relationships as mathematical and statistical laws, yet heaven knows how easy it is to say this, and how appallingly difficult and laborious it is to gather the necessary data and to formulate social laws!   The sociologist is, unhappily, not often in the position to control and experiment upon his material, as is the physicist; he so often must wait for wars, strikes, trade depressions, and other calamities to do it for him.

6.2. SOCIAL FIELDS AND NETWORKS

It is not unnatural that in the technology of telecommunication many aspects of this subject have received clear mathematical treatment; there are three specific developments which undoubtedly are filtering through into social studies:[84] (a) the theory of networks, (b) statistical communication theory, and (c) the theory of feedback (sometimes called cybernetics). The latter has been adequately dealt with in literature,[349] and we shall here refer mainly to *networks*.

In telecommunication, the notion of an isolated discrete link is exceptionally pertinent; such links take the form of telephone and telegraph lines, for example, forming patterns of connections between pairs of transmitting and receiving points (*nodes*). In such systems, messages are essentially canalized. The flow of signals along the lines of communication which enmesh the globe—the telephone lines, submarine cables, radio links, postal services—has a profound effect upon our social organization and patterning. The increase in sheer scale of social organization is one of the most significant trends of our times, a growth possible only by modern telecommunication technology. And it is concerning such networks that a great deal of mathematical theory has been constructed.

This notion of canalized messages may be of far less value, on the other hand, in studies of crowd behavior; the microscopic point of view may reveal nothing of the character and patterning of large and closely knit congregations, which may perhaps more effectively be treated as "fields." Students of crowd behavior[259] have been concerned with the manner of propagation of ideas or "potential reaction patterns"—starting perhaps from a single individual, spreading as a "wave" over the whole crowd, growing and decaying—and with the dynamic spread of popular crazes (e.g., diabolo and other games and puzzles), new slang, rumor,[4] fashions, panics, and fervors. Such "wavelike" rise and fall has been compared, in some detail, with the epidemiology of infectious diseases.[259]*

J. B. S. Haldane's most interesting remarks about animal *ritual* behavior, to which we have referred in Section 5, suggest that such study may cast light upon human crowd behavior. The intention movement of an animal (insect, bird) is not to be considered "purposive," but it may set up imitative action, eventually becoming concerted, until a flock or swarm

---

* A modern remarkable instance of news spread, afforded by television, is the occasion of President Kennedy's assassination. The news was learned by 68% of population in the U.S.A. within half an hour.

is formed.[139] Perhaps human crowds attending football matches or watching processions or other displays are remnants of our own animal behavior; the whole crowd may be described as having purpose, but each member merely imitates.

We have mentioned two extremes of social structure, the true network and the "field." How far can the concepts and methods of network analysis be extended toward more general structures? To take a rough analogy, the relation between electrical networks and electromagnetic fields is known precisely; but we have no such exact relation in the case of the social phenomena. Still, in the next section (section 6.3) we shall comment upon one brave attempt to extend the theory of networks to social structures in which messages are not canalized so precisely from one individual to another.

Business, industries, and armies are not mobs, or crowds. They have defined purpose, they have formal structure—a skeleton of rules relating one part to another, and relating one individual member to others, which determine on the whole how messages (orders, instructions, etc.) shall flow and communication unite the parts into a whole, purposeful, goal-seeking "organism."[256] Such highly organized units possess a *constitution* (a set of rules, usually imposed, though they may be modified by experience) which defines a "network" in which messages have been intended to flow. But the fact that messages are frequently found to flow in other paths, short-circuiting or by-passing "the usual channels," is itself quite revealing. In this connection there are two recent developments in social studies, at which we shall glance later (Section 6.3), that represent the *observation* and *experimentation* approaches. The first involves prolonged observation of some particular business, office or factory, to find out the principal paths of internal communication:[303] the flow of orders, instructions, chasings, requests for advice, et cetera; the frequency, nature, and cause of blockages; who consults who and for what purpose; and other aspects of the *true* communication network, to be compared with the assumed formal one. For the formal rules, as laid down "from without," may not necessarily be the most practical and efficient; the social organism may itself determine another set for achieving its purpose. Such a study is analytical, but a second is synthetic. This concerns *group networks*, an experimental study of the self-organizing potentialities of very small social groups, when set to solve specific tasks. At present, such studies are highly abstracted from real-life organizations, but in such a way that the mathematical theory of networks has direct relevance. We shall return to this later.

In point of fact, when a young man enters a large business or industry, filled with zeal, he imagines that above him there is an Ordered World;

but as he climbs the ladder and reaches the giddy heights of Administration, only then does he slowly come to realize that the "machinery" may be very nebulous—an affair jerked along by clash of personalities and given momentum by ambitions.

6.3. ON MECHANICAL ANALOGIES TO SOCIAL STRUCTURES

Popular parlance uses many analogous mechanical terms in reference to social matters; we commonly speak of: "swing of the pendulum" (of public opinion), "government machinery," "forces of reaction." Mechanical analogy forms a basis for a great deal of our thinking. In the social field, "forces" are not the forces of mechanics, nor are social groups to be compared with machines in the Newtonian sense. For in simple mechanics, time can be reversed; but we cannot reverse the course of history.

It is true that certain social and biological studies have concerned the interactions of abstracted quantities, often represented mathematically by differential or integral equations, and such representation may suggest a "machine" analogy (for example, the growth of populations and the interaction of populations). In such mathematical work, the important quantities singled out are macroscopic, average quantities and rates; in biology we may be dealing with numbers of males and females, average birth and death rates, et cetera. But the solution of such equations does not give the life history of any one individual. Again, economics is concerned with abstracted quantities like average incomes, investment rates, scales of taxation, prices and their interactions. But such calculations are concerned with averages and aggregates, and do not describe precisely the budgeting systems which are yours and mine. In all such calculations the related quantities, the parts of the "machine," must be regarded as subject to variations, frequently random, coming from an immense variety of causes which have been ignored in detail by the conditions of analysis, that is, by the necessary abstraction of the interacting quantities.[84]

In view of the necessary abstraction, and of the great residue of uncertainties facing us in analysis of material so varied and so numerous as human populations, it would seem that statistical mechanics[325] may be more relevant and applicable than ordinary (determinate) mechanics; this suggestion has occasionally been put forward.[120] Ordinary mechanics deals with simple rigid bodies like levers, wheels, frameworks, and with their motions and the various forces in equilibrium which act upon them, where *forces* is a clearly defined mathematical term having nothing whatever in common with the "forces" that control our destinies. On the other hand, statistical mechanics deals with the properties of *systems* consisting of such enormous assemblages of component elements (such as a volume of gas) that exact determinate calculations become impossible. It abstracts certain macroscopic properties and ignores other data entirely, so that the life history of the system cannot be specified precisely, but only statistically —on an *average*. The founders of statistical mechanics seem to have been aware of the wide interpretation of their concepts and results, though they were expressly interested in certain well-defined physical problems. Today the principal concepts are finding application in many fields where vast assemblages or "systems" are studied.[349]

Nevertheless, this attractive proposition possesses many difficulties. For one thing, statistical mechanics deals adequately only with truly enormous assemblages, whereas most social groups are only moderately numerous. A second difficulty, which may eventually prove not insurmountable, is that statistical mechanics has mostly been applied to systems of particles having zero or very weak interactions, whereas the people composing a social group exert a great deal of influence upon one another. However, recent study of the theory of liquids and solids has considered particles which "co-operate" or exert strong interactions one upon another —as in, say, metals and crystals. Fürth suggests that the theory of such "co-operative" phenomena may assist in the understanding of certain social behavior problems.[120] A third trouble is that a human population does not normally form what a statistician would call a "stationary" system; that is, statistics gathered at one period of time may be quite inapplicable at a later period, for the major controlling conditions may be altered by plagues, windfalls, new regulations, currency devaluation, political reversals, international treaties, or wars. Social organisms are rarely in true "equilibrium," for evolution continues.

It should be understood that physical models and analogies are of no use if they merely "liken" people to atoms, molecules, and particles but lead to no further inferences. Such blind-end comparison would carry us no further than have the analogies of Herbert Spencer.[307] The laws which determine true forces between atoms or particles, and the various physical properties of gases, solids, or liquids, have nothing to do with the "forces" or natural influences exerted upon human beings—and the great difficulty lies just there, to discover by observation and experiment what are the important parameters, and the laws relating them, in social fields. It is the mathematical methods *per se* of statistical mechanics which may eventually prove of some value in the study of social and other systems, rather than the (extensional) semantic relations of the method to the problems of physics. The mathematical methods exist in their own right.

If the methods of physics are considered in relation to social problems, two further points should be borne in mind. In the first place, society may require not one model but many, depending upon what attributes are to be portrayed. Then again, and more delusive, the concepts of time and space in physics are highly abstracted and universal, whereas *time and space in sociology mean history and geography.* We cannot take a model of some social phenomenon and transplant it to another epoch, or another part of the world.

To many laymen the notion appears strange that material so varied and willful as human beings is subject to any laws; but we should remember that at the time of Newton the idea may have seemed laughable to many, that the complex motions of solid bodies of all different shapes, sizes, and weights could be given mathematical expression. Although human beings are individual personalities, they are all subject to certain appetites, needs, and desires; and we are simply *not* free to do what we like; to say, to spend, to beget, in complete independence of the actions of our fellows. A man who breaks *all* the rules is not a member of the social group—he is a lunatic or an anarchist.

Governments spend enormous sums on gathering census data, the better to predict and cater for future social needs; there are other sources of data too—public opinion polls, market research, radio listener research, and various social surveys. As computing machine techniques improve, so more and more facts may be extracted from this mass of material, concerning economic matters, population trends, opinions, habits, and preferences, and their various relationships. But we sadly lack techniques of similar power for analysis of the psycho-social or communication problems which so concern our social health—the acceptance and spread of slogans, the propagation of rumors,[4] the building up of national attitudes out of the daily blast and counterblast of accusations in press and radio. How is it that a crowd can listen to and applaud with enthusiasm, a string of clichés and platitudes which no one member would waste a thought upon in the privacy of his own home.* Why are mobs violent? What distinguishes news from propaganda? What is the difference between competition and conflict? Why does society continually split into two, like the two opposing teams in a game: capital and labor, the two parties of stable democracies, the two sides in war, believers and infidels? Within each side there is sense of cohesion, loyalty, and rectitude. Our side is wholly good, the other wholly evil. Is such dualism inherent in the way we think?

7. GROUP NETWORKS

Who does not remember seeing, in his school history books, diagrams with arrows, dots, and little shaded rectangles representing armies arrayed

* Television is a far more critical medium for political personalities than any we have had before.

against each other in battle? All the vast mêlée, the terrors and agonies of the day, reduced to the neatness of geometry.

Such diagrams represent a simplified, abstracted pattern of relationships, a formalized skeleton. Equally familiar must be the organizational charts stuck on the walls of offices and factories: little blocks labelled "President," "Sales Manager," "Chief Engineer," with connecting lines showing their functional relationships—the rules of the institution. Family trees form another example. Again, flow charts are commonly used by engineers, to illustrate the functional relations between the various functions of complicated machines.

This type of representation, and the mathematical system which goes with it, is called *graph theory* (an aspect of combinatorial topology), and it has received elaborate application and interpretation in the theory of electrical networks. Recently, "social networks" have also been studied by the methods of graph theory from two aspects, theoretical and experimental (work which has perhaps received some inspiration from Kurt Lewin's use of topological concepts for expressing psychological situations).

Although it has been concentrated upon very simple social structures, this work is nevertheless interesting, especially since it represents a genuine attempt at *synthesis*, breaking away from the long tradition of analysis in social studies.[17,18,65,111,211,213]

Roughly speaking, a *topological graph* is the mathematical name given to a set of lines connected together into any kind of network. We may imagine a number of wires, having hooks at each end, which can be hooked together into different network patterns; the hooks, or ends of the wires where they are united, are called *nodes*. The distinction between networks and true geometrical figures is that the former consist of lines which have no specified shapes or lengths but are merely connected together by their ends; magnitudes are not involved, but only number and connection. A fishing net is a topological graph; so are the various flow charts or *sociograms* to which we have referred. One of the best illustrations of the distinction between a geometric figure and a topological graph is provided by the two kinds of railroad maps we use; one is the normal survey map, using correct scales of distance and compass bearings, and the other is the stylized map showing only the *connections* between the stations, such as is sometimes used for a subway or the Underground.

In a sociogram the nodes may represent people, and the connecting lines channels of communication—the passage of messages, instructions, orders, and so on.[211] Such connections may be unidirectional (e.g., the passage of orders) shown by arrows on the lines; the network is then called a *directed graph*. As a representation of a social group this is of course highly idealized, but any application of mathematics to physical problems is idealized to some degree; the question is always: How much idealized, and what factors does the idealization conceal or eliminate?

Such networks are admirably suited to analysis by the use of matrix algebra. If the various connections, or channels of communication between the nodes, can have only one of two *states* (a message is or is not sent; a relationship or its opposite exists, etc.), then the problem becomes one of two-valued logic. The connections are either made, or not made (*yes* or *no*), and the matrix representing the properties of the network consists of an array of two distinct numbers, for example, 1 (*yes*) and 0 (*no*).[211] The whole network and the social situation it idealistically represents become closely analogous to an electrical network consisting of interconnected switches which are *open* or *closed*. Experience with electrical network analysis, using similar mathematical methods, suggests that general, overall properties of large social networks may possibly be found, provided the communication between nodes (people) is restricted to well-defined types of message. Such properties are not restricted to networks of specified size or complexity; and it may be possible to set up a system of *classification* of sociograms. But, of course, the whole success of such an approach will depend upon the precision with which messages can be controlled and objectively defined. Such theoretical work cannot stand alone, based entirely on conjecture and mathematical deduction; it must be paralleled by experimental findings.

On the experimental plane, work has been carried out on comparatively small social groups, under such controlled conditions that the idealized nature of the network representation is thrown into relief. In typical experiments,[17,65,150] a number of people sit alone in small adjacent cubicles and communicate with one another by passing written messages through slots in the walls between the cubicles; the slots can be arranged so that any required network of connections may be set up, ad initium. Such a pattern of communication, regarded as a "social group," is of course highly artificial; the very mechanics of the method which has had to be employed to canalize the flow of messages into a true network emphasizes this. Such networks do not represent real-life social situations, but invented or set-up systems with formalized rules; we shall later be referring to the analogous case in language study, where invented or set-up "language systems," having formalized syntax rules, are developed in the same spirit of synthesis. The analogy in methodology here is very close, arising from similarity of difficulty. Both language and social pattern are evolved systems, not imposed from outside or designed on any logical basis. In both cases, the synthesis of artificial but "logical" structures may eventually help understanding of the natural phenomena, partly by throwing into relief the very failures of the synthetic systems;

just what can these systems *not* do that the natural systems perform very efficiently?

There are numerous examples of social working groups set up to perform specific tasks, for which Authority has planned and imposed what it thinks to be the best internal patterns of communication. Frequently, these patterns are of a comparatively rigid type, not readily changed by the individual group members themselves: army units, business offices, factories, and so on. Yet working groups may show a tendency to depart from the formal imposed pattern of communication: "One may take the view that this departure is due to the tendency of groups to adjust towards that class of communication patterns which will permit the easiest and most satisfying flow of ideas, information, decisions, etc."[17]

In group-network experiments, the tasks to be performed frequently require the group members to obtain data from one another. Externally imposed communication patterns are set up by the arrangement of slots through which written questions or answers may be passed: star patterns, rings, chains, et cetera. What is subsequently observed throws light upon the emergence of a "leader" and his position in the group pattern, the relative times taken to complete tasks, and the degree of satisfaction or irritation (questions of "morale") experienced by members at different positions in the network. In other experiments, message exchange is left completely free, and the preferred patterns of communication are observed as they develop when tasks of various types are set for the groups to tackle.

Popular speech suggests that definite skeleton structures are recognizable in large social organisms. For example, we use words such as "dictatorship" to imply a strong central authority with branches radiating to all its servants (a star pattern); or "commercial ring" to imply that the members use one set of rules among themselves and quite another for their attitude toward the public; again "bureaucracy," implying "pass to you, please" (a chain pattern). Popular fancy clings to such simple imagery. It would be extremely dangerous to generalize from network experiments upon small groups, especially since such studies are in a very early stage. Nevertheless, armies, factories, banks, ministries, and many of our most important organizations possess highly formalized networks of communication which, although much more complex than those used in the experiments, may eventually benefit from this work.

Rather than think of real-life organizations as single "networks," it may be more realistic to regard them as a number of networks superimposed. For example, in an army the pattern of relationships is clearly laid down, but this pattern is not a simple network. There is a network for *supplying* the army in the field; there is a patterning of flow or orders and directives, relating to the *movement* of troops; another may represent the flow of *intelligence* signals. Each network would represent the flow of messages of a particular class: messages concerning materials, quantities, messages representing orders on troop disposition, messages representing secret information. Such patternings are not necessarily independent parts or subsections of the entire system but have rather the nature of projections; they exist simultaneously and are superimposed.

It has become a cliché to refer to man as "the communicating animal." Of all his functions, that of building up systems of communication of infinite variety and purpose is one of the most characteristic. Of all living creatures he has the most complex and adaptable systems of language; he is the most widely observant of his physical environment and the most responsive in his adjustment to it. He has organized ethical, political, and economic systems of varied kinds; he has the greatest subtlety of expressing his feelings and emotions, sympathy, awe, humor, hate—all the thousand facets of his personality. He is self-conscious and responsible; he has evolved spiritual, aesthetic, and moral sensibilities.

A man is not an isolated being in a void; he is essentially integrated into society. The various aspects of man's behavior—his means of livelihood, his language and all forms of self-expression, his systems of economics and law, his religious ritual, all of which involve him in acts of communication—are not discrete and independent but are inherently related, as sociologists have continually stressed from the time of Adam Smith.

Evolution
of Communication Science—
an Historical Review

There can never be wanting some . . . who will consider that . . . he, whose design includes whatever language can express, must often speak of what he does not understand; . . . that what is obvious is not always known, and what is known is not always present; . . . that sudden fits of inadvertancy will surprise vigilance, slight avocations will seduce attention, and casual eclipses of the mind will darken learning; and that the writer shall often in vain trace his memory at the moment of need, for that which yesterday he knew with intuitive readiness, and which will come uncalled into his thoughts tomorrow.

Samuel Johnson (1709–1784)
Preface to the *English Dictionary*

Note. This chapter is based upon a paper which first appeared under the title "An History of the Theory of Information," presented at the first London Symposium on Communication Theory (see reference 167). This paper subsequently appeared in the *Proceedings of the Institution of Electrical Engineers* (*London*), *98*, Part III, September 1951, and the material is used here with their kind permission. A further version appeared in the *American Scientist, 40*, No. 4, October 1952.

A quarrel which your author makes with many people today is not that they think "history is bunk," but that they regard it as funny. The doings of the alchemists can indeed make us smile; yet set against the whole background of their time, in their historical context, alchemists become utterly reasonable people (and, in fact, they laid the foundations of modern chemistry). Many early writers in alchemy, in astronomy, anatomy, and other sciences stumbled upon discoveries and truths *in spite* of the philosophy of their time, a state of affairs not unknown today (though, we pride ourselves, perhaps not to the same degree).

Real understanding of any scientific subject must include some knowledge of its historical growth; we cannot comprehend and accept modern concepts and theories without knowing something of their origins—of how we have got where we are. Neglect of this maxim can lead to that unfortunate state of mind which regards the science of the day as finality.

1. LANGUAGES AND CODES

Man's development and the growth of civilizations have depended, in the main, on progress in a few activities—the discovery of fire, domestication of animals, the division of labor; but, above all, in the evolution of means to receive, to communicate, and to record his knowledge, and especially in the development of phonetic writing. Man is essentially a communicating animal; communication is one of his essential activities. Whereas the lower living creatures cope with their environment on a moment-by-moment basis, the higher animals possess the faculties of learning, in varying degrees, and their actions are influenced by their past experiences. Man has developed such faculties to the most pronounced degree in coming to terms with a hostile world; he possesses the unique powers of speech and writing. Human experience is not a moment-by-moment affair, but has continuity; man has contact with his ancestors and descendants, and a sense of history and tradition. Such powers of communication have rendered possible his organization into the most complex societies and keep him in a continual state of change. Unlike the simple "releaser" stimuli and the fixed behavior patterns of the lower animals, human language is ever-changing. Language and other social activity are mutually related; the interests and needs of the day force changes upon the language and, in turn, the language is dominant over our thoughts. We think and we see the world as our language conditions us to do.

Communication essentially involves a language, a symbolism, whether this be a spoken dialect, a stone inscription, a Morse code signal, or a chain of binary-number pulses in a modern computing machine. Language has been called the "mirror of society"; truer perhaps of speech than of writing, especially of colloquial speech. A detailed history of spoken and written languages would be impossible here; nevertheless there are certain aspects which we may take as a starting point for this review.

The early scripts of Mediterranean civilizations were in pictographs, ideographs, and hieroglyphs; simple pictorial representations were made of objects and also, by association, of names, actions, and ideas of all kinds. But the step of greatest importance was the invention of phonetic writing, with which sounds were given symbols. Speech and writing were linked. The civilizations which did not adopt such symbolism, but which continued with one form of language for writing and another for speech, have been handicapped throughout their history, more so today than at any time. We make relatively few *significantly* different sounds when we speak, so few symbols are needed to represent them and writing is efficient, flexible, and adaptable. With the passage of time, picture writing became reduced to more formal signs, as dictated by the economy of using a chisel or a reed brush. Phonetic writing became simplified into a set of two or three dozen alphabetic letters.[A,*]

Egyptian inscriptions and papyri have presented the greatest difficulties of decipherment to scholars, partly because they so commonly used mixtures of phonetic signs and pictograms, together with many otiose signs and embellishments. The Rosetta stone, for example, contained hieroglyphic, demotic, and Greek transcriptions, with many *redundant* signs (presumably both phonetic and pictographic signs were included to make sure that more people could read and understand[B]). The gradual evolution of true phonetic writing, during the Coptic period, and the establishment of regular syntax built redundancy into language in a really useful way. "Redundancy" means additional signs or rules which guard against misinterpretation—an essential property of language, which we shall discuss further in Chapter 3.

The Semitic languages show an early recognition of redundancy in writing. Ancient Hebrew script had no vowels; modern Hebrew uses them only for children's books. Many other ancient scripts show no vowels. Church Slavonic, especially in its Russian recension, went a step further in condensation: in religious texts, commonly used words were abbreviated to a few letters, in a manner similar to our present-day use of characters such as the ampersand (&), abbreviations such as lb, $, and the

Fig. 2.1. Roman shorthand (orthographic).

* These letters refer to the lettered bibliography at the end of each chapter.

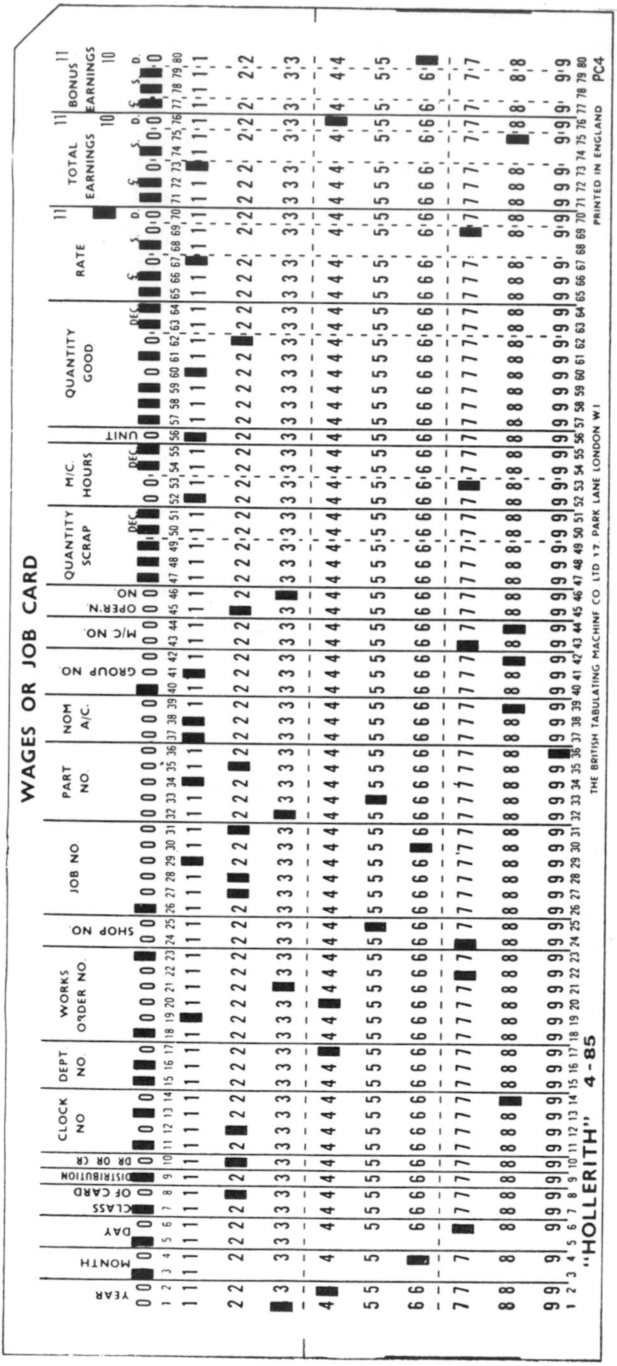

Fig. 2.2. A modern example of punched-card (binary-code) storage of information.*

* The card shown here is one manufactured in England by the British Tabulating Machine Company and is reproduced with their kind permission.

increasing use of initials like, for example, UNESCO, NATO, U.S.A. The more common a word is, the more easily it is guessed or predicted and so the less need be said about it.

Abbreviated writing seems to have been used by the Greeks as early as the fourth century B.C., gradually evolving into a true system of shorthand, or "tachygraphy." The freed slave Tyro has been credited with inventing the first true shorthand, about 60 B.C., apparently for recording the speeches of Cicero (Fig. 2.1). This system is known to have continued in use in Europe until the Middle Ages.[B]

Related to the structure of language is the theory of cryptograms and ciphers; ciphering, of vital importance for diplomatic and military secrecy, is as old as the Scriptures.[16,128] The simple displaced alphabet code, known to every schoolboy, was most probably used at the time of Julius Caesar.[273] There are many historic cases of the use of cipher; for example, Samuel Pepys' diary[B] was entirely ciphered to "secrete it from his servants and the World"; also certain of Roger Bacon's scripts (1214–1294) have as yet resisted all attempts at deciphering. A particular cipher, important to our present context, is one known as "Francis Bacon's Biliteral Code"; Bacon (1561–1626) suggested the possibility of printing seemingly innocent lines of verse or prose, using two slightly different fonts (called say A and B). The order of the A's and B's was used for ciphering a secret message: each letter of the alphabet was coded into five units, fonts A and B being used as these units.[B]

Now, this code illustrates an important principle which seems to have been understood for centuries: *information may be conveyed in a two-state code*.[86] There are numerous examples: one is the bush telegraph, the "talking drum" of Congo tribes, which uses drum beats with high and low pitch. The two notes, which are called "male voice" and "female voice" (for they may not have the metaphorical concepts of "high" and "low" pitch) do not operate in an artificial code; the drums are truly talking drums and imitate the human voice.[54,55] In some *tone languages*, each syllable has either a high or a low tone.[152,274] Nowadays we still have Morse code, using dots and dashes, and many similar two-state codes.

These historic two-state codes are the precursors of what is nowadays called *binary coding*, as used in many punched-card filing systems, in coded telegraphy, and in high-speed digital computing machines. Fig. 2.2 illustrates a typical punched card record (hole/no hole). Computers operate likewise with electrical impulses (pulse/no pulse)—binary. Now it happens that the electrical signals which pass along the nervous systems of animals and men, both from the sense organs (receptors) and to the controlled organs and muscles (effectors), take the form of triggered pulses which are either *on* or *off;* there is no half measure. (This is, in principle

also a binary code, and this fact is partly responsible for analogies sometimes being made between the nervous system and digital computing
machines, a comparison which is in fact very misleading.[38c]) The importance of the binary code to modern technology lies chiefly in the
ease with which mechanical and electrical devices may
be made to switch from one state to another, such as
holes punched in cards and on-off relays and switches,
for instance, which are either open or closed circuits.
This is purely a question of practical convenience, and
it should not be thought that there is anything particularly magical about the binary code.*

The ancient Celts, some 1500 years ago, invented a
script of interest in this connection, known as the Ogam
script,[B] which is found carved upon stone pillars in
Ireland and Wales (Fig. 2.3). Most scripts have developed into structures of complex letters, with curves,
angles, and various ornaments, difficult to chip in stone,
but the Celts seem to have consciously invented this
script, for making hasty inscriptions on warriors grave-
stones, using the simplest symbol of all—a single chisel
stroke—discovering that this is all that is necessary.

With the introduction of the famous dot-dash code,
by S. F. B. Morse in 1832, the *statistical* aspect of language
economy seems to have been realized. In an earlier
paragraph, attention was drawn to the shortening of
words as they come into increasing use. For there are
two diametrically opposed "forces," metaphorically
speaking, governing language; there is the "force" set
up by the desire to be understood ("*social* force"), lead-

Fig. 2.3. The Ogam
(Celtic) script.

ing to the insertion of redundancy, and there is the other
"force" of personal laziness ("*individual* force"), leading
to brevity or simplification. Morse realized that the
various *letters* of the English language are not used equally often; a visit to a
printer's office and a count of the quantities of type used gave him an
estimate of the relative frequencies of the letters. He then designed his
code so that the most commonly used letters were allocated the shortest
dot-dash symbols (Fig. 2.4). In this way the coded messages use fewer
total symbols, on an average. Today there is a revival of interest in this
aspect of coding; the need for a statistical view of language and code has
been appreciated for more than a hundred years, and as time has passed

* Any number-base could be used in theory (2, 3, 4 . . .). Most of us use the base
ten (decimal). But 2 is merely the first plural number.

this has assumed increasing importance. Another example may be cited; certain types of message are of very common occurrence in telegraphy, such as commercial expressions and birthday greetings, and these are often coded into a simple number. (By the year 1825 a number of such codes were in use.) Language statistics[273] have been of greatest importance for centuries, especially for the purpose of assisting decipherment of secret codes and cryptograms, to satisfy military and diplomatic needs. The first table of letter frequencies to be published was probably that of Sicco Simonetta of Milan in the year 1380; another, used by Porta in 1658, included digrams also (letter pairs, such as *ed, st, tr*).

The modern view is that messages having a high probability of occurrence contain little *information*, and that any mathematical definition adopted for "information" should conform to this idea —that the information conveyed by a sign, a message, a symbol, or an observation, in a set of such events, must decrease as their frequency of occurrence in the set increases (see Chapter 5). Morse's appreciation of a statistical law of this kind was purely descriptive; an exact *measure* of information, on a statistical basis, only emerged after recognition of communication as a statistical concept, by Wiener[349,350] and by Kolmogoroff,[193] and was developed extensively by Shannon in work to which we shall have occasion to make further reference in Chapter 5.

Letter	Frequency
E	12,000
T	9,000
A	8,000
I	8,000
N	8,000
O	8,000
S	8,000
H	6,400
R	6,200
D	4,400
L	4,000
U	3,400
C	3,000
M	3,000
F	2,500
W	2,000
Y	2,000
G	1,700
P	1,700
B	1,600
V	1,200
K	800
Q	500
J	400
X	400
Z	200

Fig. 2.4. Morse's original code, showing relation to quantities of type found by him in a printer's office. The modern International Code shows a similar appreciation of this statistical aspect of coding.

A great deal of statistical analysis of written languages, but far less of spoken ones, has been carried out in recent years; it is of interest to linguists, psychologists, and telecommunication engineers in particular. Such analysis of language behavior brings out definite laws. In particular, Morse's letter-frequency law shows one tendency, but is purely descriptive; the precise form of this and other relationships was explored experimentally by Zipf, who made an extensive collection and study of statistical aspects of speech and writing, carrying further into many other types of human behavior.   Zipf showed, for example, that P_n, the frequency of use of words in American newspaper English, and $n*$, the rank order, are closely related; he investigated also the laws relating to the lengths of words, the different meanings, and other factors.[367].   Nowadays, statistical analysis is one important method of linguistic study.[344]   Apart from letter and word frequencies, observations have been made also concerning the frequencies of syllables,[85] and of parts of speech (nouns, verbs, etc.),[114] of the stressing and inflection habits of telephone speakers,[27,114,†] and of many other statistical laws.‡

Modern mathematical symbolism illustrates a language system possessing a high degree of compression of information.   The Greeks had been limited largely to geometry, algebra eluding them because of their lack of a symbolism.   The great triumph of Galileo and his day was the recognition of mathematics as a universal language for the description of physical systems; but the books and writings of the first post-Aristotelian scientists were long and wordy affairs, even after the time of Newton. Descartes' application of formulae to geometry and, even more important, Leibnitz's great emphasis on the importance of symbolism are two outstanding developments in the compression of mathematical language systems.   The importance of symbolism is indeed prominent throughout the modern growth of mathematics, as its generalizations have increased; Russell and Whitehead's treatment of the bases of mathematics (1910) as a generalization of ordinary logic was written almost entirely without words.§   During the last century, the idea has emerged of mathematics as the "syntax of all possible language" and as the language of logic.   In particular Peano invented the symbolism used for symbolic logic.[265]

Leibnitz considered mathematical symbolism as a universal "language of logic"; but he is probably less well known for his advocacy of language reform.   Already, in 1629, Descartes had considered the possibility of creating an artificial, universal language, realizing that the various languages of the world were, by virtue of their complex evolution, utterly illogical, difficult, and ambiguous.   However, his dream did not materialize until 1661, when a Scotsman, George Dalgarno, published his *Ars Signorum* with the support of Charles II.   All knowledge, he proposed, should first be grouped into seventeen sections, such as "politics," "natural objects," and so on, each section being represented by a Latin consonant.   Each

---

* By "rank order" we mean the position of a word in the list, when all the words are tabulated in order of their frequency of occurrence.

† See Berry in reference 166.

‡ For extensive bibliographies of statistical data relating to languages, see references 235 and 367.   We take up Zipf's law again in Chapters 3 and 5.

§ *Principia Mathematica.*

section would be further divided into subsections, represented by vowels; and again, into sub-subsections, repeatedly as required, consonants and vowels alternating.[A,B,*] Every word, always pronounceable, thus denoted an object or an idea by a sequence of "successive approximations" represented by letters denoting selections from the prearranged sections, subsections, et cetera. Another attempt at classification of human knowledge, of amazing scope and ambition, was made by John Wilkins[B,†] in 1668, with the encouragement of the Royal Society; again this classification involved invention of a new "language," with special grammar, and for this purpose a study was made of the basic sounds of speech and of their representation by a phonetic script. The notion of *selection* or *classification*, emphasized by George Dalgarno for the specification of ideas, together with its logical representation by a symbolism, is very relevant to the modern theory of communication. We shall be discussing further historical aspects of such work in the next section. Dalgarno envisaged arriving at an "idea" (a thing, action, relationship—a *referent*) by a series of successive *selections* out of the whole gamut, or totality, of such "ideas," which his language set out to describe ("the universe of discourse").[‡] These selections were to be made from the first seventeen categories, and from successive subcategories, sub-subcategories, and so on. Similarly in the theory of communication today, the symbols transmitted (words, letters, code signs) are considered to be selected from a defined set (the gamut, alphabet, code book, etc.). Such theory, in the restricted form used by telecommunication engineers, is not concerned with meaning or "semantics," but is applicable only after the various ideas have been expressed in a language, as words and sentences or other successions of signs.

In his work on the theory of communication[F] Shannon has illustrated the idea of building up a written "message" as a *stochastic* process, that is, as a series of signs (letters or words), each one being chosen entirely on a probability basis, depending upon the one, two, three or more signs immediately preceding. Stochastic series in which only digram structure is considered, that is, in which each sign is probabilistically related to one of its neighbors, are called Markoff chains; they are named after A. A. Markoff who, in 1913, published a statistical study of Pushkin's poetic novel

* Herbert Spencer, in his *Classification of the Sciences*, argues that the various sciences cannot be arranged in serial order, either on logical or historical grounds, and proceeds to classify them by dividing "Science" into three categories (Abstract, Abstract-Concrete, Concrete), and then to break each down into subcategories, sub-subcategories, and so on. Much modern classification follows such a principle.

† John Wilkins, *An Essay Towards a Real Character and a Philosophical Language*, 1668, and *Mercury, or The Secret and Swift Messenger*, 1641.

‡ Dalgarno is noted also for his original publication (1680) of a deaf-and-dumb manual language; see reference B.

Eugène Onĕgin, in which he considered only word digrams.[225]   That such sequences of words can bear some resemblance to an English text merely illustrates the accuracy of the statistical tables used, although no "sense" is conveyed by the resulting message.   It keeps wandering from the point! A great deal of nonsense has appeared in the lay press, concerning "machines which can write sonnets," so perhaps a word of warning may not be out of place here.   The gathering of monogram and digram statistical data involves an immense amount of labor, and with trigram, quadrigram, and so forth, this becomes increasingly prohibitive; lest the reader should feel that we are merely quibbling and avoiding a point of principle, that given time, patience, unlimited cash, and computing machines, we could collect 10-gram, or 100-gram word transition probabilities of Shakespeare's writings, the following point should be stressed.   The limitation is not the mere labor of letter or word counting; it is the fact that *there are not enough books*.   The data gathered would not be statistical; they would be Shakespeare's actual lines and verses, for each sequence would occur only once. In this connection there is a certain historical interest in the following quotation from Jonathan Swift's *Gulliver's Travels*.   Gulliver has paid a visit to the Academy of Lagado, and, among a series of abusive descriptions of imaginary research programs, describes that of the Professor of Speculative Learning:

> The professor observed me looking upon a frame which took up a great part of the room; he said that by this contrivance the most ignorant person may write in philosophy, poetry and politics.   This frame carried many pieces of wood, linked by wires.   On these were written all the words of their language, without any order.   The pupils took each of them hold of a handle, whereof there were forty fixed round the frame and, giving them a sudden turn, the disposition of the words was entirely changed.   Six hours a day the young students were engaged on this labour; the professor showed me several volumes already collected, to give to the world a complete body of all the arts and sciences.   He assured me that he had made the strictest computation of the general proportion between the numbers of particles, nouns and verbs. . . .*

Such examples of historical precedence as we have been examining are not to be thought of as mere curiosities, as fascinating relics of a dead past, or as amusing glimpses at the vague fumblings of our forefathers for ideas beyond their grasp.   No; study of the history of science shows over and over again the *cyclic* process of its evolution—ideas and theories coming to a stop because of a lack of technique, and the later reciprocal effect of new techniques upon revival and extension of earlier theory. We cannot escape our past; it continually shapes our ideas and our actions.

* "The Voyage to Laputa," 1726, Chapter 5.   The extract above has been condensed.

We hope we have shown illustrations of the truth of such remarks in relation to our subject. What is being witnessed today, in the form of different studies of the communication process, is a logical continuation of activities which we see stretching back into the past. Man has continually sought to improve his communicating abilities, by development of language and improvement of techniques; the full possibilities were beginning to be appreciated in the seventeenth century and much of our discussion at the present day, concerning communication and the ultimate possibilities of machines and techniques, represents a revival of an intense interest of seventeenth-century philosophy.

2. THE MATHEMATICAL THEORY OF COMMUNICATION

Having glanced at the historical origins of the principal concepts of human communication, let us now examine some of the modern technical work in which they have been treated mathematically. The material in this section must necessarily be rather technical, and may be omitted at first reading.

It is in *telecommunication* that a really hard core of mathematical theory has developed; such theory has been evolved over a considerable number of years, as engineers have sought to define what it is that they communicate over their telephone, telegraph, and radio systems. In such technical systems, the commodity which is bought and sold, called *information capacity*, may be defined strictly on a mathematical basis, without any of the vagueness which arises when human beings or other biological organisms are regarded as "communication systems." Nevertheless, human beings usually form part of telephony or telegraphy systems, as "sources" or "receivers"; but the formal mathematical theory is of *direct* application only to the technical equipment itself, from microphone to headphones or loudspeaker, and is abstracted from specific users of the equipment. This is not to say that the mathematical concepts or technique are completely forbidden elsewhere but, if so used, this must *not* be regarded as a simple application of existing "theory of (tele)communication" by extrapolation from its legitimate domain of applicability.

Perhaps the most important technical development which has assisted in the birth of communication theory is that of telegraphy. With its introduction, the idea of speed of transmission of "intelligence" arose. When its economic value was fully realized, the problems of compressing signals exercised many minds, leading eventually to the concept of "quantity of information" and to theories of times and speed of signaling.

In the year 1267, Roger Bacon suggested that "a certain sympathetic needle" (lodestone) might be used for distant communication. Porta and Gilbert, in the sixteenth century, wrote about the "sympathetic telegraph" and, in 1746, Watson, in England, sent electric signals over nearly two miles of wire. Thus not only did the notion of distant communication, by invisible means, arise at an extraordinarily early date, but the first practical achievements were made at a date which astonishes many telecommunication engineers.* In 1753 an anonymous worker used one wire for each letter of the alphabet, but in 1787 Lomond used one wire pair and some code. The introduction of "carrier waves," during the First World War, was made practicable by G. A. Campbell's invention of the wave filter. This principle of allocating simultaneous signals into "frequency bands" has been the mainstay of electrical communication and remained unchallenged until the Second World War.

Related techniques which have greatly urged the development of general communication theory are those of telephony and television. Alexander Graham Bell's invention of the telephone in 1876 (anticipated by Reis and by Bourseul, it is believed[B]) has particular significance in relation to the question of analogies between mechanics and physiology, to which we shall be making further reference later (Section 3) when discussing both the value and the dangers of *anthropomorphic* or *animistic* analogy; otherwise the telephone is, from our present point of view, purely a technological development, setting up problems similar to those of telegraphy. However, early in the history of television broadcasting (Baird and the B.B.C., 1925–1927 in my country), the very great channel capacity required for detailed "instantaneous" picture transmission was appreciated; at that time the normal sound-broadcasting bands† were used and the narrow signal spectrum was a serious restriction. The difficulty was brought to a head with the introduction of the techniques of cathode-ray tubes, mosaic cameras, and other electronic equipment which rendered a high-definition system practicable (1937). Great masses of information had to be read off at high speed at the camera end, transmitted, and reassembled in the receiver. Major theoretical studies were forced by the great channel capacity required for television; in particular the *noise* problem received much attention. In this technical sense, "noise" refers to any disturbance or interference, apart from the wanted signals or messages selected and being sent. Apart from man-

---

* For an historical sketch see *Encyclopædia Britannica* under *telegraphy*.

† It will be assumed that the reader has some knowledge of the terminology of signal analysis. The terms used are similar to those used in optics and diffraction theory. For example, *frequency* is a number of oscillations per second; *band* or *bandwidth* means a spectral spread. Chapter 4 is devoted to signal analysis.

made noise, similar unwanted disturbances come from the random motions of electrons in amplifier tubes; such "noise," sometimes called "Brownian motion,"[G] has been given extensive mathematical and statistical study. These interfering factors are always present to some degree, in all types of communication system whether electrical or not.* "Noise" is the ultimate limiter of communication (see Chapter 5, Section 3).

But to return for a moment to the First World War. Wireless had been developed from the laboratory stage to a practical proposition, largely owing to the field work of Marconi and the early encouragement of the British Post Office, at the turn of the century.[B]† Analysis was eventually applied to problems of "modulation," or superposing a signal upon a radio carrier wave; the mathematical representation of such waves as spectra of "sidebands" first caused some confusion, and fruitless arguments were heard as to whether such sidebands did or did not physically exist. In the early use of wireless for telegraphy, many people naively imagined that a carrier wave was merely switched "on" or "off" for the dots and dashes; an understanding of Fourier spectral analysis grew slowly. Nevertheless, in the case of speech telephony, the advantages of reducing the (spectral) bandwidth required for transmission were in fact recognized, but the early theories of modulation were vague and lacked mathematical support. In 1922 John Carson[56] clarified the situation with a paper showing that the use of frequency modulation did not compress a signal into a narrower bandwidth (this is the F.M. with which radio listeners today are familiar). He also made the important suggestion that all such schemes "are believed to involve a fundamental fallacy," a fact now well known.

In 1924, Nyquist[248] in the United States and Küpfmüller[195] in Germany simultaneously stated the law that, in order to transmit telegraph signals at a certain given rate, a definite bandwidth is required, a law which was expressed more generally by Hartley[C] in 1928. Hartley showed that in order to transmit a given "quantity of information," a definite product (bandwidth × time) is required. We may illustrate this law in the following way. Suppose we have a gramophone record of a speech; this we may regard as a "message." If played at normal speed, the message might take 5 minutes for transmission and its sound bandwidth might range 100–5000 cycles per second. If the speed of the turntable were doubled, the time would be halved; but also the pitch and hence the bandwidth would be doubled. However, Hartley went further and defined *information* as the successive selection of signs or words from a

* For another discussion of "noise" see Section 6.1 of Chapter 5. For a simple description see reference G.

† An early account of these experiments, written in 1899, is contained in reference 405.

given list, rejecting all "meaning" as a mere subjective factor (it is the signs we transmit, or physical signals; we do not transmit their "meaning"). He showed that a message of N signs chosen from an "alphabet" or code book of S signs has S^N possibilities and that the "quantity of information" is most reasonably defined as the logarithm, that is, $H = N \log S$.

We shall later be considering the more modern and detailed aspects of this theory of Hartley's, which may be regarded as the genesis of the modern theory of communication. The factor we have called (bandwidth × time) is a fundamental one which has its counterpart in all systems of communication, whether electrical or not. It may loosely be interpreted to mean "the more elements of a message we send simultaneously, the shorter the time required for their transmission."

All the early modulation theories took as a basic signal the continuous sine wave, or pure tone such as that produced by a sustained tuning fork. Such "Fourier analysis" is essentially timeless, since the waves are imagined as lasting forever; such analysis gives a "frequency description" of signals. The opposite description of a signal as a function of time falls into the reverse extreme, as if the values of the signal at two consecutive instants were independent. Practical signals, whether speech or code, are of finite duration and, furthermore, must occupy a certain bandwidth. The longer the time element ΔT, the narrower the frequency bandwidth, or, as we may say, the more *certain* is its frequency. (The longer the duration of a tone, the more certain we are of its pitch.) We shall discuss Fourier analysis further in Chapter 4.

Gabor[D] took up this concept of *uncertainty* in 1946 and associated the uncertainty of signal time and bandwidth, in the form of $\Delta T \cdot \Delta F \simeq 1$, by analogy, with the Heisenberg uncertainty of wave mechanics, $\Delta p \cdot \Delta q \simeq 1$. In doing this, he is most careful to point out that he is not attempting to "explain" communication in terms of quantum theory, but is merely using some of the mathematical apparatus. A great deal of analogy, as a valid part of scientific method, is of this kind. Later (1948) MacKay, in lectures, generalized this concept of uncertainty in scientific observation and, in Section 4, we shall be discussing this work, which may be regarded as the genesis of what we now call the "theory of (scientific) information."

Gabor pointed out that our physical perception of sound is simultaneously one of time (duration) *and* frequency (pitch), and that a method of signal representation may be used which corresponds more nearly to our acoustic sensations than do either the pure frequency description or time description. The basic signal elements, into which complex signals such as speech may be analyzed and upon which such a representation must be based, must be finite in both frequency and time. Such a basic element is the smallest which can be considered; it is regarded as a "unit of structural information" and is called by Gabor a "logon."[D.]*

By this stage in the evolution of communication technique, it had been realized for several years that in order to obtain more economical transmission of speech signals, in view of the bandwidth × time law, something drastic had to be done to the speech signals themselves to remove those elements which do not contribute markedly to the speech intelligibility. These considerations led to what is known as the Vocoder, an instrument for analyzing, and subsequently resynthesizing, speech; a "talking machine" which requires only control signals to be transmitted and received in order to reproduce intelligible speech. Such control signals are inherently simpler than the speech signals but need to be produced automatically, by electronic analysis of the speaker's actual voice.[E] It is fair to say that such an approach to the problem of speech compression arose out of a study of the human voice and the composition of speech, which itself is of early origin; for example, Alexander Graham Bell and his father had studied speech production and the operation of the ear,[B] and more recently there has been the work of Sir Richard Paget[254] and of Harvey Fletcher.[108] In the year 1939 Homer Dudley[88-90] demonstrated the Voder at the New York World's Fair. This instrument produced artificial voice sounds, controlled by the pressing of keys, and could be made to "speak" when controlled manually by a trained operator. In 1936 Dudley had demonstrated the more important Vocoder; this apparatus gives essentially a means for *automatically* analyzing speech and reconstituting or synthesizing it. The British Post Office also started, at about this date, on an independent program of development, largely due to Halsey and Swaffield.[141] In simple terms, it may be said that the human voice employs two basic tones: those produced by the larynx operation, called "voiced sounds," as in *or, mm, oo*, and a hissing or breath sound, for which the larynx is inoperative, as in *ss, h, f*, etc. Speech contains much that is redundant to intelligence and therefore wasteful of bandwidth; thus it is unnecessary to transmit the actual voice tones, but only their fluctuations.† At the transmitter these fluctuations are analyzed and sent over a narrow bandwidth, while at the same time another signal is sent to indicate the fundamental larynx pitch or, if this is absent, the hissing, breath tone. At the receiver these signals are made to modulate and control artificial, locally produced tones from an oscillator or a hiss

---

* It is important to appreciate that the *structural* aspect of communication theory has nothing to do with probability theory. The logon is a unit which relates to a specified *channel*, but not to any one particular signal transmitted. Such matters will come under discussion in Chapter 4.

† Chapter 4 gives an outline of some modern studies of speech structure.

generator, thus reconstituting the spoken words to such a degree of intelligibility and naturalness as may be required.

Another method of reducing the bandwidth of the signal, called "frequency compression," has been described by Gabor.[126] At the transmitter a record of the speech is scanned repeatedly by electrical "pickups," themselves running, but with a speed different from that of the record. Thus a kind of Doppler effect[G] is produced, reducing the bandwidth of the signal, which at the receiver is expanded to its original width by a similar process. It is of course impossible to reduce *all* frequencies in the same ratio, since this would imply stretching the time scale; rather the apparatus reduces the acoustical frequencies, leaving the syllabic periods unchanged.

It must not be thought that studies of voice production and an interest in "talking machines" is of modern origin. Far from it. Although the Greeks were very concerned with the theory of language and grammar, they do not seem to have got far in their understanding of the physical nature of speech, beyond the explanation by Lucretius, the Epicurean poet, of the production of words: "when atoms of voice in greater numbers than usual have begun to squeeze out through the narrow outlet, the doorway of the overcrowded mouth gets scraped. . . ." Lucretius considered that different voice sounds are produced by differently shaped atoms. It was not until the eighteenth century that serious attention was given to this physical aspect of speech production; the most prominent work of the time was that of von Kempelen, who invented a pneumatic "speaking machine," described in 1791, which was manipulated with the fingers.[187,*]

Even at this date the important function of resonance in the vocal tract was appreciated. At first *one* resonance was considered sufficient, when suitably varied by muscular control of the vocal tract, to produce the major distinct vowel sounds. It was Helmholtz[151] who first put understanding of speech and hearing on a firm scientific basis; he suggested the existence of more than one vocal tract resonance and the part played by these in the control of the larynx tone for the production of vowels. On such foundations our modern theory of speech has been built; the broad ideas have changed little; the major progress has been due, to a large extent, to the availability of electronic and oscillographic technique.[E]

We have so far considered, in the main, the *frequency* aspect of the transmission of signals; questions of bandwidth, of frequency spectra, and so on. This frequency aspect absorbed the most attention during the rapid development of telecommunication during the nineteen-twenties and early nineteen-thirties. However, within the past few years it has been the *time* aspect of which we have heard much: we hear of pulse

* See also Chapter 4.

modulation, of pulse-code modulation, and of "time-division multiplex" —techniques of sending different messages over the same system, separated not into frequency bands but rather by interleaving in time.

Referring back, we find that the earliest suggestions for the simultaneous transmission of two messages over one line, without frequency (spectral) separation, seem to have come independently from Heaviside (1873) and Edison (1874), who introduced the "duplex" and "quadruplex" systems. With this system one message, sent in Morse code, was read at the receiving end by a polarized relay; a second message was transmitted, by allowing it to modulate the amplitude of the first one, which thus acted only as a "carrier wave"; this second message was read by an unpolarized relay.

The important principle inherent in this system is relevant to modern communication theory, namely that two messages can be sent simultaneously over the same bandwidth that is required for one, and in the same time, if the power is increased. The factor bandwidth × time is therefore not the only determinant of communication rate; signal power is another. Although not explicitly stated in his paper, Hartley[c] implied that the "quantity of information" which can be transmitted in a bandwidth F and a time T is proportional to the product $2FT \cdot \log S$, where S is the number of "distinguishable (power) levels." The number of such levels clearly depends upon the incremental power step between each. Hartley considered messages consisting of discrete signs, such as letters or Morse code and dashes, and also messages consisting of continuous wave forms, such as speech and music. He observes that the latter signals do not contain infinite information, because "the sender is unable to control the wave form with complete accuracy." He approximates the wave forms with a series of finite-sized steps, each one representing a *selection* of an amplitude level (Fig. 2.5). The successive amplitude levels S simulate an "alphabet" by which wave forms convey messages, and these levels are "selected," just as letters are selected in written messages.

Such a discrete level representation is nowadays referred to as *amplitude quantization* of the wave form. The words "quantum" and "quantization" have become adopted with specialized significance by physicists, but are used in the present context with their original meaning of "allowed amount," "sufficient quantity,"* or more precisely "significant change of quantity." The concept is really very broad; quantization is a logical necessity of description.[I] For example, we "quantize" people into political parties, into age groups, social classes, and the like, though in truth their opinions, their ages, and their fortunes are as varied as the winds. We merely do this for the *purposes of discussion*, that is, for communication. In our present case, a wave form may be quantized into arbitrary steps (Fig. 2.5), meaning

* *Oxford Dictionary, quantum.*

that smaller steps will be *considered* to be insignificant, and not transmitted. For example, imagine a wave form to be traced out on a rectangular grid as in this figure; the horizontal mesh width representing units of time equal to $1/2F$ (where F is the bandwidth) in order to give the necessary $2FT$ data, in time T and the vertical mesh width representing the amplitude quanta. If we assume this vertical mesh width to equal the noise level n, then the quantity of information transmitted in time T may be shown to be proportional to:

$$FT \cdot \log \left(1 + \frac{a}{n}\right)$$

where a is the maximum signal amplitude, an expression given by Tuller,[328] being based on Hartley's definition of information, to which we have already referred. That this expression bears superficial resemblance to a

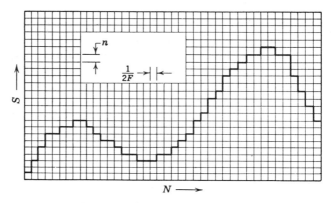

Fig. 2.5.   Quantizing of a continuous wave.

formula for the "information capacity" of a communication channel, under certain conditions, as given later by Shannon, is somewhat fortuitous.[F]   The assumption that the noise has a definite level, equal to the wave-form vertical steps n, is ignoring the fact that noise has an amplitude distribution; it has a certain probability of having *any* amplitude level. We shall be referring again shortly to this work of Shannon in Chapter 5.

The total transmitted quantity of information may be held constant, while the magnitudes F, T, and a are changed; thus bandwidth or time may be traded for signal amplitude (that is, power).   This principle has been given practical embodiment in various systems of pulse modulation and time-division multiplex.   Particular reference should be made to the pioneer work of Reeves* and Deloraine,[82] who patented time-division multiplex systems of communication in 1936, as practical alternatives to frequency division already established.   In such time-division systems the wave form is not transmitted in its entirety but is "sampled" at suitable intervals (about $1/2F$), and the samples are transmitted in the form of pulses, suitably modulated in amplitude, width, number, or time position.[†] Reeves[‡] also proposed another system, which uses directly the idea of amplitude quantization, as envisaged by Hartley; the wave form is automatically restricted, at any instant, to one of a number of fixed levels, as illustrated in Figure 2.5, before being sampled and transmitted as a pulse-train signal.   This assimilation of telephony into telegraphy becomes even more complete if the quantized pulses are coded.[82]   Thus the information to be transmitted is given by the *number* of quanta s in any one pulse-amplitude sample, and this number having one of S possible values, may be coded, for example, into a binary-number code; that is to say the pulse amplitude may be written as a binary number using 1 or 0 only.   The binary code is one of the simplest codes and may take several forms but, in all, the number of "distinguishable levels" is reduced to two.   Information cannot be communicated with less, a fact that has been known concerning language since early historic times, as we have already had occasion to observe in Section 1.

A wave form quantized in amplitude and time, as in Fig. 2.5, can have S^N possible "states."   By regarding these states as an alphabet of all the possible wave forms, Hartley's law gives the information carried by one of these wave forms as $H = KN \log S$, which is finite.   Since Hartley's time this definition of information as *selection* of symbols has been generally accepted, variously interpreted and gradually crystallized into an exact mathematical definition.

This chapter purports to present an historical review and it would be out of place to enter into mathematical discussion here; rather we should make reference to the most important steps in the development of theoretical work and to the relations between them in an attempt to trace the continuous historic thread.   Readers who may be unfamiliar with the various formulae for representing "information" are asked to be patient and to accept them for the moment.   We shall be enquiring further into them in Chapter 5.   It may interest the reader to note here that the Henry system

* Reeves, A. H., British Patents Nos. 509,820 and 521,139 (U.S. Patent No. 2,262,838), British Patent No. 511,222 (U.S. Patent No. 2,266,401); French Patents Nos. 833,929, and 49,159.

† For the so-called "sampling theorem" in mathematics as presented by Whittaker, see reference 347.

‡ Reeves, A. H., British Patent No. 535,860 (U.S. Patent No. 2,272,070); French Patent No. 852,183.

of classifying fingerprints, as used by Scotland Yard, follows precisely the ideas now formulated as Information Theory, even including probabilities —yet it was invented at the turn of this century.[373]

A quantitative description of the information from a source of messages must be given in statistical terms; the information conveyed by a sign must decrease as its probability of occurrence increases. With probabilities* attached to the symbols of an "alphabet," $p_1 p_2 \cdots p_i \cdots$ (or, analogously, to the "states" of a wave form), Hartley's law may be reinterpreted so as to define the average information in a long sequence of n symbols as:

$$H_n = -\sum_i p_i \log p_i$$

an expression which has been evolved in various ways by several authors[328] during the past few years, in particular by Shannon[F] in the United States† whose work is based upon the statistical concept of communication, first emphasized by Wiener[349,350] and Kolmogoroff.[193] (The minus sign in the formula above makes H_n positive, since it involves logarithms of p_i which are fractional.)

In his extended treatment of this measure of information rate, Shannon[F] refers wholly to *averages*; he does not consider the information conveyed by single signs. The formula given above is itself an average; it may be written as $H_n = $ avg (log p_i). It represents what statisticians would call the "expected value of the log-probability" of the signs from the source; it measures their statistical rarity. Any message which is expressed in language may be written in binary code, as a series of *yeses* and *noes*, or 1 and 0; it is said to be *logically* communicable. For example, if it is written in words, we may identify each word by asking a series of questions such as: "Is it in the first half of the dictionary or not—*yes* or *no?*" Given which of these sections, then, "Is it in the first half of this section or not—*yes* or *no?*" And so on; the word is then identified by a chain of numbers such as 10011101. For a dictionary of a quarter of a million words, at most 18 questions with the answers 1 or 0 would suffice, since 2^{18} is greater than 250,000. Such binary digits 1, 0 are called *bits* for short.‡

Perhaps we should emphasize, at this point, the fact that such a measure of information relates only to the signs themselves and does not relate to what they "mean." In his original work, Hartley defined *information* as the successive selection of signs, rejecting all meaning as a mere subjective factor. He was not concerned with the meaning or truth of messages;

---

* *Probability* here means *relative frequency*, estimated from sampling the source of symbols (e.g., counting the letters or the words, as required, in a suitable number and variety of books written in, say, English).

† In Great Britain also, by W. S. Percival, in unpublished work.

‡ See Chapter 3, Section 3, for a fuller description of such logical coding.

semantics does not enter into the theory at this stage. The signs must not be confused with the things they "stand for."*

However, attempts have been made to measure "semantic information," in particular by Bar-Hillel,† who bases his approach on the theory of inductive probability of Carnap.[49,52] He stresses that the recent success of statistical communication theory in elucidating a number of basic problems of telecommunication has led a number of impatient scientists to apply the terminology and the theorems "to fields in which the term *information* was used, presystematically, in a semantic sense; that is, one involving contents or designata of symbols; or even in a pragmatic sense, that is, one involving the users of these symbols." We shall discuss this semantic theory again in Chapter 6.

The measure for H_n in the form given above, from Wiener and Shannon, is applicable to the signs themselves, and does not concern their "meaning." In a sense, it is a pity that the mathematical concepts stemming from Hartley have been called "information" at all. The formula for H_n is really a measure of one facet only of the concept of information; it is the statistical rarity or "surprise value" of a source of message-signs.

But let us return to our theme of a few paragraphs back. The expression for information, H_n, given there, happens to be similar to that for the entropy‡ of a thermodynamical system with states of probabilities, $p_1 p_2 \cdots p_i \cdots p_n$, using the term in the Boltzmann statistical sense. Probably the first detailed discussion of the relation between information rate and entropy was that made, as early as 1929, by Szilard,[318] who, in a discourse on the problem of "Maxwell's demon," pointed out that the entropy lost by the gas, because of the separation of the high- and low-energy particles, was balanced by the information gained by the demon and passed on to the observer of the "experiment." Boltzmann's order-disorder notion is directly applicable to the process of communicating information; it is a notion of extraordinary scope and is rapidly finding interpretation in many, widely diverse, studies of *systems*.§

* See Chapter 3 for further discussion of the syntactic, semantic, and pragmatic aspects of language.

† See Bar-Hillel and Carnap under reference K. (Quotation by kind permission of Butterworth Scientific Publications.)

‡ The relation of information rate to the entropy concept of statistical mechanics is a little indefinite; for example, there is a subtle distinction between the ordinates of spoken language sounds, which possess energy, and the letters of a written language, which do not. The term "selective entropy" has been suggested for this application to communication theory. Brillouin discusses the validity of this interpretation of statistical entropy in several papers (see reference 35); we shall make further comments in Chapter 5, Section 8.

§ See reference 28 for a discussion of the universality of different scientific laws, and for similarity or correspondence between different sciences.

One of Shannon's principal contributions to communication theory has been his expression for the maximum *capacity* of a communication channel to communicate information. This represents the greatest rate of information which may be communicated per second over bandwidth W, in the presence of uniform, random (Gaussian) noise as

$$W \log \left(1 + \frac{P}{N}\right) \text{ bits/sec,}$$

where P and N are the mean signal and noise powers, with amplitude modulation.

This formula superficially resembles that given above, from Tuller, which was derived from Hartley's definition of information. Shannon's formula, however, gives a true absolute maximum; it states the greatest rate in binary digits (bits; *yes-no* decisions) at which the channel can transmit per second, with a vanishingly small probability of error which can be approached but not exceeded as the coding is improved. This channel capacity concept is somewhat analogous to the notion of the conservation of energy; it is a definite limit which no practical system can exceed, and its principal value is that it provides a standard against which efficiencies may be assessed. Many practical telecommunication systems are found, in fact, to be highly efficient; once again practice has preceded theory. Nevertheless, such conservation laws have great value, for they prevent us from trying to attain the impossible. Coding has received considerable attention in recent years, not always for specific practical ends but, in common with much of the theoretical work upon communication, in a search for general guidance where otherwise we would have been fumbling in the dark.[K] In particular, attention has been given to the design of error-correcting codes.[142]

In this section we have tried to put the principal theoretical studies of *tele*communication into historical perspective. Such studies, we have seen, are of precise mathematical character. We are not primarily concerned, in this book, with exposition of such mathematical work in detail (though it is hoped we may serve as a guide through the literature) but with a broader interpretation of the concept "communication." This mathematical work nevertheless has significance and considerable relevance to domains outside telecommunication though, as we have stressed, it should then be interpreted with very great care.

3. BRAINS—REAL AND ARTIFICIAL

The operation of a modern high-speed digital computing machine is of similar nature to that of any electrical communication channel; information is supplied by a "source," suitably coded, transmitted, operated upon in various ways, and passed to the output. This relationship with telecommunication systems, added to the fact that many writers have drawn comparisons between the functions of such machines and of human brains, suggests we might inquire a little into the origins of such analogies, with advantage, as having some bearing upon our subject. From the communication theory point of view, there are certain differences between calculating machines and telecommunication systems. First, a computing machine is usually "noiseless" in that it cannot be allowed to make a single mistake,* since this mistake would render all subsequent calculations invalid; it does, however, possess a limiting accuracy, set by the limited digital capacity. Second, the machine comprises many individual communication channels.† Third, questions of language statistics and coding, such as arise in telecommunication, are replaced by problems of "programming." The development of the early digital computing machines[33,276] such as the ACE and EDSAC in Great Britain and the WHIRLWIND and UNIVAC in America soon led to the popular usage of term "electronic brains."[25] These machines raised complex problems in programming, that is, in the breaking down of the mathematical operations into elementary steps and the logical feeding of the steps into the machine together with prior data referring to the particular calculation.‡ For this purpose the punched-tape or card system is commonly employed. This system of coding data was first conceived by Herman Hollerith in 1889 and was based upon a scheme used for ordering the patterns woven into cloth, by the Jacquard loom,[B]·§ which is itself a problem in "programming." The surprising thing is that, once the programming of a calculation has been carried out, both the fundamental steps and the types of actions required of the machine are few in number and elementary in principle; such simple processes as discriminating, adding, and subtracting form the basis of calculation. It is the automatic feeding-in of the sequence of "instructions" which distinguishes these modern machines from the older manually operated desk types, and especially the facility of changing the sequence of operations according to criteria evaluated during the course of calculation.

Pascal constructed an adding machine (using numbered wheels) in 1642; Leibnitz built a digital multiplying machine in 1694. The modern desk computers have originated from these. However, Descartes, and

* Self-checking procedures are now a recognized essential part of high-speed digital computer operation.

† Either the *serial* system may be used, in which all the digits of a binary number are transmitted in time sequence, or the parallel system, in which they are sent simultaneously over different channels; this is analogous to the time or bandwidth alternative in communication channels.

‡ For historical accounts of calculating machines, see references 7, 19, 146, 276.

§ The invention of several people, from 1725 onward.

again Leibnitz, had visions of "reasoning machines," dealing with problems of logic rather than with arithmetical computations. But the lack of technique prevented practical construction until Charles Babbage, while Professor of Mathematics at Cambridge University between 1829 and 1838, commenced construction of two different kinds of automatic digital computing machine (unfortunately never completed), one of which in basic structure corresponds to our modern machines.[7] This "analytical engine" possessed three component parts: a store for data or for the intermediate results of a calculation, which could be read off as desired; a "mill" for performing arithmetical operations; and an unnamed unit (nowadays called a "controller") for selecting the correct data from the store, for the required operation in the mill, and for returning the result to the store.

Over a hundred years elapsed before the first successful mechanical digital computer was operated, the Harvard Mark 1 calculator by Professor Aiken,[147] using the fundamental principles envisaged by Babbage.[7] The first electronic machine was the ENIAC (by Eckert and Mauchly), with its inherent advantages of speed. Although the choice of a suitable scale or radix is quite arbitrary for the representation of numbers in a machine, great advantages are offered by a binary scale, using only the digits 0 and 1, since the physical elements used in the machine then require only two mutually exclusive states. For example a relay or a switch can be either *on* or *off*. Such a two-valued logical method of representing numerical information is another example of the age-old language, or coding, principle which we examined in Section 1—logically communicable information may always be represented by a two-state code.

During the past ten years or so it has been meaningless to speak of "a modern computer," so great has been the pace of development. The same thing may be said of other technologies, for example aircraft. But computers have become a growth technology of a new kind in industrial experience for three reasons: (*a*) the truly explosive growth of their data capacities and speeds, (*b*) their immense diversity of uses,[394] and (*c*) great advances in man-machine "communication" by the use of so-called "automatic languages" for programming, thereby permitting use of computers by people who understand their problems but who may not necessarily be versed in the details of computers nor, indeed, of mathematics.[390] Originally conceived as automatic arithmetic engines, as aids to computations of all kinds, they are now used not only for scientific research but for business accountancy, for mechanical design leading to machine drawings, for simulating otherwise expensive trials and experiments, for control of industrial plant, for predicting needs for raw materials, for social census analyses. It is this flexibility and universality which makes them have such social importance.[411]

A diagrammatic notation suitable for representing schematically the functional operation of these digital machines was suggested by von Neumann and later modified by Turing, being adapted from the notation proposed by McCulloch and Pitts for expressing the relations between parts of the nervous system. The latter workers[229] had applied the methods of mathematical logic to the study of the union of nerve fibres, by synapses, into networks, while Shannon had applied Boolean algebra to electric circuit switching problems.

Now the nervous system may be thought of, crudely speaking, as a highly complex network* carrying pulse signals, working on an on-off basis; a neuron itself is thought to be a unit, like a switch or a relay which is either on or off. This development of a common notation for expressing the actions of the nervous system and also of binary computing machines at least recognizes a crude analogy between them. It is this analogy which has been greatly extended today, but "models of the brain" have shown more profitable development since this false trail was abandoned. For the brain is really nothing like a digital computing machine.[38a,216,217,408,410]† There is more serious interest in the possibility of "reasoning machines," thus fulfilling the dream of Leibnitz. Just as arithmetic had led to the design of desk computing machines, so we may perhaps infer that symbolic logic may lead to the evolution of "reasoning machines."

Such possibilities, together with the success already achieved by the automatic digital machines, caught the popular imagination during the 1950's. But we should again learn a lesson from history; this interest in machine-brain analogies goes right back to the machinist-vitalist controversies of the seventeenth century.[G,246] We are today witnessing a revival of a number of interests of the days of Descartes[H] relating to animals and machines. The ideas arose in the seventeenth century but techniques for executing practical experiments were lacking; today we have the techniques and are casting back for threads of old ideas. The history of science shows countless examples of such theory-technique cycles.

On the whole, the approach of the scientist to this field has been wise and cautious, but its news value has somewhat naturally led to exaggerations in the lay press; thus, phrases such as "electronic brains" and "machines for writing sonnets" have been used. However, the question "Can a machine think?" is a pseudo-question, if for no better reason than that the words "machine" and "thinking" themselves do not have unique referents

---

* Strictly it has more the characteristics of a field than a network. In the nervous system the potentials are not confined rigidly to single nerve fibres as though these were wires; rather there is a certain spill-over into a region surrounding fibre bundles. See references 149, 337, 338.

† This question is discussed in Chapter 7, Section 7.

(i.e., "meanings").* Again, some people experience a feeling of intense irritation when such questions are raised. "A man is a living thing," we are told, "but a machine is dead matter." Perhaps again, this suggests a wrong emphasis; it may well be, not that people have too great a respect for living matter, but rather that many people have too ready a contempt for "mere" dead matter—a stuff, devoid of mystery.

Much analysis of "mechanized thinking" has been prompted by the theory of intellectual games.[247] Machines which play "noughts and crosses," and incidentally can always win or draw, are comparatively simple;† the existence of such machines does not often cause surprise, because this simple game is considered determinate, whereas chess and card games (such as bridge) give one the feeling that "judgment" is involved. However, Shannon and others have also considered the problem of programing a computer for playing chess,[295] concluding that a machine is constructible, in principle, which could play perfect chess, but owing to the astronomical number of possible moves involved, it would be impracticable. Nevertheless, one could be made which would give a mediocre player a very good game. It is conceivable also that such a computer could be programmed to "learn," by storing up data from all its past games, relating to its moves, wins, and losses; again it might be programmed to classify its human opponents into types by the opening moves they make and then to select its strategy accordingly. A machine of such a character need not operate determinately;[216,217] indeed, the mechanism and stored data needed would be fantastically complex, in the face of the permutations of moves which are possible in chess. Rather the machine could be built on a predictive or probabilistic basis, so as to maximize its likelihood of winning or stalemating at any stage of a game, depending upon the two or three moves which have preceded that stage.

There are two important points which are emphasized by most writers on the subject of "mechanized thinking." First, the machine acts on instructions given to it by the designer; as an illustration, Shannon observes that at any stage in a game of chess, played against his machine, the next move which the machine will make is calculable by its designer, or by one who understands its programming. Again, every single step in a calculation, carried out by a digital computer, could be well done by a human; the machine is merely far quicker. But the class of machines which is of most interest, in the analogies to human behavior which they set up, is the non-determinate class; the machine may be given only some general, overall guiding or goal-seeking rules of operation, and provided with statistical

* This question is discussed again in Chapter 6, Section 4.1.

† See, for example, D. W. Davies, *Science News No. 16*, Penguin Books, Ltd., Harmonsworth, England, 1950, p. 40.

elements giving *random choice* of action, together with storage facilities for recording its past actions and their consequences. The behavior of such a machine would form a stochastic chain of actions. A second point of emphasis is the importance of the *programming* rather than the machine in the metal. As Wiener has been most careful to stress, it is not the machine which is mechanistically analogous to the brain but rather the *operation* of the machine plus the instructions fed into it. The process of programming a digital computer can be long and laborious, and usually it is by far the most serious limitation to the speed of a calculation. As Fairthorne has put it: "The use of high speed devices creates a state of affairs similar to that arising in a rocking-horse factory when the spots are painted in by hand, but the tails are inserted by a high-speed tail-inserter at the rate of several megatails a second."[98].* For this reason, in recent years, a great deal of attention has been given to design of programming methods which can be used by less expertly trained operators—programming such as Algol, Fortran, Autocodes, and others.[390]

To digress for a moment, it was apparent during the years immediately preceding the Second World War that the ideas, basic concepts, and method of communication engineering were of wide applicability to other specialized branches of science. The lead was taken by Norbert Wiener who, with Rosenblueth, called attention to the great generality of the concept of *feedback*, which had been studied intensively by communication engineers for twenty years, and emphasized that this concept provided a useful relationship between biological and physical sciences.[349] They referred to this general study as *cybernetics*, from the word κυβερνήτης (a "steersman"), a word first used by André Ampère in the form *cybernétique*, in his "Essai sur la philosophie des sciences," 1834, to mean the "science of government or control." The simplest feedback systems with which most people are familiar are the Watt steam governor, which regulates the speed of a steam engine, and the thermostat, which controls the temperature of a room. The needs of the War forced attention to feedback theory with the urgency of developing automatic predictors, automatic gun-laying mechanisms, and many other automatic-following, "self-controlling," or "goal-seeking" systems. Weiner and Rosenblueth called attention to the need for a general study that would cover not only these automatic mechanisms but also certain aspects of physiology, the central nervous system, and the operation of the brain, and even certain problems in economics concerning the theory of booms and slumps.[323,332].†.‡

---

* With kind permission.

† J. M. Keynes's theory of economics (1935) is based upon a feedback pattern of action. [189]

‡ See reference 322 for graphs.

The common thread linking these topics, whether mechanical, biological, or electrical, is the idea of communication of information and the setting up of self-stabilizing control action.* Apart from a study of the Watt governor by Maxwell in 1868, the first mathematical treatment of the stabilization of a dynamic system by feeding information signals back from the output or "receiver" end to the input or "transmitter" end was made by H. S. Black, in a study of electrical feedback amplifiers in 1934, and later developed, largely by the efforts of Nyquist and of Bode, into an exact mathematical method and system of design.† The extension of the principles to electromechanical or to purely mechanical systems was a logical one, and has been widely studied; the design of automatic error-correcting ("goal-seeking") systems, such as those for anti-aircraft gun laying, for automatic pilots in aircraft, etc., need no longer proceed on a trial-and-error basis. Much modern so-called *automation* derives from this principle of feedback.

For these automatic control systems the term "servo-mechanism" has been coined. The existence of numerous controls in the body accounts partly for a common interest with physiology. For example, there is homeostasis, or involuntary regulation of body temperature, of heart rate, blood pressure, and other essentials for life; voluntary control is involved in various muscular actions, such as those required for balance when walking along a narrow plank; the simplest motion of a limb exercises multiple feedback actions. If a stabilized servo-mechanism has its feedback path broken, so that the magnitude of its error cannot be measured at the input end and automatically corrected, it is liable to violent oscillation; an analogous state of affairs in the body has been mentioned by Wiener, a nervous disorder called ataxia, which affects the control of muscular actions. The analogies in physiology are countless; Wiener goes even so far, in developing the *functional* analogy between the operations of feedback machines and of the brain and central nervous system, as to compare certain mental functional disorders (the layman's "nervous breakdown") to the breakdown of a machine when overloaded with excess of input instructions, for example, when the storage or "memory circuits" cannot store enough instructions to be able to tackle the situation. Note again the emphasis is on *operation;* no material damage may have occurred. The philosopher Rignano[B,281] had earlier laid great emphasis on the goal-seeking, purposeful activity of man; such a teleological view of life stresses man's powers of choice, of selection of what actions he

* The word "cybernetics" is little used in Britain, but rather the term "control systems" is employed. The French often use "la cybernétique" to correspond with "information theory" in Britain.

† There are many references, but see, for example, reference 175.

shall take for self-preservation or for self-development. It is again the "goal-seeking" behavior of servo-mechanisms which throws into relief their functional analogy to living organisms.

We are led instinctively to ask whether such analogies are not modern examples of a kind of animism, in the sense in which Lewis Mumford uses that word[246]—our readiness to attribute human form or spirit to the machine which can perform functions commonly carried out by humans.* Writers have often criticized the use of expressions such as "memory," "instructions," "decision making" in connection with computing machines. I have. The fault, for example, in referring to the data-storage unit of a machine as a "memory" is not that this implies human personality or character (the engineer is not that naive) but rather that it is an extremely bad analogy. The human memory has properties far more complex and flexible than those of a mere static store of data.[15] Indeed, such analogies as we have discussed do not attempt to "explain" life mechanistically or even to describe the body as a machine in the sense used by Descartes, who observed that "the action of the body, apart from the guidance of the will, does not appear at all strange to those who are acquainted with the variety of movements performed by the different automata, or moving machines fabricated by human industry. . . . Such persons will look on this body as a machine made by the hands of God."[H]

Early invention was greatly hampered by inability to disassociate mechanical structure from animal form; the invention of the wheel was one outstanding early effort of such dissociation. The great spurt in invention which began in the sixteenth century rested on a gradual awareness of the functions of machines, void of all remnants of animal form or of controlling spirits. The development of machines had a converse effect and the body came to be regarded as nothing but a mechanism: the eyes as lenses, the arms and legs as levers, the lungs as bellows, et cetera. Julien de la Mettrie, in about 1740, wrote, "[he thought] that the faculty of thinking was only a necessary result of the organisation of the human machine," a materialist view which greatly disturbed the vitalists of the time. The mention of *organization* here is significant and has a modern ring about it. There has been speculation as to whether a fundamental difference between a living and a dead organism, in scientific terms at least, is that the former constantly reduces its entropy (increases organization) at the expense of that of its environment; here, entropy is identified with information which the living creature is constantly taking in.[36,37,289,318] Since "animistic thinking" has been recognized as such by inventors and

* Sometimes the word "anthropomorphism" is used in texts treating the dangers existing in machine-brain analogies; strictly, however, this word means "attribution of human form and personality to God" (*Oxford English Dictionary*).

scientists, its dangers are largely removed and turned to advantage, though amongst laymen it exists today (as in the use of the expression "electronic brain").

Physics and biology have gone hand in hand; for example, Harvey's discovery of the circulation of the blood (*circa* 1616)[G.265] owes much to his rejection of "animal spirits" and to his interest in the. work on air pumps being carried out at that time. In a more recent age Helmholtz attempted to unify physics, physiology, and aesthetics in his studies of music and hearing.[151] Electrical communication owes a debt to physiology; Alexander Graham Bell,[B] the son of A. M. Bell, who was an authority on phonetics and defective speech and who invented a system of "visible speech," became professor of physiology at Boston in 1873; he invented the telephone microphone after constructing a rubber model of the tongue and soft parts of the throat. The telephone receiver also was modeled on the structure of the human ear.

Although the reflex response had been observed in the sixteenth century and the essential function of the spinal cord discovered in 1751, the relation between function and structure remained elusive until the dawn of the nineteenth century. In 1861 Broca fixed on the area of the cortex concerned with speech, and Thomas Young, in 1792, had already settled that part associated with the eye.[265] The "on-or-off" impulse action of nerve cells was first discovered by Bowditch in 1871, but the neuron theory, that the entire nervous system consists of cells and their outgrowths, has been developed only in our own generation. That the intensity of nerve signals depends upon the frequency of nervous impulses was observed by Keith Lucas in 1909—work which Adrian subsequently carried to an extreme elegance with the assistance of modern amplifier and oscillographic technique in the late nineteen-twenties.

It is most certain that further studies in physiology will lead to new developments in electrical techniques, which in turn will reflect back; new theories and generalities may emerge, leading to greater understanding of machine capabilities. The study of the behavior of these machines and methods of their control or programming may cast new light on logic, as Turing has suggested. Already there are signs of far-reaching developments.*

The philosopher John Locke considered the content of the mind to be made up of ideas, not stored statically like books on a shelf, but by some inner dynamic process becoming associated in groups according to principles of "similarity," "contiguity," or "cause and effect." The word "idea" meant "anything which occupied the mind" or "any object of the under-

---

* See Minski, reference 395, for a very extensive bibliography covering the whole cybernetics field, up to the year 1961.

standing" (*Essay Concerning Human Understanding*, 1690). The first major experimental work, inherently implying a physiological basis for operation of the mind, was carried out by Pavlov, starting about 1898, who studied "patterns of behavior" of animals.[G,265] He produced salivation in a dog by showing it certain objects which, by previous repetition, had become associated in the dog's mind with food—the *conditioned* reflex. Wiener has taken the view that conditioned reflexes enter into the field of cybernetics, or theory of control systems; that, to give the extremes, the encouragement of actions which lead to pleasure in the body and the inhibition of those which lead to pain may possibly be regarded as feed-back actions, suggesting interconnection between different parts of the nervous system. Further, he observed that a conditioned reflex is a "learning mechanism" and that "there is nothing in the nature of the computing machine which forbids it to show conditioned reflexes." Again, the word *machine* here includes instructions.[349]

Experimental work on what may loosely be termed the "behaviorism of machines" was originated, at least in Britain, by Ashby[5] and by Grey Walter.[340] The inaccessibility and complexity of the central nervous system and of the brain render direct analysis overwhelmingly difficult; the brain may contain more than 10^{10} nerve cells, whereas the most complicated computing machine may have up to a million switches, so how can they possibly be compared?* Grey Walter, in his experiments, has started on the simplest scale, building a moving machine having only two "effector" units (linear and rotary motion) and two "receptor" units (by light and touch), and has observed that "behaviour is quite complex and unpredictable." The use of this toy is justified on the grounds "not that it does anything particularly well, but that it does anything at all with so little." One principal method of direct analysis of the workings of the brain is the electro-encephalographic method; the wavelike rise and fall of potential on the surface of the brain, the "alpha rhythm," first observed by Berger[265] in 1928, have been found to possess a complex structure, which varies with the mental state of the subject—asleep or awake, relaxed or concentrating. Study of these wave forms is slowly leading to a detection of "pattern," crudely analogous to the decoding of a cipher by search for its structure.[340] The brain is a highly adaptable instrument; there is considerable flexibility in its functionings and plasticity, or give-and-take between its parts, as forced by circumstances such as damage, or difficult or unusual circumstances. The computing machine on the other hand is a relatively simple instrument; this simplicity restricts its adaptability in the face of faults or of requirements for which it has not

* When the first edition of this book was published, in 1956, the figure given here was 10,000!

been designed, and so calls for infallibility of its various parts. Some attention has been given to the design of error-correcting codes, and to inclusion of routine tests for faults during the operation of these machines.[142]

One of the most important and humane applications of these theoretical studies of communication, which concerns both the biological and the mechanistic fields, is the substitution of one sense for another which has been lost.   Early work in this field[B] includes A. M. Bell's system of "visible speech" for the education of deaf mutes.*   Braille, invented in 1829, involves the tactual learning of a raised-dot code which employs permutations of six positions.†   The first machine to convert print directly into sound was the Optophone, invented by the Frenchman Fournier d'Albe in 1914; Naumberg, in the United States, designed the Visagraph for transcribing a printed book into embossed characters, which unfortunately was slow in operation and costly.‡

The possibility of machines which can directly read printed type and convert this to standardized sounds or "feels" is restricted by the fact that the print may have different sizes and types of font; this therefore raises the difficult psychological question of *gestalt*, or perception of form.   How do we recognize print or, even more puzzling, handwriting which is not even in precise standard form, and which we may never have seen before? How do we recognize a friend's voice?   Or the shape of a ball by its "feel"? Such questions lie at the root of the whole problem of communication and will be discussed in Chapter 7.   In the field of telecommunication, most of the attention has been given to the design of efficient apparatus for carrying signals; yet these signals eventually reach a human being, at the terminal of the channel, who "recognizes" the signals as messages.   Can this process of recognition be described in physical and mathematical terms;—that is, can we build a "machine" capable of receiving, say, speech and of typing it down in some standard script?   (The nature of this basic problem will be given some attention in Chapter 4.)

4. ON SCIENTIFIC METHOD

In this brief history we have attempted to trace the idea of "information" as it existed in early times and gradually entered into a variety of sciences, to some limited extent suggesting a coherent and intelligible study.   Nowa-

---

* "Visible speech" is discussed further and illustrated in Chapter 4.

† In Great Britain, work on the design of reading devices and guiding devices is carried on at St. Dunstan's.   In the United States such work is co-ordinated under the National Research Council.

‡ For discussion of the difficulties inherent in "reading machines" see Beurle p. 323 reference I.

days, the concept of information would seem to be of value to many research workers, and as universal and fundamental as the concepts of energy or entropy.   Speaking most generally, every time we perform any experiment, or make any observation, we are seeking for information; the question thus arises: How much can we know from a particular set of observations or experiments?   The experimenter is really not forming a "communication-link" with Mother Nature.   He is not receiving signs or signals, which are physical embodiments of messages, not words, pictures, or symbols.   The stimuli received from Nature—the sights and sounds—are not pictures of reality but are the evidence from which we build our personal models, or impressions, of reality.   Another distinction between observation and communication is implied by the fact that Nature, as a source of information is uncooperative—in the sense (which we set up in Chapter 1) that she does not select the signs to suit our particular difficulties of observation at any time.

In his classic work, R. A. Fisher[L] considered the extraction of information from experiments, largely from the point of view of using the correct statistical methods.   The experimenter always assumes that it is possible to make valid conclusions from the results of an experiment; that it is possible to argue from effects to causes, or from a particular observation to a general hypothesis.   That is, inductive reasoning is involved essentially, after an experimentation has been made: "inductive inference is the only process . . . by which new knowledge comes into the world."[*][†]   The experimental method implies uncertainty, and the subsequent generalization of conclusion and extraction of systematic laws involves inductive reasoning. Such procedure is essentially forward-looking, as opposed to deduction which looks backward and sorts out, reclassifies, or reorientates what we know already.   But induction cannot tell us new things with certainty; there is always some margin for error or incompleteness, which subsequent deduction and new experiments assist in clearing up.   To some purists there is a certain intellectual unsatisfactoriness about the inductive method but, nevertheless, in physical science it is a principal method of advance. (There exists even today a Society of Flat-Earthists; they are, of course, perfectly right in refusing to accept any evidence as *proof* that the world is round.)   A physical experiment supplies us with information; it assists in narrowing the range of uncertainty of hypothesis.   The information gained, concerning a hypothesis, may perhaps be thought of as the ratio of the *a posteriori* to the *a priori* probabilities (strictly the logarithm of this ratio), as will be argued next.

* This sentence is reprinted from Fisher, *The Design of Experiments*, published by Oliver & Boyd, Ltd., London, by permission of the author and publishers.

† An idea first expressed, I believe, by John Stuart Mill, in *Logic II*.

The importance of the inductive method in science, arguing from observed facts to theories, then back to new experiments, seems to have had its beginnings in Hobbes's doctrine of cause and effect; in his insistence that if a set of "laws," such as Newton's laws of motion, be assumed true, then it is logical to deduce all the inherent consequences mathematically. David Hume stressed how important it is to correlate these calculated consequences with experience. This process of discovering Nature was based upon an act of supposition, or faith, "that the course of nature will continue uniformly the same" (in the future).

The mathematical basis of induction seems first to have been expressed in 1763 by the Reverend Thomas Bayes,[20] who considered the following problem: If H_1, H_2, $\cdots$, H_i, $\cdots$ represent various mutually exclusive hypotheses which can "explain" an event, what are their relative probabilities of being correct? He assumed certain data to be known before the event happens; if E represents some additional data, or evidence, provided by the events, then Bayes's theorem of "inverse probability" gives:

$$p(H_i|E) = \frac{p(E|H_i)p(H_i)}{\sum_i p(E|H_i)p(H_i)}$$

where $p(H_i|E)$ = probability of H_i after the event,
$p(H_i)$ = probability of H_i before the event,
$p(E|H_i)$ = probability of obtaining the data E if the hypothesis H_i be assumed correct.

Although this theorem is generally accepted, its applicability is questioned by some mathematicians on the grounds that the prior probabilities are, strictly speaking, unknown. Bayes put forward an axiom, in addition: If there are no prior data, then all hypotheses are to be assumed equally likely. That is $p(H_i) = 1/n$. The point about this axiom which really matters, as regards the *practical* use of this inverse probability method in physical science, is that the results of applying the theorem to successive events, and the resulting hypotheses' probabilities, are not very "sensitive" to wrong weightings of the original probabilities $p(H_i)$ and Bayes's axiom is as useful an assumption as any. The practical unimportance of the original probabilities has been stressed by I. J. Good.[136] This author expresses Bayes's theorem logarithmically:

$$\log p(H_i|E) - \log p(H_i) = \log p(E|H_i) - \log \sum p(E|H_i)p(H_i)$$

If we remember that the log $\sum$ term here is usually a constant, this equation represents the statement made a few paragraphs back: the information gained (about a hypothesis), by the receipt of some evidence E, is given by the logarithm of the *a posteriori* to the *a priori* probabilities of the hypothesis.

This theorem clearly is of direct application to the theory of telecommunication systems, and in fact may be taken as one starting point for statistical communication theory. The signals received at the end of a communication channel, such for example as a telephone, are relatively imperfect or distorted versions of the "perfect" message signals transmitted. They can only be regarded as evidence (E) about the various messages sent (hypotheses H); all the receiver can do is to assess the relative probabilities of the received message being H_1, H_2, $\cdots$, H_i, in the face of this received, distorted signal evidence E, and perhaps assume the most probable one to be true. In Chapter 5 it will be necessary to examine such notions more closely.

If both sides of the equation above are averaged, over all possible H's and E's, then the result corresponds to the expression for the average rate of communication of information through a noisy telecommunication channel, as given first by Shannon.[F]

In a series of lectures delivered in 1948, at King's College, University of London,[218] MacKay sought to obtain a logical, quantitative, definition of the information given by an experiment or scientific proposition. He observed: "Many scientific concepts in different fields have a logically equivalent structure. One can abstract from them a logical form which is quite general and takes on different peculiar meanings according to the context. . . . It is suggested that the fundamental abstract scientific concept is 'quantal' in its communicable aspects."

MacKay applied this formal logical view to scientific concepts, observing that they are based on limited data given by sets of observations and concluded that a scientific statement may be dissected into elementary ("atomic") propositions, each of which may be answered by *true* or *false*;[356] a "unit of information" is then defined as that which induces us to add one elementary proposition to the logical pattern of the scientific statement. MacKay then drew attention to two complementary aspects of "information." First, the *a priori* aspect, related to the structure of the experiment; for example, a galvanometer may have a response time of 0.01 second; so to describe readings at closer intervals is impossible, for the instrument is capable only of giving information in terms of these small, but finite, (quantal) intervals. This structural aspect corresponds to the *logon* concept of Gabor,[D] originally framed to define the response characteristics of a telecommunication channel (see Section 2 of this chapter). Experimentation abounds with such uncertainties: "Each time that a compromise has to be struck, say between the sensitivity and response time of a galvanometer, or the noise level and bandwidth of an amplifier, or the resolving power and aperture of a microscope. . . ." Secondly, the *a posteriori* aspect, related to the "metrical information content" of the experiment; for example, a galvanometer may be used to record a set of values of a variable, each reading representing a certain "amount of metrical information." These recordings being capable of only a certain accuracy, the amount of metrical information obtained may be thought of as a dimensionless measure of precision, or weight of evidence.

MacKay's "metrical information" is related to Fisher's definition of an amount of statistical information, as the reciprocal of the variance of a statistical sample.[L] It is this definition of information which statisticians most readily call to mind, at least in Europe, when they hear the word. Briefly, if $p_\theta(x)$ is a distribution function, with some parameter θ (for example, a mean value) then, by writing $L(x|\theta) = \sum \log p_\theta(x)$, where $x_1 x_2 x_3 \cdots$ are independent samples, the "information" about θ which these samples give is defined as the mean value of $\partial^2 L/\partial\theta^2$. In MacKay's illustration of galvanometer readings, $x_1 x_2 x_3 \cdots$ represent successive readings and θ is the mean; so the "information" $\partial^2 L/\partial\theta^2$ here is information concerning this mean θ, provided by the evidence $x_1 x_2 x_3 \cdots$.

Barnard[14] has investigated the relation of this "information" with that of Shannon and others in telecommunication; further, he describes another interpretation of "information," in a third sense, as a measure of the "difficulty of a mathematical problem." He stresses that: "the elements ... of a basic set ... can variously be interpreted as (a) 'messages' ... (b) 'propositions' ... (c) 'problems' ... to emphasise the abstract character of the theory which resides in the fact that the symbols and axioms in the theory are capable of bearing more than one interpretation."

BIBLIOGRAPHY

A. Bodmer, F., *The Loom of Language*, George Allen & Unwin, Ltd., London, 1944.
B. *Encyclopædia Britannica*, Cambridge University Press, London, 11th Ed., 1911.
C. Hartley, R. V. L., "Transmission of Information," *Bell System Tech. J.*, 7, 1928, p. 535.
D. Gabor, D., "Theory of Communication," *J. Inst. Elec. Engrs. (London)*, 93, Part III, 1946, p. 429.
E. Potter, R. K., G. A. Kopp, and H. C. Green, *Visible Speech*, D. Van Nostrand Co., Inc., New York, 1947.
F. Shannon, C. E., and W. Weaver, *The Mathematical Theory of Communication*, University of Illinois Press, Urbana, 1949.
G. Dampier, Sir William Cecil, *A History of Science*, Cambridge University Press, London, 4th Ed., 1948.
H. Descartes, René, *A Discourse on Method* (and other philosophic essays), 1637. Edition in English by J. M. Dent & Sons, Ltd., London, and E. P. Dutton & Co., Inc., New York.
I. Poincaré, Henri, *Science and Hypothesis* (in English), The Walter Scott Publishing Co., Ltd., London and New York, 1905.

J. Jackson, Willis, Editor, *Proceedings of a Symposium on Information Theory*, London, 1950, published by the Ministry of Supply and later by the American Institute of Radio Engineers, 1950.

K. Jackson, Willis, Editor, *Proceedings of a Symposium on Applications of Communication Theory*, London, 1952, published by Butterworth Scientific Publications, London, 1953.

L. Fisher, Sir Ronald, *The Design of Experiments*, Oliver & Boyd, Ltd., London, 1935.

CHAPTER THREE

On Signs, Language, and Communication

Language is called the garment of thought; however,
it should rather be, language is the flesh-garment,
the body, of thought.

Carlyle (1795–1881)
Past and Present

The *Oxford English Dictionary* contains about half a million words; the seeds of all our great literature and poetry, of the expressions of our novelists, our historians, and our humorists; they may be used for trivial gossip, or for the fire of rhetoric to inflame a mob; for the most bitter polemic and for hymns of praise.   From these fertile seeds have grown the majesty of Milton, the poignant wit of Swift, the terseness of Army Orders, and the banality of business English.

Words can arouse every emotion: awe, hate, terror, nostalgia, grief. . . . Words can demoralize a man into torpor, or they can spring him into delight; they can raise him to heights of spiritual and aesthetic experience. Words have frightening power.[404, 369]

All that we have to do is to pick them out of the dictionary and string them in the right order. . . .

1. LANGUAGE: SCIENCE AND AESTHETICS

When I first visited America, I was startled to see standing in the middle of the highway a signboard which read:

CARS MUST BE KEPT
ON THE PAVEMENT

Fortunately I was not driving, or perhaps I might have broken the law unwittingly by parking my vehicle on the "sidewalk";* that is, I should have behaved in an anti-social manner.   Language performs an essentially social function; it helps us to get along together, to communicate and achieve a great measure of concerted action.   Words are signs which have significance by *convention*, and those people who do not adopt the conventions simply fail to communicate.   They do not "get along" and a social force arises which encourages them to achieve the correct associations. By "correct" we mean "as used by other members of the social group." Some of the vital points about language are brought home forcibly to an Englishman when visiting America, and vice versa, because our vocabularies are nearly the same—but not quite.[45]   It was Oscar Wilde who observed "England and America are two countries separated only by a common language."

Not all words represent things, or even classes of things.   Words such as "in," "whether," "good-bye," "yes" clearly do not.   But for the purpose of this simple discussion let us restrict our present examples to words which do.   The word "pen" denotes a class of thing, such as that which I am now holding in my hand; *la plume* means the same thing to a Frenchman and *die Feder* the same to a German.   When we think about such words, as when we are learning a foreign language, we are conscious of them as mere empirical signs; but in our everyday speech we are so familiar with the words of our own language that we may tend to forget this empiricism, and we may unconsciously regard the word as being part and parcel of the thing it represents—the referent.   It is not difficult to imagine how magical properties may become attributed to the names of those objects which themselves set up feelings of wonder, awe, or fear.   As Frazer has remarked, taboo words, spells, and passwords have terrible power.†   Nor need we pride ourselves that we have shaken off all such primitive superstitions.   Today we ourselves recognize many taboo words, though we may cloak our superstitions by calling them decency, delicacy, or humility.

But if all the words we used were names of things—words like "pen," "table," "floor"—then the study of language would be far simpler than it is.   Each word would represent a thing (or class of things) empirically, and their exact uses might be agreed to by all of us.   As it is, however, most words do not stand in such unique relationship with simple things.

* "Pavement," in England, means "sidewalk."

† See *The Golden Bough*, Chapter XXII, p. 244 (abridged edition), by Sir James Frazer, MacMillan & Co., Ltd., London, 1941.

For example, nouns such as "democracy," "civilization," "education" have different significance to different conditions and classes of men; nouns like "freedom" and "happiness" are interpreted differently by almost every individual. Indeed, with continued use a good many words have lost their significance and no longer act as symbols of specific things, or even of specific ideas. Some have become verbal emotive stimulants, arousing passion without reason, bemusing or stiffening the hearer into attitudes. Words such as "Fascist," "Communist," "nigger," "bitch" are bandied about as mere terms of abuse, without thought to their formal significance. The prefix "atomic-" suggests only bombs to most people and nothing more. Many scientific sounding expressions, like "chlorophyll," "nerves," "vitamins" are used by commercial advertisers of patent medicines merely to impress the layman who has no notion of their meaning; he may become "blinded by science." Senseless clichés and platitudes, hammered in by continual repetition, form the practiced art of the propagandist, of the crowd-swaying orator and the charlatan. Language may be set to work upon an accumulated body of past experiences and past misunderstandings employed for deliberate deceit or for arousing prejudices of all kinds.

One important point concerns emotion; to speak about an emotion is not the same as to experience it. Emotions may be shown by signs, by tears, blushes, whitening, shudders.[380] When someone says "I was terrified!" he refers to a past experience but may be quite stable and happy at the time of speaking.

These remarks may serve to show the various degrees of vagueness associated with words, even nouns. The simplest word-signs that we have are those which *denote* unique referents—such, for example, as the names of people, the index numbers of automobiles, the reference numbers of books in a library or in a filing system. Such symbols enable us to have access to the things denoted without any vagueness or error; they form exact *denotations*. A great deal of *descriptive* language, though not purely denotative, serves a sorting or classifying purpose: words as "big," "blue," "round"—the longer the description, the more precisely may the object be pigeonholed (see Chapter 6, Section 1.2). The commonest nouns, words like "man," "house," "box," refer not to things but to classes of things, and the boundaries of these classes are more or less clearly understood by convention, though with some vagueness; when does a boy become a man, or a bush a tree? Other nouns, such as "freedom," "beauty," "progress," are even less definite and, in fact, lie open to an infinite variety of interpretations. Again, as already stressed, many nouns do not name anything at all to their hearer, but act as little more than emotive stimulants or even mere expletives. "When we begin to fix by means of words . . .

abstract ideas . . . there is a danger of error.   Words should not be treated
as adequate pictures of things; they are merely arbitrary signs for certain
ideas—chosen by historical accident and liable to change."*

Then how do we communicate?   If words of a language do not name
things, actions, events, relationships, and so on, with precision, then
language itself must be a source of imprecision in communication?   Indeed
it is.   And the degree of this imprecision depends to a great extent upon the
choice of words by the writer or speaker, upon his skill in selecting words,
and upon his artistic sense in using them to set his audience into the right
frame of mind.   Language cannot give precise representation of things or
ideas because there are simply not enough different words to express the
subtlety of every shade of thought.   If we had words for everything, their
numbers would be astronomically large and beyond our powers of memory
or our skill to use them.[G]   The entry of new words into a language is
resisted, with the result that "one word has to serve functions for which a
hundred would not be too many";[250] again, combinations of words into
phrases may have to be employed where a single word might serve, if it
existed.   But language is kept alive by common use, by the "vulgar," and
a few thousand words may provide the limit of vocabulary of the majority
of English-speaking people or other Europeans.

Words are conventional signs; they are empirical but not wholly arbitrary.
Thus a spade is called a "spade," not with any particular reason or in any
calculated manner, but by virtue of historic circumstance.   A spade is
equally well called *une bêche*, or *ein Spaten*, where history has been different;
if everyone agreed, it could well be referred to as a *shnoppel!*   The word, as
a written chain of letters or, in far more cases, as a spoken sound pattern,†
need be no more than empirically chosen, at least for its purely *denoting* or
sorting purpose.   However, the acceptability of a word and its effectiveness
and aesthetic value in communication are greatly enhanced by a happy
sound patterning; happy, not because the sounds themselves are particularly
beautiful (they may seem ugly to listeners of another language), but because
of the host of mental associations which they call up.   Onomatopoeia,
alliteration, rhythm of syllabic flow, and a dozen other devices play their
part.   If words were mere empirical signs, arising from no historic or
artistic reason, all our writings would read like textbooks of algebra (or
like the bulk of legal documents). Poetry would be a void.

A word in a dictionary is explained in terms of other words, but such
explanations, or illustrations, do not constitute definitions in any logical or
scientific sense.   The dictionary supplies phrases more or less synonymous

* John Locke, *Essay Concerning Human Understanding*, 1690.
† Only a small fraction of the world's languages have any written form.   Professor
A. S. C. Ross has estimated it as no more than 5 per cent (private correspondence).

with the word, as judged by common usage. All the words that are employed in these explanatory phrases are themselves listed in the dictionary, which thus forms what might be called a "closed system." But not quite. The etymological roots are given as well; Greek, Latin, Middle English, and so on. Words are partly known by their backgrounds, their pasts, like men; and like men they do not have their full significance when standing alone but are known by the company they keep. A word is essentially contained in a context and the full effect of the word is felt only when it appears in context. The word "knit," standing alone, as in the dictionary, is nothing but an empirical sign; but in the line, "Sleep that knits up the ravell'd sleeve of care," the word becomes a different creature.

Literary style is influenced by the broad choice of vocabulary; the predominant use of classical words may give an air of seriousness, a sonority, or even a grandeur, as opposed to the blunter and more homely words of common English. Again, the continual use of archaic words sets an atmosphere which influences the reader's thoughts ("wench," "ere," "perchance"); just as does, in another way, the importing of foreign words (*élan, ennui, chic*) not yet truly assimilated into our language. At a closer range, words are known partly by the type of context in which they customarily appear. Thus, the words "silica" and "sodium chloride" may put the reader in a scientific frame of mind whereas their equivalents, "sand" and "salt," may give a whiff of the seaside. The English language is very rich in its possession of near-synonyms, words which have similar referents but which usually appear in different types of contexts; having such past associations, these words achieve greater subtlety of meaning. "Fat," "obese," "stout," "podgy," "swollen," "rotund," "bulbous," "puffy," "portly," "bloated," "gross," "corpulent," "bulky," "tubby," "chubby," "plump," "fleshy," "pursy," "brawny," "gigantic," "stuffed," "gargantuan," "inflated," "paunchy," "giant," "large," "elephantine," "big," "balloon-like," "bulgy" are all used to suggest large size in people, yet each suggests some extra quality, from past usage.

A word is more than an arbitrary written or spoken sign; it is all that it carries in association as well. Words can play upon our feelings and tap our memories. A text, when translated from one language into another, may lose or change a great deal of its emotive force. When I read French I need to become as a different person, with different thoughts; the language change bears with it a change of national character and temperament, a different history and literature. The translator of poetry really has an impossible task.[279] Nevertheless there have been those with remarkable powers to breach cultural boundaries and to produce fine translations of poetry.

A language has not been invented or set up arbitrarily at some point in time, by authority, like a card-index coding system, but has steadily moved with the history of the community, changing as social conditions change. It has been described as "the mirror of society." It represents a *continuous* growth, for all human experience is a continuing process. In analogy to the growth of living plants and creatures, subject to the continual influence of natural forces, language may be said to have *form*.*

The concept of form[319,348] is one of those rare bridges between science and art. It is a name we may give to the source of aesthetic delight we sometimes experience when we have found a "neat" mathematical solution or when we suddenly "see" broad relationships in what has hitherto been a mass of isolated facts. Form essentially emerges from the continual play of governing conditions or "law." An artistic mode of expression, such as music, painting, sculpture, represents a "language"; through this means the artist instills ideas into us. His creation has form inasmuch as it represents a continuity of his past experience and that of others of his time, so long as it obeys some of the "rules." It has meaning for us if it represents a continuity and extension of our own experience. Modern music would have fewer bitter things said about it by some people if they approached it gradually instead of jumping into it. The language of a people largely constrains their thoughts. Its words, concepts, and syntax, out of all the signs people use, are the most important determinant of what they are *free* and *able* to think. It makes their particular epistemology, their special view of the world, what they notice or do not notice.

Pictures and sculpture may be regarded as signs—*icon signs* or *icons* as Peirce has called them. But pictures are not true copies, not duplicates of real scenes and people; portraits are not models or duplicates of people's faces—not even in the sense that a photograph is a one-to-one, two-dimensional projection.† A portrait acts as an icon by virtue of certain inherent attributes or characteristics (e.g., Fig. 7.7). We may be so accustomed to the classical paintings of Gainsborough and Watteau as to imagine that they are "natural" or "life-like," but a moment's thought and close examination show many distinctions from reality; and there is a continuity of artistic development from their time to, say, the "unnatural" cubists. The more we comprehend the past, the better we apprehend today.[134]

* The use of the word "continuous" here should not be taken to imply that languages develop along some predestined course, or to deny that development may be random, as some linguists hold.

† Prof. E. H. Gombrich's essay[348,388] "Meditation upon a Hobby-Horse" is a delightful development of such ideas. This same essay reappeared in a more recent collection of his essays.[388]

Every individual word in a passage of prose or poetry can no more be said to denote some specific referent than does every brush mark, every line in a painting have its counterpart in reality. The writer or speaker does not communicate his *thoughts* to us; he communicates a representation for carrying out this function, under the severe discipline of using the only materials he has, sound and gesture. Speech is like painting, a representation made out of given materials—sound or paint. The function of speech is to stimulate and set up thoughts in us having correspondence with the speaker's desires; he has then communicated with us. But he has not transmitted a copy of his thoughts, a photograph, but only a stream of speech—a substitute made from the unpromising material of sound.

The artist, the sculptor, the caricaturist, the composer are akin in this, that they express (make representations of) their thoughts using chosen, limited materials. They make the "best" representations, within these self-imposed constraints. A child who builds models of a house, or a train, using only a few colored bricks, is essentially engaged in the same creative task.* Metaphor can play a most forceful role, by importing ideas through a vehicle language, setting up what are purely linguistic associations (we speak of "heavy *burden* of taxation," "being in a *rut*"). The imported concepts are, to some extent, artificial in their contexts, and they are by no means universal among different cultures. For instance, the concepts of *cleanliness* and *washing* are used within Christendom to imply "freedom from sin." We Westerners speak of *the mind's eye*, but this idea is unknown amongst the Chinese.[279] After continued use, many metaphorical words become incorporated into the language and lose their original significance; words such as "explain," "ponder," "see (what you mean)" we no longer think of as metaphorical.[113] Metaphors arise because we continually need to stretch the range of words as we accumulate new concepts and abstract relationships.[380]

A printed text is not simply a chain of individual words, picked one at a time; it is a whole. It has a structure, but it has meaning for us only if it represents a continuity of our experience of past texts. A text in some strange foreign language sets up an abrupt change in our experience, a discontinuity, and we make nothing of it. Given a translator's dictionary we may decipher some of the words and attain some understanding, though this understanding through translation has been achieved by projecting the text onto our own language;[208] that is, we are looking at it with the eyes of our English-speaking culture. A grammar book may help us to decipher the text more thoroughly, and help us comprehend something of the language structure, but we may never fully understand if we are not bred in the culture and society that has molded and shaped the language.

* See Gombrich in reference 348.

Clearly, such difficulties with foreign languages do not enter in the translation of simple direct statements, such as we meet when traveling abroad. "*Non sputare nella carroza*" or "*Rechts fahren!*" have very direct interpretations! Again, it is a major triumph of science to have evolved a language largely independent of culture. But the majority of texts use language with much greater subtlety, and understanding is far less readily attained. The full effect of a word upon its hearer may depend not only upon the context but upon the whole physical and psychological environment and, on many occasions, upon his experience of the culture of which the language forms an integral part. The study of language (linguistics) has both its scientific and aesthetic sides, and partly for this reason it is a most valuable study.

Dualism, or twin-thinking, seems to be a natural human quality. Controversies continually rage: science versus humanities as a vehicle of education; technology and the arts; the material and the spiritual; mind and body. Yet in truth the cleavage is never perfect, the two sides are never complete in themselves. The division is a convenience but is not part of the structure of the world. In the study of language the nullity of any such divorce is made particularly prominent.

The scientist is a man who puts himself under a particular discipline. In the so-called "exact sciences" he takes up a position as far to one side of the science-art union as he can—deliberately. But this does not make him fit only for "treasons, stratagems and spoils." He is aware that the scientific way of thinking is not the only way, but rather that it is the only way relevant to his restricted purpose. The scientific study of languages may need to tear apart the writings and utterances of people, the prose and poetry, the profound and the trivial; to reduce them to elements, to pieces, to classify and catalogue, so that each unit and its relations may be examined. Just as a man may be dissected, reduced to bones, tissue, and organs; yet assembled and with the breath of life in him, he is a man for all that.

In their *Meaning of Meaning*,[250] Ogden and Richards distinguish between the symbolic and the emotive uses of language. The first, they say, serves for identifying or cataloguing things, actions, or relationships. Many scientific words perform this function. Thus in mechanics the primary words *gram*, *metre*, *second*, refer to physical standards of mass, length, and time; other scientific words such as *velocity*, *momentum* are defined in terms of these primary words and through them they are connected to the physical things, the referents. And so the complex system of language is built up for discussing mechanics. Such words, used in this way, are truly empirical and arbitrary; any other words could be invented and used instead, like the index numbers of a filing system, provided that everybody agreed to them. For its scientific use, a word such as "metre" is merely *correct* for the physical standard of length; there is no question of this word's being a *good* choice.

At the other extreme, poetry may largely dispense with such symbolic, logical use of words. When the words were wrung from Macbeth—"Tomorrow, and tomorrow, and tomorrow, creeps in this petty pace from day to day"—he was not speaking of time and velocity! Words in poetry are selected, not for their "correctness" but to achieve certain results, to produce certain effects upon the reader's mind.

The point we wish to make, in this present discussion, is that these two "polar extremes" of the whole sphere of language, the symbolic and emotive, which we may in extreme call the scientific and the aesthetic, are not mutually exclusive and antagonistic. In all speech and writing, something of both uses is called into play. At one end of the intellectual scale, mathematics and the so-called "pure" sciences provide the most severe disciplines in their demands for symbolic language.* But the more recently developed sciences, like psychology, sociology, or economics, have not as yet built up a consistent vocabulary of universally accepted words having precise referents and a special syntax. Such sciences so far are not highly formal, deductive systems, and misunderstandings can arise; speakers may be guided by their particular habits of language, and linguistic argument may be mistaken for scientific controversy. The poet Shelley has summed up the difference between these two attitudes to language in the words: "Poetry is not like reasoning, a power to be exerted according to the determination of the will. A man cannot say 'I will compose poetry.'"†

The artist is sometimes offended by what he imagines to be the scientific view and the scientific use of language; the scientist so often fails to appreciate the importance of the literary value of his writing to its *scientific* comprehension and acceptance. But writing poetry and writing *about* poetry are different activities; and the scientific analysis of language is not to be confused with literature. The scientist prides himself that he uses words in a special way; that he chooses them, not for their emotive value, or for their beauty of sound patterning, or in any way private to himself, but rather in conformity with a public use amongst all his fellow scientists. That is, scientific language has a *public* utility, whereas poetry may have significance which is personal to the reader. This scientific language is relevant only to the *corpus* of the scientific structure; but its rigid discipline need not restrict the freedom of the scientific writer in his desire to communicate his ideas to others. The writer may use all his powers of

* The very word *pure*, in this scientific context, is highly emotional, even suggesting virginity!

† "A Defence of Poetry."

persuasion, all his wit and imagination, to clarify and convince—only the nucleus of scientific concepts require strict adherence to the "public" scientific language. A scientific treatise can well be a work of art, too; and indeed we have a great inheritance in this respect, which no young scientist can afford to overlook.

The powers of persuasive language are required for the "putting over" of new ideas, for explaining new generalizations convincingly. But for presenting purely deductive arguments, highly formalized language systems serve the purpose. In mathematical texts, this formalism reaches a climax; not only is the bulk of the symbolism completely standardized and universal, as a scientific *lingua franca*, but so too are many of the connecting phrases: "consider the function . . . "; "let us assume that . . . "; "necessary and sufficient conditions. . . ." In normal life we call such standardized phrases clichés. Mathematics rarely has literary value! On the other hand some of the most important advances in science arise from generalization, by *inductive* reasoning, to the production of new concepts. Such reasoning requires the reader to extrapolate beyond his present knowledge. His imagination and faith must be called upon to accept something hitherto quite out of his ken. He must be put into the right attitude of mind, and the full artistry of the writer is called upon to augment his formal symbolic use of language.

2. WHAT IS A LANGUAGE?

Language is an aspect of culture which is common to all human societies. Languages are in a continual state of change, as social conditions change; as contacts between classes, peoples, and races touch and go, as ideas pass and repass. Language has been compared to the shifting surface of the sea; the sparkle of the waves like flashes of light on points of history.

Language makes a hard mistress and we are all her slaves. It is difficult to exaggerate the influence which she exerts upon our lives, yet she is aloof and mysterious. Anyone who would consort with her, to study and understand her, lays himself open to a severe discipline and much disappointment.

2.1. SPEECH AND WRITING—ESSENTIALLY HUMAN FACULTIES

At the beginning of the seventeenth century, Ben Jonson wrote:

Speech is the only benefit man hath to express his excellency of mind above other creatures. It is the instrument of *Society*. Therefore Mercury, who is the President of Language, is called *Dearum hominumque interpres*. In all speech, words and sense are as the body and soul. The sense is as the life and soul of Language, without which all words are dead. Sense is wrought out of experience, the knowledge of human life and actions, of the liberal Arts, which the *Greeks* called Ἐγκυκλοπαιδείαν.

Man has the unique gift of speech. To the young child the babbling sounds he makes may afford him pleasure and may serve biological functions by exercising the speech organs. But these sounds do not form a social communication process and cannot strictly be called language.[170] They may be said to be *indicative* to the mother. As the arbitrary symbolic function of words comes into the child's awareness and vocal sounds begin to acquire value, his mental activity undergoes adjustment and he becomes integrated with the social community. With words he can not only communicate with others, but he can soliloquize (a secondary, not a social function[130]). He can have thoughts framed into words and so gains great advantages for cataloguing things and ideas, for relating them and for arguing and reasoning with himself.

The case of Helen Keller[186] provides an interesting human story. Helen became blind and deaf at the age of eighteen months, before she had developed speech habits or the abstract concepts of an adult. She could neither see nor hear, but was cut off. Most people in her situation, at that time, had become complete idiots, but Helen developed into a remarkably intelligent personality, largely through the patience of her nurse, who taught her to make the sounds of speech; Helen felt the motions of her nurse's throat and mouth with her hand. Up to the age of about nine Helen learned to speak words and phrases but—and this is the point— such speech sounds were quite meaningless to her, no more than verbal play; they gave her pleasure to utter, as it pleases a parrot to speak, but such words and phrases were irrelevant, purposeless, and empty. She achieved some measure of communication by pushing and pulling, nodding and shaking her head, and by direct imitative action—all the time accompanied by her senseless gibberish. But one day Helen was playing with the water coming from the pump when her nurse vibrated out the word "water." Immediately, in a flash of revelation, Helen saw the idea of words. "Everything has a name!" she cried.* She made a remarkable inference, developing the new concept, or universal, of "words," a thing no animal can do. From that moment on, Helen became human and her mental life became organized. She could communicate and become a social being. Since her day there have been many others taught in a similar way.

All of us have the experience of thoughts and ideas growing in our minds; for example, relating to our own fields of study. Yet we all know how difficult it can be to state the exact instant when an idea was born in us. Like Topsy, it "just grow'd." We are aware that some idea is beginning to take shape, but for some time it may be vague and misty, seen dimly

---

* This is the story.   It can only be assumed that she used this phrase (being meaningful) when *later* describing her experiences.

through the depths of "feeling," "intuition"; we are in acute mental discomfort until the idea is expressed in words, formulae or diagrams, that is, until it is *formulated*. The only way to pin down a thought before it can slip away and fly out of the window, is to jump on it with both verbal feet, to pin it down with language, by diagrams, or by mathematical symbols—though such language may be inadequate. When the thought has such form and substance, it may be communicated and discussed with others.

We cannot necessarily put all our mental experience into (existing) words. Many thoughts and experiences are extremely difficult to express so. But language gives us undoubted ability to organize thoughts, for collecting, sorting, relating, and recording ideas. We pay a price with the possession of language, for we become prone to verbal habits. It is only too easy to use clichés, proverbs, and slogans as a substitute for reasoned statements; to accept the smooth persuasion of well-sounding humbug; to misunderstand a difficult passage in a book by misreading into it our own preconceived ideas. The broad pastures of our minds are crisscrossed by pathways of verbal habit.[c, 321.]*

If speech is our first, it is not our only mode of communication. Most human beings, but *not* most societies (see footnote, p. 69), have some form of writing or scribing. The present times might well be called the Age of Paper; without the written word civilization, in the form we know it today, could not be sustained. Compared to speech, writing is relatively clumsy, lengthy, and slow. We can introduce great expression and flexibility into our vocal utterances by stressing, speed, pitch, and articulation. (There are a hundred ways of saying "Yes.") It may take a page of finest prose to convey the spine-chilling effect of one piercing scream. Even more subtle and compact are gestures—a shrug, a turn of the head, or a look of despair. There can be worlds in a wink. In the ballet and the theater, communication and understanding are as dependent on movement and gesture as upon words and music. When we speak to a friend on the telephone, sight plays no part, and normal gesture reinforcement is lost, which we partly replace by changing our habits of speech.[c, 114, 226.]† Again, if a speech is literally transcribed into print, a great amount of information is lost; conversations in novels are rarely like real-life talk, but are constructed by the author to convey the right impression.

* One amusing illustration of how our scientific thinking may be confused by habit is given by the problem: When we look into a mirror, why is it that we see ourselves the right way up, but the wrong way round? (The answer is not to be found in the laws of optics; the "puzzle" is left to the reader.)

† Studies have been carried out by J. Berry at the British Post Office Research Station (Dollis Hill, London), as yet unpublished except in the form of an internal report. See also Berry in reference 166.

Spoken language may well be enhanced in effect by stressing, by changing speed or pitch of speaking, together with reinforcement by gestures. But signs such as frowns, smiles, tears, bared teeth, and blushes do not constitute part of human language; they are not arbitrary symbols but are signs evoked by a situation or environment. They are akin to the signs used by birds and animals, their cries of alarm, their postures of threat, and their attitudes of defense. These various releaser stimuli, the signs indicating friend or foe, are not to be thought of as "language." The writer has argued elsewhere that there is one specific situation in which we humans are "reduced" to animals, inasmuch as we are bereft of human language and are forced to use a determinate alphabet of preformed signs—namely, when we are driving our motor cars. We cannot speak to one another, show gestures of sympathy, apologise, discuss, give opinions, etc. We must *conform* to the externally determined rules of the Highway Code Book. The street and road signs, our car blinkers, policeman's signs, etc., do not constitute language, and we are held *incommunicado*, as we are when in prison, or if "sent to Coventry" by our colleagues. And a man incommunicado is not part of our society; we must expect motorists to show their present amoral attitudes and behavior until they can speak to one another.

2.2 Phonetics—a written description of speech sounds

Speech is not spoken writing. It is a stream of sound, which cannot strictly be said to consist of words and which has a most loose grammatical structure. Anyone who has ever had an impromptu address taken down by a stenographer will see the truth of this last remark. Speech is usually personal, for conversation, and is composed during the course of speaking. Most writing is premeditated and is read in the absence of the author.

Speech is bound to the time continuum; we must receive it as it comes, instant by instant. For the purpose of observing speech and making scientific analysis, we record it and examine segments in a search for structure. Such recording implies an *a posteriori* examination, the speech being examined out of its natural time continuum. The study of the physical speech sounds is called "acoustic phonetics." Once speech has been recorded, say as an oscillogram,* it is in a form having some analogy to writing; it can be examined as a whole, and broken down into segments or elements. It may then be interpreted as a chain of syllables, or of smaller segments, and it may be transcribed into phonetic writing. It is important to realize that such representation into discrete elements is made for the purpose of talking *about* speech. Speech itself is a continuous stream; there are no razor-sharp boundaries between successive sounds; the phonetic transcription is a written symbolic representation, quantized

* Or running-spectrum, preferably. See p. 145.

into a chain of distinct symbols like the letters of print. Such symbols are the quantized units of the phonetician which serve his particular purpose, for recording those basic properties of a speaker's voice which are of significance to him.[179,180] All human tongues may be recorded in phonetic script of some kind.

If I read aloud the word "stronger" from a book and a phonetician* writes down [stɾɔŋə], he is not recording my exact speech wave form. He is making a sufficient model of my sounds to enable him to compare my pronunciation (a southern English one) with, say, a Scottish one. Such a model would convey to a Scotsman some idea of my pronunciation. A gramophone recording would tell him more, reproducing within fine limits my actual voice, not a segmented model. The symbols "stɾɔŋə" can no more be said to be the sounds of my voice than an architect's plans can be said to be a house; they are merely a sufficient guide to the builder.

The reader may feel that this distinction between the physical entity and its representation by discrete elements, as a model, has been overstressed here. But it is an example of a distinction which arises at many different levels in the study of communication. So long as our discussion is confined to any one of these levels, say this level of acoustic phonetics, the distinction may be of less importance; but it is when we wish to compare the ideas of the phonetician with, for example, those of the psychologist (as in connection with the problem of recognition of speech) that we need to take special care to note the different types of model by which a physical event may be represented, and the different discrete, or quantized, elements from which such models are built up.

In his massive work *Of the Origin and Progress of Language*, the eighteenth-century student of language, Lord Monboddo, wrote:

> ... for the pleasure of the ear contributes not a little to persuasion; and setting aside that consideration, language spoken may be said to be a living *language*, compared with *written language, the dead letter*, being altogether *inanimate* and nothing more than marks or signs of language, wanting that chief beauty of elocution, which is given it by pronunciation and action.[241]

2.3. TALKING LANGUAGE—AND TALKING ABOUT LANGUAGE

Quantization is a logical necessity of describing any physical phenomenon, for example, the process of communication, and we shall give further attention to this important concept in a later section (Section 3.1). (This of course is very different from asserting that we "think logically." Logical considerations enter into the *description* of a system.) All spoken languages are tied to the time continuum, streams of sound, but must be segmented for the purpose of description; the segments may be chosen to be of different

* See reference 164 for a guide to phonetic transcription, with examples in many languages.

lengths, and given names such as *phrases, words, phonemes.* As an example relevant to our present theme, the words in an English dictionary may be regarded as types of segment or quantal elements with which we transmit messages one to another in printed form. With these words—including their various syntactical forms, et cetera—the various messages may be constructed. (This is very far indeed from saying that these listed words "are the English language.") Equally well, though with less popular use, dictionaries of phrases, or of syllables; might be compiled which could be regarded as the quantal elements.[235] The important point is that all such quantization is entirely arbitrary—a form is chosen on some occasion which suits the particular purpose of that occasion. The linguist breaks down the raw material of his subject—language—into elements, units, or segments. He speaks of phonemes, morphemes, words. Such elements are conceived for the purpose of talking *about* language. The language used for talking about language is called a *meta-language.*

What is a language? Your author will not presume to answer such a question by attempting a formal definition. But if he be allowed to express any personal opinion, it would be this: If we accept that the concept "language" serves useful purposes (and if it does not, a good many people are wasting a great deal of time!), then descriptions or definitions of some kind are required; but the linguist, the phonetician, the psychologist, the telecommunication engineer, and all those concerned may not be thinking of exactly the same thing when they use the word "language" in discussion. The concept is a many-sided one and many descriptions or models may be needed; such descriptions are not independent. Speech, as a means of communication, cannot strictly be divorced from the rest of Man's communicative activity. The operations of the speech organs and of the ear form an integral part of the functioning of the whole body and brain. When we hear a man speak, we usually see him too, his facial expressions and gestures; we communicate in a complex physical environment, against a particular social and cultural background. But the study and understanding of the whole communication process is, as yet, an unattainable ideal. The division of the field into "subjects," and the concentrated study of these as separate and almost independent interests, must come before the process of synthesis into an intelligible whole can be attempted.

In the following sections we shall consider language from two aspects in particular: (*a*) language as the complete corpus of all the utterances made by a specific group of people over a specific period (the physical aspect); and (*b*) language as a collection of habits, described as a set of signs and rules (the abstracted, linguistic aspect). These two aspects correspond also to the object-language and the (linguist's) meta-language. We shall attempt to show the relation between the two aspects.

Utterances serve as stimuli and set up patterns of behavior. The stimuli-behavior relations show a considerable measure of correlation, or agreement, when observed among different members of the group. This complete corpus, if it could be gathered, would then represent the result of physical, psychological, and social observation. Such an unwieldy mass of physical data is of course beyond our powers of collecting *in toto*, let alone of analyzing. Such data can merely be sampled and then only certain attributes of these samples can be recorded. Nothing else is practicable. From these samples and recorded attributes, various different sets of abstractions and analyses are made, which are distinguished by names such as "phonetics," "phonemics," "semantics," and so on; their distinction lies in the method of sampling and in the types of attribute recorded. Such abstractions are then essentially statistical. No one of these aspects or sets of abstractions, by itself, is fully descriptive of "language," but each serves some specific purpose; to the complete study of communication, *all* these aspects have relevance.

In a similar way the "average man," beloved of the statistician, may be described by various sets of abstractions inferred from sampling a population; he may be described "physically" (by height, weight, age, etc.) or "socially" (married or no, children, education, etc.) or "economically" (earnings, savings, spending on food, tobacco, etc.). There are many different ways, essentially interrelated, of talking about the average man—but we have never met him.

A phonetician has his primary interest at the physical, articulatory, and acoustic level.* He observes the physical sounds of people speaking and how they produce these sounds; he records symbolically those sounds which his trained ear, perhaps aided by instruments,† tells him are distinctly different. The quantal elements into which he divides sounds, as being "distinctly different," are empirical. No two people speak in exactly the same way, and even the sound wave forms of a word, spoken by one person on successive occasions, cannot be exactly the same. So the phonetician must make a compromise in order that his system does not become so unwieldy as to defeat its own object. He is particularly interested in comparing the speech of people in different localities, and he symbolizes the spoken sounds into printed letters, using just enough letters to record the aspects of interest. Sometimes he wishes to draw more minute distinctions

---

* Speech is basically an articulatory process; it is the motions of the lips, tongue, uvula, etc., together with pulsation of the breath by the chest muscles and the diaphragm which produce the sounds of speech—not vice versa. Phonetics, however, is studied at both the articulatory and acoustic levels. We shall say more about the forms in Chapter 4.

† For a condensed study, commencing at elementary level, see references 108, 182.

than the standard letters allow, such as particular values of stress, intonation, or length of speech sounds; then he embellishes the phonetic letters with "diacritical marks." The phonetician essentially tries to symbolize the sounds of speech into a type of writing, irrespective of "meaning." Once the speech of a particular speaker has been recorded in this manner, a great deal of the original utterances has been thrown away, such as those nuances which identify the speaker; the remainder, written on paper, contains all the attributes of interest to the phonetician. The statement just made—that the phonetician is primarily interested in transcribing the physical speech sounds, irrespective of "meaning"—needs some qualification. For this is an idealization. First, if the speaker under study happens to come from the same language group as the phonetician, the latter is himself "inside the system"; he cannot help but be aware of the meanings and significances of the spoken sounds he hears. He is to some extent "culture bound." Much as he may wish to regard the system he is observing objectively from the outside, he cannot entirely shake himself free.G·* Second, if he is studying speech in a language new to his experience, he is aware of acting from specific practical motives. His purpose may be to teach others the language subsequently; or it may be to compare the phonetic structure to that of some other language; or again it may be purely for the purpose of learning to speak the language as well as possible, in order to view some other aspects of the culture. Although his prime interest may be the transcribing of speech sounds, this activity is carried on with a realization that the sounds which are of real importance are those which serve some communicative function. Third, although the speech he studies may be new to him, the phonetician nevertheless has a great knowledge of the phonetic structure of other languages and also has had experience of those social and cultural interests which commonly, though not inevitably, are reflected in the structure of spoken language. He is still not wholly "outside the system."

The phonetician's interest then centers around the smallest segments of speech which play any part in communication, and in transcribing these into written symbols; other aspects of language, such as grammatical or syntactical structure, do not come directly under his microscope though he certainly sees them out of the corner of his eye.

Once the utterances of a speaker have been symbolized by a phonetician, they are in the form of "writing," a chain of phonetic signs. Such "writing" bears direct relation to spoken sounds and in this aspect is distinct from normal writing—goodness knows that English spelling has little relation to

---

* This is certainly true of many descriptions of cultural structures (e.g., ceremony, kinship systems, etc.). A description formulated by one who is outside the culture may be unintelligible to those within it. See also references 198, 261.

the sounds! Occasionally it is required to make reference to individual phonetic signs, and then they are written in square brackets thus: [p], [b], and so on. Such reference to single signs is frequently made when comparing complete spoken words or syllables, as the [p] and [b] in *pen* and *ben*; but the writing of these isolated signs does not imply that such sounds, [p], [b], are spoken in isolation. In fact the particular sounds represented by these signs, and many other consonantals cannot be uttered without at the same time giving rise to some measure of an adjoining continuing or vowel sound. But more about *transitions* anon (Section 3.5).

Discussion of the specification of speech, both instrumentally and physiologically, together with the difficulties, will be deferred until Chapter 4.

2.4. PHONEMES; LINGUISTIC UNITS

The linguist, or philologist, is concerned with speech not only as sounds, but in all its communicative functions; he is intimately concerned with the phonetic, psychological, social, and cultural facets. Again, the physical evidence from which he gathers his data and forms his abstractions is the corpus of utterances made by a specific group of people, together with observations on how the individuals react to these utterances. Besides having an interest in the smallest phonetic units, the linguist studies grosser segments of utterances and seeks to describe the whole structure of a language, so that it may be compared to others. He observes how utterances are constructed, how one differs from another and, by comparing them, interprets the relations between these utterances and the behavior patterns of the speakers and listeners. He compiles dictionaries and describes grammatical systems; he makes statistical studies.

One of the linguist's prime interests lies in a search for the simplest description of a language. At the phonetic level, it frequently occurs that some compression of the raw phonetic transcriptions is possible, and a further reduction of description may be achieved. For example, it may happen that two phonetic elements regularly occur together, without exception, in a particular language (much as, to use an analogy, the letter u always follows q in written English). As an illustration, all words in English which commence with [p], [t], [k] sounds have these sounds aspirated.

Once such redundant elements have been trimmed off, after careful examination of the transcribed phonetic data, the linguist is left with a minimal list of phonetic elements with which it is possible to represent and to distinguish one word from any other in the language. Such minimal elements may be called *phonemes*.[B, D, *] These elements may be insufficient to represent phonetically all the nuances of pronunciation, and they do not purport to do this; they are sufficient for a description of the language

* See a discussion of different possible definitions, reference 335.

element sounds because they form the minimum essentials for distinguishing between one *word* and another (or one "meaningful segment or utterance" and another). The communicative functions of all the various utterances in the language are, in principle, inherent in such phonemic representation. Phonemes, as individual elements, are meaningless; but they serve to distinguish meanings.* The phonetician is eager to note differences in pronunciation as slight as his trained ear can detect, or as it may serve his purpose to record; but the linguist takes note of such differences as give the utterances different meanings, or distinguish their phonetic transcriptions.

As another example, in English, the sounds [ŋ] and [n] are phonemically distinct because they distinguish between pairs of words such as *sing* and *sin*; but in Italian these are not distinct phonemes, since there are no words which can possibly be converted one into another by the sole exchange of these sounds. So one sign serves for both. In fact, an Italian with a cold in his head may pronounce [n] as [ŋ], but this alone, though detectable, would cause no confusion! A phoneme represents the smallest change which can convert one word into another, or one meaningful utterance into another; but moreover certain changes of stress, duration, or pitch, impressed upon the same dictionary word, may be said also to have communicative significance,[262] especially for denoting a speaker's attitude or emotion.[F] For example, the word "what?" (a mere interrogative) is distinct from the sudden shouted exclamation "WHAT!" (denoting amazement), both phonetically and semantically. In certain languages, the prosodic features of stress, duration, and pitch serve major communicative roles.[B, 180] It would be possible, though quite impracticable, to expand the list of words in the *Oxford English Dictionary* by listing many of them in all their variations of emphasis; again it would be possible in principle to give corresponding dictionary "definitions" (synonymous forms) of each. But such a method would produce a tome so massive as to serve little purpose, and it is more practical to list "neutral" forms. Again, in phonetic writing it is more economical to restrict the phonetic signs to neutral forms and to embellish with diacritical marks as required, to indicate stress, duration, or pitch.

(The story has been told of the director of the Moscow Art Theatre, Stanislavsky, that he required his pupils to speak the one word "tonight" in some fifty different ways, while an audience of assessors wrote down their impressions of what sense was conveyed.†)

---

* We use the word "meaning," at present, with our tongues in our cheeks! Some discussion of this illusive concept will be taken up in Section 6.2 of this chapter; and again in Chapter 6 and elsewhere.

† Professor Jakobson, in private correspondence.

Phoneme signs are distinguished from phonetic signs by slanting lines, thus: /n/, /ɛ/, /ʃ/. When a linguist records his observations in such discrete, symbolic form, he has made a representation which suits his particular purpose, a practical purpose.   This model does not represent the utterances of any one speaker on any one occasion—physical sounds *per se*—but only gives a minimal description, representing the conformity of these utterances to a system, "the language."   Nevertheless, the physical evidence which the linguist examines and from which he extracts his stock of phonemes is not the precise sound made by any one member on a particular occasion; it is a linguistic unit abstracted from the utterances of many people.   We shall take up the relation between utterances and linguistic phonemes again later, in Section 4, with reference to Fig. 3.4.

Phonemes are one particular set of *segmented* units of language, and we have here picked upon phonemes, not for the purpose of stressing any one theory, but rather to illustrate the logical necessity of segmentation when describing utterances, with some of the attendant difficulties.

Your author has no mandate to legislate upon what are essentially linguistic concepts, and such is certainly not his intention.   Rather he wishes to make it clear in what sense terms such as *phoneme* will be used in this present text.   Considering the multi-faceted nature of language, we must expect differences of opinion in different schools of thought.

A set of purely linguistic definitions is an ideal target for the building up of a system of structural linguistics; this is a vital academic problem.   But linguistic analysis has always had a practical purpose too; "However varied were the definitions of the phoneme offered by different scholars and schools, all of these formulations aim at essentially one and the same thing, and in broad outline the practical task of enumerating the stock of phonemes for any given language found its approximate solution."[262].*   The amount of academic argument may provide a measure of the present inexactness of a science, but it need not arrest completely its practical utility.

3. TOWARD A LOGICAL DESCRIPTION OF LANGUAGE

Various elements of a language may be classified in a logical manner. Such a statement will need clarification, but let it be emphasized here and now that this is not the same as saying "that we communicate logically" or, even less, "that we think logically."   It is the language itself, a description of its various symbols and elements (in meta-language), not its use during a live communication, that we are discussing here.

To illustrate, any letter in the alphabet may be identified by asking the question: "Is it in the first half, A through M; yes or no?"   When this is

* With kind permission of author and publisher.

answered, say by *yes*, a second question follows: "Is it in the first part of this first half; yes or no?" And so on, until identified. Such dichotomy, or two-valued "logical" identification results in a chain of *yeses* and *noes*, called a *binary symbol chain*. For example, *yes*, *no*, *no*, *yes*, *no*, might identify a particular letter; such a chain of *yeses* and *noes* is a ciphered version of the letter, similar to the dots and dashes of Morse code. Of course for such a cipher to identify a letter uniquely, the letters must first be listed in some agreed manner, and the successive points of division into two parts agreed upon. In a similar manner we might identify words instead, by taking them as ordered in the dictionary and asking the same questions: "Is it in the first half? The first half of the first half?" And so on. Again, in the familiar game called "Twenty Questions," we identify some object by asking question which may be answered only by *yes* or *no*. In all such cases, the binary symbol chain is of no use whatever—is not decipherable—unless the precise manner of questioning is stated beforehand.

There are many interesting historic instances of binary ciphers and codes, to which we made some reference in our historical review, Chapter 2, where we noted that it appears to have been appreciated for many centuries that information may be transmitted by a two-symbol code. But again it should be stressed that this does not mean that in practice we *do* communicate in this manner; it means that the symbols of which messages are composed may be *transcribed* into binary chains (may be ciphered) if we so wish. When I converse with a friend we do not fire yes-no questions at one another!

We shall be returning to these points later, but first some attention should be given to the *a priori* setting up of message categories (letters, phonemes, words, and so on) and to the agreed ordering and "method of questioning." Let us take a few points from the theory of description.

3.1. THE LOGICAL NECESSITY OF QUANTIZATION

When we speak or write about anything, we can say only a finite number of things about it. We cannot describe and convey ideas with infinitesimal precision; we cannot classify or pin-point with absolute accuracy but must always be content to do so within some arbitrary limits of practical utility. For the purpose of talking about people, we classify them into groups; into political parties, into countries, and into trades, where fine variations within these groups is considered to be of no immediate consequence. If greater precision is required and more subtle differences to be discussed, then more has to be said; but we cannot continue indefinitely. Such a logical necessity of description is one example of *quantization*. The *Oxford English Dictionary* describes the word "quantum" as signifying "... required, desired, or allowed amount ... "; the word is not the prerogative of the physicist. It is convenient to distinguish three aspects, or levels, of quantization: (*a*) descriptive, or linguistic level; (*b*) instrumental or observational level (see Chapter 2, Section 4); and (*c*) quantum theory of physics.

The quantum may be likened to the size of the slit through which an observer views the world; the nature of the slit is quite different for the three levels listed above. At present we are discussing only the first level and, in this case, the world we are viewing here is the world of our own experience. When we frame our thoughts* into speech or writing, we have to be content with an imperfect model; we cannot express our entire thoughts in language but only a certain number of their *attributes*.

When we are expressing ourselves in language and other signs, our words, phrases, and utterances may be said to form a "pattern"—a pattern of relationships. The attributes of such patterns which we choose to represent verbally are arbitrary; as many or as few as we please, sufficient for our immediate purpose. They are the columns in our mental notebooks in which we assemble data for subsequent verbal representation.

As a simple example, suppose we are describing a man, whom we know well, to a friend who has never seen him; we can refer to his height, his stoutness, the color of his hair, his complexion. These might represent the attributes we choose. If we wish our description to be more detailed, we could add others; his age, color of his eyes—as many and finer details as we wish. But we must stop somewhere. Associated with many such attributes there is a magnitude; *how* tall, *how* fat, *how* old, et cetera, and such magnitudes must also be quantized. We can refer to his height in feet, in inches, in millimetres; but on no account can we communicate his *exact* height.

(One is reminded of the story of an inspector in a ball-bearing factory who, for many years, had consistently rejected every ball that came to his hands. Either they were too large to pass through his gauge or they were so small that they fell through; but none ever fitted exactly.)

Of course, much of this attribution, or patterning, function of language does not rest in the choice of words alone, but in the whole syntax of the language. But for our present purpose, this important factor does not matter.

Such a description may be given pictorial representation (Fig. 3.1) by a set of mutually perpendicular axes, forming what we shall call an *attribute space*. Figure 3.1 (*a*) shows such axes of *height, weight, age,* on the assumption that we wish to discuss people only in terms of these three attributes. If we wish to consider also *complexion, girth,* or other attributes, we should need other axes, forming an imaginary hyperspace which we cannot, however, draw in this simple form on a flat sheet of paper.

---

* All words and utterances may not be "framing thoughts." Talking in one's sleep for example, or ejected cries like *help*! Thoughts may *follow* such reflex cries.

The three-attribute space in Fig. 3.1 (*a*) has divided the field of discussion into three independent types of attribute. The simplest scales which can be attached to the axes are binary ones; in such a case height is recognized only as *tall* or *short*, weight as *heavy* or *light*, age as *young* or *old*; then only eight different kinds of people are being recognized here, and they can be represented as cubic *cells*, in this space. For example, the cell shown shaded in Fig. 3.1 (*b*) describes a person who is classed as *short, old,* and *heavy.* Greater precision of specification is attained by dividing the axes into more than two, using scales of units chosen to be as small as desired [Fig. 3.1 (*c*)]. Then the whole space is considered to be divided into smaller quantal cells, little square prisms with sides corresponding to these units. These finer divisions may be denoted either linguistically (*extremely* tall; *very, very*

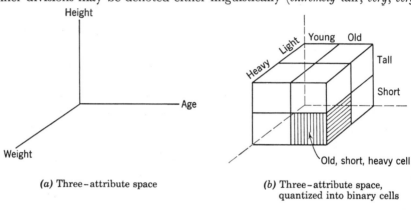

(*a*) Three–attribute space

(*b*) Three–attribute space, quantized into binary cells

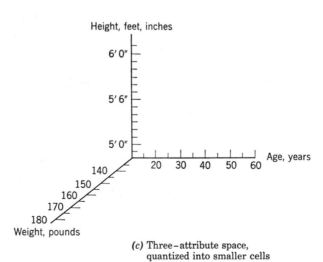

(*c*) Three–attribute space, quantized into smaller cells

Fig. 3.1.   Three-attribute space for describing "a man."

tall; *very, rather . . . short, minute*) as suits our immediate purpose, or numerically (feet, inches, etc.). Discussion is restricted to these quantal units; no finer specifications are admitted, for the purpose of the immediate discourse. Naturally far more people may be distinguished now, represented by the cells in the space; the finer the units of division, the smaller the quantal cells, and the finer the distinctions which can be brought within the "field of discussion."

An apology should perhaps be offered, if we appear to have strayed rather far from the track of our subject—language—but this type of pictorial view of the process of classification or description has some usefulness and we shall have occasion to refer to such diagrams again.

It may perhaps be as well to comment here on a common point of misunderstanding about *numerical* description. A man's height may be quoted as being between say 5 and 6 feet, or, with greater accuracy, as between 5.7 and 5.8 feet, depending on the size of the quantal cell chosen; but his height cannot be given *exactly*. Against this, it may be thought that we can talk about irrational numbers, such as $\sqrt{2}$. But we can only talk *about* them, and can never state their values or magnitudes. The subject has been discussed extensively by the mathematicians Kronecker and Poincaré,[266] in relation to the unreality of mathematical "continuity"; they stress the fact that we cannot *communicate* the irrational number $\sqrt{2}$, but only rules about it. The expression $\sqrt{2}$ is merely a symbol, signifying an instruction, or rule ("conceive a number, which, if multiplied by itself, gives the number 2"). It is not a magnitude.

3.2. OBJECT-LANGUAGE AND META-LANGUAGE

Let us return to our real subject and apply these arguments to the description of language itself. We can only describe attributes of an observed language in terms of another language and it saves much confusion if the two are kept distinct. The natural human language being observed and studied (English, French . . .) is usually called the *object-language*, whilst the scientific language with which the observer describes this is called the *meta-language*. Figure 3.2 illustrates the distinction; here, two communicants (*A* and *B*) are shown in conversation as forming an *object-channel* of communication, while they are being observed through the *meta-channel*, or channel of observation. In other circumstances the observer himself acts as one communicant, as Fig. 3.2 (*b*). We shall return to this later:

The observer (say, a linguist) observes the object-language utterances, then forms various hypotheses about what he hears and sees and expresses these in meta-language. Hypotheses, theories, descriptions are metalinguistic.

The linguist describes certain attributes of the observed object-language of various different *categories*. Examples are: phonemes, morphemes, words; syntactical structure elements. All such categories are linguistic concepts, elements of the meta-language with which to discuss the mass of physical evidence—the utterances of people.

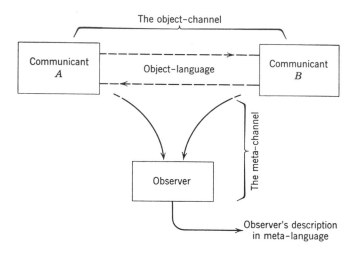

(a) External observation of a conversation

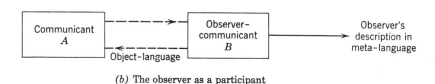

(b) The observer as a participant

Fig. 3.2. Object-language and meta-language.

With various categories distinguished, structure of language may be discussed. In *structural linguistics* an important technique used is that of *substitution*; substitution of one phoneme for another, for example, thereby converting one word to another. And substitutions can be made only if the elements substituted are finite (quantal).

The linguist makes substitutions of finite segments of words in order to compile his catalogue of phonemes—the minimal segments which, when substituted for one another in pairs, convert one word to another. A single such substitution produces a pair of words differing only by one phoneme (*bill-bull, list-lisp, same-sane*).   Phonemes then have a mutually exclusive property and distinguish one context from another; in this way they have a semantic significance.   A comparison of two things, differing only in one attribute, is the simplest kind of comparison; it is a logical, *yes-no*, or binary, comparison.   Let us now return to an earlier discussion and see how this logical point of view may be adopted for various linguistic categories.

3.3. BINARY DESCRIPTION OF LANGUAGE

Attention has already been called to the way in which binary division arises naturally in our thoughts and language.   Antonyms form a very important class of words, playing a more practical (sorting) function than synonyms.   We have many word pairs which suggest that we like to make binary comparisons, that this forms part of our thinking habits: *high-low*, *hot-cold, good-evil, war-peace, rich-poor*.   But truly there are many shades of value in between these.   Other classes of word pairs arise from a distinction we draw between material things and properties, thoughts or abstractions: *fact-fiction, substance-form, body-soul, real-apparent, material-spiritual*.   A further class consists of words which arise from our intuitive ideas of mutual exclusiveness: *inside-outside, and-or, yes-no, with-without*.   Many other classes of antonyms may be considered, but language does not consist entirely of such doublets or duals; if it did, then we might be said to communicate logically, by yes-no binary word symbols.   As illustrated in Chapter 2, there are many historical examples of *invented* binary languages.   For centuries it has been realized that all communicable information *may* be communicated entirely in a binary code—only there is no compulsion, and real languages have not in fact evolved this way.   Natural human languages have not developed as binary codes, but it is possible to take any aspect of the language which serves a communicative function (phonemic, morphemic, syntactical, etc.) and to represent it in a binary code.   Now the terms *cipher* and *code* have no one single formally accepted meaning but are used in slightly different senses by different writers.   Edward Sapir[G] has referred to writing or phonetic symbolism as *coding* of its spoken counterpart; symbols for spoken sounds.   He treats Morse or other telegraph codes as special cases.   The spoken language is then the "real language," and all other representations are called codes.   Even more broadly, Martin Joos defines all language as a "code" because it is both symbolic and organized.[183] But it will serve our purpose here merely to make a distinction between a "language" and a "code."   By "language" we shall mean those organically developed systems, whether spoken or scribed, by which humans transmit messages; but the word "cipher," or "code," will be used to mean any invented, self-consistent system, whereby one set of symbols may be transformed into another for certain special stated purposes (i.e., Morse code which converts printed letters into dots and dashes).

The linguist is faced with a situation of appalling complexity; he wishes to describe the structure and evolution of a system, the evidence for which consists of all the utterances of thousands of different people. He is constantly searching for valid simplification, to reduce the raw data, yet he has to guard against taking simplicity as an end in itself.[262] One form of simplification which has found a certain use is this binary symbolism, but it does no more than code or present data in a simple and economic form.

There are two particular aspects of binary coding of linguistic data to which we shall refer in this book. The first of these concerns the employment of certain concepts of Statistical Communication Theory in connection with written communication. In particular a measure may be attached to the *rate of information* conveyed by the signals or signs transmitted along a communication channel, in terms of the average minimum number of *yes-no* answers required to describe the selection of the signals from the set (dictionary, list, alphabet, etc.).[297] We shall outline this theory in Chapter 6.

The second use of binary coding relevant to our theme arises from the concept of *distinctive features*, which we shall discuss next. A linguist, in his search for structure, breaks down whole utterances into segments of various sizes—into phrases, into words, into phonemes. The phoneme is the smallest segment to which we have so far made reference; but why stop there? Further analysis may reveal the basic materials of which these phonemes are constructed—their attributes. The independent (or autonomous) attributes, chosen for unique description of the phonemes of a language, are called *distinctive features*.[172] The great significance of this concept lies partly in a certain lack of empiricism that it possesses and partly in its function of relating the phoneme to its articulatory production. Both these aspects will need some closer examination because, as stated thus, they are not wholly true, and some qualification is called for.

3.4. DISTINCTIVE FEATURE; BINARY ATTRIBUTES OF PHONEMES

Music has both a melodic and an harmonic structure, the melody being a time sequence of sounds and the harmony a set of simultaneous sounds. By analogy, speech may be regarded as a stream of sound, segmented into a time sequence of phonemes for purposes of linguistic analysis; or it may well be viewed as a series of concurrent activities corresponding to muscular control of the vocal cavities, the larynx, lips, tongue, and teeth. The linguist's transcription then has some likeness to a musical score; the phonemes represented by a sequence of chords, conveying not a single

eater, part "harmony."[172]   Such
continue with the comparison, the
f a phoneme.   A phoneme may be
butes.

iving apparatus of extraordinary
s; it is surpassed in delicacy and
s "engineering products," built of
e and bone!   When we speak, a
operated by neural controls, which
mouth, the lips, and tongue, sets
ns the nasal cavity to the throat
parting of the teeth—all with the
rmed by a number of concurrent

es of speech sounds with readiness;
f the larynx, called *voicing*, heard
see, etc.) and in certain consonants
(as in *h*ard, *sh*ort, *th*ink, etc); the
); the nasal quality (which appears
cteristics of speech sounds are less

based upon such evident charac-
us as early as 300 B.C.   Modern
ent Indian inquiry into the nature
of speech—work carried out to a great extent prior to Greek science, which
itself accomplished very little in this field.   In particular, the Hindus had
identified certain phonetic elements such as vowels, fricatives, continuants,
and stops; furthermore they had achieved some measure of classification
into characteristic forms of articulation—*closure, opening, constriction, voicing,
aspiration, nasality*—and to some extent they had the notion of binary
oppositions.[3]

The interesting feature of this description is that it was in part binary,
though not quite.   The first linguists to present a fully binary description
of phonemes were Roman Jakobson and his collaborators.[F, 172]

It is not our business here to discuss or even to comment upon the particular set of attributes of phonemes which were in fact chosen for this binary
classification; many different sets might have been used, but this one has
advantages in two respects: it is correlated fairly closely to the articulatory
process and, as a logical description, it is quite efficient.[62]   There is no
question of a *unique* set; the problem is a practical one, that of describing
and distinguishing between the phonemic stocks of the world's various
languages.

The attributes chosen by Jakobson and his associates[F,*] have been called *distinctive features*; they distinguish 12 such features, or binary oppositions, which "we may detect in the languages of the world and which underlie their entire lexical and morphological stock...." They name them: (1) vocalic/non-vocalic, (2) consonantal/non-consonantal, (3) interrupted/continuant, (4) checked/unchecked, (5) strident/mellow, (6) voiced/unvoiced, (7) compact/diffuse, (8) grave/acute, (9) flat/plain, (10) sharp/plain, (11) tense/lax, (12) nasal/oral. Such features may be regarded as forming a set of orthogonal axes of an attribute space (phonemic feature space) in the manner of Fig. 3.1 (*b*); the various phonemes are then representable by cubic cells lying in a hyperspace of 12 dimensions. Of course, we cannot visualize such a space, but the idea may be illustrated by a three-dimensional projection, as in Fig. 3.3. But we may calculate the

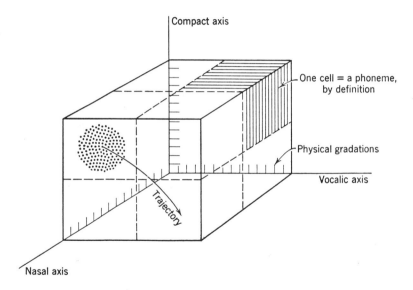

Fig. 3.3. "Features" as "general co-ordinates." Phonemes as quantal cells, and speech as a trajectory of system points. Only three features can, of course, be illustrated.

number of cubic cells contained in a twelve-dimensional space and thus the number of phonemes which may be represented distinguishably in such a space. Each attribute (or feature) has two possible states, so that N features may have 2^N states. In our present case, $N = 12$, and a set of 12 features could serve to distinguish 4096 different phonemes, if called upon

* A full treatment of the "distinctive feature" theory of Professor Roman Jakobson is to be found in his *Selected Writings*, Mouton, The Hague, 1962, Volume 1, and in his forthcoming book in this series, *Sound and Meaning*.

to do so.   Such a complete system of features enables us, in principle, to describe the phonemes of any language; but when restricted to one particular language, the full freedom of choices is not required.   Most languages use only a few dozen phonemes.   English may be considered to contain 28, if the prosodic features are excluded[F] (or about 40 otherwise).   For describing the phonemes of any one language then, the 12 feature oppositions offer a highly redundant set of attributes.

As a useful alternative to the hyperspace model, the feature system may be illustrated in tabular form.   Figure 3.4 represents a phoneme feature pattern of English (Received Pronunciation);[F,181] in this diagram the binary signs, +, −, relate to the various oppositions: vocalic/non-vocalic, consonantal/non-consonantal, interrupted/continuant, and so on.   It will be seen that a number of spaces are left blank; these correspond to *redundant*

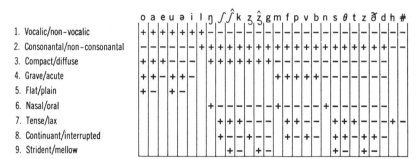

Fig. 3.4.   The Phoneme pattern of English (Received Pronunciation)
after Jakobson, Fant, and Halle.

Key to phonemic transcription: /o/–p*o*t, /a/–p*a*t, /e/–p*e*t, /u/–p*u*t, /ə/–p*u*tt, /i/–p*i*t /l/–*l*ull, /ŋ/–lu*ng*, /ʃ/–*sh*ip, /ʃ̂/–*ch*ip, /k/–*k*ip, /ʒ/–a*z*ure, /ʒ̂/–*j*uice, /g/–*g*oose, /m/–*m*ill /f/–*f*ill, /p/–*p*ill, /v/–*v*im, /b/–*b*ill, /n/–*n*il, /s/–*s*ill, /θ/–*th*ill, /t/, –*t*ill, /z/–*z*ip, /ð/–*th*is /d/–*d*ill, /h/–*h*ill.   The prosodic opposition, stressed vs. unstressed, splits each of the vowel phonemes into two.

features, to questions which do not have to be answered.   It is important to appreciate that such a table does not tell us precise *sounds*; rather it represents a cipher which describes the minimal distinctions between the various phonemes.   Just because one feature opposition is left blank, such as the nasal-oral feature of all the vowel phonemes, this does not mean that English speakers necessarily differ in their nasalizing of their vowel sounds.   It implies rather that we do not need to know whether or not they do, to be able to identify the vowels, provided that we know certain other features (numbers 1 to 5 in the instance).   The table as shown represents a cipher of *minimal distinctive features*; examination will quickly show that each phoneme is distinguished from every other by its binary chain of $+$, $-$ feature oppositions, and that the distinction is everywhere at least one feature opposition. For example, /b/ and /d/ differ only in the grave/acute feature; similarly /s/ and /z/ correspond to the single opposition tense/lax. On the other hand, /b/ and /t/ differ by two feature oppositions; /t/ and /v/ by three.

The minimal distinctions between words may also be defined in terms of these oppositions. If we take the word *bill* and commute the initial phoneme /b/ with various others to form different words in the English language, we could draw up the list: bill, pill, vill, fill, mill, dill, till, thill, sill, nil, gill/gil/, kill, gill/ʒil/, chill hill, ill, rill, will. The minimal distinction between any pair is then expressible in terms of feature oppositions.

This "logical" feature description of phonemes may be interpreted as a set of rules—linguistic rules, which a speaker must obey if he is to conform to the language. Of course, he is not normally aware of such rules of language. Rules are expressed in meta-language; the speaker may be described *as though* he obeys such rules.

It may be of interest to note that the blank spaces in Fig. 3.4, corresponding to redundant feature questions, do not really make this cipher a three-valued one, because these questions need not be given $+$, $-$ (yes-no) answers; consequently the feature description is strictly a binary one. It can be shown that all these blank spaces may be eliminated by a simple transformation of the ordering of the feature oppositions.[62]

Of course, the whole success and value of this distinctive-feature concept depends upon the choice of the features, the attributes of phonemes, and the possibility of basing these on some kind of physical measurements. As they have been set out here, they are derived essentially from the linguist's accumulated experience of the world's languages and their phonetic structures. Such experience may well be correlated eventually with physical acoustic measurements, and specifications; this work is still proceeding. As stressed at the commencement of this section, the list of feature oppositions is chosen empirically, to serve an essentially practical purpose in as simple a manner as possible; the features or attributes of phonemes are no more unique or absolute than are the attributes chosen for other descriptions—such as the height, weight, age, birth and so on which we chose for distinguishing between men. The attributes are chosen in both cases to bear some correlation with "natural" physical data which have been singled out for other purposes in the past.

In a typical laboratory speech test, a card containing an assortment of printed words is handed to a speaker who reads them out, in his own peculiar accent, to a number of listeners who identify and write them down. A cycle of communication is formed, and a comparison of the speaker's and listener's cards may reveal errors. Such a cycle may be regarded at a number of different levels. Those levels which concern us at present are, first, the physiological level of speech production; second, the articulatory level involving observations of the positions and shapings of the speech organs, the dimensions of the vocal cavities, et cetera; third, the acoustic level, at which physical sounds are analyzed by spectrographs and other instruments; fourth, in terms of physiology of the ear and of the whole hearing neural process; fifth, the psychological level concerning the problem of the recognition of words from the aural stimuli in a complex environment. The problem of the specification of speech involves any or all of these levels. In the order presented here, there is a certain irreversibility about the levels. Thus, proceeding in the reverse order, a listener's final identification and written transcription by no means specifies the precise sounds he heard (and again the identity of the speaker and the peculiarities of his speech are lost); similarly, a specification of the sounds does not uniquely specify the articulatory process—positions, shaping, or dimensions of the speaker's vocal organs.

At the purely physical levels, there are two approaches toward the problem of specification of speech, the analytic and the synthetic. Briefly, the former proceeds through direct measurements upon speakers, with the aid of X-ray photography, the laryngoscope, and all the technique and method of the physiological laboratory, together with measurement and analysis of the sounds themselves with the aid of oscilloscopes, spectrometers, and all the apparatus of the acoustics laboratory.[271]   The latter approach, the synthetic, is through the construction of mechanical or electrical "synthetic speakers," which can imitate human speech; devices such as the Vocoder,[89,90,141] artificial vocal tracts,[92] the hand-painting of speech energy spectra,[68,69] and other experimental means.* The specification of speech sounds, by such synthetic methods, would be made in terms of those physical parameters which determine the construction and adjustments of these devices. Speech analysis and specification is a major study in itself, and we shall turn to the subject in the next chapter, in more detail.

3.5. THE FLOW OF SPEECH: PHONEME AND FEATURE SEQUENCES AND
     TRANSITIONS

The character of flowing speech is determined neither by the phonemes individually, nor by their feature structures. Speech is a flow, a dynamic affair. The whole acoustic effect of a language in part rests upon the particular *successions* of sounds; certain sequences may commonly occur, others never at all. Given a complete stock of phonemes, an immense variety of possible sequences could be envisaged, formed of all possible

* See Lawrence in reference 166.

permutations; yet any specific language uses only a small fraction of these possibilities.

When we have learned to speak our language, we have developed the faculties both of making the required sounds and of patterning them into sequences. We acquire deeply ingrained habits of speaking these sequences —habits that are betrayed by the difficulty we experience in pronouncing a foreign language. The acoustic qualities we associate with particular languages (qualities which our ears can often distinguish, though we may not understand the language) are accounted for partly by the phonetics, partly by the durations of vowels, partly by syllabic patterning, and by many other sequential factors. In addition, the ear readily detects a characteristic rise or fall in pitch of a speaker's voice.

The stock of phonemes, or their distinctive feature descriptions such as those of Fig. 3.4, does not describe the phonemic structure of a language completely. It is intended only to describe the units out of which the structure is built. To each of the various phonemes, or to each of their feature descriptions, a probability may be ascribed—the relative frequency of its occurring in normal speech. Again, probabilities may be attached to stated *sequences* of phonemes. To collect such data demands immense labor,* but they are descriptive both of the phonemic structure of a language and of its average acoustic effect upon a listener. Further, in connected speech the successive sounds are not simply phonemic elements standing side by side like the letters of a printed text. The whole important question of *juncture*[D, 327] arises; the manner in which the elements flow one on to another and how they affect one another. The sequences of phonemes, with their relative frequences, may be interpreted directly in terms of their distinctive features, only if each phoneme is regarded as a separate distinct event. Each phoneme is represented as a bundle, or more exactly a superposition, of features. Two successive phonemes may have several features in common—each of these features then forming a "supra-segmental continuation"; or they may have none in common, such as the successive /f/ and /e/ in the word "fetch." The degree of "continuity" of each feature could be assessed partly from its probability distribution in time (probability of a stated feature remaining $+$ for n phonemic successions) and partly from transition probabilities (probability that, after remaining $+$ for n successions, the sign remains $+$ for the $(n + 1)$th phoneme). Such statistical analysis of transcribed speech is now rendered possible with the aid of modern computing machines, and perhaps we shall soon see the method developed more extensively.[62]

Although the bulk of the phonemic structure of a language could, in principle, be described by such a set of probabilities and transition proba-

* See Fry in reference 167.

bilities, certain sequences occur, and certain others are absent, with *unfailing* regularity, so that they are determinate (probability unity or zero). Thus, all weak English verbs (except those ending in t or d in the present tense) which end with an unvoiced consonant add the unvoiced /t/ in the past participle; in other cases they add the (voiced) /d/.

For example:

$$\begin{cases} \text{miss} \rightarrow \text{missed, /t/} \\ \text{slap} \rightarrow \text{slapped, /t/} \\ \text{live} \rightarrow \text{lived, /d/} \\ \text{grab} \rightarrow \text{grabbed, /d/} \end{cases}$$

One final, and rather subtle, point which bears upon the acoustic flow of speech should perhaps be mentioned. The concept of words as juxtapositions of phonemes is a linguistic concept; in real speech the successive segments of sound are not truly independent but may condition one another in their formation.[287] For instance, a consonant sound may slightly alter its form in *anticipation* of the following vowel. Thus the English "coo" and "key" employ different /k/ sounds, which can be detected in the manner of their formation; yet this distinction is not phonemic (that is, linguistic), since no two words differing only by these two sounds are to be found in the English language.[F]

4. FEATURES AS THE "GENERAL CO-ORDINATES" OF SPEECH

"Distinctive features" form a linguistic concept; they have been set up for the purpose of describing language, but not the utterances of any one person. The feature oppositions *nasal/oral*, for example, represent a logical distinction, a choice which must be made when a spoken word is identified in the language. But the speaker's voice does not itself operate at such extreme polar points; rather does it lie somewhere in between, on a whole scale of gradation of nasality. But a sound is not *identified* phonemically until one or the other polar extreme is selected by the listener as being "what the speaker intended." However, we may regard the *physical*, acoustic evidence for a phoneme as a distribution of sounds, a cluster of points, one point for each speaker in the population, but not as a single, unique, physical sound. The cluster of points may then be represented in a multi-dimensional space, such as that shown in Fig. 3.3, the axes of which are acoustic attributes (or their physiological counterparts) corresponding to the distinctive features. In the figure, a three-dimensional projection is shown which has axes of *vocality*, *nasality*, *compactness*, graded as desired. This space may then be quantized into cells, by binary division of each axis; these cells then represent the binary distinctive features. The full space would require more dimensions, one for each feature opposition; this is conceptually possible, but cannot, of course, be drawn.

In this way the linguistic concept of phonemes becomes identified with a co-ordinate system, whilst the spoken utterances are represented by *system points* distributed within the space.* As one speaker speaks, his system point executes a continuous and irregular trajectory within the space, passing from cell (phoneme) to cell (phoneme).

It is hoped that such a description of the relationship between a sound and a phoneme does not cause offense to linguists. But, if it be acceptable, it may be of some value to make analogous comparison with a familiar concept of physics—that of "general (orthogonal) co-ordinates." In dynamics, a set of general co-ordinates may be thought of as a chosen set of independent variables by which the motion of a dynamical system (such, for example, as the particles of a gas) may be defined. Being independent they are represented diagrammatically as orthogonal (compare Fig. 3.3). A single point in such a co-ordinate space then represents the configuration of the dynamical system at a certain instant. A large number of similar systems would require a cluster of points (ensemble). As time varies, the points, and hence the clusters, move about the co-ordinate space and represent the motions of the dynamical systems. Analogously with speech, as time varies, the single point representing the speech sounds of one person moves about feature space (Fig. 3.3), and the locus of trajectory represents the dynamical movements of the whole vocal organs, setting up the speech sounds. Many speakers, saying the "same thing," are represented by the whole moving cluster (an ensemble of speakers requires an ensemble of points).

5. STATISTICAL STUDIES OF LANGUAGE "FORM"

Some reference has already been made, in Section 1 of this chapter, to the quality resembling "organic form" possessed by human languages. Languages are not inventions, designed by individuals to suit particular purposes. They are systems evolved from the *continual* interplay of the multifarious needs of thousands or millions of people. They grow. They are molded by social needs and become adapted as social conditions vary. A major war can wreak havoc upon colloquial language, as upon other institutions. Man-made systems, whether they be machines or card-index files, are designed and built to serve specific functions, whereas by contrast

* The "generalized co-ordinates" here are only those necessary and sufficient "distinctive features" of the language; again, only the corresponding physical attributes of speakers' utterances are to be assessed, while redundant features and other phonetic variations are ignored. If these are considered to be included, extra dimensions will be needed.

a natural organism grows and has as one principal characteristic a great adaptability to different situations. The human leg, as against the wheel, is a convenient illustration of this point; the "form" of the natural organism is an exhibition of the variety of functions it serves. And how many purposes does language serve!

5.1. ZIPF'S LAW

One of the most illuminating ways in which the form of language may be exhibited is through statistical study, the classic exponent of the method, applied not only to language but to other forms of behavior, being G. K. Zipf.[E] If only for historical reason, we should take some note of his ideas. Zipf collected a large body of statistical data, referring principally to language, and attempted to show that this and other human activities are subject to a single overriding law, which he has called the Principle of Least Effort. Man is a goal-seeking organism; the whole of his striving, his manner of organizing tasks, the mental exertion involved—the paths along which he directs his actions, the whole means of attaining his ends, so Zipf would hold, is governed by a single dynamical law. Such a law, corresponding to a minimization principle, is strongly suggestive of certain "stationary-value theorems" in the physical sciences. To refer to an analogy we have already used—dynamics—the whole motion of the parts of any (energy conservative) physical system, such as the planets around the sun, may be described by one single law; for example the Principle of Least Action implies that such a system will move so as to minimize the total *action* (a definable physical quantity) integrated between any two instants of time. The planets in their courses are following "natural" orbits; any other orbits would be "unnatural" and would imply a greater quantity of action.

What is applicable with such generality to an inanimate system, it is tempting to extend to the living organism, so pressing is the need for valid concepts and means of description. Zipf is emphatic that the course of human activities, whether singly or collectively, need not minimize the total *work* required, physical and mental. When we set about a task, organizing our thoughts and actions, directing our efforts toward some goal, we cannot always tell in advance what amount of work will actually accrue; we are unable therefore to minimize it, either unconsciously or by careful planning. At best we can but predict the *total likely* work involved, as judged by our past experience. Our estimate of the "probable average rate of work required" is what Zipf means by *effort*, and it is this, he says, which we minimize.

The planning of our actions, with modification as they proceed, involves thinking. A great bulk of what we do in life involves us in talking, arguing, soliloquizing. Our courses are charted on a sea of talk. Language too, requires effort and represents an integrated part of the whole effort involved. Zipf draws heavily upon experimental evidence, gained from statistical studies of language, in support of his theory; but it is toward this *evidence*, rather than toward any theory, that we wish here to direct the reader's attention. We shall not presume to summarize the mass of data presented, but would refer the reader to the original work.[E]

When designing his code, Samuel Morse gave the shortest symbol, dot, to the most frequent English letter, e, and the longest, dot, dot, dot, space, dot, to the least frequent, z, with a graded scale of length between.* In so doing he showed a recognition of the economy of effort; that is, he minimized the average number of dot, space, or dash symbols involved. It has been discovered that languages evolve similar structure, in many of their aspects, under the natural stress of human economizing; the most frequently used words are the shortest; when a word comes into frequent and popular use we tend to abbreviate it (UNESCO, NATO, gas).[C, 158]

When we express ourselves in speech, we may regard ourselves as subject to two opposing forces; a *social* force (the need to be understood) and the *personal* force (the desire to be brief). But such "forces" are not like physical forces; analogy to a pair of weighing scales would be very poor. Zipf speaks of the Force of Unification and the Force of Diversification, as acting between *one* speaker and *one* listener, thereby sailing very close to this analogy. But he observes that it is rather the language itself which may be observed and analyzed, objectively and numerically. The relevant data may be gathered, though only by most tedious and painstaking work on the part of many people.† Such data are far more readily gleaned from printed books than from spoken language, partly because print is so accessible.

It will be sufficient for our purpose to give one single illustration of the type of relationship studied by Zipf. Figure 3.5 shows, curve *A*, the result of a statistical word count made upon James Joyce's *Ulysses*; the volume contains about a quarter of a million word *tokens* with a vocabulary of nearly 30,000 word-*types*.‡ This curve *A* results from plotting the frequencies of the various word-types against their rank order.§ (Note

---

* See Fig. 2.3 and Section 1 of Chapter 2. This is true of his *original* code. The modern one is different but illustrates the same point.

† In this book, by Zipf, will be found a bibliography of statistical counts of various elements of speech and writing—letter frequencies, word frequencies, syllable frequencies, and hosts of other data. See also reference 344.

‡ *Token* is the name given to every individual word that actually appears in a printed text; *type* refers to the entries in a vocabulary list of the text (dictionary).

§ *Rank order:* in statistical studies, if a number of elements are listed in the order of their frequencies of occurrence, $f_1 f_2 f_3 \cdots f_n$, then they are said to be *rank-ordered*, in frequency. The suffixes $1, 2, 3, \cdots, n$ may be regarded as units on a linear co-ordinate scale of rank-order.

that the co-ordinate scales have been made logarithmic, for convenience.) Several aspects of this curve are remarkable. Naturally, this curve must slope downward from left to right, but we have no right whatever to assume that any part of it would be at all smooth—let alone straight. It might well descend from left to right in a series of irregular jumps; again, rather than approach a straight line of unit slope, it might take the form of a dotted curve such as *C* or *D*.*

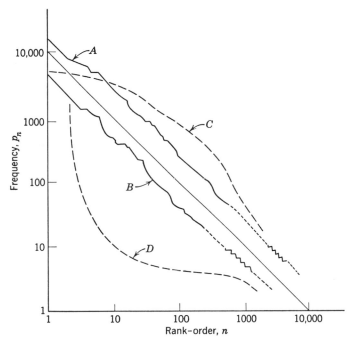

Fig. 3.5. The rank-frequency distribution of words: *A*, James Joyce's *Ulysses;* B, American newspaper English; *C* and *D*, hypothetical (after Zipf).

Such a linear law is derived from empirical data; if the source of data be changed markedly, it may be felt that the change would be reflected in the form of law. But Zipf takes some different data, corresponding to samples of American newspapers, as analyzed by Eldridge, and plots them as in curve *B*. Considering the divergent natures of these sources of language, the two curves *A* and *B* are surprisingly similar. Zipf reinforces his evidence for the existence of a definite "law" by amassing similar data

* It has been reported that the curve for persons suffering from schizophrenia may correspond more to the form *C* (see reference E). We quote Zipf here as the collator of many people's work; the reader will find an extensive bibliography of statistical counts in his book.

from widely different languages of the world and from texts covering a thousand years of history.   Not only words but other segments of text have been studied in such a statistical manner; phonemes, syllables,[c, E] morphemes[184]—and even Chinese characters, and the babblings of babies.[E]

When speaking or writing, people show marked preference for certain phrases and sentences, but statistical analysis of such longer segments has not yet been made.   Such data would involve immense labor in its initial gathering, though modern computer techniques may be of great assistance.

Such statistical data relate to language *form*—to the verbal material itself, to words, syllables, letters, et cetera—rather than to function or meaning.   But language exists for meaningful purposes, to set up thoughts or responses in the recipient, and we may expect that various semantic aspects of language also exhibit some kind of statistical "law."   Two particular cases should be mentioned.   First, the meaning-frequency relation for single words.   In language, we do not have a different word for everything; consequently we must use either strings of words (phrases) for an idea, or a word may take on several distinct functions.   Zipf has made an analysis, based upon Lorge's *The English Semantic Count*, of the number of distinct meanings possessed by words as a function of their frequency rank order (*words* here mean *lexical units*, as listed in the dictionary, ignoring affixes indicating number, tense, and case); he shows the relation to be a linear one.   Secondly, Miller[c] has emphasized the value, as a social study, of making statistical analysis of the *contents* of texts—of what ideas people talk or write about.   A good deal of analysis is made today concerning people's habits, preferences, and fashions,[198] based upon organized census or "social survey" returns; not only their material needs but their educational and cultural trends are studied too.[196, 198]   To such statistics, it has been suggested, might be added the results of frequency counts of references to specific ideas or topics, made from newspapers, magazines, books, advertisements[c]—favorable or unfriendly references to foreign powers or to their social structures, to internal minorities, to institutions, to rearmament, to wage pegging, to any matters which excite public interest, which set up definite currents in the sea of public opinion, and which affect our happiness.   Such statistical content analysis might reveal something of the nature of the verbal constraints which canalize our thoughts and writing.

It may well be that Zipf's law is one case of a more general "logarithmic law" of ecology; one biologist at least has found interest in comparative study of literary statistics and the statistics of insect and animal populations.[352, 353]

The type of analysis we have been discussing, which exhibits definite "laws" as applying to our writings and sayings, may suggest that we are not free to say what we please; that we are bound in some mysterious way to conform to rule. Indeed this is true; we are not completely "free." We never make wholly original remarks nor can we truly "speak our minds"; the nature of language is such that we are, to greater or lesser degrees, slaves to convention. But the existence of such statistical laws of human utterances has nothing whatever to do with free-will.[284]

First, the statistical laws refer to language—written or spoken—and to the constraints of language which we call vocabulary and syntax, not to our wills or thoughts. We do not transmit our thoughts but are free only to represent them as well as we are able, using the language we happen to possess by chance of birth or by dint of hard work. Second, statistics are *averages*, the norms toward which we tend when we use the language, averaged over a great many samples. All the various statistics of language relate to our powers of predicting what a person is likely to say, in certain defined circumstances—but when he says it, *then he communicates with us only by virtue of departing from these predictions.*

Let us return for a moment to our comparison of a language, as a "system," with a physicist's concept of a closed system—taking for example the dynamics of an isolated mass of gas particles. The mass of gas is subject to the laws of statistical mechanics; the particle motions are defined *on an average*, by a minimal condition such as the Principle of Least Action. But the movements of any one particle (if they could be followed) are unrelated to the movements of any other particle—they are all random, individually, yet conform to law, on the whole. So, analogously, with language; the multitudinous conversations which are going on in this country at this moment, all the chatter and gossip, are largely independent individual events; yet as a whole they have a conformity which statistical analysis would reveal, corresponding to current topics and interest, conventional greetings, clichés, and platitudes. But each person is only as "free to speak his mind" as his language allows. He may depart more and more from the statistics, from the rules, and his originality increases. So far but no farther; for if he departs too far, he fails to communicate. If social "forces" are considered to act upon language, their balance must be taken to imply *statistical equilibrium* of the whole system, rather than simple "forces" acting on each individual. On this point we find ourselves in slight disagreement with Zipf, who refers to the two opposing "forces" (Force of Unification and Force of Diversification) as acting between *a* speaker and *a* listener—the individuals.

The equilibrium is of course not perfect, the language continually changing with history, but it is stable over relatively short periods. However, as Zipf has evidenced, the form of certain statistical laws at least has stayed remarkably constant as the macroscopic (cultural) conditions have altered during the past thousand years.

Such analogies should not be carried too far or be taken too seriously. It is really the *experimental* evidence of simple statistical structure existing in language, such as Zipf and others have amassed, which is important; all else is at present wordy conjecture.

5.2. MANDELBROT'S EXPLICATION OF ZIPF'S LAW

Zipf's law relating the frequency of words and their rank order was discovered experimentally, and presented in the first place as an empirical fact. Later an interesting theoretical explication has been put forward by Mandelbrot.[221-224].* As illustrated in Fig. 3.5, the empirical law may be expressed:

$$\log p_n = A - B \log n \tag{3.1}$$

giving
$$p_n = Pn^{-B}$$
where A and B are constants and $B \simeq 1.$ $\left.\right\}$ (3.2)

Mandelbrot does not assume this law but aims to show that it follows from simple premises. He, too, is concerned only with the *formal* aspect of language and not with its function or questions of "meaning."

Mandelbrot expresses his point of view, in this connection, by reference to de Saussure,[286] and to the comparison of written language with coding, which uses either *analog* or *digital* forms of representation. An analog language would be an imitative, pictorial language, whereas civilized writings have evolved as empirical symbolisms; the signs, letters, words are like a digital coding, using letters or other "digit signs" and sequences of these. Mandelbrot's theory is based upon the *word* as a sequence of letters, separated by spaces.†

Against him, the argument can be applied that the concept of "word" may be natural to those bred upon printed languages (e.g., European), but that the concept is far less valid in some other cultures.‡   Nevertheless the counter-argument applies equally, that both Zipf's experimental law and Mandelbrot's theory relate only to those languages which *do* use words. But this point is very penetrating.

Another counter-argument might be to say that the law and the theory are statistical in character, and that we cannot have statistics without elements to be counted. The elements of the printed languages, summarized in Zipf's law, are words, and words are sequences of letters. There is no *a priori* reason to suppose that the whole question cannot be reconsidered, both experimentally and theoretically, and based upon other segments than "words"; but it remains to be done.[224]

* Read Mandelbrot first in English, reference 222, and then see reference 26.
† See Ross, footnote, p. 69.
‡ For example, see Ross in discussion after Mandelbrot under reference 166.

Mandelbrot starts with the concept of *cost*; all signs, letters, words "cost" something; in time, or effort, for example. This cost "includes everything and anything which enters into the expense of sending (the sign) properly weighted." Without referring to any empirical and numerical data of real languages, the theory first shows how to assign probabilities to words in such a way that their total cost will be minimized on an average, keeping a certain property (their "information rate") invariant. The concept of cost is then examined more closely, and the question of measuring it is considered. In a purely mathematical treatment, Mandelbrot shows that the resulting relation between frequency p_n and rank order n corresponds to Zipf's experimental law.

We shall defer summary of this mathematical treatment to Chapter 5, Section 8, because it lies partly within the field of statistical communication theory and, in the writer's opinion, is more properly discussed as such.

5.3. LANGUAGE AND ENVIRONMENT; LITERARY STYLES

Languages continually change; their statistics are "non-stationary." Not only do they change continually with history, as social conditions in general alter, but they may show a difference, at any particular time, as the environmental conditions differ. Telephonic speech differs from tête-à-tête conversation,[114, 226] the whole of mimic and gesture reinforcement being removed;* in particular the commoner words, at least, shift their frequency rank orderings, and stressing of words† and repetitions of phrases[226, 232] assume new importance.[E]

But the term "non-stationary" must be interpreted with care. One of the conclusions drawn from Zipf's collected statistics,[E] at least of written language, is that certain statistical laws appear to have held over hundreds of years, and to be applicable to diverse cultures; again these laws appear to be independent of environment—that is, they apply almost equally to newspapers, to drama, to novels, and to *Ulysses*. In particular the law relating to word frequency and rank order (Fig. 3.5) seems to be universal in this way; it is partly on such a law that Zipf bases his thesis of the minimal principle he calls the Principle of Least Effort in determining the "balance of forces" acting on the users of language. Or, as we prefer to express it here, this law is evidence that macroscopic conditions exist which determine the "statistical equilibrium" of the language. It is, however, the *microscopic* aspects of the language which shift with time and place; the vocabulary alters, and the frequencies or rank orderings of *specific* words change. It is such microscopic aspects of which we are aware when we sense the difference

---

* A speaker continues to gesture, to smile or grimace, unseen, of course—as we often observe whilst waiting outside a telephone booth.

† See Berry in reference 166.

between, say, Jane Austen and James Thurber—though both may be subject to similar macroscopic conditions which determine the production of language itself. "Macroscopic" aspects concern how many words, et cetera; "microscopic" aspects concern *which* words. Again such ideas apply mainly to *print*.

The gathering of statistical data relating to conversational *speech* is a matter of extreme difficulty. The problem is mainly one of sampling. The interests of every group of speakers differ and the differences are reflected in their vocabularies. Every conversation is "specialized," inasmuch as it refers to interests peculiar to the speakers. How can samples be taken, sufficiently scattered as regards subject matter and sufficiently lengthy, to be considered truly representative of "conversational English"? The difficulty has been underlined by Berry,* who remarks upon the results of a statistical count of 25,000 words of telephone conversation which showed the word "mudguard" to be one of the more frequently used words in English! Sampling is the problem.

In contrast to speech, written language is more readily analyzed statistically, though still with enormous labor. Writing is produced for public consumption; it is premeditated and less varied by the specialized and momentary interests of speakers. The different conditions under which speech and writing are performed and their different purposes reflect in their different structures.

Within one community the various classes and institutions often develop different language structures, dependent upon their distinct needs and circumstances. Thus "business English" shows a highly formalized cliché language, about 800 of its words being used with high relative frequency;[138, 257] "journalese" exhibits a peculiar grammatical and word-order structure; the language of an army camp differs from that of the Law Courts, though both are "English." Basic English[249] represents an attempt to take advantage of statistical facts about the language; by restricting the vocabulary to 850 lexical units, the idiomatic structure will necessarily be altered.[c]   Again, Professor Ross has attracted great interest with his exposure of what he calls U-words (popularly believed to be symptomatic of the British "upper classes") and non-U words, which are shuttled between the classes, back and forth.

The brain is a great averager. When we read a text, or listen to speech, we are aware not only of the individual words and phrases but also of a broad, overall effect. We appreciate the word or syllabic patterning and rhythm, the prevailing length or shortness of words, the simplicity or complexity of the grammar; we may glean some understanding of a writer's or speaker's social background. All such broad properties may be

* See Berry in reference 166.

brought to our attention, though we may not perform detailed analysis while reading or listening. The quality called "style" is describable partly in statistical terms, by the comparative extent, richness, or poverty of vocabulary, by the syllabic lengths of words, the relative frequencies of sentences of different length,[353] and by different grammatical structures.[365] Wilhelm Fucks has made a certain mathematical examination of literary style. (This need cause no offense to the aesthetically sensitive reader, for, as we have remarked already, speaking poetry and speaking *about* poetry are quite different activities.) In particular, Fucks seems to have found a set of highly selective statistical operations for distinguishing between languages, writers, and periods. We shall attempt no summary here, but would refer the reader to the original.[119] We recognize styles as "rich," "ponderous," "archaic," or "light." We all possess immense mental stores of statistical data* against which to judge a text; and we can readily distinguish broad differences of style. We can separate Milton from Shakespeare, Swift from Bunyan, though we may not know the particular passages, just as surely as we can tell Bach from Mozart.

6. WORDS AND MEANING: SEMANTICS

What should be said in a short space concerning "meaning," a subject so controversial and upon which some of our greatest philosophers have spent so much energy? I can do little but make a naive sketch indicating the nature of some of the difficulties which surround the word "meaning," lead the reader up to some of the literature, and leave him there.†

6.1. THOUGHTS, SIGNS, AND DESIGNATA

When we speak to one another we do not transmit our thoughts. We transmit physical signals, speech sounds; or, if we communicate in writing, paper and ink. We do not transmit "words"; they are linguistic, not physical, entities. In fact we have never heard or seen "words," in this linguistic sense, but only physical signals ("tokens" or physical embodiments of words). In this book, we use the term *signal* or *sign* to mean any

---

* Not in the form of numerical data but as approximate rank orderings, built up from our past experiences of texts. We shall refer to experimental evidence of this in Chapter 7 when considering the psychological problem of "recognition."

† The newcomer to the subject of semantics is advised to read the short article by Lady Welby in the *Encyclopædia Britannica* (11th Ed.) under the heading *signifies*. Significs refers to *meaning* in every form; not only to language but to every human form of expression; not only to the sense or signification of words and phrases, but to "what people mean" when they do or say something (intention, volition) and, at another level, to meaning as "significance," "worth," "moral value," etc., of all forms of expression (of propositions, doctrines, theories, etc.). Significs, inasmuch as it relates to *linguistic* form, includes semantics.

physical stimulus, such as uttered "word-tokens" (visible or audible signs), used in communication.   The term *message*, on the other hand, may apply to a thought, as it is constructed; it is the orderly *selection* of the signs, but not the physical signs (word-tokens, utterances) themselves.   The signs are then physical embodiments of messages.*

The concept of "meaning" is frequently discussed within the strict bounds of logic and mathematics, concerning whether sentences are "meaningful" or not, inasmuch as they conform to *specified* rules, or can be operated upon by such rules, or whether they are consistent or not with other sentences, etc.   But in our present study we are not so concerned with formal logic; for human everyday thoughts and conversations have little to do with logic.[6]   We shall merely make a few points about "meaning" as this word is employed widely in common speech.

Going back about a century in time, it seems to have been Charles Peirce[129, 258] who first stressed the essentially triadic nature of "meaningful" situations, situations involving relations between thoughts, signs, and designata (roughly "what is referred to").†   This triadic nature has been examined in the now classic work of Ogden and Richards,[250] and represented by their well-known "triangle diagram" [Fig. 3.6(*a*)].   Here, the idea of "meaning" is considered to involve three elements: a person having *thoughts*, a *symbol*, and a *referent*, which are represented by the three corners of a triangle.   Thought/symbol corresponds to one side, thought/referent to a second side, whilst the third side, symbol/referent, represents a less direct and non-causal relation.[250]   (The term *symbol* is better replaced by *signal*, *sign*, or *token* in our present context and terminology; Fig. 3.6(*b*) shows the triangle modified to suit our discussion here.)   Both the symbol (or, as here, *token*, *sign*, or *signal*) and the referent set up a thought and become associated in thought.   To quote these authors: "Symbols direct and organise thoughts . . ."   Speech cannot organize things; it organizes thoughts in people, and people organize things.   The trouble is, of course, that we have no direct access to other people's thoughts; we cannot observe them, but only the physical signals and the people uttering them.

We have used the word *referent* (Ogden and Richards) to signify "what is referred to" (i.e., thought about) when a specific word is used, as we saw in Section 1 of this chapter, with various degrees of vagueness.   We shall use the term *designatum* in a more general sense, to imply "any attribute of the outside world (thing, property, event, relationship . . .) which is referred

---

* The various terms used here are unfortunately not employed consistently in different disciplines; consequently an attempt has been made to set out a set of consistent definitions, in the Appendix, to which the reader's attention is directed.   See p. 305.

† See Appendix for definitions.

to when a signal is employed." However, reference is frequently made to non-existents (unicorn, phoenix, Julius Caesar); the designata in such cases correspond to memories, resulting from past experiences, or readings, tellings, et cetera; for human language, unlike animal signs, can refer to the past.[139] Figure 3.6(b) shows "memories" as part of the functional flow

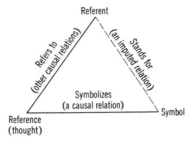

(a) The thought–word–thing triangle (after C. K. Ogden and I. A. Richards, *Meaning of Meaning*, Routledge & Kegan Paul, Ltd., by kind permission).

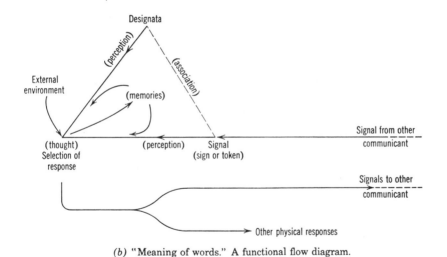

(b) "Meaning of words." A functional flow diagram.

Fig. 3.6. Words and meaning. Signal-thought-designata relations.

diagram—memories of designata or of signals from the past. When we use such a term as "designatum" to signify "what is referred to," this is not necessarily a *thing* of course. Meaning emerges from whole utterances, whole phrases or sentences, and frequently these do not signify things (e.g.,

"How do you do?"; "Are you awake?"; "What an idea!"). In some cases these reduce to single-word phrases ("Indeed!"; "Yes"; "Good-by"). Nevertheless, the term designatum is conveniently used in discussion of meaning to signify "what is referred to" by words ("indeed" might be said to refer to surprise; "good-by," to the act of parting), but it should be appreciated that the sole physical evidence of words/designata associations are *from what people do* when they hear speech. It is upon such physical evidence that a linguist builds his description of a newly observed language, compiles a dictionary, and constructs a grammar—by patient listening to speech and watching behavior, by imitating the speech sounds and the behavior, and then by observing reactions.

There is a move today to avoid "meaning" so far as can possibly be done, in communication studies. In linguistics, for example, some would aim to deal only with context, to observe utterances and how they are constructed, to study distributions and describe the *formation rules* of languages.[144] Again, Statistical Communication Theory sets out to analyze and measure the information content of messages, also abstracted from all meaning (Chapter 5). On the other hand, a movement has grown up to place semantics upon a formal basis, abstracted from human users of language and disciplining the looseness of "meaning." In particular, we have Carnap's conception of *logical syntax*,[47-53,*] with its emphasis upon the formulation of sentences and the dependence of logic upon *formal* rules of language (see again Chapter 6); and there is the work of Tarski and the Polish school of logicians with its extensive use of symbolic logic.† But let us return to the popular use of the word "meaning."

6.2. SOME DIFFERENT MEANINGS OF "MEANING"

"Meaning" is a harlot among words; it is a temptress who can seduce the writer or speaker from the path of intellectual chastity. There are many like her. Our language is filled with such words of easy virtue; words like "true," "value," "instinct," "entity." These are everyday words, and their ambiguity is such that high-sounding statements may easily be made, having little content.

This is not to say that such words cannot be turned to honest employment. "Meaning" has been seized upon by Ogden and Richards, in their classic work, and its uses in various contexts scrutinized and compared. The great lesson of their book is that the word "meaning" serves many functions, a lesson which they drive home with a multitude of examples quoted from texts of philosophy, science, criticism, and psychology. The words "means" and "meaning," if used too freely in a text, may bespatter the linguistic

---

* Read first his "popular" *Foundations of Logic and Mathematics*, reference 47.

† For a discussion of semantics and linguistics, see reference 11.

window through which we view the writer's thoughts; his muddying is, in so many cases, performed unwittingly. In brief, the word "meaning" has many meanings, and such have been the fruitless philosophic speculation, the misunderstanding, and scientific error set up by this word that we should almost blush to use it.

To take a few examples of its everyday use, the following are typical:

(1) *"Saltpeter" means "potassium nitrate"* (i.e., "denotes the same substance as" or "is a word more or less synonymous with").
(2) *George means mischief* (i.e., intends to cause).
(3) *He means his father* (i.e., wishes to refer to).

Then again, on quite a different plane, there are its aesthetic, or emotional, connotations:

(4) *Picasso has no meaning for me* (i.e., arouses no specific emotion in).
(5) *Life has no meaning for me now* (i.e., interest, purpose, worth, significance).

The word "means" often replaces the expression *is a sign of*, or perhaps *is a consequence of*, for example, in "Smoke means fire."

The following examples of typical uses of the word by a speaker in conversation are more relevant to our present theme:

(6) *"I mean what I say!"*
(7) *"I know what I mean, but can't think how to say it."*
(8) *"Is my meaning clear?"*
(9) *"What do you mean?"*

The word "means" is too often slipped into our speech and writing, from laziness. So often will a moment's thought provide a more precise word or phrase, for example: "designates," "denotes," "signifies," "symbolizes," "portrays," "represents," "stands for," "indicates," "portends," "interprets as," "translates as," "implies," "intends," "purports to show," "connotes," "expresses," "is a synonym for," and perhaps others. Charles Morris sifts out four terms in particular, as distinguishing quite different classes of meaning: "designates," "signifies," "indicates," "expresses."[243, 244,*]

The examples 6 to 9 above are of course drawn from object-language; all involve the personal element: *I mean, you mean*, and so on. Such uses are distinct from the so-called dictionary meanings, for example:

(10) *"I wonder what 'prestidigitator' means?"* ("I want a good synonym for . . .").

As stressed earlier (Section 1), dictionaries do not "give meanings" or even give definitions; they give more or less synonymous words and phrases, as judged from a survey of many texts.[c] Rather than say "*X* means *Y*," it would be a happier choice of phrase to say "The meaning of a sentence, *to*

* Read reference 243 first.

someone, is substantially unaltered if X and Y are interchanged"—cases such as 1 and 10 above.   When people use the word "mean" or "meaning," in such contexts as 6 through 9 above, they are referring to some utterance that has been made (or is about to be made).   Essentially an *intention* is involved; the reference is volitional; an utterance has meaning *to* someone, to the speaker or to the listener.   The speaker intends by his utterance to set up some specific response in the listener—to change the listener's physical and mental state (e.g., his behavior and also his attitude in relation to some designata).   On the other hand, the listener actually responds to the utterance according to his estimation of the speaker's intentions.   The meanings of an utterance, to the speaker, or to the listener, are to be distinguished.   (I am reminded of the story of Captain Cook who, when he asked a native, "What's that silly-looking animal?" received the answer "kangaroo," which I understand is Aborigine for "I don't know.")   A speaker may tell a deliberate lie, with the intention of deceiving the listener, who may, in turn, either see through this lie or be deceived by it; the listener would then either interpret the utterance as a sign of "the speaker's intention of deceiving" or not, and respond accordingly. *

Referring to Fig. 3.2 (*a*) again, this shows two people A and B in conversation and an observer.   There are two people under observation here and two meanings may be attached to an utterance which passes from A to B, its meaning to the speaker, or its meaning to the listener. A's utterance is a sign, chosen from his repertoire, serving as a stimulus to B; B may respond in many ways, depending upon his entire environment and experience. Then we shall here accept that "the meaning of the utterance to the listener, B," is the selection of the particular response he actually makes; and that "the meaning of the utterance to the speaker, A," is that selection of a response in B which A intends his utterance to evoke.   Notice that in both cases this does not identify the meaning of the utterance with a physical response, but rather with the selection of a response.   Charles Morris, to whose work we shall be referring in Chapter 6, speaks of signs as "*selecting responses in their interpreters*" (italics mine).[244]   The "meaning of the utterance to the speaker," as we have expressed it here, is substantially the formulation of Gardiner,[130] although it is also referred to by Ogden and Richards.[250].†   These authors single out the meaning to the *speaker* of his utterance, whilst here we wish to stress the distinction between the meanings

---

* We shall continue this discussion of "meaning"—to a speaker or to a listener—in Section 4.2 of Chapter 6.

† Ogden and Richards distinguish *five* functions which an utterance performs: (1) symbolization of a reference (thoughts about designata); (2) expression of speaker's attitude to listener; (3) expression of his attitude to the referent (designata); (4) the promotion of effects intended; (5) support of reference.

to the two parties, speaker and listener. Warren Weaver[297] refers to the "semantic problem of communication" as being "concerned with the identity, or satisfactorily close approximation, in the interpretation of meaning by the receiver, as compared with the intended meaning of the sender."

Very little has yet been accomplished in formulating descriptions or making physical and mathematical "models" of real human communication processes. But two particular problems stand out: that of mechanization* of translation from one language to another,[8, 10, 12] and that of *perception* or recognition of speech (popularly referred to as the "automatic speech-typewriter" or "mechanical stenographer"—see Chapter 7). Machine translation is of course not concerned with "meaning" at all, in our present sense of that word, not with meaning *to* someone but purely with "syntactic transformations"—textual substitutions, from an original to a target language. The machine must store word stems, prefixes, and affixes and be provided with rules governing alternatives as conditioned by the context.[208] Perhaps scientific texts, with their "public" language and narrow ranges of semantic variations, will be the first to be translated by machine; this would indeed be useful. The problem of machine translation is to transform from a source language A into a target language B, using rules expressed in a *third* language C; it sets a really scientific question to the linguists.[363] And the scientific study of translation has social importance, for it may force us into greater intercultural understanding.[279]

This has been an extremely brief and simple sketch of "meaning," a subject upon which volumes have been written. It sets out to do no more than indicate that "meaning of an utterance" is an ambiguous phrase. Indeed, to speak of utterances *and* their meaning is almost to make a dualism, like body *and* soul, substance *and* form. The meaning and the utterance form a unit: a "meaningful utterance"; the meaning is inherent in transmission or receipt of the utterance.[1] A "meaning" is not a label tied round the neck of a spoken word or phrase. It is more like the beauty of a complexion, which lies "altogether in the eye of its beholder" (but changes with the light!)

6.3. "REDUNDANCY" IN LANGUAGE

The complex syntactical rules of a language represent a set of constraints.† As with all human laws or rules, such constraints give structure to the

* Here, and elsewhere, when we speak of "mechanization" or the "making of models," we do not refer to actual physical construction. The terms should be taken to signify "the discipline and language of physics and mathematics." Nevertheless, if such descriptions can be formulated, of phenomena which are at present describable only in the language of psychology and linguistics, there would be no lack of enthusiasm for the practical construction of reading, translating, speech typewriting robots!

† We use the term *syntax* in its broad sense of "signs, and relations between signs." See Appendix.

system and determine a conformity, by which predictions of behavior can be made. The syntactical constraints of a language ensure that, *to some extent*, we know already what will be said, or written, in a given situation or at a certain point in a speech or text. We do not know exactly what, but we know something about it. Bodmer[A] refers to syntax as the "traffic rules of language."

We have glanced, in Section 5, at certain macroscopic aspects of language form, at the various statistical constraints which exist, or the rules which we obey on an *average* when we speak and write. But such constraints as Zipf's law do not give us much assistance in trying to follow a speaker, moment by moment. Let us now take a brief look at some of the microscopic aspects of language form, at some of the rules which we follow and which help us in communication.

The syntactical constraints which exist in language are said to introduce *redundancy*—a rather unfortunate term in view of the important role it plays. Redundancy may be regarded as two levels, the syntactic and the semantic. Syntactic redundancy implies additions to a text; something more is said or written than is strictly necessary to convey the message. But immediately the question arises: Additional to *what*? "Additional to the bare bones of the message," we might say. But what are the bare bones of a message? Such a question concerning the magnitude of the redundancy in human languages cannot be anwered with any accuracy, at least not in this form. We cannot say what elements may be stripped off a given text before the message will fail to be conveyed to a given recipient; there are so many different ways in which such stripping could be done. On the other hand, Shannon has described a technique for assessing the redundancy in printed texts (of a given class) on an *average*, by observing how much is predictable, or guessable, by the reader.[294] Any individual has an enormous storehouse of his language statistics, as habits and conventions, at both syntactic and semantic levels. He stores rules of spelling, word orders, grammar, idioms, and clichés; again he stores typical vocabularies and phraseology which are used for specific subject matters, and he can predict to some extent from his knowledge of topics or of the writer's point of view. All such prior information is brought to bear on the reading of a text; but the text redundancy is distributed in a most complex way amongst the various factors.

Briefly, Shannon's experimental technique is to ask a person to guess an unseen text, letter by letter. As he guesses correctly, the letters are written down for him to see; if he guesses wrongly, a note is made and he is informed correctly before proceeding. An alternative technique is to refrain from correcting the recipient's errors, but to require him to guess until the correct letter is found, noting the number of guesses he needs. From the results, Shannon makes a numerical assessment of the redundancy.[294]

Such guessing faculties which we all possess in varying degrees might be explained in terms of our knowledge of letter and word-chain statistics; of digram, trigram, et cetera; of letter or word transition probabilities (if not of their actual frequencies, then of their rank orderings). Rather than speak of "knowledge," it would be better to speak of "habits"— habits of response we have acquired from years of verbal experience.

This store of verbal habits, if averaged over a large number of people drawn from a particular population, who habitually communicate in the same language, provides a source whereby the statistical properties of the language may be estimated. Miller[235] has taken advantage of this, in order to construct passages of English text which conform (in the long run) to the statistical structure of English. Such passages he uses for various psychological tests. He constructs them as follows. A common word is chosen from the dictionary and shown to someone, who is asked to suggest a "suitable" word to follow it; this done, this second word is written down whilst the first word is covered over. This new word is shown to a second person, with the same instructions. And so on, to a third, fourth, fifth . . . person until long word sequences are obtained. Such a technique results in texts typical of the *word* monogram structure of English. It reads like rubbish, of course, each word being chosen by a different person who has seen only the preceding word. Alternatively, instead of one word, two could be shown each time to each person, resulting in texts typical of word digram structure; or three words, for trigrams, and so on. This short extract comes from such a text based upon showing *two* words only each time:

> A big leakage of secret information which should help you cross the road to destruction is what must be inevitably the case of bacon and eggs for breakfast with the bishop who said we might go there next Thursday week is soon enough for me to understand the question of the hour hand of my watch chain swinging along. . . .

And so on. The ramblings of a moron with a memory of two words' duration. It grips you for a line or so, but it never seems to get to the point. It is at least a way of being funny, if you don't know a better. The important thing here is that it grips you *at all*—this tremendous tenacity of language is a remarkable property. You will always grope "for sense."

Such texts could as well be constructed on an *n*-gram *letter* basis, by showing 1, 2, . . . , *n* consecutive letters each time. This experimental technique may be easier and more practicable than using published frequency tables—besides which, such tables do not go above trigram letter frequencies.

The statistical theory of communication has, as part of its aim, the setting up of a measure of the redundancy in *codes*, such as telegraph codes. In this theory (Chapter 5), the messages are assumed, *a priori*, to be expressed in signs (i.e., to exist as physical signals); then the amount of redundancy which is added or subtracted when the code structure is modified may be assessed quantitatively.[297] It is difficult to apply this measure to the redundancy in human language texts (though approximate upper and lower bounds may be set).[294]

Why do we need redundancy at all, whether syntactic or semantic? Mainly, as we have already discussed, because of the various disturbances from the external environment, the uncertainties of accent or handwriting, and the inadequacies of language itself. This latter requires that we expand our phrases and sentences until we are content that we have "conveyed our meaning"; so we may need to express a thought in several different ways. This semantic redundancy then calls for extra signs; that is, for syntactic redundancy. Basically, redundancy implies some kind of repetition, or additional signs to be used. The various affixes, spelling rules, conjugation rules, in English, for example, do this.

The simplest manner of adding further signs might be to repeat everything we say—word by word, or phrase by phrase—thereby reducing the chance that the recipient will make errors, in spite of the various uncertainties or disturbances. In fact such direct repetitions do play a major part when we communicate under difficulties—for example over a noisy telephone.[226, 232]

When we send a telegram we deliberately reduce the redundancy, because words cost money. This is possible owing to the restricted purpose which a telegram usually serves, and because the writer can take his time in composing it so as to draw the maximum advantages from his knowledge of the intended recipient's prior knowledge, both of syntax and of the subject matter or situation. A few moments' thought enables the writer to remove those words which he judges will be guessed correctly; nevertheless, in so doing he is running the risk of ambiguity. Newspaper headlines achieve such compression to a high degree—and frequently the ambiguity either does not matter, or perhaps whets the reader's appetite! "RUNNING WATER CAN DEFY WEIGHT AT SANDOWN" referred, on closer reading, to a racehorse, not to some miraculous levitation.*

The relationship between the whole structure of a language (the morphemic, syntactic, grammatical formalism) and the outside world associations (its semantic functioning) is extremely complicated; it is essentially

* A London evening paper.

empirical and, above all, varies between different languages.* Again, redundancy is built into the structural forms of different languages in diverse ways.   No general laws exist.

Most of us are taught, during our school days, that certain sentence structures are "good" and to be accepted as standard; such structures are illustrated by examples from set books.   We may be taught also that different parts of speech serve different but very specific (semantic) functions. Nouns, we are told, are "names of people or objects"; "verbs present their content as processes, adjectives as properties," and so on.   Perhaps we are even told that a sentence is not a sentence unless it contains a verb, or even that a sentence cannot start with *and*!   Classification into parts of speech certainly has its uses and the functions we commonly attribute to nouns, verbs, adjectives, and so on are fairly widely applicable; but most of these semantic functions cannot be laid down as definite universal rules, even within the bounds of one language, such as English.   All the rules we are taught, as schoolboys, for identifying a word as a noun, verb, or adjective, may be violated and yet meaning conveyed.   Indeed not only do newspaper headlines break such rules, but the bulk of everyday conversational speech does too.[A, 250]

It is essentially experience with our own language that ensures this identification of "parts of speech"; familiarity with common types of sentences and with the ways in which different semantic categories are built into them.   Indeed, so deeply engrained is our experience of such conventional forms and of word affixes that we have no difficulty in analyzing "nonsense" sentences of simple types:

The ventious crapests pounted raditally.
(adjective) (noun) (verb) (adverb)

We can readily translate this into French:

Les crapêts ventieux pontaient raditallement.

but we cannot carry over these parts of speech, or the sentence structure, to more remote languages, any more than we can translate each word into a word.   Thus, this nonsense sentence could not be put into, say, a Chinese dialect![279]

Nonsense sentences, such as the one above, do in fact communicate something; at the least they convey a standard sentence construction.   We might guess, for instance, whether a statement is being made, a question being asked, or an order given.   This illustrates one manner of introducing

* For example, Sapir stresses the independence of form and function: "acoustic patterning is one thing; its semantic use is another and varies with different languages." See reference G.

redundancy, by adhering closely to standard sentence structures, at least in written texts.

But to pass to the other extreme, we can strip off all grammatical clues to sentence structure, all affixes and prepositions, and yet still achieve communication. Thus restricted to nouns, simple "stories" can be told in word chains: *Woman, street, crowd, traffic, noise, haste, thief, bag, loss, scream, police.* . . . Again, the reader's past experience of his language is sufficient to restore the missing elements, sufficiently accurately for the purpose. But of course, not only does the reader have experience of sentence structure, enabling him to supply the missing syntactical elements, but also he has experience of typical contexts in which the various words are used; many words bear an aura about with them. It might be more difficult to tell a tale about a policeman who robbed a woman, for instance, with so little redundancy!

Not only are the individual words in a text significant, but so is their order: "When a dog bites a man that is not news, but when a man bites a dog that is news."* One source of ambiguity in language is the existence of *homophones*, which sound alike but have different meanings ("gate," "gait") and *homonyms*, which are even spelled alike ("ward": a dependent child; part of a key; a hospital room). But more subtle than these are the varied functions which prepositions serve, especially in English, "of," "with," "in." *I am in my right mind* (answers question: "How?"); *I am in bed* (answers question: "Where?"); and a host of other uses (*in the meantime, in such a case, in so far, in no way*). We overcome such word ambiguity by adhering to standard forms of phrase in standard situations. But ambiguity of this nature is by no means limited to prepositions: "The bride wore a dress of white satin and carried a bouquet of roses; the bridegroom wore a happy smile and carried himself well."† These examples illustrate one of the principal difficulties of describing translation. Surprising as it may seem at first, the great difficulty which faces the designer of a "translating machine" (either conceptually or in the metal) is not the problem of grammar but that of vocabulary, the problem of words serving a variety of semantic functions.[8, 10, 12, 253] A relatively small and closed vocabulary (such as that of Basic English) would be utterly inadequate for such machines.

When we speak to a friend, we carefully construct our words and phrases, building in redundancy, as we judge to be necessary for him to understand; but speech is a running affair, because we are watching and listening to his reactions, and redundancy may be put in, in a changing, patchwork manner, moment by moment. Conversation is rarely "correct" in

* C. A. Dana, *New York Sun*, 1882.
† Condensed from a local newspaper report.

grammar or syntax; sentences may remain uncompleted, words may be repeated, or phrases uttered several times in different ways.   With writing it is another matter; the writer cannot observe his readers and can only make prior judgment of their difficulties.   His writing is therefore premeditated and usually conforms more closely to the rules. A writer can take as long as he wishes to select the most suitable words and to try the effects of alternative grammatical structures.   By contrast, conversation is built out of a relatively small vocabulary (statistical studies of telephone speech have suggested that 96 per cent of such talk employs no more than 737 words);[114] but the words may be arranged with great fluidity into varied patterns, with repetitions, stressings, gestures, and a wealth of reinforcing "redundancy."   Writing must make up for the lack of gesture or stress, if it is to combat ambiguity, by introducing redundancy through a wider vocabulary and closer adherence to grammatical structure.   How easy it is to *write* an ambiguous sentence!

"Do you think that one will do?"

When spoken, stressing of each of the seven words here results in seven distinct meanings; each meaning could be conveyed less ambiguously in writing by restructuring the sentence.

BIBLIOGRAPHY

A. Bodmer, F., *The Loom of Language*, W. W. Norton & Co., Inc., New York (George Allen & Unwin, London), 1944.
B. Bloomfield, L., *Language*, Henry Holt & Co., Inc., New York, 1933.
C. Miller, G. A., *Language and Communication*, McGraw-Hill Book Co., Inc., New York, 1951.
D. Bloch, B., and G. L. Trager, *Outline of Linguistic Analysis*, Linguistic Society of America, Waverley Press, Baltimore, 1942.
E. Zipf, G. K., *Human Behavior and the Principle of Least Effort*, Addison-Wesley Publishing Co., Inc., Cambridge, Mass, 1949.
F. Jakobson, R., G. Fant, and M. Halle, "Preliminaries to Speech Analysis," *M.I.T.*, *Acoust. Lab. Rept.*, *13*, 1952.
G. Sapir, E., *Language*, Harcourt, Brace & Co., Inc., New York, 1939.
H. Carnap, R., *Introduction to Semantics*, Harvard University Press, Cambridge, Mass. 1946.
I. Price, H. H., *Thinking and Experience*, Hutchinson & Co., Ltd., London, 1953.

On Analysis of Signals, Especially Speech

The problems discussed in Chapter 3 are largely the affair of the linguist, and to a great extent of the phonetician too. In this current chapter we shall consider further some interests of the latter and also of some of those of the communication engineer; we shall discuss the physical signals themselves, and how they are described and analyzed, but without referring to their function in language.*

1. THE TELECOMMUNICATION ENGINEER COMES ONTO THE SCENE

When we communicate, one with another, we make sounds with our vocal organs, or scribe different shapes of ink mark on paper, or gesticulate in various patterned ways; such physical signs or *signals* have the ability to change thoughts and behavior—they are the medium of communication. Telecommunication engineers have as their business the transmission of such signals, and the preservation of their forms, in such systems as tele-

* Attention is drawn to the International Congress on Acoustics which, under Unesco, meets every 4 years. For its proceedings, see Bibliography, reference 368.

phones, telegraphs, facsimile, television. The engineer succeeds in spanning vast distances, in bringing distant friends into contact in a twinkling of an eye; he has changed the size and shape of the world, and the social impact has been immense.

An engineer is concerned not only with the design of apparatus, but with its operation by human beings. The civil engineer builds bridges for people to use. The mechanical engineer designs a motor car to operate with its driver as an integrated mechanical-human unit; a unit, we notice, not a man *plus* a machine—and a unit with its own set of reaction times, its own behavior, unlike those of a normal man (incidentally, since its freedom of action is so different, we should expect this unit to have its own moral code). A telecommunication system too is designed to work together with human users, and the engineer is concerned that it should work successfully as a unit. As part of his business, he analyzes signals mathematically, in various ways, which we shall glance at in this chapter. But although it is 200 years since the first telegraph line was set up,* it is only during recent years that engineers have considered how they may measure not only the signals, their wave forms, and their spectra, but the *information* which their electrical channels have the capacity to transmit. The "measurement of information" will be deferred until the next chapter, whilst at present we shall confine attention to the analysis of physical signals, as an essential preliminary. Then in the final chapters of our book, we shall return to the broader aspects of human communication, with the intention of showing that this mathematical theory is quite *basic* to the whole study, yet at the same time quite insufficient.

1.1. SIGNALS IN TIME AND SIGNALS IN SPACE

The sounds of speech are tied to the time continuum—and the hearer must accept them as they come; time is the current of the vocal stream. But with sight it is different; the eye may scan a scene, or may sweep over the phrases and lines in a book, at varying speeds, as may suit the viewer or reader (and the obscurity of the text being read); the stream of words and phrases may be dammed or checked at will.

There are then two distinct classes of signal. There are signals in *time*, such as speech or music; and there are signals in *space*, like print, stone inscriptions, punched cards, and pictures. Out of all these, we shall select speech and reading as being typical of the aural and visual senses—temporal and spatial signals—and our illustrations will be confined to these.

* Stephen Gray and Granville Wheeler, in Scotland, about 1753; see *Encyclopædia Britannica* (11th Ed.), under *telegraphs*.

The eyes, when they scan the lines of a printed page, or in fact any scene, do so in a series of extremely rapid jerks (called *saccades*) between points of comparative rest (*fixation pauses*) at which they take in information.[46].* Such a scanning process converts the spatial signal to a temporal one but, as mentioned, in a manner unique to each occasion.

Temporal signals are then of principal interest—the complicated fluctuations of air pressure which evoke the sensation of sound, or of electric current in a telephone line. All such wave forms are conveniently regarded as varying continually with time. For illustration, Fig. 4.1(*b*) shows the wave form of sound pressure when the writer spoke the word "kin" into a microphone.

In contrast to the ears, the eyes do not receive one single fluctuating signal when they rest on a scene, or on a printed word, but a great many indeed; the whole retina in each eye, with its mosaic of rods and cones, represents a great number of receptors operating simultaneously, each stimulated differently when the pattern of light from the scene is focused upon it. The complex neural "mechanism" associated with the retina certainly "recodes" the spatial pattern of light—but we cannot regard the eye as reducing this spatial pattern to one single wave form, in any manner analogous to the simple television scanning process.

Other types of signal are regarded conveniently as sequences of *discrete* events in time; the successive depressions of the keys of a typewriter sets up a sequence of letters, in time; the successive positions of the arms of a semaphore also form a sequence in time. For certain types of analysis, such signals are treated as a chain, or sequence of events, but without making reference to any "wave forms"—only their sequence, or *time-ordering* matters. (We shall be concerned more with such signals in Chapter 5.)

1.2. Physical signals are distinct from sense impressions

Physical signals should not be confused with the sensations they set up in the mind of the recipient; yet this is a common error. For instance, when middle C is gently sounded on a piano, the string is vibrating 261 times a second.† We may quote its *frequency* (as measured, say, by a phonic motor or a stroboscope^c) as 261 cycles per second. But the sensation we call its *pitch* is mental. As the notes of a piano are sounded, successively from the base to the treble, the frequency steadily increases, note by note, and we have sensations of *rising* or *increasing* pitch; such words are deceptive because they suggest a simple relation between the sensation of pitch and the frequency of a note. But the two are categorically distinct

* We shall look more closely at this fascinating process in Chapter 7 (see Fig. 7.6).
† "English concert pitch" (see reference 177).

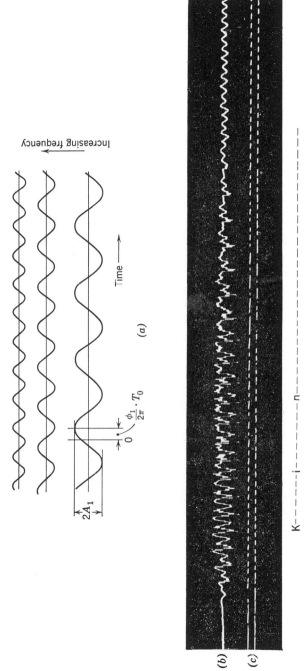

Fig. 4.1.   (a) Sinusoidal wave forms of pure tones; (b) wave form of male voice saying "kin"; (c) centrally clipped version of (b).

—*pitch* is a sensation, private to a listener, whereas *frequency* is a physical attribute of the sound, measurable by instruments. Similarly the magnitude or *intensity* of sound should not be confused with *loudness*. There are similar distinctions with our other senses, the sight, the touch, and so on.

Corresponding to this categorical distinction, there are two classes of measurement carried out in the experimental study of communication. First, there are measurements upon physical signals themselves—frequencies, magnitudes, wave forms, et cetera—carried out instrumentally, and leading to actual numbers, or magnitudes, according to definite calibrated scales or standards of reference. Secondly, there are observations and comparisons made of the sensations which such signals can set up in people. Then the first class consists of objective measurements (usually numerical), while the second class includes measurements involving subjective effects. "Measurement" involving "subjective" effects suggests a contradiction in terms, and so it is unless the recipient of the signals, who is experiencing the sensations, is considered also as a *participant* in the experiment. He can participate in two ways. He may act as a self-observer and gauge his sensations against the dial readings of instruments which are measuring the physical signals. Alternatively an external observer may carry out the measurements, if the recipient of the signals co-operates (e.g., he may say when two sounds seem alike to him, or different in some specified way). Such *indirect* measurements, involving a recipient's responses, may then attach actual magnitudes to the sensations. But the recipient himself, in whose mind the sensations arise and who is unaided by instruments, cannot *measure* his sensations; he cannot say how loud a sound is, how brilliant a light is, or what is the heaviness of a stone he is holding. Nevertheless he can compare and *rank-order* the associated sensations; he can compare and mentally place them in order of magnitude along a subjective scale. It is this which enables reliable, repeatable observations and studies to be made of human perceptions.

The faculty, sometimes possessed by those of musical ear, called "absolute pitch" does not deny this. Such people are able to name accurately a musical note, upon hearing it.[G] But such judgment consists of *relating* the sensation (pitch) to past sensations; at some stage the frequency has had to be measured instrumentally. Similarly, many people can judge weights, or colors, with remarkable accuracy.

But examples are often worth a deal of argument; let us first take the sensation of *aural harmonics*.

1.2.1. THE SENSATION OF AURAL HARMONICS. The electrical oscillator is commonly used as a controllable source of audible tones, for acoustic experiments.[c] With this instrument, tones may be generated in headphones, or loudspeakers, having any specific frequency and intensity—with a purity of wave form like that of a tuning fork.

Should a listener, possessing a fairly musical ear, be stimulated by a pure audible tone from an oscillator, he may report that he hears *harmonics*, or overtones.[275] These are created within the hearing organs themselves. Harmonics are tones having frequencies at exact multiples $(2,3,4,\cdots.)$ of the principal, "fundamental" tone. Moreover, as the intensity of the pure-tone stimulus is increased, the listener will say that, to him, the harmonics appear also to be magnified.   This is one illustration of the fact that we cannot make a strict one-to-one comparison between a physical stimulus and the sensation it sets up.   Here the stimulus is a pure tone, while the sensation is complex.

These aural harmonics may, with the listener's co-operation, be referred to an external scale of measurement.[G] If, in addition to the first (fundamental) oscillator, an auxiliary one is introduced, tuned to two, three, or more times the fundamental frequency, it will be heard by the listener to interfere, or *beat*, with one of his aural harmonics.   The relative intensity of the auxiliary oscillator tone may be adjusted until the listener reports it as giving the loudest beats, thus seeming equal to the aural harmonic in volume; it then gives a measure of the loudness of the aural harmonic. The various aural harmonics may be measured in this way, and their dependence upon the intensity of the pure-tone stimulus determined.   The results differ, among different people.*   Many other tests of similar character also show this lack of simple relationship between stimulus and sensation.   One most striking test shows that the pitch depends not only upon the frequency of the sound stimulus but upon its intensity as well.[G]

1.2.2. RESPONSES TO SHORT-DURATION TONES.   Aural sensations also show remarkable complexity when the ears are stimulated, not by continuous tones of constant frequency, but by tones switched suddenly on and off.   If an audible tone of 1000 cycles per second is switched on for, say, 5 seconds and then switched off, the listener reports a sensation of constant pitch during that interval; for that 5 seconds this pitch may be assessed objectively by reference to an auxiliary oscillator operating continuously.   But as the duration of the switched tone is made shorter and shorter, the character of the sensation changes.   At the very short duration of about 20 milliseconds, the pitch appears definitely lower than before, and, at the same time, the listener may report that the sound seems more like a "click."   As the duration is lessened further, the "click" gradually predominates, until all sensations of pitch are lost.[G, 42]

* Rather than quote a large number of references of specialized interest, we give reference G as itself a valuable source of other references on the subject of hearing. Another useful source is reference 315.

But another factor enters in here, our "sense of time." A steady note continuously maintained gives rise to a definite pitch sensation (perhaps with added aural harmonics); on the other hand, an extremely sharp acoustic impulse appears pitchless though it marks a definite *instant* in time. It is an *event* (sometimes referred to as an *epoch*), and our ears are sensitive and discriminatory not only toward pitches but also toward the timing of events. When we listen to speech, or to other complex sounds of everyday life, we may need to discriminate pitches (e.g., as of the vowel tones or the notes of a singer) and events as well (as of the syllabic rhythms and sequences). Both *frequency* and *time* are important attributes of speech and other acoustic signals.

The shortest note which sets up any sensation of pitch has a duration, very approximately, of 10 to 20 milliseconds.[42] This figure occurs again and again in subjective tests upon hearing and, for certain purposes, may be regarded as a rough boundary at which our sensations pass from pitch to events in time.

1.3. OUR SENSE ORGANS ARE NOT "CONSTANT PROPERTIES" MECHANISMS

As we have had occasion to mention before, the historical precedence of the science of mechanics has led to the natural consequence that its concepts are commonly carried over, and used for scientific description, in other fields. We may speak of the ears, or the eyes, as "mechanisms" (using terms taken from mechanics, electrical engineering, or physics). Whatever may be the adequacy, or validity, of such description, all that I wish to stress here is that if such description is made, we must not expect the "mechanism" to possess the same structure for different tests. Such a model may be adequate for one series of tests, yet be found to fail, as a description, with other tests.

However, this is not to say that the properties of, for example, the ears cannot be described by sufficient physical measurements, recorded data, graphs, et cetera. Rather it implies the risk of false conclusions if the results of one series of tests are generalized and assumed to be relevant to other sets of conditions.

In all experiments carried out upon people, involving their sensations, it is of the greatest importance to record all the conditions of the test; only too frequently, results are vitiated because an experimenter has neglected to record some significant attribute of the stimulus or of the environment. The human senses (above all, that of hearing) do not possess one set of constant properties, to be measured independently, one at a time. It is even questionable whether the various "senses" are to be regarded as separate, independent detectors. The human organism is one integrated whole, stimulated into response by physical signals; it is not to be thought of as a box, carrying various independent pairs of input terminals labeled "ears," "eyes," "nose," et cetera.*

2. SPECTRAL ANALYSIS OF SIGNALS

Those readers who find even simple mathematics tedious should pick up the thread again at Section 2.4 and accept the next sections as read. Let us look at some of the ways in which physical signal wave forms have been analyzed and described mathematically. Such analysis bears only upon these *signals*, and may be carried out without any reference whatever to sensations.

We are at present concerned not with the communication process *per se* but with physical signals as functions of time, and with their spectra; such analysis, we may imagine, is carried out by the external observer [type (*a*) Fig. 3.2].

2.1. Fourier series and Fourier integrals

As a basis for analysis of signal wave forms, the simple harmonic motion, *sine wave* or *sinusoid*, Fig. 4.1(*a*), has reigned supreme for several decades; telecommunication engineers have depended largely upon it for many very good reasons: (1) it leads to simple mathematics, widely taught and readily understood; (2) a great deal of acoustic and electrical measuring apparatus exists, employing sine waves; (3) analogous aspects of wave motion exist in physics, for example in optics or in electromagnetic wave theory, and again, many familiar vibrations approximate to "simple harmonic motions," for example, water ripples, gently swinging pendulums, tuning forks, et cetera. Analysis in terms of continuous sine waves (Fourier analysis) is certainly very important but, as we hope to show later, inadequate for the full description of communication signals.

The continuous "simple harmonic motion," or sinusoid, represented by:

$$s_1(t) = A_1 \cos\left(2\pi \frac{t}{T_0} - \phi_1\right) \tag{4.1}$$

is sketched, in part, in Fig. 4.1(*a*); it has a peak amplitude A_1, and phase angle, with respect to the chosen origin, ϕ_1 (giving a *time delay* of $\phi_1 T_0/2\pi$). Such a wave form corresponds to a "pure" musical note—as of a tuning fork or a gently blown flute—with a frequency $1/T_0$ cycles per second. But it is important to notice that time has no limit in this equation; the wave here lasts forever and from all time past—from creation to eternity—

---

* For instance, the responses to an aural signal may be conditioned by visual stimuli because of inhibitory effects taking place in the central nervous system (e.g., see Rawdon-Smith, under reference G).

an unrealistic notion, but adopted for its simplicity, like many ideas in applied mathematics.

Many other sustained tones may be regarded as built up by adding to this *fundamental* wave a series or *band of harmonics*, having frequencies of $2/T_0$, $3/T_0$, $4/T_0$, $\cdots$, N/T_0 cycles per second; the highest frequency N/T_0 determines the *bandwidth*. The acoustic quality of such wave forms will

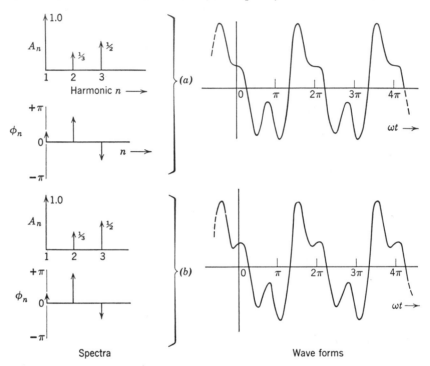

Fig. 4.2. Addition of pure sine waves to form compound periodic wave forms. Wave forms and their amplitude and phase spectra. (The phases in (b) here are $\phi_1 = 45°$, $\phi_2 = 140°$, $\phi_3 = -80°$.)

depend upon the number of harmonics and upon their relative amplitudes. Such wave forms are nevertheless periodic, with the cyclic periodic time T_0 being that of the fundamental component. For example, Fig. 4.2(a) shows such a non-sinusoidal wave, obtained by adding to the fundamental wave in Fig. 4.1(a) two harmonics:

> Fundamental; amplitude A_1, phase $\phi_1 = 45°$
> 2nd harmonic; amplitude $A_2 = A_1/3$, phase $\phi_2 = 120°$
> 3rd harmonic; amplitude $A_3 = A_1/2$, phase $\phi_3 = -90°$

The actual shape of any periodic wave depends upon both the relative amplitudes and phases of all these component waves[c] (the fundamental and the harmonics). We may then write any periodic wave form as a *Fourier series*:

$$s(t) = \sum_n A_n \cos\left(2\pi \frac{nt}{T_0} - \phi_n\right) \qquad (4.2)$$

The amplitude spectrum A_n and the phase spectrum ϕ_n are usefully represented by diagrams; Fig. 4.2(a) shows the spectrum for our simple example, quoted above.

It is a remarkable fact that the mechanism of our ears is such that they are rather insensitive to phase angle; we cannot readily hear the effect of shifting the phase angles ϕ_n of the component waves of such periodic waves —at least over considerable excursions (Ohm's law[C,*]). Thus the two wave forms (a) and (b) in Fig. 4.2 possess the same amplitude spectrum, but have slightly different phase spectra; yet, as aural *sensations*, the two would sound very alike. The ear tends to hear a complex sound as a number of superposed tones. Ohm's law of hearing is frequently quoted as though the ear were absolutely insensitive to phase—but this is not the case.[C,G,275,†]

With the eye, the effect is quite otherwise. The phase spectra are most significant; the eye readily perceives the difference between (a) and (b) in Fig. 4.2.

Though the ear is relatively insensitive to phase, it is most sensitive to the number and magnitudes of the harmonics. The *quality* of aural sensation depends markedly upon the amplitude spectrum of the sound stimulus.

A periodic wave form having any frequency lower than a certain threshold (between 10 and 20 cycles per second) is perceived not as a tone, or musical note, but as a sequence of *events* (see Section 1.2.2). The sensation changes in character; at such very low frequencies the individual surges may even be counted. In such cases, a large shift of the phases of certain harmonics can be made to split each cyclic surge into two parts, which then appear as discrete events.‡ (Such an effect proved a nuisance in fact in the early days of submarine telegraphy.) For illustration, Fig. 4.3(a) shows a single surge, or *transient* wave form; a suitable phase distortion can convert this to the wave form (b), and such a change would be detected by the ear, if the time scale is slow enough or if the period of repetition of such transients is of suitably long interval. The ear then sometimes appears

---

* Those readers who require further reading on elementary wave motion, or who wish to make a study of acoustics, are referred to reference 358, and those interested in spectra of musical instrument tones are also advised to read reference 177.

† For those who do not read German, an English translation of Helmholtz's classic work exists, reference 151.

‡ E.g., the peaks on the waveform in Fig. 4.2(b).

to operate as a *frequency*-sensitive organ and sometimes as a *time*-sensitive one; in practice, especially with speech, it acts both ways in a complicated manner. Our diagram of the spoken word "kin," Fig. 4.1(*b*), illustrates this; the wave form to the extreme right, corresponding to the [n] sound, is periodic for many cycles, but the wave form nearer to the start of the word, the sound [ki], appears partly periodic but with irregular transient variations superposed. Speech sounds are partly tones and partly transients.

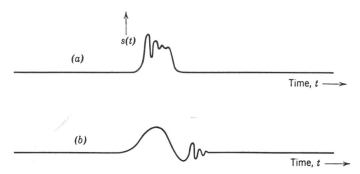

Fig. 4.3. A transient wave (showing effect of excessive phase shift of high-frequency harmonics).

A musical chord, gently played on a piano with the damper raised, consists of a number of fairly pure tones sounding concurrently. Yet any reasonably musical ear is able to hear each note separately[151]—though it can also hear the chord as a whole, as a *gestalt*.[177] A trained phonetician can perceive the individual resonances of a speaker's voice, too.[A] Although phases cannot be dismissed entirely, it is the magnitudes (or rather the powers) of the various components of a composite sound which are most important.

The instantaneous power of a signal $s(t)$ is given by $s^2(t)$, squaring the amplitude scale of the intensity wave form. The *average* power of the complex signal may be expressed in terms of the amplitudes of the constituent harmonics. Thus, squaring both sides of Eq. 4.2:

$$s^2(t) = \sum_n \left[A_n{}^2 \cos^2 \left(\frac{2\pi nt}{T_0} - \phi_n \right) \right]$$
$$+ \sum_{n \neq m} \sum \left[A_n A_m \cos \left(\frac{2\pi nt}{T_0} - \phi_n \right) \cos \left(\frac{2\pi mt}{T_0} - \phi_m \right) \right] \quad (4.3)$$

If now we average both sides over a whole cycle of duration T_0 (using a bar to indicate such time average):

$$\overline{s^2(t)} = \frac{1}{T_0} \int_0^{T_0} s^2(t)\, dt = \sum_n \overline{\left[A_n{}^2 \cos^2 \left(\frac{2\pi nt}{T_0} - \phi_n \right) \right]} = \sum_n \frac{A_n{}^2}{2} \quad (4.4)$$

since the average of the cross-spectral terms on the right-hand side of Eq. 4.3 ($m \neq n$) is of course zero.

Now the average power of the signal, $\overline{s^2(t)}$, must equal the sum of the average powers of the constituent harmonics. Equation 4.4 expresses this; if we write $i_n = A_n/\sqrt{2}$ (the *effective* value of the nth harmonic), then

$$\overline{s^2(t)} = \sum i_n^2 \qquad (4.5)$$

So far, we have considered only the addition of given harmonics, with specified amplitudes and phases, to form a composite wave form $s(t)$; we now carry out the reverse process. Given a periodic non-sinusoidal wave form, we may analyze it into a set of harmonics by Fourier's theorem.[D] With a given time origin, the amplitudes A_n and phases ϕ_n of these harmonics will be unique, for any given wave form $s(t)$, but may be infinite in number; any specified harmonic, the nth, may be calculated.*

It is convenient to express the right-hand side of Eq. 4.2 in terms of a separate sine and cosine series; thus, writing $a_n = A_n \cos \phi_n$ and $b_n = A_n \sin \phi_n$, we have:

$$s(t) = \sum_n a_n \cos \frac{2\pi nt}{T_0} + \sum_n b_n \sin \frac{2\pi nt}{T_0} \qquad (4.6)$$

This splits the wave form $s(t)$ into a sum of two wave forms, an *even* function of time and an *odd* function of time, respectively symmetric and skew-symmetric about the chosen time origin. Figure 4.4 illustrates a periodic wave form split into such even and odd components. Calling these components $s_c(t)$ and $s_s(t)$, then:

$$\left.\begin{array}{l} s(t) = s_c(t) + s_s(t) \\ s(-t) = s_c(t) - s_s(t) \end{array}\right\}\text{from Eq. 4.6}$$

Adding, or subtracting:

$$s_c(t) = \tfrac{1}{2}[s(t) + s(-t)] \text{ and } s_s(t) = \tfrac{1}{2}[s(t) - s(-t)] \qquad (4.7)$$

To determine the harmonic spectra of these odd and even component wave forms, multiply both sides of Eq. 4.6 by $\cos 2\pi mt/T_0$ (where $m = 1, 2, 3, \cdots$) and integrate over a period T_0; this gives the expression for the cosine harmonic amplitudes a_n. Again, multiplying by $\sin 2\pi mt/T_0$ and

* We need not be too pedantic and rigorous with the mathematics here; actually the functions $s(t)$ must be finite, continuous, and single-valued for Fourier's theorem to be applied, but all physical temporal signals in fact conform to such requirements.

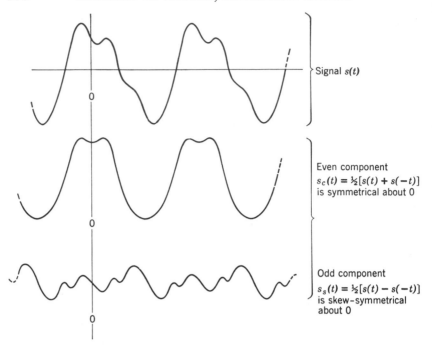

Signal $s(t)$

Even component
$s_c(t) = \frac{1}{2}[s(t) + s(-t)]$
is symmetrical about 0

Odd component
$s_s(t) = \frac{1}{2}[s(t) - s(-t)]$
is skew-symmetrical
about 0

Fig. 4.4.   A wave form divided into even (cosine) and odd (sine) components.

integrating gives the sine amplitudes b_n:

$$a_n = \frac{2}{T_0} \int_{-T_0/2}^{+T_0/2} s(t) \cos \frac{2\pi n t}{T_0}\, dt$$
$$b_n = \frac{2}{T_0} \int_{-T_0/2}^{+T_0/2} s(t) \sin \frac{2\pi n t}{T_0}\, dt$$

(4.8)

since integrals of the form $\int \cos \dfrac{2\pi n t}{T_0} \cos \dfrac{2\pi m t}{T_0}\, dt$, taken over whole periods, vanish, except when $m = n$.

Then Eqs. 4.6 and 4.8 go together as a reciprocal pair. The first expresses the signal $s(t)$ as a sum of harmonics; the second enables the harmonics to be calculated from a knowledge of the signal's periodic wave form $s(t)$.

Let us now convert this pair of equations, 4.6 and 4.8, to a form suitable for *transient*, or non-periodic, wave forms. For instance, Fig. 4.3 shows an impulsive type of transient wave form; how may we calculate its Fourier spectrum?[D]

We could first of all imagine this impulse to be repeated periodically, but with a very long cyclic period T_0; its spectrum would then, as with any periodic wave form, consist of harmonics having frequencies $2/T_0$, $3/T_0$, $4/T_0$, $\cdots$ where $1/T_0$ is the fundamental repetition frequency. The harmonics would be spaced apart by $1/T_0$ cycles per second or, as an *angular frequency*, $2\pi/T_0$ radians per second. If now we imagine T_0 to be extended indefinitely "toward infinity," we see that the harmonics crowd closer and closer together, because $2\pi/T_0$ becomes infinitesimal. Let us call this harmonic angular frequency spacing $\delta\omega$; then we may represent this limiting process by:

$$2\pi/T_0 \to \delta\omega \qquad \text{the "harmonic" spacing} \qquad (4.9)$$

Also write $n\delta\omega = \omega$, the angular frequency of the nth harmonic. Then we can eliminate T_0 from Eq. 4.8, which now becomes:

$$\left.\begin{aligned}
a_n/\delta\omega &= \frac{1}{\pi} \int_{-\infty}^{+\infty} s(t) \cos \omega t \, dt = a(\omega) \\
b_n/\delta\omega &= \frac{1}{\pi} \int_{-\infty}^{+\infty} s(t) \sin \omega t \, dt = b(\omega)
\end{aligned}\right\} \qquad (4.10)$$

the integral limits $\pm T_0/2$ in Eq. 4.8 are now $\pm\infty$. Notice that, as we let $\delta\omega$ become indefinitely small, the "harmonics" eventually form a *continuous spectrum*, which we have called $a(\omega)$ and $b(\omega)$ in the equation above. The idea of harmonic *number* now disappears; there are spectral components at *any* conceivable frequency $\omega/2\pi$. As we approach the limit, any harmonic, say a_n, becomes an element $a(\omega) \, \delta\omega$ of the continuous spectrum; thus $a(\omega)$ and also $b(\omega)$ have the natures of spectral *densities*. Figure 4.5 illustrates such continuous spectra, drawn from imagination, for the transient shown; at present we shall ignore the dotted parts of the spectra in this figure.

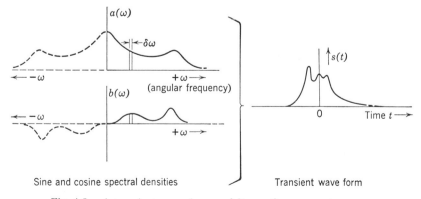

Sine and cosine spectral densities   Transient wave form

Fig. 4.5. A transient wave form and its continuous spectra.

We may make similar substitution for T_0 in the other Fourier series, Eq. 4.6. Then:

$$s(t) = \sum a(\omega) \, \delta\omega \cos \omega t + \sum b(\omega) \, \delta\omega \sin \omega t$$

and, as $\delta\omega$ becomes indefinitely small, the $\sum$ here become integrals.

$$\left.\begin{aligned} s(t) &= \int_0^\infty a(\omega) \cos \omega t \, d\omega + \int_0^\infty b(\omega) \sin \omega t \, d\omega \\ &= \quad s_c(t) \quad\quad + \quad\quad s_s(t) \end{aligned}\right\} \tag{4.11}$$

Again, the two Eqs. 4.10 and 4.11 form a pair. The latter, 4.11, represents a transient signal $s(t)$ as a continuous sum of sinusoids, of every conceivable frequency $\omega/2\pi$; the two integrals correspond to the even and odd components of the transient, $s_c(t)$ and $s_s(t)$. The other equation, 4.10, determines the spectral densities $a(\omega)$ and $b(\omega)$ from a knowledge of the signal $s(t)$.

Such expressions are called *Fourier integrals*; a glance at Eqs. 4.10 and 4.11 shows there is a measure of symmetry between them. Such symmetry is one beautiful property of Fourier integrals, but it may be shown more strikingly by converting the trigonometrical cosine, sine, notation to the *conjugate exponential* form; thus writing $\cos \omega t = (\epsilon^{j\omega t} + \epsilon^{-j\omega t})/2$ and $\sin \omega t = (\epsilon^{j\omega t} - \epsilon^{-j\omega t})/2$; in Eq. 4.11:

$$s(t) = \int_0^\infty [a(\omega) - jb(\omega)] \frac{\epsilon^{j\omega t}}{2} + [a(\omega) + jb(\omega)] \frac{\epsilon^{-j\omega t}}{2} \cdot d\omega$$

But notice this may be written very neatly with a *single* exponential term, $\epsilon^{j\omega t}$, by changing the limits of the integral to $-\infty$ and $+\infty$; that is, we allow ω to be positive *and* negative. The Fourier integral for $s(t)$ then becomes:

$$s(t) = \int_{-\infty}^{+\infty} \alpha(\omega) \epsilon^{j\omega t} \, d\omega \tag{4.12}$$

where $\alpha(\omega) = [a(\omega) - jb(\omega)]/2$, the *complex* spectral components. These negative frequency spectral components have been shown dotted in Fig. 4.5. The negative side of the $a(\omega)$ spectrum is a symmetrical continuation, since $\cos(-\omega t) = \cos \omega t$, while that of the $b(\omega)$ spectrum is skew-symmetrical, since $\sin(-\omega t) = -\sin(\omega t)$; there is nothing mysterious about "negative frequencies." The spectral components go in *pairs*; a negative term $\epsilon^{-j\omega t}$ and a positive term $\epsilon^{j\omega t}$ constitute one true sinusoid. The amplitudes $[a(\omega) + jb(\omega)]/2$ of the negative frequency terms $\epsilon^{-j\omega t}$ are *conjugate* to $\alpha(\omega)$ and are usually written $\alpha^*(\omega)$; "conjugacy" implies having the same real part $a(\omega)$ but imaginary parts $\pm jb(\omega)$ of opposite signs. Note, then, that $\alpha(\omega) = \alpha^*(-\omega)$.

Again, making the identical substitution for cos ωt and sin ωt in Eq. 4.10 results in the other Fourier integral:

$$\alpha(\omega) = \frac{1}{2\pi} \int_{-\infty}^{+\infty} s(t)\epsilon^{-j\omega t}\, dt \qquad (4.13)$$

As before, these Fourier integral relations 4.12 and 4.13 form a pair, but now the symmetry between them is very obvious. Apart from the constant, the two integrals have the same form, except for the sign of the exponent.

This symmetry between *time* and *frequency*, or between functions of time and functions of frequency, runs right through Fourier analysis and is extremely important, as we shall see; it usually happens that any theorem, or rule, which can be established in the *time domain* has its counterpart in the *frequency domain*.

If a newcomer to this subject of transient wave forms and their frequency spectra, the reader will glean little understanding from this simple outline presented here. It is essential to have practical experience of analyzing wave forms into their spectra, using Eq. 4.13, or of synthesizing wave forms when presented with their spectra, using Eq. 4.12. Many textbooks exist which give courses upon this subject, with worked examples, and the reader is referred to one of these.[D] It is not the purpose of this book to replace such a text, but rather to point out some of the limitations of Fourier analysis, when it comes to describing the acoustic, or other physical, signals used when communicating.

2.2. SOME LIMITATIONS TO SIMPLE FOURIER ANALYSIS, FOR DESCRIBING COMMUNICATION SIGNALS

The classical principles of Fourier analysis have served the communication engineer, and his friend the acoustician, in good stead for many years. Some of these people have become increasingly aware of the unrealistic nature of the infinite scale of time involved; signals $s(t)$ must be known for all time ("static time"), before they can be analyzed into spectra in the way indicated. But it is characteristic of communication signals that we can only have access to their *past* values, as functions of ("running") time; their exact forms, in the future, are not known with certainty—otherwise, it can be argued, there would be no need to communicate them! Considerable ingenuity has been shown, for example by Gabor[125] and by Fano,[100] in extending the concepts of Fourier analysis so as to take account of the difficulty. But full appreciation of this restriction was first shown when communication signals began to be examined on a statistical basis. This recognition of the essential need for a statistical approach to the subject of telecommunication represents a maturity which was attained earlier in other sciences—in statistical mechanics, the biological studies, meteorology, for instance.   In fact, in those studies which involve extremely large assemblies of individual elements, the behavior of each and every one being impossible of observation or description—systems whose macroscopic properties are irreversible in time.[349]   The newer statistical communication theory, at which we shall glance in the next chapter, has, however, not ousted Fourier analysis, which still forms an essential part of the whole theory.   Signal analysis both historically and logically precedes the statistical theory.

Consider an instant of time, during a certain communication process, at which a signal is just about to be transmitted—this channel of communication being observed by an external observer who is describing the process as in Fig. 3.2(a).   It is important to distinguish all that has taken place before this event (*a priori*) and known to this observer, from what the observer can say afterwards (*a posteriori*) about the transmitted signal. Between these two states, a signal has passed and has been observed, as a communication event.   Fourier analysis, if used by the observer as part of his description, can be applied only to *a priori* knowledge.   *The place of Fourier analysis then is rather for describing properties of the channel itself—the acoustic or the electrical medium (e.g., a telephone channel)—and the signals which it can convey*, as judged from past observations.   It forms part of *a priori* knowledge.   It can say something about the structure of the signals that will, in the future, be transmitted (e.g., their spectral bandwidths); but it cannot be used for *determining* these actual future signals.

2.3. An example of Fourier spectrum calculation

A simple example may serve to illustrate a typical use of the Fourier integrals and, at the same time, will provide a result which we shall need later.   Figure 4.6(a) shows a rectangular Morse dot $u(t)$; let us calculate its spectrum $\alpha(\omega)$.   We have

$$u(t) \text{ defined as } \begin{Bmatrix} 1 \text{ for } |t| < T \\ 0 \text{ for } |t| > T \end{Bmatrix} \tag{4.14}$$

the pulse duration being $2T$. secs.   Then, from Eq. 4.13,

$$\alpha(\omega) = \frac{1}{2\pi} \int_{-T}^{+T} \epsilon^{-j\omega t} \cdot dt$$

since the integrand is zero beyond the limits of time $\pm T$.   Then

$$\alpha(\omega) = \frac{1}{2\pi} \left[\frac{\epsilon^{j\omega T} - \epsilon^{-j\omega T}}{j\omega} \right]$$

which may be written

$$\alpha(\omega) = \frac{T}{2\pi} \frac{\sin \omega T}{\omega T} = \frac{T}{2\pi} \frac{\sin 2\pi f T}{2\pi f T} \tag{4.15}$$

which is a function of considerable importance in Fourier analysis. This spectrum $\alpha(\omega)$ is plotted in Fig. 4.6(b). Since the corresponding wave form $u(t)$ is an even function, symmetrical about the origin, the spectral terms here must be cosines.

Let us now deal with the opposite case and start with a rectangular *spectrum*, as in Fig. 4.6(c), having an angular-frequency bandwidth $\pm 2\pi F$ radians per second (with "negative frequency" conjugate 'band, $-2\pi F$).

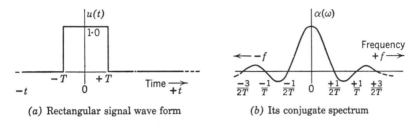

(a) Rectangular signal wave form   (b) Its conjugate spectrum

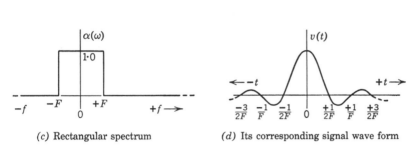

(c) Rectangular spectrum   (d) Its corresponding signal wave form

Fig. 4.6.   The inversion of Fourier integrals (signal elements and their spectra).

Then, from Eq. 4.12 the corresponding signal is:

$$v(t) = \int_{+2\pi F}^{+2\pi F} \epsilon^{j\omega t} \cdot d\omega = 2\left[\frac{\epsilon^{2j\pi tF} - \epsilon^{-2j\pi tF}}{2jt}\right]$$

$$= 2\pi F \cdot \frac{\sin 2\pi tF}{2\pi tF} \qquad (4.16)$$

which is plotted in Fig. 4.6(d), being identical in *shape* with Fig. 4.6(b).

This little example illustrates the remarkable symmetry between time and frequency functions, as represented by the similarity of the Fourier integrals 4.12 and 4.13, to which we have already alluded. We see that the forms of a signal and a spectrum may be interchanged, with consistency. In this example, a rectangular signal was found to possess a spectrum of $\sin x/x$ form; conversely a rectangular *spectrum* was seen to represent a *signal* of $\sin x/x$ form.

This example of a Fourier integral calculation may give the impression that all such integrations are equally simple. But this is by no means the case; a great many similar integrations prove to be extremely difficult, or in many cases impossible. The method is of particular value in two fields: first, for analysis of simple wave forms or spectra ("idealized" cases), and secondly, for establishing general theorems.

One further important result follows from Eq. 4.15. If the rectangular signal $u(t)$ is allowed to become shorter and shorter in time, $T \rightarrow \delta T$, then its spectrum

$$\alpha_\delta(\omega) \rightarrow \frac{\delta T}{2\pi} \qquad \text{a constant} \qquad (4.17)$$

over any finite frequency band, $f \ll 1/\delta T$. That is, in the limit, an infinitesimally short impulse has a spectrum of cosine terms, all of equal amplitude.

Our example illustrates another fact which is generally true: the longer the duration of a signal, T, the narrower its spectral bandwidth, F (given the signal wave-*form* invariant), and vice versa. That is, with a signal of fixed form, stretching its time scale compresses its frequency scale. Time and frequency scales are inversely related. If we regard the "effective" bandwidth of the spectrum $\alpha(\omega)$ as $\pm 1/4T$ [Fig. 4.6(b)], then the *product* of (signal duration) × (effective bandwidth) = a constant (unity). The choice of the "effective" bandwidth is arbitrary, but merely affects the value of the constant.

2.4. THE UNCERTAINTY PRINCIPLE IN SIGNAL ANALYSIS

The inverse relationship between signal duration and effective spectral bandwidth, which we have just noticed in the previous section, suggests an uncertainty principle, on which attention has been focused by Gabor.[E] If signals are received through a channel having a bandwidth ΔF, then the shortest impulse signal which may be communicated through that channel is ΔT, where

$$\Delta F \cdot \Delta T \approx \text{a constant of order unity} \qquad (4.18)$$

the exact constant depending upon the arbitrary definition of ΔT and ΔF. No shorter signals can be communicated; such simple elements are the bricks out of which practical signals are built, whether they be speech, television, etc. We may then imagine that the time scale is graduated in intervals of ΔT; no briefer event than ΔT is measurable. The so-called "continuous" signal is a mathematical fiction, and a very useful one; but a mathematical description of the physical signals, in such discrete terms as these, is more realistic. Gabor compares this principle of uncertainty represented by Eq. 4.18 to the Heisenberg Principle of Uncertainty, and goes further by illustrating how some of the mathematics of quantum theory may be applied to signal analysis—though he is careful to stress that he is not "applying quantum theory," but only some of the mathematical apparatus. He calls such elements of uncertainty, $\Delta F \cdot \Delta T$ *logons* [E,*] with reference particularly to signals of Gaussian form.[†]

The mathematical idea of a signal as a continuous function of time, $s(t)$, is then unrealistic when related to the physical process it describes, since it would suggest that an independent value can be attached to $s(t)$ at every instant of time. But an "instant" of time cannot be communicated *through* the channel, of bandwidth ΔF, to an accuracy better than about $\Delta T = 1/\Delta F$. Conversely, to communicate any special group, having a bandwidth of ΔF, requires a time of at least ΔT. We cannot be certain of *both* an instant (epoch) and a frequency of a signal, jointly, to a less amount than one logon.[‡]

MacKay[218] has referred to the generality of such a logon concept, pointing out that many instrumental measurements show an analogous uncertainty: for example, the aperture and the resolving power of a microscope, or the sensitivity and response time of a galvanometer. Again, Woodward[360] has recently shown that the resolving power of radar, for moving targets, is uncertain with regard to discriminating target positions and velocities.

Signals and their spectra may then be considered to be broken down into a finite set of logons; these are the bricks with which signals may be regarded as constructed. Signal analysis reduces to the handling of a finite set of data (numbers, magnitudes). The apparently "continuous" signal wave forms $s(t)$ may be regarded as discrete—in the same way as a time sequence of token signals (Section 1.1). But this statement needs qualification.

2.5. THE SAMPLING THEOREM

Figure 4.7 shows part of a "continuous" wave form $s(t)$ representing a signal which has been received through a channel of finite bandwidth, F cycles per second. Then the Sampling Theorem states that this wave form is completely specified by its ordinates, at successive time intervals equally spaced by $1/2F$ second. From a knowledge of these data, and the bandwidth F, the "continuous" wave form may be reconstructed. *Through a bandwidth of F cycles per second it is impossible to communicate more than 2F independent data (logons, magnitudes) per second.*[E, 343]

---

* Gabor expresses this uncertainty relation in more rigorous form than we attempt here; the reader is referred to the original text, reference E. In particular, the "effective durations" ΔT and bandwidth ΔF are defined in terms of their root-mean-square deviations from their mean instant t and frequency f.

† See Fig. 5.7 for illustration of a curve of Gaussian form.

‡ This principle played an important part in the history of telegraphy; see p. 42. Also see references 195 and 248.

If we did not know the theorem, the following question might have been asked about this signal wave-form function $s(t)$: How many independent data does the signal convey in the time T? Infinity perhaps?—since it is "continuous" and has an infinite number of ordinates. This absurdity is rationalized when it is appreciated that all these infinity of ordinates are not independent; only N are independent, where $N = 2FT$.

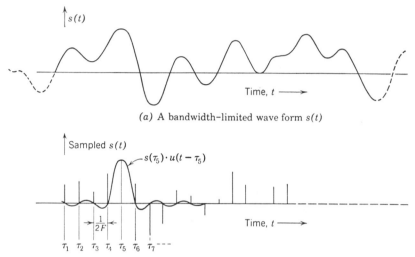

(a) A bandwidth–limited wave form $s(t)$

(b) The sampled $s(t)$ and the sin x/x interpolation function

Fig. 4.7.   Sampling of a bandwidth limited signal.

The N independent data which the signal communicates in time T, through a band F, may be chosen in an unlimited number of forms and ways. At present, we are thinking of ordinate samples or, alternatively, Fourier coefficients. In such terms, the proof of the theorem is elementary.

From the continuous signal function $s(t)$, let us select a portion of duration T seconds. Imagine, now, this portion alone to be repeated periodically, forever. Such a periodic wave form would, of course, have a Fourier-series spectrum of cosine and sine harmonics, a_n and b_n, spaced by the fundamental frequency $1/T$ cycles per second. Thus, in the limited bandwidth F there would be $2FT$ such harmonic amplitudes (a_n, b_n). From a knowledge of these data we could reconstruct the periodic wave form, *any one cycle of which* corresponds to the portion of duration T from the signal $s(t)$. Similarly for any other portion of signal $s(t)$.

Then $2F$ independent data, per second, are all such a band-limited signal can communicate. Successive equally spaced ordinates, as shown in Fig. 4.7(b), are the simplest form of such data; this diagram (b) shows the samples; how do we construct the "continuous" wave form $s(t)$?

Such sampling is in fact commonly used by telecommunication engineers* as a practical method of communicating speech and music signals by transmitting not the whole wave forms but only the samples, as very short impulses $(\delta T \to 0)$ having the successive amplitudes $s(\tau_1) \cdots s(\tau_n)$; then our mathematical "sampled $s(t)$" is an ideal description of such physical impulses. We have already shown that such short impulses have spectra which are constant, $\alpha_\delta(\omega) \to \delta T/2\pi$ (Eq. 4.17); but when this sequence of impulses is transmitted through the channel, limited in bandwidth to F cycles per second, *each individual* impulse sets up a response signal at the receiver of the form $u = \sin x/x$, as given by Eq. 4.16 and as illustrated by Fig. 4.6(d). For example, the response set up at the receiving end of the channel, by the impulse at τ_5 in Fig. 4.7(b), has been drawn in on this figure.

Each impulse $s(\tau_1) \cdots s(\tau_n)$ sets up a similar response and if these all be added together it may be proved that the composite signal is identical with $s(t)$, the original signal (at least substantially within the interval T, if $s(t)$ is bounded to T). This proof is simple and follows from the Fourier integrals 4.12 and 4.13; it has been presented by several authors, and we need not duplicate it here.[252,†]

The diagram Fig. 4.7(b) illustrates the independence of these ordinates, or impulses, as the $2F$ data per second capable of being communicated through the channel of bandwidth F cycles per second. We see that the $\sin x/x$ *interpolation function* wave form crosses the axis at every sample instant $\tau_1, \tau_2 \cdots \tau_n$ and so contributes nothing to these other sample amplitudes. Thus adding or removing, any one sample will not affect $s(t)$ at the other sample instants—whereas samples taken closer together would interfere with one another.‡

This is the Sampling Theorem in the time domain, which was used by Hartley in his classic paper[F] on signals and their information content. It sometimes causes confusion because of the reference to a *finite* bandwidth F since, it is argued, frequency bands in practice are not so sharply bounded. But it must be remembered that we are applying the theorem here to a physical problem, including an observer. The observer, with his instruments, can only measure frequencies up to a certain limit—say that limit set by the fact that the signal spectral amplitudes become too small to, measure. In the absence of any more clearly defined bandwidth (e.g.

---

* As described very briefly on p. 46. See references 67 and 82, or any good book on pulse-modulation telephony.

† The theorem was originally Whittaker's; see reference 347.

‡ Such functions are said to form an orthogonal set; thus if $u(t - \tau_r)$ and $u(t - \tau_s)$ are any pair of these $\sin x/x$ functions, with their peaks at τ_r and τ_s respectively, then

$$\int_{-\infty}^{+\infty} u(t - \tau_r) \cdot i(t - \tau_s)\, dt = 0 \text{ except when } \tau_r = \tau_s.$$

such as is commonly used in telephony), it will be this observer's limiting bandwidth which we take as F. But an "infinite bandwidth" is non-physical. There is a dual theorem for sampling in the *frequency domain*, which is: The spectrum of any wave form $s(t)$ having a duration only of T seconds [$s(t) = 0$ outside this interval] is specified completely by its values at successive points equally spaced by $1/T$ along the frequency axis (not $1/2T$, notice, because a spectrum has itself two components (sin, cos) at each specified frequency).[360]

The $2FT$ independent data communicated through a bandwidth F, in a time T, need not, however, be restricted to the two forms we have so far discussed—first, the Fourier co-efficients a_n, b_n, or second, the equally spaced samples, $s(\tau)$. It happens that these two forms are the simplest and most familiar but, as Gabor[E, 125] has indicated, other orthogonal functions would serve (e.g., Bessel functions, or Legendre polynomials).

It is valid to regard the set of $2FT$ independent Fourier data as forming the co-ordinates of a space of $2FT$ dimensions.[297] Such a hyperspace corresponds to an "attribute space" for describing signals (e.g., compare Fig. 3.1, Chapter 3), though the axes (logons) have, as yet, not been quantized, since we have said nothing about the accuracy with which each of the $2FT$ data may be measured.

3. SPEECH REPRESENTATION ON THE FREQUENCY-TIME PLANE

The $2FT$ independent data describing a wave form, in a bandwidth F and time T, may also be represented as a kind of matrix.[E] Figure 4.8 shows the frequency-time plane, divided up into a grid of cells of *unit* area, but arbitrary aspect (length-side) ratio; there are thus FT cells, so that two independent data may be associated with each. The aspect ratio of the cells is a matter of choice, or convenience, in a practical analysis; only the areas are fixed. If the bandwidth F is fixed and divided into bands ΔF (Fig. 4.8), then as time proceeds more and more cells are added along the time axis, at intervals $\Delta T = 1/\Delta F$. The actual instants of location of these cells on the time axis are of course arbitrary; only their spacings (i.e., number in unit time) are determined.

3.1. "RUNNING" SPEECH SPECTROGRAMS, OR "VISIBLE SPEECH"

Such a diagram is given a very practical and valuable interpretation, in an instrument known as a speech spectrograph.[271] This instrument is used for producing what have been called "visible speech" patterns, or "sono-grams," which are photographs of the energy spectra of speech (or, of course, music or other sounds) "running" with time. Figure 4.9 shows a typical sample, recorded when the author spoke the words "*My name is Colin Cherry.*" The intensity of the photograph represents speech *energy*, and the axes of the plane are again frequency/time.

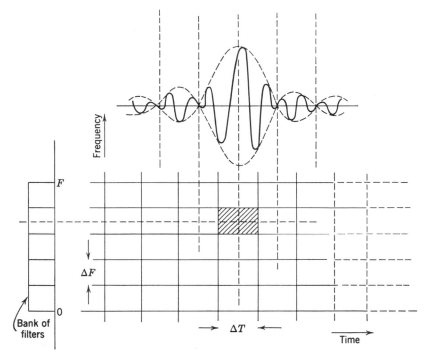

Fig. 4.8. Representation of signals on the time-frequency plane, divided into FT cells.

Such an instrument[192] contains, in effect, a bank of wave filters, each of which selects a narrow band of frequencies in the audio spectrum; ideally these bands form a contiguous series, occupying the full audio bandwidth as illustrated in Fig. 4.9, here using 17 filters, but the most satisfactory results have been obtained with more practical electric wave filters. (Readers who are unfamiliar with electric circuits may imagine a bank of resonant reeds, or acoustic resonators; but in modern instruments, electric circuit equivalents are normally found to be more convenient.)* Then

---

* *Technical note:* In practical spectrographs, a damped resonant circuit may be used as a filter, for cheapness and simplicity. Again, it is more usual to employ a single filter and to scan its center frequency over the whole audio spectrum, periodically, using the variable superheterodyne principle. If this is done, the speech to be analyzed must be recorded (e.g., on magnetic tape) in order that it may be scanned the requisite number of times. More modern spectrographs use active filters.

the fluctuating energy of the speech is divided into a number of separate, adjacent bands by these filters, and is caused to control the brightness of a row of small lamps, placed side by side, so as to vary the intensity of photographic reproduction (or other technique, such as brightness on a cathode-ray tube, or electro-sensitive recording paper).[306]   Two different filter bandwidths ΔF are commonly used, one about 30–50 cycles per second

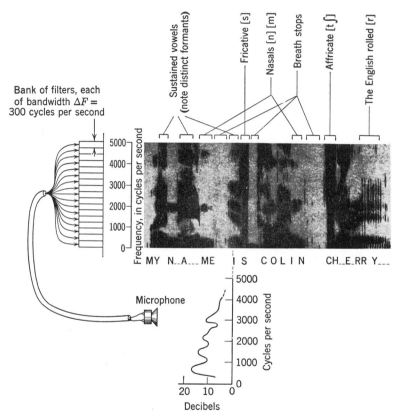

Fig. 4.9. A "visible speech" spectrogram (sonogram).

and the other 300 cycles per second, a fact which we shall comment upon shortly.   Then from the uncertainty principle (Eq. 4.18), the resolution along the time axis is of the order of 25 millisecs, or 3 millisecs, respectively. We can imagine a "grid" of cells (like that in Fig. 4.8) to be superposed upon the sonogram of Fig. 4.9, but arbitrarily located.   There is an interesting analogy between this idea and that of a visual scene photographed by the pinhole camera with its inherent aperture distortion;[234]

there are in fact many close analogies between optical problems and acoustic ones, inasmuch as both are describable in terms of Fourier analysis.

For precise measurements of the "running" spectra of speech, reliability cannot be placed upon reading the photographic density of sonogram patterns; nor should linearity be assumed between speech energy and brightness. Consequently a device called a *sectioner* is sometimes provided to plot the graph of energy against frequency at any selected region on the time axis.[272,]* Figure 4.9 also shows one such section, or "instantaneous spectrum," at the [i] sound. Sections taken closer together on the time axis than ΔT seconds cannot be independent.

Such an instrument is one of the most valuable tools we have today for research into the sounds of speech, as an aid to the phonetician and the linguist in their comparisons of the sound elements of different dialects and languages,[174] as an aid to the teaching of speech production (especially for the deaf[271]) and for correlating the sounds of speech with their articulatory production.[81,182] A glance at the example of Fig. 4.9 shows that such a running spectrum does not consist of a collection of casual smudges; the thousands of spectra which have been made, by many people during the past 20 years, bear out the fact that the spectra form very distinct visual patterns, closely correlated with phonetic data, and closely similar for different people with the same dialect. They form a kind of "natural" phonetic writing—the ideal of A. M. Bell[A,22,23]—which people, deaf or not, may be trained to read.[270] The idea that signals, designed for aural recognition, can set up intelligible visual patterns, unambiguously, is not obvious. Such visual speech patterns, *sonograms*, are set up in an artificial manner—unrelated to the natural process of speech production—and their remarkable facility of *visual* recognition is on a level quite different from that of lip reading, where the visual signals are the gesture signs of actual speech sources. This property of "visible speech" sonograms strongly recommends their study as quasi-natural representations of the articulatory production of speech.

3.2. SPEECH AS AN ARTICULATORY PROCESS

The sound spectrograph measures frequency spectra of physical sounds (sonograms)—those of musical instruments or singers[271] as well as those of speech. These spectra, if used alone, then give an *acoustic* description. But the spectra of speech show a very definite structure, which is characteristic of the articulatory process itself.

Speech is basically an articulatory process; this process produces the sounds, not vice versa. The sounds may be used by the speaker himself, for monitoring his own speech production; but the sounds serve their chief

* See Peterson in reference 166.

functions in communicating to the listener evidence of the articulatory activity of the speaker.   The congenitally deaf may speak and communicate; yet sound, as sound, is beyond their experience.   If the breath be held, lips, tongue, and jaw may be given all the motions and gestures of speech— and may be "lip-read" by the deaf.   But in normal speech these motions and gestures operate upon the breath and larynx tones which make them audible and so serve to carry them greater distances (and round corners).   Speech is both a visible and an aural set of signs.   Phonetics is studied extensively at the acoustic level, for convenience and simplicity, but the acoustic data must at some stage be correlated with tongue, lips, uvula, vocal folds, breath—and the whole vocal apparatus producing the sounds.[B]

In order to make any sense of the speech sonograms, therefore, it is necessary to study the production of speech by the vocal organs.   The two aspects (acoustic and articulatory) really go together; first one and then the other have advanced our understanding of the whole process.

3.3. THE VOCAL ORGANS

The vocal organs are sometimes compared, functionally, with the operation of a church organ pipe (*vox humana?*), but perhaps the comparison does not bear very close examination.   For one thing, Stetson questions whether our lungs supply our "windpipes" with air at constant pressure, but rather in a pulsating manner, controlled by the inter-rib muscles of the chest, so as to aid the syllabic rhythm.   These rapid pulses of breath, forming the syllables, would deflate the lungs, but equilibrium is maintained by grosser and slower movements of the larger chest muscles, abdominal muscles, and the diaphragm.   These slower movements also contribute to patterning groups of syllables and in adding stress; the whole action produces the characteristic rhythm of our speech.   Measurements have been made upon speakers, of the fluctuating pressures in the windpipe, of the movements of the inter-rib muscles and those of the abdomen, together with the compensating movements of the diaphragm.[B]

The reader may care to try a few simple experiments.   If so, purse your lips and *whisper* in fairly rapid succession: *oo, oo, oo, oo*; four gentle pulses of breath are expelled through the lips.   Now, using a similar rhythm, whisper the phrase: *How do you do?*   The pulses of breath are now different.   At the [d] you will find your tongue has completely blocked your mouth; holding your tongue in this position, you are able to breathe only through the nose.   During the dynamic articulation of this phrase, the air pressure behind your tongue builds up at the [d], to be released with a sudden rush at the following vowel.   A [t] is similarly formed, as in: *too*.   Thus the pulsations of breath, characterizing syllabic rhythm, are controlled not only at the lungs, but also by closures at the other (mouth) end of the vocal tract.   The sounds [p] and [b] require the lips to be closed momentarily, so as to build up a small burst of breath.   Similarly, in English, [g] and [k] require the top of the throat cavity to be closed by the back of the tongue on the soft palate.   (This you may readily see, in a mirror, if you hold your mouth wide open, tongue flat, so as to expose the uvula; then say *uck* very slowly; notice the soft circular orifice at the back of your mouth first constricting, before being blocked by the back of the tongue.)   All such sounds are aptly called plosive, and the brief closure, during which pressure builds up, produces an acoustic stop, or temporary silence (e.g., see the brief empty bands, just before the C in Fig. 4.9, as well as before the CH, or [t ʃ] sound).[179, 181]

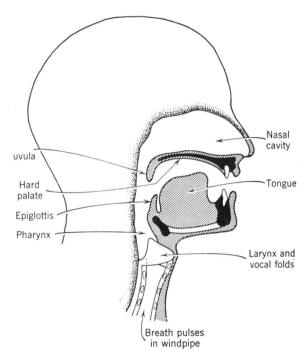

Fig. 4.10.   The vocal organs.

Figure 4.10 shows a simple cross-sectional sketch of the vocal organs, indicating these principal ways of making closure: by the lips, the tongue, or the soft palate, epiglottis, the teeth—the articulators.   The nasal cavity does not form part of the principal vocal tract; breath may enter it, as controlled by the backward and forward movement of the uvula or soft palate. If you pinch your nose tightly, you will find you can still utter all the sounds of English speech without difficulty, except [m], [n], [ŋ]—the so-called nasals—as in *him*, *pin*, *sing*, because these sounds again require closures of the lips, of the tongue on the roof of the mouth, or against the soft palate, respectively; breath is then released only through the nose.   Still pinching your nose, hum these three sounds [m], [n], [ŋ] steadily, until you are forced to stop as the nasal pressure builds up.   Place the tips of a thumb and finger lightly in your nostrils and say: "'Tis mightiest in the mightiest: it becomes the throned monarch better than his crown," and you will feel the nasal cavity vibrations at each [m] and [n].

Yet another form of (partial) closure is afforded by the tongue-palatal gap, as in the sounds [s], [ʃ]—when we say *soon*, or *hush*.   Air turbulence and friction around the teeth and alveolar region produces such fricative sounds.   Other fricatives are produced by placing the tongue against the upper teeth as in *thin*, or by placing the upper teeth against the lower lip as in *fin*.   Such "rushing" sounds are produced by large numbers of random turbulent motions—as when the surf shifts the stones on a beach.   It is characteristic of such sounds that their energy is diffused over a wide band of frequencies (see the spectrum, Fig. 4.9, at the S and CH).

Incidentally, the curious periodicity seen in the spectrum, Fig. 4.9 at the extreme right, is due to the "rolling" of the [r] sound;* the uvula, the tongue, and the lips, being highly mobile, may be vibrated rapidly.

During the so-called "vowel" sounds, the vocal tract is left comparatively unobstructed, the different acoustic qualities arising from different sets of resonances, as the mouth and the pharynx are molded into different shapes, by movement of the jaw and of the highly flexible lips, tongue, and soft parts.   Sometimes the nasal cavity is opened, to add a resonance or "nasalization."   The resonance of a simple cavity is well illustrated by blowing gently across the mouth of a bottle.   The smaller the cavity, the higher the resonance, as we hear when a bottle is left under a dripping tap and gradually fills with water.   A simple mouth cavity resonance may be detected in this way: whisper the word *who* (a gentle blowing action), and the stream of breath sets up a distinct musical note; hold your mouth in that position and, lightly tapping your cheek, you will hear the same note.

But the human vocal tract is not rigid in form like a bottle; the lips and the tongue may be molded, to introduce constrictions which separate the tract, more or less, into two "cavities" joined by a smaller neck.   These cavities may be shaped into many forms with great precision and control; resonance depends upon shape, and not entirely upon the volume of a cavity.   The tongue has almost a constant volume, irrespective of its molding,ᴬ yet with the jaw and lips held firm in one position, you can whisper several different vowel sounds (you can say *hee-haw* like a donkey—

* The speaker being Southern English.

notice your tongue constriction moves from front to back of the mouth, altering the ratio of the two "cavities"). The vocal tract is capable of resonating at more than one frequency simultaneously, the frequencies selected depending upon the whole shaping and particularly upon the place where the tongue provides any constriction (the "point of articulation")* and upon the shape of opening formed by the lips too.

Vowel sounds may be uttered, in a sustained manner, such that the shape of the whole vocal tract is held unchanged (and may be steadily sung until you are out of breath). The various shapes for different vowels have been studied extensively by X-ray photography.[64,157,282] Though not providing a complete specification of the shapes or volumes of the cavities, the distinct positions of the tongue are widely used as a convenient method of classifying the vowels[A,179] (the so-called "vowel quadrilateral"). Not only the vowels but many of the consonants may be steadily maintained; the plosives of course cannot, since these depend upon a definite breath-stopping action. You can hum [m], [n], [ŋ], or breathe [h] or [ʃ] (as in hush), or say [l] (as in full) or [r] (as in read), and others, in a steady manner.[B,271] However, when uttering connected speech, truly sustained sounds are the exception rather than the rule; even the vowel sounds are not steady for long, but change with the restless motion of the articulators.

Besides the use of X-ray photography for observing the vocal tract formation during vowel utterance, there exists an extensive technique for the study of the dynamics of speech production—for measuring shapes and sizes of the cavities, the fluctuating air pressures within the tract, the muscular action potentials, the movement of jaw, uvula, and lips.[B] The segment of speech we call a *syllable* is not a simple sound; there has in the past been considerable discussion upon its structure for, like the consonant-vowel distinction, it seems to be universal in human speech. From the articulatory point of view, the vowel may be regarded as a shaping of the vocal tract, thereby adjusting the frequencies of the resonances, whereas the consonants launch pulses of breath through the tract, or arrest them, by control of the articulators. Sustained consonants, such as we have noted, [s], [ʃ], [n], et cetera, then become classified as "semi-vowels" or "vowel substitutes." Again, at articulatory level, the term *syllable* has been applied to a vowel delimited by launching and arresting consonants or, in some cases, by action of the chest muscles in controlling the breath.[B,30]

During a syllable then, the breath pulse, forced into the vocal tract by the chest muscles, becomes "modulated" (modified, operated upon) in various ways; in particular by arresting actions of the lips, tongue, teeth, and by resonances in the vocal cavities. But there is one prominent type

* The great importance of this constriction, "the point of articulation," seems to have been recognized, well back in ancient phonetic history. See references 3, 91.

of modulation to which we have made no reference as yet—the larynx vibrations.

3.3.1. VIBRATION OF THE VOCAL FOLDS; PHONATION OR VOICING. All that has been said so far concerning syllable formation—the transmission of breath pulses along the vocal tract and their modulation by shaping the cavities and by the articulators—might be applied to whispered speech. But whispered speech does not carry far. We have another way of modulating the breath stream which greatly reinforces the acoustic effect; this is by vibration of the vocal folds (often misleadingly called vocal "cords"). You can feel such vibration by placing a thumb and forefinger on either side of your Adam's apple and singing aloud [m], [n], or any vowel in normal English speech, or various stops like [b], [g], or fricatives like [v], [z], and many other examples. This action is called voicing or phonation, and vastly increases the acoustic energy of the sounds so modulated.

Situated at the top of your windpipe is the larynx which, as one of its functions, may act as a valve for shutting off the air in your lungs, either momentarily so as to initiate a breath pulse, or steadily as (with some people) when "holding the breath." The valve action is provided by the vocal folds, which are not "cords" or "strings," but a pair of substantial fibrous lips which, when relaxed, leave a V-shaped opening termed the glottis, but which may be folded together so as to touch and press upon one another. They have been photographed through a periscope[A] and even filmed in action.[103,242] When pressed together they may be set into relaxation vibration, by air forced between them.[342] Crudely analogous relaxation vibrations, with which we are all familiar, are set up by blowing between two sheets of paper. The reed of a clarinet or of some organ pipes serves to excite the resonances of the pipes; the lips of a trumpet player act as a kind of "vocal folds" for exciting the instrument. But real vocal folds have this advantage over the reed of a musical instrument: they may be altered in tension and form with extreme facility, rapidity, and accuracy. Extreme is indeed the word.

It is characteristic of such relaxation vibrations that they do not produce pure tones but a rough "saw-toothed" or pulse shape of periodic wave form, rich in harmonics.[64,342] The periodicity of the wave form is controlled by tensioning and compacting the vocal folds, which enables us to sing or hum notes of various pitches. The harmonics of the larynx tone energize the resonant cavities of the vocal tract, according to the vowel being sounded, so that certain frequency bands are accentuated, giving rise to the characteristic vowel qualities. The question then arises: What are the prominent tones which we hear when a vowel is sung? Are they the harmonics of the larynx tone, reinforced by resonance, as first advocated by Helmholtz[151] and Wheatstone, or are they the natural resonant frequencies of the vocal tract itself, as originally suggested by Willis?* Some considerable controversy grew around this question during the earlier development of vowel theory.[c,†] The answer is really: neither. In Rayleigh's words "the disagreement between the theories is only apparent."[275] The question may have arisen from a misunderstanding of the process of acoustic excitation; the transmission frequency-response characteristics of a tract multiply or "operate upon" the spectrum of the excitation energy—they do not add together.[B,88,‡] Moreover, the spectrum of the larynx tone is truly a discrete harmonic *series* only if the tone be steadily maintained (Section 2.1); but in connected speech, transient excitation also occurs, owing to sudden launch or stop of vowels, by the consonants. (Press your lips together, teeth apart, then *suddenly* open your mouth; notice the "pop" or natural resonant frequency of the mouth cavity.) Prior to the development of accurate speech spectrographs, vocal resonances were observed, and their frequencies assessed accurately by a trained ear, by tapping the cheeks or throat.[A]

3.4. THE FORMANT PATTERNS OF SPEECH

For a moment let us confine our attention to steadily maintained and whispered vowel sounds. The breath stream is constituted of a myriad of turbulent motions, each of minute energy, and so it would set up an acoustic spectrum of uniform energy at all frequencies—at least over the audible range—were it not for the selective resonant characteristics of the vocal tract. These resonant characteristics differ for every vowel sound, and the particular frequency regions which they reinforce most strongly are called *formants*; their relative positions on a scale of frequency determine the spectrum of each vowel, and hence their acoustic quality. All vowels may be whispered, and their constituent resonant-frequency regions identified by a listener of good musical ear.[A] Although the tongue divides the vocal tract more or less into two cavities, the formant resonances are not the individual resonances of these two cavities; the cavities are coupled together and resonate as one whole system.[275] The formants continually shift about in frequency, as the tongue wags, and the relative size of the front and back cavities varies, but there is no simple mathematical relation between the formant frequencies and the dimensions of the cavities.

Some selective characteristics of the vocal tract, for a pair of sustained vowels, are illustrated in Fig. 4.11(*a*); the peaks of these curves constitute the formants or regions of strongest acoustic resonance (see arrows).

* R. Willis, "On the Vowel Sounds and on Reed Organ Pipes," *Proc. Cambridge Phil. Soc.*, 1829 (British Museum Shelf Mark 7895. S. 12).

† For example, see reference 290 for a history of vowel theory.

‡ On a decibel scale, commonly used in acoustics, this amounts to adding, of course.

If, instead of whispering, you now sing (phonate, voice) these vowels, the selective characteristics will remain similar in form since the vocal cavities do not appreciably alter, but the feeble energy of the turbulent breath stream is replaced by the strong vibrations of the vocal cords. Being a steady tone, these vibrations possess a periodic Fourier (line)

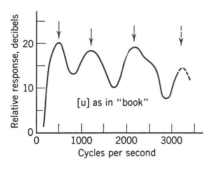
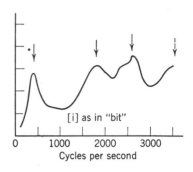

(a) The "selective characteristics" of the vocal tract, for two sustained vowels, showing formants (corresponding to the energy spectra of the *whispered* vowels)

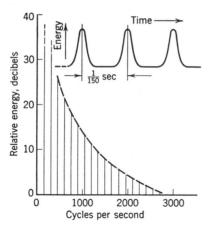
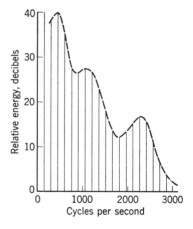

(b) Wave form of larynx source energy and its approximate spectrum

(c) Spectrum of phonated (voiced) vowel [u]

Fig. 4.11.   Spectra of sustained vowels (male voice).

spectrum of harmonics.   This spectrum cannot readily be measured in the absence of the vocal tract's selective characteristics (unless the singer's head be cut off!), so we can but infer it from a knowledge of the larynx and its mode of vibration;[64,102,311,342] Fig. 4.11(b) shows a line spectrum with a fundamental frequency of 125 cycles per second (male voice) which will serve our purpose here.*   This series of harmonics is then operated upon (multiplied) by the vocal tract characteristics (a), the vowel [u] here, giving the resultant vowel spectra which the listener hears (c).[102,160] Notice that larynx harmonics may or may not lie *exactly* at the same frequency as the peaks of the formants.   On the "visible speech" diagrams, the formants show up as dark bars, representing concentrations of energies in regions which differ in distribution for different vowels, or for continuant (non-plosive) phonated sounds (Fig. 4.9).

Speech is a continual dynamic activity, interrupted at plosive sounds, or as phrase formation and breath control demand.   It produces a stream of sound.   The discrete phonetic symbols are quantal elements of *description*, for the physical sound of speech is not a string of independent and discrete elements,[30] joined like a train of acoustic railway trucks!   Synthetic speech of this discrete character has in fact been produced, but it is readily detected as such by the ear.[143,202,271,272]   The successive sounds of speech exert a considerable influence upon one another[143] as, by analogy, do the "successive" letters of handwriting as opposed to the stark independence of printed letters.   Two examples may illustrate this point.   The first calls attention to diphthongs, where the formant bars of the preceding vowel continue in a smooth transition to become the formant bars of the latter vowel[271] (e.g., in Fig. 4.9, notice the flow between the words "my name," though "y-n" here is not strictly a diphthong).   A second example is provided by the way some plosive consonants, such as [p], [t], [k], show slight traces of the formant bars of the *following* vowel (the CH shows traces of the following E, in Fig. 4.9) because the shaping of the cavities, to sound the plosive, is conditioned by the vowel to follow.[202]   Sing the vowel [a], as in *far*; keeping the mouth and tongue steady, you can change the pitch by tensioning the vocal folds.   The vowel is still recognizable, over quite a wide range of pitch.   As the phonation rises in frequency, the harmonics exciting the vocal cavities move apart in frequency, though their spectral envelope remains unchanged, being determined by the vocal cavities; so the formants stay fixed.   Vowel identification under such conditions seems to rest upon the formant positions, though changes do appear to occur if the phonation is carried too high in frequency.

But again, we recognize a vowel whether it be spoken by a man or a woman; not only do the larynx vibrations differ in frequency, but so do the formants.   Without stressing this point too strongly, it would appear

---

* This approximate spectrum was obtained from two sources: first, Chiba and Kajiyama, reference 64, show wave forms of glottal openings during phonation, from which we have estimated the energy-pulse wave form shown in Fig. 4.11(b); alternatively, Stevens, Kasowski, and Fant, reference 311, have shown the spectrum produced by an artificial larynx.

that vowel identification (when sung in isolation, and apart from other clues afforded by the context in connected speech) rests upon the *relative* positions of the formants, in a manner analogous to the notes of musical chords.   But this is not the whole story, for the relative formant positions are not exactly the same, especially for the higher formants;[271] it may be that we learn to associate a low phonation pitch with a male set of formants and a higher one with a female set.

Again, Lawrence has suggested that a listener judges the relative formant positions against the long-term average pitch of all the formants of the speaker.*   Or, to adopt another point of view, it may be that we recognize the "gestures" of speech, the sounds merely acting as carriers of evidence; from our accumulated past experience of hearing vocal tracts excited in many different ways (and of speaking those sounds ourselves) we may learn the characteristic shapes of the tracts themselves.[A,160]

A given musical chord, such as a major triad, is composed of notes having definite frequency ratios, no matter what the key.†   A gramophone record of music, or of speech, may be changed in speed, at least over a few per cent, without serious effect upon recognition.[275]   But this parallel between music and speech should not be drawn too closely; the whole purposes of the two are different.   And the scales of musical notes are identical over the whole Western world, whilst the formant frequencies and other parameters of speech shift with every dialect and every individual. The notes of music are specified exactly, the phonetic elements of speech only statistically.[272]

3.5. "Visible speech" spectrographs are not "models of the ear"

Such spectral analysis of speech is an acoustic, physical analysis.   It requires no perceptive actions to produce a visible-speech spectrum such as Fig. 4.9 but only a speaker and some instruments.   Nevertheless, diagrams of this kind, and others, have *phonetic* importance because a trained person may read them visually (with a lot of intelligent guessing) and reproduce them vocally.   It is this *reading* of the spectra which involves perception, of course.   In 1873, Graham Bell traced the wave forms of speech sounds upon smoked glass, following on, in idea, from a device called the "phonautograph" (Scott and Koenig, 1859), a kind of early oscillograph.   These wave forms represented speech in "visual form," and Bell proceeded to develop, from this instrument, a model of the ear; later, it was suggested to him that a real ear might be used, for converting the acoustic vibrations into movements of a stylus upon smoked glass.[70]

* See Peterson and Lawrence's comment in reference 166.
† In the equi-tempered (piano) scale.   See reference 177.

But "ear," here, means (part of) the ear *mechanism*, and includes no part of the aural nervous system, nor any questions of perception.

Before the development of modern electronic spectrographs, attempts had been made to represent running spectra of speech by painstaking measurement of spectra, at successive instants of time from recorded speech, and putting these together; one form consisted of cutting cards to the profiles of these spectra and stacking these actual cards to form a hill-and-dale model—closely analogous to the visible-speech spectrograms.*·† Other, and quite different, methods have also been proposed for the instrumental production of visible records of speech (as automatic "phonetic writing"[87]·‡).

All such representations of speech signals are made in terms of physical attributes, either acoustic attributes (frequencies, intensities, time instants) or anatomical ones (positions and movements of the articulators), but not in terms of subjective sensations. Although, as was stressed in Section 1.2, care must be taken to distinguish between physical attributes and mental sensations (e.g., frequency/pitch, intensity/loudness, etc.), it has been adequately demonstrated that the visible-speech running spectra provide a basis for a specification of *physical* speech sounds, as judged by results of perceptive tests. People can read the spectra, and identify the syllables, words, or sentences visually. But it should not therefore be concluded that the instrument which produces these spectra is a model of the ear, although, as Potter and Steinberg,[272] and again Gabor,[E] remark, this type of analysis goes a long way toward representing the process in the ear.

A number of subjective aural sensations—aural harmonics and difference tones, beats, the effects of masking one sound by another,[235]·§ fatigue,§ for instance—have no counterpart on visible-speech spectra, as must be expected. Again, the spectra represent acoustic *energy*, and all phase information is missing (only *FT* data are represented). Although it is true that, broadly speaking, the ear is insensitive to phase changes, it is not correct to say that such changes are quite undetectable.§ "Ohm's law" of hearing (Section 2.1) referred originally to the fact that the ear tends to perceive a complex periodic and continuous wave as a group of harmonic tones;[c] it is sometimes wrongly interpreted as implying that the ear is absolutely insensitive to phase.[275] This is not so; visible-speech spectra give a specification of speech signals; they may, with suitable training, be read by the deaf, but they do not purport to describe "how the ear works." For one thing, when measuring a spectrum, the instrument is set up as a

* See Dudley and Schuck and Young in reference 306.
† See Licklider and Miller in reference 315.
‡ For example, see Huggins in reference 166.
§ See Licklider and Miller in reference 315.

constant-parameter system, with a fixed set of filters; the parameters of the instrument are not controlled in any way by the signals themselves. A comment was made, in Section 1.3, upon the remarkable way in which the ear can apparently change its mode of operation depending upon the type of signal to which it listens. On one occasion it may discriminate between two tones, very close together in frequency; on another, for instance, it may discriminate between two rapidly successive acoustic "clicks."[G,42] But the spectrum analyzer is restricted by the $\Delta F \Delta T \approx 1$ principle and can either distinguish the two frequencies, or the two clicks, but not both, unless its filtering system be changed. This limitation has been well recognized by the designers and users of visible-speech spectrographs, for on some occasions wide-band (300 cycles per second) filters are used which enable rapid time transitions to be measured, whilst at other times narrow bands (40 cycles per second) enable sharp frequency discriminations to be made. Both are of great value in speech analysis.[271,121] Plosives, fricatives, vowels, et cetera may require different filtering in the spectrograph for their different characteristics to be displayed most prominently. It would be more accurate to compare the ear to a set of such visible-speech spectrographs, rather than to one of fixed parameters—or to one which has the power of varying its own parameters according to the signals being received[E,126,270] (e.g., the $\Delta F/\Delta T$ "aspect ratio" of its logons).[300]

Gabor[E,126] has analyzed some of the published data[42,300,168,203] concerning the time and frequency discriminability of the ear, in order to determine, first, the minimum $\Delta F \Delta T$ areas on the frequency-time plane which must be exceeded if the ear is to discriminate between such data, and, second, how sensitive an instrument is the ear to the ratio $\Delta F/\Delta T$ of such elementary areas. He concludes that the ear can adjust its time constant between at least 20–250 milliseconds, according to the act of discrimination it is performing, whether this is basically in pitch or in time, and dependent upon the region of the audible spectrum. He further concludes that whereas an *ideal* instrument (filter) can detect individual logons, or elementary areas $\Delta F \Delta T$, the ear requires several to make its discriminations. The ear efficiency varies between about 50 per cent (the theoretical maximum of a phase-insensitive instrument) at frequencies below 500 cycles per second, dropping to 20 per cent at 5 kilocycles per second and, of course, to zero at the limit of pitch audibility.

4. THE SPECIFICATION OF SPEECH

The question of specification of physical speech signals is not to be equated with the problem of aural perception, or "recognition." How the ear and brain carry out their task is a psycho-physiological matter.

Nevertheless, specification of the speech stimulus is basic to the psychologist's work. Another question concerns quantitative measurement of the degree of "intelligibility" of speech, when it is distorted or noisy, which is particularly the concern of telephone engineers.

All these problems impinge upon one another; before speech signals can be specified, we must know what basic attributes assist in recognition, and so need specification; for these to be determined, we must know how to design reliable and meaningful experiments involving listener's responses; then again, we must know what constitutes a "response" and how these responses can best be correlated with the text used by the speaker.

In the past, the sharp ear of the phonetician has to a major extent decided the specification of speech sounds, but with the passage of time it has become increasingly urgent to provide instrumental means, in addition, and to express the whole matter in the language of physics and statistics. All human languages may be recorded by phonetic symbols,[164] and visible-speech spectra too show promise of discriminability amongst the various tongues.[271]

When attending to a speaker, a listener may operate upon the speech he hears in a great variety of ways; the significant attributes of the speech may be microscopic acoustic clues, general acoustic qualities, syllabic rhythms, et cetera, or he may be guided by syntactic structure, or by knowledge of subject matter and of the speaker's interests, of seasonable topics—a whole hierarchy. The speaker's utterances play upon the entire past experience of the listener, stimulating him into response at all these levels. If addressed by a stranger, the listener may change his mode of operation, as the conversation proceeds, and while he is learning something of the speaker's accent, speech habits, phrasing, and interests.

It is this greatly varied experience that renders difficult the design of "listening tests" and other experiments involving perception of speech or measurement of its "intelligibility." If the text used consists of readings of connected prose, the listener's responses are dependent upon contextual clues of all kinds; if isolated words at random be used, his knowledge of vocabulary is operative; if "nonsense words"* are employed, emotional or other associations may be set up.[39,94,108,132,154,161,237]

At least two further major factors enter into such measurements, adding to the difficulties. First, different types of communication channel may be used under entirely different conditions, imposing varied requirements upon "intelligibility." For instance, domestic telephones are normally used for personal conversation, with all its verbal redundancy aids, whereas, in contrast, intercommunication between aircraft or tanks may proceed

---

* That is, invented words, not in the dictionary. We shall argue later that there is no such thing as a "nonsense word," if it elicits any response whatever.

under the most severe noise conditions, using military vocabulary interspersed with battle code words, numbers, distances, et cetera, with few contextual clues.   Secondly, a measurement of "intelligibility" made in a particular way, under certain conditions of noise or distortion, may lose all significance if these conditions be changed.   The whole question is most difficult.*   Before deciding upon the type of text to be used, and the method of carrying out the tests, it is necessary to consider carefully what is the "intelligibility" that is to be measured.

4.1. ARTICULATORY SPECIFICATION

Traditionally, phonetics has viewed speech as an articulatory process. The phonetician has applied his critical ear to distinguishing the various sounds of speech, correlating these with the motions of the speech organs— so far as he has been able to judge or to observe these.   The various shapes of the cavities, the mouth openings, tongue positions, et cetera, would, if they could be measured and reduced to a set of numerical data, constitute an objective specification of articulation.   But the vocal organs, in action, were singularly inaccessible before the coming of X-rays, palatographs, air-pressure recorders, periscopes, and all the paraphernalia of the modern phonetics laboratory.[B]

The intellectual stirrings of the seventeenth and eighteenth centuries in Europe awoke a curiosity concerning the workings of the body, including the production of speech.   There was much conjecturing about the movements of tongue and lips; many gruesome cut-away pictures of the vocal organs were drawn.   But it is not surprising that these early inquiries into the mysteries of voice production led toward the making of models—a technique which has continued and is paying dividends today.

4.1.1. ARTIFICIAL VOCAL TRACTS.   One of the most remarkable working models of the human vocal organs was that of Wolfgang Ritter von Kempelen (1734–1804).[91,187]   The instrument, which he developed in a series of experiments lasting over twenty years, was manipulated in the fashion of a bagpipe, with a bellows under the right elbow and the fingers of the right hand operating controls for producing consonants, by a series of flaps simulating the lips and tongue stops.   The left hand was manipulated inside, and in front of, a bell-shaped mouth for producing the vowels; two fingers of the right hand covered two holes simulating the nostrils.   The instrument seems to have been fairly successful, but was not given very extensive demonstration.[A]   At this period in history, scientific experiments were still associated with conjuring tricks; throughout the Middle Ages there has been attempts made to construct "talking machines," some serious, some for entertainment and showmanship.   Automata for playing

* For further notes, see Chapter 1, Section 4.

chess, for acting as oracles, for singing, writing, flying, telling fortunes, and other human interests were popular and were shown widely in the Courts and Societies of Europe*—though perhaps we have the same instincts today. We are always looking for the Geni in the Lamp. But von Kempelen's work was modern in concept; it was essentially functional, not made as an automaton to *look* like a man speaking, but as a model producing the sounds of speech. In contrast to earlier eighteenth century interests in automata, all resemblance to the person had been removed.[246] Von Kempelen considered controlling such a talking instrument from a keyboard, though this does not appear to have been constructed.

From this time onward there have been numerous serious attempts made to produce synthetic vowels,[70] of which the most notable were due to Professor Kratzenstein of Copenhagen[A,91,97] (1779) who built five odd-shaped cavity resonators, excited by metal reeds, and Robert Willis of Cambridge[A,†] (1829), who stated that the exact shapes of these resonators were not important, and that straight tubes could be set to different lengths to give distinct vowel sounds. Willis seems to have regarded vowels as being characterized by *single* resonances of such tubes; Helmholtz also refers to a single resonance as "sufficient to characterise the vowels," as judged from his measurement of oral cavity resonances by holding tuning forks close to the lip opening.‡ It was the classic work of Sir Richard Paget which finally established the *two* dominant resonances (formants), and sometimes three, which characterize the vowel and other sounds, although multiple resonances had in fact been suspected by Graham Bell, Helmholtz, and others. Paget made models of the human vocal tract using children's modeling clay, showing clearly the multiple resonances which arise when a constriction divides one hollow space into two cavities, coupled together acoustically. He related the true vowels, and the so-called sonorants such as [m], [n], [r] et cetera, as depending upon the resonant tones, and he demonstrated that the qualities of the plosive consonants [p], [b], [t], [d], et cetera, depend not only upon the noisy burst of breath but upon the resonances excited by the bursts, in a transient manner. The consonants are as "essentially musical" as the vowels.[A]

It is a natural and simplifying step, to pass from such direct oral models to their electric circuit analogs. The making of circuit analogs to given mechanical structures has become an established technique today;[C] such models of course are only *functional* analogs, exhibiting a behavior, in

---

* See *Encyclopædia Britannica* (11th Ed.), under (1) *automata* and (2) *conjuring*.

† "On the Vowel Sounds and on Reed Organ Pipes," *Proc. Cambridge Phil. Soc.*, 1829 (British Museum Shelf Mark 7895. S. 12).

‡ See reference 151, Chapter V.

electrical currents or voltage, identical with the behavior of the mechanical model, as expressed in pressures and velocities.

But such electrical analogs are frequently easier to make than their mechanical counterparts and, what is more important, easier to control dynamically. I would refer particularly to the work of Gunnar Fant.[383,382,406]

The close association today between phoneticians and telecommunication engineers has naturally led to carry-over of technique. One particular point of view which has been opened up regards the vocal tract as a dynamical system having an input end to which signals are applied (larynx tones or breath excitation) and an output end, giving out the speech sounds. The larynx or breath then provide "driving signals" to the response characteristics ("system-function") of the vocal tract which "responds," or gives out, the speech we hear.[102] Then the vocal tract "system function" may be specified, in principle, either by mechanical model tracts such as Paget's, or by their electric circuit analogs. Work of this kind on the practical design of electrical simulators of the vocal tract, has largely been restricted to the production of sustained vowels.[92,311]

The mechanical "speaking machines" of earlier centuries, and the resonator models of Paget and others, had been controlled with the fingers and hands; the modern electrical vocal tract simulators are controlled by pre-set electric signals. What the telephone engineer would like to be able to do, to reap advantage of this work, is to control such devices by varying electric control signals, obtained automatically from the speaker himself. We might imagine, perhaps, a set of muscular action potentials[B] to be picked up from small electrodes placed upon the articulators, and these potentials to be transmitted for the purpose of controlling an electric analog vocal tract at the receiving end. Such a proposal may be impracticable (and uncomfortable for the speaker!) but illustrates the idea. It is only such *control* signals which need be transmitted; all the elaborate acoustic vibrations, as picked up by a microphone, are inherent in these simpler control signals. Other approaches to this problem of telephone *channel compression*, such as the Vocoder,* attempt to derive the basic control signals not from the articulatory motions but instead from the *sounds* of speech themselves.

4.2. ACOUSTIC SPECIFICATION OF SPEECH

Speech is extraordinarily resistant to distortion and disturbances of many kinds. Not only does it provide a most effective means of communication in the clash and din of street noises, or amid the chatter of a crowded room,

---

* See also pp. 44, 97.

but it may be deliberately distorted in the laboratory, yet remain intelligible. Large portions of the spectrum may be filtered off in many different ways;[108,115] again the speech signal may be interrupted randomly, or regularly, yet communication proves only slightly hampered.[238] It seems that normal speech contains many more clues than are barely necessary to convey a message. It forms a highly "rendundant" signaling system. If some clues are removed, by filtering, distortion, or noises, then sufficient others remain for effective conversation.

Everyone's voice is different; and so are their visible-speech spectra to some extent, although the same text be used. But the spectra show remarkable constancy (far more than do the wave forms of speech), and it is the invariants of the spectra which, if they can be found and described, may serve as a phonetic specification. Such invariants may still possess elements which are redundant to a *minimal* specification, and it is the removal of these which is sought, to leave only the "basic attributes" of the speech sounds to be specified.

In Chapter 3 (Section 4) we described the acoustic correlates of phonemes as distributions (clusters) of points in an attribute space—points corresponding to a great number of people, saying "the same thing."[272] It is these attributes, or axes of the space, which are required to be isolated and defined in terms of the physical properties of speech—at present *acoustic* properties.

What are the "essential attributes" of such spectra, for an accurate yet non-redundant phonetic description? How much may be pared off? Students of speech today are active in their search for such basic spectral attributes, both for the benefit of pure phonetics and for utilitarian reasons. For if such basic attributes could be described physically, then the reader who reproduces the speech from them need not be a human being; such a description would amount to a specification of a machine for doing the same thing, and such a mechanism would have a multitude of uses. It might enable the "automatic-stenographer" to be made, which could set down verbal dictation in phonetic script; in reverse, it might realize the ancient dream of a "reading machine." But it is perhaps the telecommunication engineer who has the biggest stake in the business, for the ability to extract automatically the basic phonetic attributes of speech spectra would imply that only these need be transmitted—and they would be simpler, and far fewer, than the signals transmitted at present on our telecommunication channels.[89,90,141,143,*] Not all channels would lend themselves to such compression, because at the receiving end the speech would be "spoken" in a standard accent, robot-like; much, or all, of the

* See p. 44 for reference to the Vocoder. See the following papers under reference 166: Davis, Biddulph, and Balashek, Fry and Denes, Lawrence, and Peterson.

personal characteristics of the original voice might be lost.*   But there are numerous instances for such impersonal communications—for example, the telegrams we now send so often, in crude and standard phrasing.

But the difficulties should not be underestimated.   It must be remembered that the human brain is able to discriminate between acoustic patterns, not only on an individual phoneme by phoneme basis, but by possession of an immense store of experience of sound sequences,[237] together with linguistic and other knowledge†—and machines possessing such astronomically large stores are going to be very expensive!   No; as with many machines, the best result may be attained not by direct imitation of human functions but by some compromise.   Machines have in fact been constructed to respond to simple words, like spoken digits, but only to the carefully modulated voice of *one* speaker.   If another speaker is to be used, the parameters of the machine must be changed.‡

It is the other side of the problem which has so far met with better success—speech *synthesis*.   Recognizable speech has been produced, electronically, from "hand-painted" spectral or other control templates,[237]·§ Fig. 4.12 shows an example.   Such templates are highly simplified and omit many of the finer details of the spectra.[68,69]   But before such highly compressed telecommunication channels are successful, the two aspects must be wedded—the automatic analysis and extraction of sufficient and simple attributes of the speaker's voice and the use of these low-redundancy signals to control and synthesize speech sounds at the receiving end.   It is the automatic analysis which is technically the more difficult.

Particular reference should be made to the work of Lawrence in this connection.§   Lawrence's early work on "synthetic speech," used prepared templates, from half a dozen parameters: (*a*) the acoustic excitation (larynx tone, amplitude, and frequency, or breath energy, controlled by start-stop signals); (*b*) vocal tract resonances (from the outline of the first three formants).   At an early stage of development, this synthesis process had been demonstrated, but there still remained the question of automatic analysis, the extraction of these control parameters from live speech, upon which Lawrence also did pioneering work.   He has also demonstrated another interesting fact; the damping of the vocal resonances is unimportant and may be varied over wide values, yet defy aural detection.

All such Vocoder methods of compressing the channel-capacity required for transmission of speech (telephony), by extraction of relatively few basic parameters, may be regarded as reducing the dimensionality of the signal

* See Lawrence under reference 166.
† See Fry and Denes under reference 166.
‡ See Davis, Biddulph, and Balashek under reference 166.
§ See Lawrence in reference 166.

space in which the speech is represented. The wave forms of speech require a space of great dimensionality; both for practical telephony purposes and also for phonetic specification, it is desirable to reduce this dimensionality as much as possible.[B,126]

Another synthesis approach to speech study, made by Cooper and his colleagues at the Haskins Laboratories, is most interesting;[68,69] it is illustrated by Fig. 4.12. They have eliminated much of the fine detail of the speech spectra, by hand-painting simple stylized versions onto film. Formants are represented by curved bars, fricatives and affricates by splashes of dots. Such "painted spectra" may be played back through a special machine and the corresponding speech reproduced. A high intelligibility is claimed. Investigations at present are carried out on a trial-and-error basis, in the attempt to find out, by such synthetic means, the functions of various elements of the spectra.

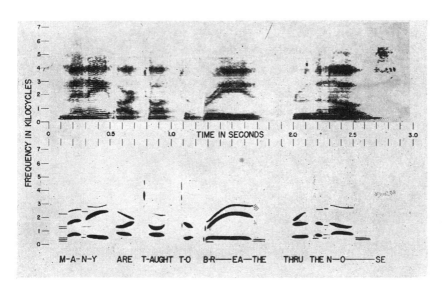

Fig. 4.12. A "visible-speech" spectrum and (below) its hand-painted equivalent (with acknowledgments to Dr. Franklin S. Cooper and the Haskins Laboratories).

The value of any particular physical attribute of the spectra, for contributing to the specification of speech, can only be judged by intelligibility (articulation) tests. The spectra, either unmodified or with various attributes filtered out or otherwise removed, may be converted back again into audible speech by an instrument which performs, effectively, the reverse function to that of the spectral analyzer.[288] Artificial spectra may be constructed by hand-painting onto film; it is experiments of this kind which have been partly responsible for highlighting the importance of the energy concentrations—the formants—and their interrupted, snake-like motions.[69]   There is evidence too that these concentrations remain largely unaffected by the types of distortion which speech may suffer, while remaining intelligible.[124,238]

We do not wish to overemphasize either the acoustic or the articulatory specifications of speech.   The former is a comparatively modern approach, the latter more traditional.   True specification can only depend upon both aspects, and upon their relationship.[B,81]

BIBLIOGRAPHY

A. Paget, Sir Richard, *Human Speech*, Kegan Paul, Trench, Trubner & Co., Ltd., London (Harcourt, Brace & Co., Inc., New York), 1930.
B. Stetson, R. H., *Motor Phonetics*, North-Holland Publishing Co., Amsterdam, 2nd Ed., 1951.
C. Wood, A. B., *A Textbook of Sound*, George Bell & Sons, Ltd., London, 1930.
D. (*a*) Franklin, P., *Fourier Methods*, McGraw-Hill Book Co., Inc., New York, 1949.
   (*b*) Carslaw, H. S., *Introduction to the Theory of Fourier Series and Integrals*, Macmillan & Co., Ltd., London, 1906.
E. Gabor, D., "Theory of Communication," *J. Inst. Elec. Engrs. (London)*, *93*, Part III, 1946, p. 429.
F. Hartley, R. V. L., "Transmission of Information," *Bell System Tech. J.*, *7*, 1928, p. 535.
G. Stevens, S. S., and H. Davis, *Hearing—Its Psychology and Physiology*, John Wiley & Sons, Inc., New York, 1938.

CHAPTER FIVE

On the Statistical Theory
of Communication

*It is a very inconvenient habit of kittens (Alice
had once made the remark) that, whatever you say to
them, they always purr. "If they would only purr
for 'yes,' and mew for 'no' or any rule of that sort,"
she had said, "so that one could keep up a conversation! But how can you talk with a person if they
always say the same thing?"*

Lewis Carroll (1832–1898)
Through the Looking Glass

1. DOUBT, INFORMATION, AND DISCRIMINATION

In this, as in other chapters, we shall make no attempt to compress a
whole study within the compass of a few dozen pages, but rather try to
convey to the reader some notion of the nature of the subject of statistical
communication theory, which has aroused such widespread interest during
recent years. We hope, too, to guide him through the literature and advise
him on a preferred order of reading.

We shall be discussing the scientific concept of *information*. Now this is
a word in everyday use; we speak of information as being *reliable, accurate,
precise, timely, valuable*, et cetera. These terms are very relevant to human
communication. But, although the scientific concept of *information* makes
no reference to these qualities, it nevertheless has a very important role in
the description of the communication process. This role will be explained
in the next chapter.

Communication theory first arose in telegraphy, with the need to specify precisely the *capacity* of various systems of telecommunication (to communicate information). The first attempt to formulate a measure mathematically was made by Hartley[A] in 1928, and his ideas are basic to the theory today. The newcomer to this subject can do no better than read his short classic paper first; it is easy reading. Engineers are concerned primarily with the *correct* transmission of signals, or (electric) representations of messages; they are not commonly interested, professionally, with the purposes of messages—whether they be trivial gossip, serious news, or racing tips. Provided the telegraph or telephone transmits the signals faithfully, the messages will have "meaning," value, truth, reliability, timeliness, and all their other properties. The signals must be correct; then all these human properties are inherent and consequential. Mathematical communication theory concerns the signals alone, and their information content, abstracted from all specific human uses. It concerns not the question "What sort of information?" but rather "How much information?"

This aspect of the theory was once described by Weaver as "bizarre," but now seems to be generally accepted as completely reasonable. The newcomer is referred to his discussion.[D,*] In this chapter we are concerned solely with this aspect—the information content of *signals*. In the following chapter we shall look more closely at the philosophical background, in an attempt to see relationships between the mathematical concept of information and other common and more human aspects.

Information can be received only where there is doubt; and doubt implies the existence of alternatives—where choice, selection, or discrimination is called for. We are continually making selections among alternatives, every moment of our lives, some consciously, but in the majority of cases unconsciously. It is a basic animal attribute; in the words of a psychologist: "discrimination is the simplest and most basic operation performable."[†]

But *selection* (or discrimination) can be carried out in non-human communication links. Perhaps the reader has seen that modern wonder, one teletype machine communicating with another. At the transmitting end, the operator selects and presses keys one at a time; coded electric signals are thereby sent to the receiving machine, causing it to select and depress the correct keys automatically. We see the receiver keys going down, as though pressed by invisible fingers.

When we ourselves communicate one with another, we transmit signals, electric, acoustic, visual—physical embodiments of messages. Now it is

* Read first Weaver's discussion on p. 95 of reference D.

† Reference 314, with kind permission of the American Psychological Association.

customary to speak of signals as "conveying information," as though information were a kind of commodity.   But signals do not convey information as railway trucks carry coal.   Rather we should say: signals have an information content by virtue of their *potential for making selections.* Signals operate upon the alternatives forming the recipient's doubt; they give the power to discriminate amongst, or select from, these alternatives. And at present the "set of alternatives" with which we are concerned is any set of distinct signs, which will be termed an *alphabet.*   They may be the

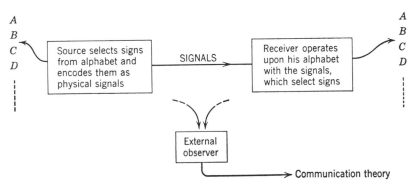

Fig. 5.1.   "Information" as the selective potential of signals.

letters of a written language, numbers, printed words, the ordinates of wave forms (Chapter 4, Section 2.5, Fig. 4.7); any set of distinct sign-types constructed for communication.   But the alphabet must be specified, before the information content of messages can be discussed numerically; further, it must be assumed that the same alphabet exists at both the transmitting and receiving ends of the communication channel.   It is then the function of the *source* of information to select the signs successively from this alphabet, thus constituting *messages,* and to transmit them in physical form as *signals,* through a channel, to the receiver.   At the receiver, the signals operate upon an identical alphabet and select corresponding signs.   Messages are then sent and received.

Note the distinction drawn here between *message* and *signal.*   A message is regarded as the "selections from the alphabet," which is then put into physical form (signals) as sound, light, electricity, et cetera, for transmission.*   (A message might, for instance, be a thought, selected from an alphabet of thoughts, but this thought is not physically transmitted.

* The nomenclature of communication theory is still not universally established. However, the system adopted in this chapter in the greater part has been widely adopted in Britain and in the United States.   A full list of definitions is given in the Appendix.

Perhaps such a naked description of this basic operation, illustrated by Fig. 5.1, emphasizes the dehumanized nature of the theory.   But we shall breathe back the breath of life again in the next chapter.

Communication theory is written in the meta-language of an external observer; it is not a description of the process of communication as it appears to one of the participants.   Figure 5.1 may thus be compared to Fig. 3.2(*a*) of Chapter 3.

2. HARTLEY'S THEORY: "INFORMATION" AS LOGICAL "INSTRUCTIONS TO SELECT"

Figure 5.2 shows, as an example, a simple alphabet of only eight signs, denoted by $ABC \cdots H$.   A source selects a sign, and signals in some way to the receiver; how much information must be signaled for the receiver to identify the sign correctly?   Let us assume that, from past observation, any sign out of the eight is equally likely to be selected.   Doubt is then spread uniformly over the "alphabet" or, as it is said, the *a priori* probabilities of the signs are all equal (in this case, to 1/8).

The signals reaching the receiver represent instructions to select.   Thus the first instruction answers the question: Is it in the first half of the alphabet, *yes* or *no*?   (In Fig. 5.2, *yes* = 1, *no* = 0.)   The range of doubt is *halved* by this.   Then a second instruction divides each half into half again, and a third into half yet again.   In this case then, three simple *yes, no* instructions (1, 0) serve to identify uniquely any one sign out of eight.

Such *yes, no* instructions are the simplest possible; each one successively halves the range of doubt.   They are called *binary digits*, usually shortened to *bits* (or by some people, *binits*), and are used as the elementary *units of information capacity*.   Notice that each sign in Fig. 5.2 is identified by a different sequence of 1, 0 digits.   Thus *C* by 101, *G* by 001, et cetera.   No two sequences differ by more than one digit; any single mistake therefore will cause ambiguity.

As we have already seen, all communicable messages (i.e., expressible by signs) *may* be coded into such binary 1, 0 sequences.   The simplest illustration is provided by Morse code (dot, dash), which can code any written message in, at least, European languages.†   We would remind the reader too of the punched-card system of storing information (hole, no-hole), illustrated by Fig. 2.2 (p. 34).

In our example, three bits of information are required for selection of each sign from among eight equally likely signs—because $2^3 = 8$ or

† Ignoring the letter- and word-space intervals; these can also be coded by a dot-dash sequence if required.

$\log_2 8 = 3$. A communication channel like this one, selecting the signs at the rate of 100 per second, would have an *information rate* of 300 bits per second.

So much for the cases where the number of signs N in the alphabet is an exact power of 2. But suppose it is not? We shall show later that the information is still equal to $\log_2 N$ bits per sign selected, though this will involve an *averaging* process. But first, let us consider, as Hartley did, messages comprising wave forms, such as speech, rather than printed signs.

Sign	1st	2nd	3rd	Selections
A	1	1	1	
B	1	1	0	
C	1	0	1	
D	1	0	0	
E	0	1	1	
F	0	1	0	
G	0	0	1	
H	0	0	0	

Fig. 5.2. Binary coding of selections.

Figure 5.3 shows (dotted) part of a continuous wave form $s(t)$, band-limited to F cycles per second, together with its representation by independent sample ordinates, spaced $1/2F$ second apart (see Section 2.5 of Chapter 4). These samples then define the wave form completely. Hartley appreciated that the amplitudes of such samples cannot be specified with absolute accuracy, in reality, although this is frequently done for the convenience of theoretical analysis. The amplitudes, being physical observations, must be quantized; in the figure, here, a comparatively coarse quantizing Δs of only eight levels has been assumed. (Such quantizing is in fact used practically in certain telecommunication systems, and the successive sample pulses are restricted to their nearest quantal levels. The wave form then assumes a step-like character, which introduces a so-called quantization distortion.[252,*]) But such steps Δs may, in theory, be made as small as desired.† The smaller Δs, the greater the

* See Chapter 2, Section 2.
† For example, good quality speech (telephony) requires 32 levels, or better, 64.

number of levels, and the greater the *precision* of transmission; as we shall see, this implies also the greater the rate of transmission of information.

If we now label these ordinates arbitrarily, $ABC\cdots H$, then the successive selection of the sample ordinates may be regarded also as selection of these letter signs; such selections closely resemble our previous case, Fig. 5.2, with a source of discrete signs.   However, it is advisable to distinguish between such (quantized) wave-form sources and sources of printed signs.   For one thing, wave forms usually represent acoustic, electric, or other physical sources possessing *energy*, whereas we cannot readily associate energy with letters or other printed signs.   The different levels, $ABC\cdots H$ represent possible *states* of this wave-form source; the successive sample ordinates select from these states.   In general, if there are N such levels, or states, each sample ordinate contributes $\log_2 N$ bits of information (about the wave-form source) analogous to our previous case.

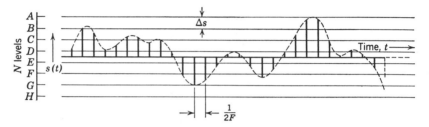

Fig. 5.3.   Hartley's theory; band-limited wave-form source.

Consider a time interval of T seconds.   This interval contains $2FT$ independent sample ordinates, each of which can have one of N levels. Thus in this interval there could be N^{2FT} different, distinct, wave forms. This set comprises all the different possible signals which such a quantized source is capable of transmitting each T seconds; it is called a band-limited *ensemble*, of duration T seconds.   Hartley defined the information rate of such a source by the logarithm of this number of different signals (number of members of the *ensemble*), as H where, expressed to the base 2:

$$
\begin{aligned}
H &= 2FT \log_2 N \quad \text{bits per } T \text{ seconds} \\
&= 2F \log_2 N \quad\ \ \text{bits per second}
\end{aligned}
\tag{5.1}
$$

which is simply $\log_2 N$ (the information content per ordinate) times $2F$, the number of ordinates per second.   This logarithmic measure is then one which permits addition of the information contents of successive independent signals.

And so, too, with any source of independent discrete signs, $ABC\cdots N$ (assuming for the moment they are equally likely).   If a source selects from these at the rate of n per second, its information rate will be $n \log_2 N$ bits per second; and again there are N^n distinct alternative sequences of signs in an *ensemble* of one-second duration from such a source.   When the term *independent* is applied to the successive signs selected by a discrete source, we mean, at present, that no one sign carries with it any information concerning its neighbors.   There are no "spelling rules."   We shall later refer to *statistical independence* in a more exact way.

This introduction to the information measure follows historical lines. Communication theory first arose in telegraphy[A] and we have used technical telegraphic terms, like *coding*.   But the reader should appreciate the basic nature of the ideas.   We are concerned not only with coding in the technical sense, but more broadly, with the *making of representations (of messages)*.   The information received enables the recipient to add to his representation at his end, and the binary-digit measure tells by how much.   The idea of "correspondence" is inherent in the concept of "communication"—the reproduction, or replication, of a representation.

2.1. Reversible and irreversible operations upon signals

Each of the sample ordinates of a band-limited wave form (Fig. 5.3) selects a level (defines a state) of the source, $ABC\cdots H$.   Each may be reduced to binary selections, as illustrated by Fig. 5.2.   In Fig. 5.4, (a) a portion of a wave form is shown, together with (b) its binary-code repre-

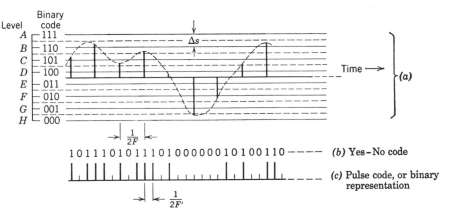

Fig. 5.4.   Binary-pulse (reversible) code.   Horizontal dotted lines represent *thresholds* of the quantization process.

sentation, according to this coding scheme of Fig. 5.2.   (A system of telecommunication coding, called *pulse-code modulation*, uses such representations practically, for transmitting speech and music;[82,252] for this purpose, *yes* (or 1) is coded as a sharp electrical impulse, whereas *no* (or 0) is coded by leaving a blank—no impulse.   Figure 5.4(c) illustrates such impulse signals.)

Such codings, or representations, are clearly reversible; from (c) we may reconstruct the wave form (a) by setting up the ordinates and using the correct interpolation function (see Chapter 4, Section 2.5).   Another, very familiar, reversible coding is the Morse code; with this, printed letters may be represented by dot-dash signals, but converted back into print without any loss or error.

The coded chain of impulses (c) may itself be regarded as sample ordinates of a wave form.   Notice then that they are now three times as closely spaced as in (a) ($\log_2 8 = 3$).   In general, with quantization into N levels, the binary-coded signal will have samples with spacings reduced $\log_2 N$ times, requiring a bandwidth F' correspondingly increased.   At the same time, the binary signal has only two levels ($N' = 2$).   Thus, from Eq. 5.1, the information content of these signals has been unchanged by such coding.

Such a reversible coding represents a change of dimensionality; that is, a "trading" of bandwidth for numbers of levels, or alternative states.

The initial quantization itself represents an *irreversible* process—information content thrown away; each wave-form sample, assumed to be known at first with an unlimited precision, when quantized is reproduced with less precision.   The original wave form then cannot be reconstructed with its original accuracy, since the necessary information has been destroyed; only the quantized wave form is recoverable.

But a more important cause of information loss (and so leading to an irreversible process) has the technical name *noise*.   Noise is the destroyer of information and sets the ultimate upper limit to the information capacity of a channel, as we shall discuss later, in Section 6.1.

Hartley did not consider what it is that limits the fineness of quantization, in practical channels of the type so far considered; he did not refer to noise, nor did he consider the *probabilities* of the various states of a message source. It is these two aspects which have received so much attention recently. The statistical theory of communication is built up upon Hartley's foundations, but the idea of a determinate source of signals has become replaced by the concept of a *statistical ensemble*.   Such a statistical approach to telecommunication may be said to have originated with studies of the phenomenon of random electrical noise, in the 1920's.   We shall return to such statistical aspects of our subject later, in Section 6.

2.2 WHEN THE NUMBER OF ALTERNATIVE STATES IS NOT A POWER OF TWO

Selection of any one sign out of an alphabet of N signs can only be specified in whole numbers.   We cannot speak of "fractions of a selection"; a choice is either made or not made—*yes* or *no*.   If then N is not a power of 2, the selective information content of any one sign out of this alphabet cannot be specified as $\log_2 N$, since this will be fractional. But it is easily shown that this measure is still relevant if *averaged* over long sequences of selections.[c]

We are still assuming that all selections out of the N are equally likely. Consider an interval of time T, during which a wave-form source gives out a sequence of $2FT$ independent ordinates (or, analogously, nT selections from a discrete alphabet). During this interval one of $S = N^{2FT}$ possible different wave forms could be transmitted; then, as before:

$$\log_2 S = 2FT \log_2 N \qquad \text{but now this is fractional}$$

$$= r + \delta \qquad \text{where } r \text{ is whole number and } \delta \text{ a fraction}$$

To select this one wave form out of the S equally likely possibilities must require a *whole* number of elementary selections. The nearest whole number is r where

$$(\log_2 S) - \delta = r \text{ bits} \tag{5.2}$$

But if we speak of *average* number of selections, per sample ordinate (or sign) of the sequence, then as the interval T becomes large, this number of bits per *sample* becomes:

$$H_N = \lim_{2FT \to \infty} \frac{1}{2FT} [(\log_2 S) - \delta] = \log_2 N \text{ bits per sample} \tag{5.3}$$

Alternatively, the information *per second* from this source is H:

$$H = 2F \log_2 N \text{ bits per second} \tag{5.4}$$

exactly as for the case, Eq. 5.1, where N is a power of 2.

Notice that H is an information *rate*; so many binary selections (*yes*, *no*) *per second*. H may be fractional, but only by virtue of being taken on the *average*. This logarithmic measure of information rate can only be applied in this average sense. We can speak of a source possessing a certain "average rate of information." There are, however, certain cases in which it is convenient to regard the incremental contribution of single signs (their information *content*), but such uses of the term information should be carefully distinguished.

The whole of the Wiener-Shannon theory is based upon average rates, whereas selections are always made as whole numbers of *yes*, *no* decisions.

2.3. STORAGE OF INFORMATION; CAPACITY FOR INFORMATION

Hartley's measurement of information rate, as we have approached it here, is seen to be in terms of the number of *yes*, *no* decisions required to specify the sample ordinates, or signs, emitted by a source, fractions arising only through averaging. One advantage of this is that it enables us to consider information storage and capacity.

Binary digits (*yes, no*; 1, 0; etc.) may readily be stored. Punched holes on large cards were used in the Jacquard loom (for coding weaving patterns),* and the method remains in common use today in computing and accounting machines. Modern computing machines use relays, tiny magnetic rings, magnetic storage drums, and other technical means.[26,33,†] All such are used as two-state devices; they are either on or off.

The output signals from a source of information may be expressed as a sequence, or *time series*, of binary pulses [Fig. 5.4(*c*)]. A source emitting H independent binary digits per second could fill a store of capacity Q binary elements in Q/H seconds on the average. But, as we have already seen, there need be no upper limit to the number of distinguishable signs, N, in an alphabet (or distinguishable amplitude levels of wave forms) were it not for noise. Consequently, a noise-free source can, in principle, have its note of transmitting information increased indefinitely, simply by increasing N.[328]

We define, then, the capacity of a communication channel as the number of independent *yes, no* digits which it may transmit per unit time. We shall return later to the question of an upper *limit* to capacity, in the presence of noise. (See Section 6, p. 198.)

3. WHEN THE ALTERNATIVE SIGNS ARE NOT EQUALLY LIKELY TO OCCUR

With most practical sources of information, the signs are not equally likely to occur. A glance back at Fig. 2.4 (Chapter 2) for example, will show the relative frequencies of the letters in "English print" as they were assessed by Samuel Morse in his day. How does the Hartley logarithmic measure of information rate apply to such a source?

3.1. STATIONARY AND NON-STATIONARY SOURCES

The relative frequencies p_i of the various signs may be estimated by an observer, if he watches the source for a long time; however, in practical cases, the possibility of making such an assessment with any pretence to accuracy depends upon the source being *statistically stationary*. This means that if the observer watches for a very long time T, the relative-frequency estimates he makes will not depend upon the actual moment of starting— the statistical properties of a stationary source are invariant under a shift of

* See Section 3 of Chapter 2.
† See punched card, Fig. 2.2, p. 34.

the time origin. This assumption of stationariness is normally required in statistical communication theory, and is one of its present limitations. Many practical communication sources are, in fact, far from being stationary; thus spoken and written languages change their statistical (micro) structure continually (Chapter 3, Section 5); again, if the source possesses learning ability, it will change its behavior with the passage of time. In most fields of real *human* communication, the assumption of stationary sign behavior cannot be made, and this is one principal obstacle to the application of the mathematical theory to individual human communicative behavior.

3.2. INFORMATION RATE OF A STATIONARY SOURCE OF INDEPENDENT SIGNS

Let $p_a p_b p_c \cdots p_i \cdots p_N$ be the relative frequencies of the N signs of an alphabet, $a, b, c, \cdots, N$, where $\sum_i p_i = 1$. Further, assume that the successive signs emitted by the source are independent, meaning that there are no rules (no "syntax", or spelling rules), by which any one sign is known to relate to another. Each selected sign is considered a separate event. In this case, the information rate of the source can be a function only of these negative frequencies p_i, and does not depend upon the *order* in which the signs are selected at the source.

This alphabet of signs, having certain relative frequencies, forms a *statistical ensemble*, upon which the source operates selectively. Figure 5.5(a) shows one way of illustrating such an ensemble; in this example there are eight signs, $abc \cdots h$, having the relative frequencies:

$$p = \tfrac{1}{2}, \tfrac{1}{4}, \tfrac{1}{16}, \tfrac{1}{16}, \tfrac{1}{32}, \tfrac{1}{32}, \tfrac{1}{32}, \tfrac{1}{32},$$

respectively. A thick line of unit length (100 per cent) beneath this ensemble is shown divided up into segments of length proportional to these frequencies. This line, with the segments, represents a "range of doubt."

The source information rate is determined as before, in terms of equally likely, *yes, no* decisions, by successively halving the range of doubt. The "range of doubt" has been redrawn vertically in Fig. 5.5(b), which may be compared and contrasted with the equally likely case of Fig. 5.2. Thus, a first selection is made such that the ensemble is divided into two groups, of equal probability $p = \tfrac{1}{2}$. The transmitted sign is equally likely to come from either group—on a long-term basis. Now the reader may object that such equal subdivision is only possible because we have chosen a most convenient set of probabilities in this example! True; this may not be possible in general, but let us assume for a moment it is, and return to this point later. A second subdivision, as shown, divides the ensemble into subgroups of equal probability $p = \frac{1}{4}$; a third, into sub-subgroups of $p = \frac{1}{8}$ and so on, until all signs are uniquely identified.   The *yes, no* codes (1, 0) are shown in this figure, which illustrates also that the lower the probability of a sign in the ensemble, the more *yes, no* elementary selections are required; that is, the rarer the signs, the higher their information content.[c,*]   Information

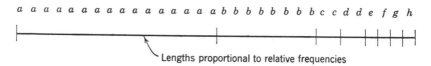

Lengths proportional to relative frequencies

Fig. 5.5(*a*).   An ensemble of eight signs, representing a "range of doubt."

Sign	Relative Frequency (p_i)	Selection	1st	2nd	3rd	4th	5th
a	1/2		1				
b	1/4		0	1			
c	1/16		0	0	1	1	
d	1/16		0	0	1	0	
e	1/32		0	0	0	1	1
f	1/32		0	0	0	1	0
g	1/32		0	0	0	0	1
h	1/32		0	0	0	0	0

$$\sum_i p_i = 1.0$$

Lengths proportional to relative frequencies

Fig. 5.5(*b*).   Binary coding of selections of unequal probabilities.

content is then measured in terms of the *statistical rarity* of the signs (likened, by some people, to their "surprise value").   This was intuitively seen by Samuel Morse (see his code, Fig. 2.4, p. 37.)

Each such division, into groups of equal probability, halves the range of *average* doubt; it therefore represents one *bit* of information.   Let a particular sign be i, requiring say K_i successive binary subdivisions to identify it. Its probability is p_i; consequently, the final subdivision, which identifies it, divided a range $2p_i$ into equal parts; the subdivision before that divided the range $2^2 p_i$; the one before that $2^3 p_i$; and so on until we arrive at the

* See Huffman in reference 166 for further treatment of such type of coding.

initial division of the *whole* alphabet, having a probability $\sum p_i = 1$. Hence:

$$2^{K_i} p_i = 1$$

or
$$K_i = -\log_2 p_i \qquad (5.5)$$

The average, or *expected* value of K_i, taken over the whole alphabet $a, b, c, \cdots, N$ (in the general case) is then:[*]

$$H(i) = \overline{-\log p_i} = -\sum_i p_i \log p_i \text{ bits per sign} \qquad (5.6)$$

We shall return to this important formula, which represents the *average* number of *yes, no* digits required, per sign transmitted—the information rate of this source of independent discrete signs.

3.2.1. WHEN THE ALPHABET DOES NOT DIVIDE INTO EQUALLY LIKELY SUBGROUPS. The argument above, due to Fano[C,101] is very descriptive, but the following method is an alternative. Consider now those cases in which the alphabet does *not* divide consecutively, so conveniently, into equally likely subgroups. The argument is rather similar to that of Section 2.2; we cannot deal with *single* signs now but only with averages, over very long sequences given out by the source.

If we observe extremely long sequences, then the various signs $a, b, c, \cdots$, N will in fact occur with almost their estimated probabilities $p_a p_b \cdots p_n$ (the source being statistically stationary); consider an ensemble of all the n possible different message sequences, each of S signs in length, distinguished only by different orders of occurrence. Then all such long sequences will have nearly equal probabilities $p(S)$ of occurring in the source, and the number of different messages in the ensemble will be $n = 1/p(S)$ where:

$$p(S) = p_a^{S \cdot p_a} \cdot p_b^{S \cdot p_b} \cdot p_c^{S \cdot p_c} \cdots p_N^{S \cdot p_N} \qquad (5.7)$$

We see this, as follows: the probability of a sequence is the product of the probabilities of all the signs forming it. Then a occurs about $S \cdot p_a$ times in each long sequence S hence, since p_a is the probability of any *one* a occurring, the joint probability of the number Sp_a occurring is $p_a^{Sp_a}$. Similarly for b, c, d, et cetera.

Now all these n messages being so nearly equally likely, the information content of any one is obtained as for our first elementary case (Fig. 5.2). It

---

[*] *Expected value:* the expression 5.6 is a way of writing average values, as used particularly by statisticians. Suppose we have a chain of the numbers $a_1\ a_2\ a_3$ (perhaps $a_1 = \log p_i$) from a source, of which the following is a sample of 12 successions: $a_1\ a_2\ a_3\ a_3\ a_1\ a_1\ a_2\ a_3\ a_1\ a_3\ a_3\ a_1$ (twelve numbers). Average of this =

$$\frac{(4 \times a_1) + (2 \times a_2) + (6 \times a_3)}{12} = (p_1 \times a_1) + (p_2 \times a_2) + (p_3 \times a_3) = \sum p_i a_i$$

is simply $\log_2 n$ bits per sequence S, or $\frac{1}{S} \log_2 n$ bits per sign. That is, from 5.6:

$$H(i) = \frac{1}{S} \log \frac{1}{p(S)} = -\sum_i p_i \log p_i \text{ bits per sign} \qquad (5.8)$$

which is identical with Eq. 5.6.

4. THE USE OF PRIOR INFORMATION: REDUNDANCY

It is one of the merits of statistical communication theory that it takes into account the effect, upon communication, of *prior information*. Though a receiver may not know exactly what messages are coming to him next, he is not necessarily in a state of complete ignorance. We have already assumed that he knows the alphabet of signs and has had experience of their relative frequencies of occurrence. In Chapter 4 we considered his knowledge of the channel itself: of bandwidth, signal power, types of coding; of the *structure* of the signals, as dependent upon the channel properties. All this must be brought into consideration in measuring information rates. But other prior information may exist, by virtue of known constraints between the signs; that is, from syntactical rules. If such "spelling" rules are known, determinate or statistical, then the signals reaching the receiver bear less information than they would if the successive signs were independent. The information conveyed by signals is always relative; it depends upon the *difference* in the receiver's doubt before and after their receipt.

4.1. SYNTACTICAL REDUNDANCY: ITS MEASUREMENT

The rules of syntax of human languages are complicated and varied; such rules introduce *redundancy* into the messages, thereby making their correct reception more certain. We have already discussed this question, in a purely descriptive way, in Section 6.3 of Chapter 3. In communication theory, redundancy is treated mathematically, the syntax being described, not necessarily as a linguist would commonly view it, but as a set of conditional probabilities.[D]

A source of information which selects signs according to probabilities is called a *stochastic source*, and the message sequences *stochastic series*. We may consider also *transition probabilities*, or the relative frequencies with which different signs follow a given sign or, alternatively, precede it. In printed English, for instance, the rule of spelling, "I before E except after C," with a very few exceptions, suggests that

$$p_C(\text{EI}) \gg p_C(\text{IE})$$

We read a transition probability $p_x(y)$ as "the probability of y given x." An alternative notation is $p(y|x)$.

Other *conditional* probabilities may be known, referring not only to adjacent signs of a sequence, but to any specified spacings or groupings such as "letter bridges" or "word bridges." Cryptographers use these.[357]

The existence of constraints, in terms of transition or other conditional probabilities will, if known *a priori*, introduce redundancy into the messages received from a source—being something known statistically about the messages beforehand (prior statistical information).

In English texts, or those of other human languages, the various transition probabilities governing the appearance of the successive letters are very unequal. As an illustration, suppose a teletype machine gives out the following sequence:

$$\cdots\cdots\cdots\cdots\cdot with\ the\ arrival\ of\ t\,|$$

where the bar represents the instant "now." The next letter is governed by a whole set of conditional probabilities, and depends, in the limit, upon *all* that has gone before. However, the influence of the letters and words several lines, paragraphs, or pages removed in the past will be very slight.

It is the few letters immediately preceding "now" which have the greatest control, with certain exceptions owing to rigid grammatical rules. But, as regards *numerical* measurement of redundancy, we have available only those conditional probabilities which have to be gathered by the patient labor of cryptographers and language students.[D,85,96,273,294,367] The task of assessing monogram, digram, and trigram frequencies is formidable, let alone going beyond this. The fact that we ourselves can guess successive letters of a text, with fair accuracy, implies that we possess immense mental stores of the *rank orderings* of letters and words; but we do not know the various transitions as numerical relative frequencies.[294]

With the help of statistical tables of letter or word frequencies, together with digrams, trigrams, or other grouping frequencies, it is possible to construct texts which resemble, say, English passages (though they may continually "wander off the point!"). But this experiment need cause no surprise, and has no philosophical interest whatever; it merely shows the correctness of the tables used. Jonathan Swift made biting comment upon this "monkeys-on-typewriters idea" (Chapter 2, Section 1).

Rather than an English message, such as that cited above, let us consider a Teletype machine operating in code* and, for simplicity, using only the

---

* It can be helpful, to the beginner, to consider examples in code, rather than in plain language, because the mind is so easily side-tracked by the "meaningfulness" of the latter. *Meaning* is quite irrelevant to our present context, but we shall consider its place in relation to communication theory later, in Chapter 6.

letters A, B, C, D.   A typical sequence might be:

$$\cdots\cdots\cdots\cdots\quad B\ A\ A\ C\ D\ B\ A\ D\ C\ D\ A\ B\ A\begin{array}{|l} A \\ B \\ C \\ D \end{array}$$

where the bar represents "now," to be followed by one of A, B, C, D, according to a whole set of conditional probabilities.   To assess any one, say the frequency with which B follows A, $p_A(B)$, we pick out all the A's, in a *very long* sequence, and observe what fraction are followed by B.   Since *some* letter must follow any given one

$$\sum_j p_i(j) = \sum_j p(j) = 1 \tag{5.9}$$

That is to say, the summation is obviously independent of the preceding sign, i.

There is a simple, yet very important, theorem concerning statistical constraints and redundancy; it should be clear from the illustration above:

If all the various transition probabilities $p_i(j)$ are equal, then the individual signs, or letters, become statistically independent and equally probable.   In such a case there are absolutely no preferred guesses as to what letters will be given out by the source; redundancy is provided by the existence of *unequal* transition probabilities.

Such a source of equi-probable, statistically independent letters or other signs has a maximum information rate (other factors being fixed).   Equation 5.8 gives the information rate for a source of independent signs, and this expression is maximized when all p_i are equal.[D]

But notice that the converse argument does not hold; it is easy to arrange that all letters should be equi-probable, yet have unequal transition probabilities.   An example will suffice; suppose this is a typical sequence:

$$\cdots\ B\ B\ B\ B\ A\ A\ A\ A\ C\ C\ C\ C\ A\ A\ A\ A\ D\ D\ D\ D\ C\ C\ C\ C\ B\ B\ B\ B\ \cdots$$

Then although $p(A) = p(B) = p(C) = p(D)$, it is possible that, say, $p_A(C) < p_C(C)$.   Given any one letter of the sequence, our best guess here, for the next, would be the same letter.

Sequences for which only pairs of adjacent signs are considered, as we have done so far, are called Markoff chains,[225] though the term is frequently used for series with known trigram or higher-order (finite) structure.

Quantitatively speaking, the redundancy of a source is assessable only *relative* to the known set of probabilities.   Thus we can quote the redundancy of a source on a monogram basis [knowing only the various $p(i)$], or a digram basis [knowing also $p(i,j)$], or a trigram basis, et cetera.   But we cannot simply give "its redundancy," on an unspecified basis.

Suppose that we have assessed the relative frequencies with which a source emits different alternative sequences of S letters; let us write such S-gram joint frequencies as $p(a\ b\ c\cdots S)$. For example, in our four-letter source used above (preceding Eq. 5.9), we may know the values of $p(A\ B\ C)$, $p(A\ C\ B)$, $p(B\ A\ C)$, $p(B\ C\ A)$, et cetera—all the trigrams. Then these may readily be interpreted in terms of successive *transition* since:

$$P(a\ b\ c\cdots S) = P(a)\cdot P_a(b\ c\cdots S)$$
$$= P(a)\cdot P_a(b)\cdot P_{ab}(c\cdots S)$$
$$= \cdots\cdots \text{ etc.} \qquad (5.10)$$

Probability constraints between successive letters may then be specified either in terms of joint probabilities $p(a\ b\ c\cdots S)$ or as different transition probabilities $P_a(b)$, $P_{ab}(c\cdots S)$, et cetera.

Knowing such conditional probabilities, we may then assess the corresponding redundancy—which is still to be defined.

The redundancy of a source may be quoted as a percentage:

$$\text{Redundancy} = \frac{H_{\text{max}} - H}{H_{\text{max}}} \times 100 \text{ per cent} \qquad (5.11)$$

where H = information rate (bits per sign, or second) of the source[D]

H_{max} = maximum information rate which it could possess if recoded in such a way as to equalise all transition probabilities, and hence equalizing all sign probabilities, thus rendering them independent.

For illustration, Fig. 5.5 shows the encoding of a redundant source; the signs of the alphabet, $a, b, \cdots, h$, having unequal probabilities are shown encoded into 1, 0 signs (digits). But there are clearly many alternative ways of doing this. The alphabet might have been divided successively into two parts, represented by a 1 and a 0, in different ways. One way, however, will give H_{max}, and will render the frequencies of the 1 and 0 signs equal, on an average, from the source. The method shown in this figure, by successively dividing the set into two groups of equal probability, ensures that this will be the case. With other sets of signs, having different probabilities, this may necessarily be only an approximation.

We have defined the rate of information of a source of signs as $H(i)$ in Eq. 5.8; this was given as minus the expected value (average, over alphabet) of the log probability of the various signs. Its maximum value $H_{\text{max}}(i)$ would be reached if all $p(i)$ were made equal by recoding. But we have not yet defined the information rate of a source of signs having known *transition* probabilities. This may be done on the same basis as before: as minus the expected value of the log probabilities of the various signs of the alphabet. Suppose, for example, that we know not only all the sign probabilities

$p(i)$ but also all the transition probabilities with which any sign j may follow a given sign i; that is, we know all $p(i)$ and all $p_i(j)$. Then at any given instant the last sign i, emitted by the transmitter, is known at the receiver (the channel being noiseless); consequently doubt about the next sign j depends upon the probability $p_i(j)$, not upon $p(j)$. Consequently the relevant "doubt measure" is $-\log p_i(j)$, which must be averaged over all the *digrams* (ij). Thus the information rate of such a redundant source $H_i(j)$ is

$$H_i(j) = -\sum_i \sum_j p(i,j) \log p_i(j)$$
$$= -\sum_i \sum_j p(i)p_i(j) \log p_i(j) \text{ bits per sign} \qquad (5.12)$$

Similarly the information rate $H_{ij}(k)$ may be calculated for a source having a known trigram structure; and so on.

Shannon has estimated the redundancy of English,[294] on a letter basis, from the published data[273] on letter frequencies, and digram and trigram transitions $p_i(j)$, $p_{ij}(k)$ [tables of higher n-grams are not available]. He gives the following figures: $H(i) = 4.14$, $H_i(j) = 3.56$, and $H_{ij}(k) = 3.3$ bits per letter. A 26-letter alphabet is used, with the word space ignored. He gives figures also for 26 letters and space, and for the information rate on a *word* basis,[85] together with an interesting experimental method of estimating rates with higher-order transition constraints (see Chapter 3, Section 6.3), showing that the information rate tends toward a limit of roughly 1.5 bits per letter.

On the other hand, suppose we know not the transition but the *joint* probabilities of adjacent pairs of signs $p(i,j)$, ranging over all signs of the source alphabet. Then the receiver's doubt about each arriving digram (ij) depends upon $\log p(i,j)$. It is as though the alphabet was considered to be rewritten as a digram alphabet, from which the source selects digrams. The information rate, relative to *a priori* knowledge of this kind, is:

$$H(i,j) = -\sum_i \sum_j p(i,j) \log p(i,j) \text{ bits per sign} \qquad (5.13)$$

4.2. REDUNDANCY: ITS FUNCTION IN CORRECTING ERRORS

"Redundancy" may be said to be due to an additional set of rules, whereby it becomes increasingly difficult to make an undetectable mistake. The term therefore is rather a misnomer, for it may be a valuable property of a source of information. If a source has zero redundancy, then any errors in transmission and reception, owing to disturbances or noise, will cause the receiver to make an uncorrectable and unidentifiable mistake.

Redundancy may be contributed in many ways; different kinds of determinate or statistical rules may be used. In human languages, such rules constitute *syntax*, where "rules" may better be called "habits," for none are inviolate (see Chapter 3, Section 6).   But with codes or invented sign systems, regular rules may be introduced.   All redundancy is, in effect, a form of addition; a larger number of instructions are sent than are barely necessary.   The simplest form of addition is plain repetition of each sign n times (hoping to be right more often than wrong), though this is not very efficient.   From a non-redundant source of, say, independent and equi-probable letters, any specified sequence of letters must be capable of occurring; none are "forbidden."   But in the English language, for example, with its 26 letters, there are many sequences which virtually never occur.   If you were to receive the following telegram, you would have no difficulty in correcting the "obvious" mistakes:

BEST WISHES FOR VERY HAPPP BIRTFDAY

because sequences such as HAPPP do not occur in the language.   By virtue of redundancy, messages may become changed by errors into some-thing *more* improbable.   Similarly with speech; speech sounds appear only in certain sequences, in language, so that extraneous noises superpose and convert the sounds into something the listener knows to be most im-probable.   He detects a mistake and asks the speaker to repeat.   If the extraneous noise, by chance, converts a sequence into something resembling a true speech sequence, the listener may mishear.   But speech perception raises other problems far beyond such simple illustrations, which we shall discuss in Chapter 7.

It will suffice here to give one elementary method of adding redundancy to coded signals, and to refer the reader to more advanced treatments of the subject of *noise-combating* codes.   Depending upon the type of noise, and the type of channel, redundancy is best added in different ways; but the whole subject is very difficult.[D,131,142,381,387,*]   Shannon has indicated a general technique of *coding* messages in advantageous ways, for combating noise, that is more subtle than mere repetition of every transmitted sign.[D]

When messages, originally expressed by some form of signs (such as the letters of printed texts), are transformed into another set of signs, in a way agreed upon between the transmitter and the receiver, and such that they may be unambiguously transformed back again, they are said to be *coded*. When transformed into code groups containing only two distinct signs, they are said to be in *binary code*.   This code, which we have seen is of basic interest, is illustrated by a simple example in Fig. 5.2.   Here, the alphabet of eight letters $ABC\cdots H$ can be expressed alternatively by *yes, no* or 1, 0 digits before being signaled to a receiver, who may recover the letters un-ambiguously.   In this example, the various 1, 0 groups, corresponding to

* See also Laemmel in reference 166.

each letter, differ from one another by one digit only; thus, any error, resulting in the conversion of a 1 into a 0, or vice versa, causes an undetectable mistake in decoding of the received letter.   But suppose we add one redundant digit to each group, as follows:

Letters		Code Groups		Letters		Code Groups	
A	$=$	1111		E	$=$	0110	
B	$=$	1100		F	$=$	0101	
C	$=$	1010		G	$=$	0011	(5.14)
D	$=$	1001		H	$=$	0000	

On inspection, it will be seen that such code groups enable *one* single mistake, in any 1, 0 digit, to be detected (but not corrected).   For instance, the group 1111, for A, might be converted to any of the following, by noise: 1110, 1101, 1011, 0111, none of which appear in the code.   With this redundancy, one digit error per letter is detectable, but not correctable; thus, the group 1110 could be produced either by a single error in the code for A, for B, for C, or for E.

To give greater safeguard against error, further redundant digits could be added, making the set of code groups differ, one from another, by as many 1, 0 digits as possible.   We may regard this as seeking to place the code groups as "far apart" from one another as can be, where "far apart" means a distance in a code hyperspace.   To visualize this, we must reduce the space to two or three dimensions, so that we can draw it.   Taking an alphabet of four letters only we can code this as follows:

$$A = 11 \qquad C = 01$$
$$B = 10 \qquad D = 00 \qquad (5.15)$$

Each code group here has only two digits to be chosen and so may be represented by a diagram in two dimensions.   Figure 5.6(a) shows two axes, representing the first and second digit, so that the four code groups may be placed at the four corners of a square.   Moving parallel to the vertical axis changes the first digit, or parallel to the horizontal axis, the second digit.   Only four distinct code groups are possible, given by Eq. 5.15, and, of these, those at the ends of either diagonal of the square are "farthest apart."   Figure 5.6(b) shows the similar case with three digits to be chosen; here eight code groups exist (corresponding to Fig. 5.2), and four which are mutually "farthest" part are shown with asterisks, lying at the corners of a tetrahedron.   Alternatively, the four without asterisks have the identical property.

This process may be carried into spaces of m dimensions, in which the code groups each have m binary (1, 0) digits. The complete set of distinct code groups would then possess 2^m members, which might be used to encode an alphabet of 2^m signs (e.g., letters), but with no chance of detecting errors. Out of this set, a number N could be selected so as to differ from one another by at least d digits. The problem is then to choose these in such a way as to maximize the number N for use as code groups.[131,142,*]

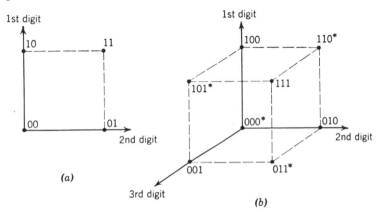

Fig. 5.6.   Binary coding: (a) with two and (b) with three degrees of freedom.

(*Postcript:* The question is often asked during student lectures on communication theory: If a million copies of a newspaper are printed, is the information content increased a millionfold? The answer is that, should any one person (a "receiver") read them all, a millionfold *redundancy* would exist!)

5. MESSAGES REPRESENTED AS WAVE FORMS: "CONTINUOUS" INFORMATION

Let us now glance at a few aspects of signal wave forms, such as those of speech, rather than sequences of discrete signs, such as letters. Notice there are two ways of regarding a source of speech; we could imagine, say, speech reduced to phonetic symbols and these treated as a finite alphabet of signs or, rather more naturally, we could treat the raw speech wave forms as the communication medium. Then, in such cases, what are the "signs"? It is here that the Sampling Theorem comes to our aid (as discussed in Section 2.5 of Chapter 4). If the bandwidth of the wave-form source is restricted to any value, F cycles per second, chosen arbitrarily or by practical considerations, then the wave forms are specified completely

* See also Laemmel in reference 166.

by the values of their ordinates spaced apart along the time scale by intervals of $1/2F$ seconds (the time origin may be chosen arbitrarily). Figure 5.3 illustrates a sampled wave form. Logically speaking, *there is no need to consider "continuous" wave forms at all in signal analysis.*[122] "Continuous" functions are the creation of mathematicians.[266] But, as we have argued before, all *observable* signals must be observed through some *finite* bandwidth F, however large. Then such signals are *completely* represented by discrete data, 2F per sec.* Mathematicians deal with mental *constructs*, not with description of physical situations. A "continuous" function is not a physical idea but a mathematical one; when solving problems in physics (or applied mathematics), such an idea need not be regarded as holy, as sometimes seems to be the case.†

Communication sources, such as telephones, are sometimes referred to as *continuous sources*. This, however, is not because wave forms are "continuous functions of time," $s(t)$, but rather because the successive independent sample ordinates $s(\tau_1)$, $s(\tau_2)$, et cetera, may have a continuous range of amplitudes; an ensemble of such wave forms (or their sample ordinate sequences) may have a continuous *amplitude distribution*.‡ Against this, it could be objected that amplitude quantization is a necessity, since the wave forms represent physical observations of signals; but to take refuge in this idea, and so make wave-form sources similar to sources of discrete signs (Fig. 5.3) is, although quite justifiable, rather distasteful to people whose interest is primarily mathematical. For the smaller we make the amplitude quantum Δs, the greater the number of alternatives in the "alphabet" of ordinate amplitudes, and so the greater the information content contributed by the selection of any one of them. Then, as $\Delta s \to 0$, in this limit, does the information rate of such a source become infinite? This is an interesting theoretical point (entirely theoretical), which we shall discuss shortly (Section 6).

5.1. The idea of "statistical matching"

Wave-form analysis concerns signals as *signs*, their properties, and relations between them. It is really, then, a "syntactic" study.§ But there

---

* For example, see reference 333. Tustin denoted a sequence of wave-form ordinates by a sequence of numbers, representing their amplitudes; he then determined the rules for addition and multiplication of such *time series*.

† All applied mathematics is necessarily approximate, of course, because we cannot describe a physical situation in its entirety. But whether it is the mathematics or the physics which is approximate is not a real question. Rather, we should say that the two can never fit one another perfectly.

‡ However, in practice, such distributions can only be estimated from a *finite* set of observations, as histograms.

§ We shall enlarge upon this notion in the next chapter.

are certain distinctions between sources of wave forms and sources of, say, printed signs, apart from the question of "continuity." One distinction is this: an alphabet of printed signs may be listed in arbitrary order; but the ordinates of wave forms are rank-ordered along a scale of amplitude, or energy. An ordinate having an amplitude $s(t) \pm \Delta s/2$, as in Fig. 5.4, specifies a wave-form sample having an energy proportional to the square of this amplitude, and so the selection of this ordinate, by the source, requires that this energy be supplied. Sources of information emitting wave forms require supplies of power, and any limitation set to the value of this power imposes a constraint upon the source. Such limitation may be set in several ways; frequently it is set as a fixed mean value (Chapter 4, Section 2) and sometimes as a peak value or as a maximum wave-form ordinate magnitude. Different types of telecommunication channel use different systems of modulation, and these, in turn, impose different types of power constraint. The power of wave-form transmitters must always be limited to a finite value.

We have now mentioned a few constraints which practical telecommunication channels impose upon the signals they transmit. In particular, they restrict the *bandwidth* (and hence the number of independent ordinates per second) and the *power*; again, the source itself, prior to encoding, possesses a certain statistical structure. A further constraint is imposed by the unwanted physical disturbances termed "noise," which must always exist, to some extent. We shall return to this subject in Sec. 6. Such constraints demand that, for efficient transmission, a source of information should be *statistically matched* to the physical channel, for transmission.[D]

This concept of statistical matching in communication theory is extremely important because it gives an exact mathematical formulation to what is otherwise a mere analogy to a universal principle of human behavior. When carrying out any goal-seeking task, the way in which this task is organized will depend upon the constraints imposed—that is, upon the individual's freedom of action. The achieving of some optimum result depends upon organization of the task, while keeping within the limits imposed. The key word here is *organize*. The encoding of messages is a process of organization, converting or transforming messages from one sign representation into another, possibly more suited to the type of communication channel employed; and the channel may impose constraints of bandwidth, or of power, (and, as we see later, noise) which determine how this encoding should best be done.

To give a simple human illustration, when I send a telegram in Britain, I am charged so many pence per word; therefore I express ("represent") my messages in certain preferred ways, omitting prepositions, et cetera, and choosing subtle words. The statistics of my language become changed.

On the other hand, when I talk to young children I am constrained to use words of one syllable, though perhaps many more of them than I would use for an adult. So the statistics are again altered. All such constraints of the channel, then, determine a preferred statistical structure for the transmitted signals. But such examples are very vague. In communication theory, this idea is given exact mathematical expression, in terms of the encoding of messages so as to *match* the physical constraints of the channel of transmission. For example, suppose a source selects messages which are represented by an alphabet of printed letters; then, as we saw before, the greatest rate of transmission (in this medium of *print*) is achieved when the letters are statistically independent and equally probable. But suppose we wish to transmit these printed messages over a telegraph channel; then the letters should be encoded into electrical signals, such that they use the limited available electric power of the telegraph channel in a most efficient manner. "Most efficient" here means that, with the given power, the electric signals shall be able to convey information at the greatest possible rate. Now the coded messages may be represented as electric wave forms in many ways; two in particular we have already illustrated, namely (a) simple amplitude variation (Fig. 5.3), in which the amplitude of any ordinate represents a sign, and (b) pulse-code modulation (Fig. 5.4), in which all the electric pulses are identical in amplitude. And it may be shown that in the former case, with the assumption that the *mean* signal power is fixed, the greatest information rate is achieved if the messages be so coded that the transmitted wave-form ordinates are statistically independent and approximate to a *Gaussian* amplitude probability distribution.[D] Briefly, in the case of a source of *printed* letters (no power consideration), the information rate is greatest when the letters are equi-probable and independent; but in the case of messages represented as bandwidth-limited wave forms, with the *mean* power limited to P_{avg}, then the maximum rate is reached with a Gaussian* amplitude distribution:

$$\sigma \cdot P\left(\frac{s}{\sigma}\right) = \frac{1}{\sqrt{2\pi}} \, \epsilon^{-s^2/2\sigma^2} \tag{5.16}$$

where $\sigma^2 = P_{avg}$, the mean power. This equation gives the probability density of s, the wave-form ordinate amplitudes, relative to their root-mean-square value σ. Here σ^2 is also called the *variance* of this bell-shaped distribution (Fig. 5.7), and it is a normalizing factor of the curve.

But this way of discussing sources of messages represented as wave forms is not wholly satisfactory. We have imagined the wave-form ordinates to be quantized into a finite number of states, possibly quite large.

---

* Sometimes called Normal Density Function (see reference E for tables), as illustrated by Fig. 5.7.

But we have so far avoided this question of a *continuous* range of amplitudes, which would seem to result in the possibility of an infinite rate of communication of information. There are certain essential distinctions between such continuous sources and discrete-sign sources. In particular, information rate can only be considered to be relative, not absolute; again, continuous sources cannot readily be discussed in a practical way unless, at the same time, *noise* be taken into account. Noise is the ultimate limiter of information rate, or capacity; it always exists in physical channels, so that infinite rates are never achieved. Let us now look at the problem of continuous sources in a slightly different way.

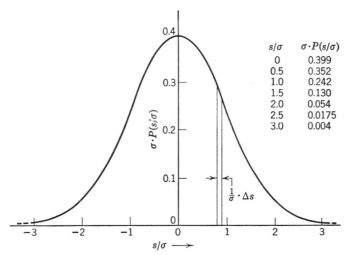

s/σ	$\sigma \cdot P(s/\sigma)$
0	0.399
0.5	0.352
1.0	0.242
1.5	0.130
2.0	0.054
2.5	0.0175
3.0	0.004

Fig. 5.7.   The Gaussian, or Normal Density Function $P\left(\dfrac{s}{\sigma}\right)$

(area lying under this curve is unity).

5.2 SOURCES OF WAVE FORMS: TIME AVERAGES AND ENSEMBLE AVERAGES

We shall now consider "continuous" sources of signals as *wave forms* having a bandwidth F cycles per second. Such wave forms may be represented completely by a series of ordinates spaced apart by $1/2F$ seconds (as in Fig. 5.3). It should be appreciated that only this *spacing* is of consequence, and the time origin of the samples is empirical. True, if a different set of points be chosen, also spaced by $1/2F$ seconds, then a different set of ordinates will result; but these will be related to the first set by transformation equations. However, if *any* sequence of ordinates be chosen, equally spaced by $1/2F$ seconds, they will specify the wave form completely.

Given the arbitrarily chosen time origin, $t = 0$ at the position of any one ordinate, the nth ordinate from this in the positive time direction will mark the instant $t = n/2F$ or, in the negative direction $t = -n/2F$.   The wave form $s(t)$ is then represented by the summation of the sequence of *interpolation functions* of sin x/x form (Eq. 4.16), having amplitudes given by these sample ordinates, as illustrated by Fig. 4.7(b).   That is:

$$s(t) = \sum_{-\infty}^{+\infty} s\left(\frac{n}{2F}\right) \frac{\sin 2\pi F\left(t - \dfrac{n}{2F}\right)}{2\pi F\left(t - \dfrac{n}{2F}\right)} \tag{5.17}$$

Here we are imagining the wave form of the source output to have unlimited duration.   If this duration is limited to a time T, then n will range over the values $1, 2, \cdots, 2FT$.   This equation, 5.17, represents the set of all the possible wave forms which can be emitted by this band-limited source.

Since a set of discrete ordinates completely defines the signal wave form $s(t)$, we should expect to be able to express all the various statistical properties of the signal in terms only of these ordinates.   "Statistics" are "averages"; and there are two distinct ways whereby such statistical parameters may be specified.   The two ways, which, in certain important cases, become equivalent, are illustrated by Fig. 5.8; let us take them in turn.

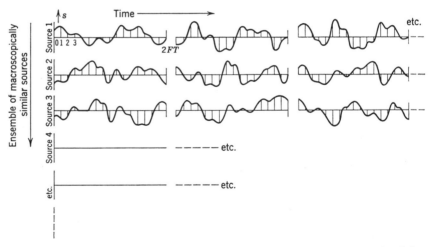

Fig. 5.8.   Time-average and (source) ensemble-average statistics.   For simplicity, we show relatively short durations T here, representing few degrees of freedom $2FT$ for the wave forms.

5.2.1. "Time-average" source statistics.   Figure 5.8 illustrates typical wave-form segments (each of duration T seconds) from a number of different sources—source 1, source 2, et cetera.   We shall be regarding Fig. 5.8 horizontally first.   Consider the output of one particular source (say source 1) to be segmented into a set of (wave-form) signals *each* of duration T, as shown; we shall assume that T is a very long time, so that each of these signals will have a large number of degrees of freedom $2FT$. Any one wave form is uniquely specified by the values of the $2FT$ equally spaced ordinates, so that, starting with the first ordinate of each or any of these wave forms, we may label the successive ordinates, as before, 0, 1, 2, $\cdots$, n, $\cdots$, $2FT$ and refer to their amplitudes as $s_1 s_2 \cdots s_n \cdots s_{2FT}$ (rather than the $s(n/2F)$ notation used in Eq. 5.17).

This set of band-limited wave forms, all of duration T, may be considered to represent alternative messages which the source may select, just as we earlier spoke of a course as selecting from alternative long sequences of printed signs (Section 3.2.1). Again, analogous to the discrete case, we may speak of this set of wave forms as a band-limited *ensemble*, defined by a probability distribution $p(s_n)$ where

$$p(s_n) = p(s_1 s_2 \cdots s_n \cdots s_{2FT}) \tag{5.18}$$

As distinct from the discrete case, this is here assumed a continuous distribution since the various s_n may have *any* values. The source of information may now be said to exert its selective action upon this continuous ensemble of wave forms. The total probability must be unity; hence the constraint, or *normalizing* condition:

$$\int\int \cdots \int p(s_1 s_2 \cdots s_n \cdots s_{2FT}) ds_1 ds_2 \cdots ds_{2FT} = 1 \tag{5.19}$$

In the case of discrete letters, a definite numerical value may be estimated for the probability (relative frequency) of any letter in the alphabet or set. But now we are speaking of continuous distributions and so we can consider only *probability densities*. As an everyday illustration of a density, we cannot speak of the probability of "a man's being exactly h feet tall in Britain"— we must consider a small interval of height, Δh, and speak of the probability of height lying between h and $(h + \Delta h)$. Figure 5.7 shows the very important type of density function—the Gaussian, or Normal (having here only a single variate s) and a typical interval $(1/\sigma)\Delta s$ is marked. The area of this thin slice, $p(s/\sigma) \cdot \Delta s$ has a definite probability value, inasmuch as it is a definite fraction of the *total* area lying under the distribution curve, which is unity. But the mean ordinate of this slice $\sigma \cdot p(s/\sigma)$ is not a probability, being a probability *density*. Similarity $p(s_n)$ in Eq. 5.18 is a probability density, whilst the

$$p(s_1 s_2 \cdots s_{2FT}) ds_1 ds_2 \cdots ds_{2FT}$$

in Eq. 5.19 is a probability.

Statistics relating to such ensembles are *time averages*; we have taken the set of all possible wave forms, having duration T and hence $2FT$ degrees of freedom, emitted from one particular source at different times.

Consequently, such a method of averaging is suited only to stationary sources; for only if the statistics remain unchanging with time can we assess them usefully from wave forms emitted at different times.

As we saw to be true of the case of a source of discrete signs (Section 2.2), the information rate of a continuous source should also be regarded as an *average* rate—averaged over long sequences of ordinates. On such a basis, the information rate may be expressed as the minimum number of *yes, no* instructions required to select the wave forms from the ensemble. In this case of a continuous source, the wave forms constituting the ensemble must have a large number of degrees of freedom $2FT$; that is, their duration T must be long. The root reason for the requirement arises from the Law of Large Numbers,[E] which concerns a deceptive point about our intuitive notions of a probability as a relative frequency. Briefly, it is this. Imagine a source of wave forms, quantized in amplitude into intervals Δs which may be made very small (Fig. 5.3, for example, though Δs is a coarse quantizing there). Then, over a very long time T, the fractions of the total number of ordinates $2FT$ which fall into these various quantum levels constitute an estimate of the amplitude probability distribution. The "true probabilities" are never attainable by real-life experiments, however small the quantum intervals Δs, but represent tendencies, or mathematical limits.* For consider what wave forms *might* occur from a sequence of $2FT$ ordinates, on the assumption that there is no mutual influence between successive ordinates (that is, if they are independent events). From a sequence of $2FT$ ordinates, quantized into N levels, we can generate N^{2FT} different possible wave forms, as was emphasized in Hartley's theory (Section 2). Any sequence of ordinate amplitudes *might* occur, to constitute a wave form. It is conceivable, for instance, that a wave form might occur for which the whole sequence of $2FT$ ordinates had equal amplitudes, or even zero amplitudes; then we should say that these were not "typical wave forms" of the source. (Again, when playing cards, you have no reason to be surprised if, one day, you draw a complete hand of spades! Such a hand is just as possible as any other *stated* hand; but it is "not typical"; a "typical" hand would contain some hearts, clubs, diamonds, and spades.) In the case of our source of wave forms, suppose we actually observe it for a long time T and make an estimate of the amplitude distribution; if a second sample, also of duration T, be observed, another estimate may be made, and a third, fourth, and so on. These different estimates, made from successive

---

* It is legitimate to question whether in fact these limits exist, or whether they are merely assumed to, as a postulate. See reference 206 for a popular discussion.

wave forms of duration T, will *fluctuate* about a mean distribution. The Law of Large Numbers states the mathematical fact that the longer the sample duration T (i.e., the greater $2FT$), the greater will be the fraction of these wave forms having amplitude distributions lying very close to the "true" probability values. That is to say, non-typical wave forms will become relatively rarer. But it is important to appreciate that non-typical ones *can* occur; they merely have, by chance, fluctuations very wide of the statistical mark.[E]

5.2.2. "ENSEMBLE AVERAGES." The classical theory of communication, as developed mainly by Shannon, was concerned with *stationary* sources.[D] It was intended for application to problems arising in the telecommunication engineer's field—to telephone systems, telegraphs, television, and other systems—together with certain analogous problems in cryptography.[293] In such systems the assumption of stationariness is not a severe limitation.

But there are certain problems (some of which arise in the engineering field too) in which the changes of the signal statistics, as time passes, are of particular interest. The communication theory of learning sources would be one case, for example, but so far as your author knows, little such theory has yet been presented.[122] Various social studies, too, such as economics and population trends, are often concerned with non-stationary statistics. Changes in the statistical structure of a system are brought about by macroscopic changes in the physical controlling factors; in the social field, the distribution of wealth may suddenly be changed by a war, a revolution, or a new system of taxation; in physics, the velocity distribution of the particles of a body of gas will be changed by application of a source of heat. But always, when dealing with the question of the relative stationariness of statistics, the time scale should be borne in mind, for all fluctuations may be smoothed out if a sufficiently long averaging time be taken. The longer this time, the more detail will be lost concerning shifts and changes taking place as the controlling factors vary.

In cases of non-stationary sources of information, time averaging cannot be used, because the estimates of the source statistics, made from successive sequences of $2FT$ wave-form ordinates, would show a steady change, the origins of these successive sequences being at different instants $0, T, 2T, \cdots$, et cetera, on the time axis. However, it can be appropriate and often very useful to replace this concept by that of an *ensemble average*.[B,79] For this purpose we regard Fig. 5.8 vertically, and imagine a large number of similar sources, all operating under identical macroscopic physical controlling conditions. The sources are not microscopically *identical*, but each emits its own wave forms or time sequences of ordinates. These sources all experience the same changes in the physical controlling conditions as time passes if, in fact, such changes occur to cause non-stationariness.   If we label the successive sample ordinates as the 1st, 2nd, $\cdots$, nth, $\cdots$, et cetera, then an *ensemble average* may be taken over *each* of these; for example, taking the nth ordinates of the (simultaneous) wave forms of all these sources, various statistical parameters may be estimated from that collection of data. The sources being non-stationary in time, the statistics relating to the 1st, 2nd, $\cdots$, nth, $\cdots$, ordinates will in general change.   Ensemble averaging is extremely useful in non-stationary system study.

It should be clear that, in stationary examples, time averaging and ensemble averaging give like results; for the successive sequences of duration T, emitted by a particular source, might well have been emitted by a succession of sources, if operating under identical macroscopic controlling conditions.   But in non-stationary cases the results will, in general, differ. These ideas are equally relevant to sources possessing redundancy, which show definite probability constraints between successive ordinates, provided that such interordinate influences extend over relatively short sequences only.

6. COMMUNICATION OF INFORMATION, WHEN NOISE IS PRESENT

The remainder of this chapter will be devoted to a barest sketch of the main concepts of the statistical theory of communication when noise is present.   This condition more closely approaches reality than the ideal "noiseless" conditions assumed hitherto.   We shall discuss in particular the concepts of "information rate," "channel capacity," and "equivocation."   These concepts are not easy to acquire, nor simple to apply correctly.   They are essentially mathematical and, what is most important, they are primarily of application to certain technical problems (mainly in telecommunication) under clearly defined conditions.   It is only too easy and tempting to use these terms vaguely and descriptively, especially in relation to human communication—"by analogy."   The concepts and the methods of communication theory demand strict discipline in their use.

6.1. Noise, disturbances, cross-talk: the ultimate limitations to communication

In real life, all communication signals are subject to disturbances, usually beyond the control of the transmitter or of the receiver.   The theory as treated so far has assumed that no disturbances are present; the source selects messages, and transmits signals, which are received without error, enabling the receiver to make an identical set of selections from his ensemble.   No question of mistakes in reception arises, for no causes have yet been cited.

Disturbances may take on many forms in practical channels.   In radio reception there may be the sporadic impulsive noise of "atmospherics"; on the telephone, there may be similar crackling and hissing noises, owing to electric disturbances; a television picture may occasionally be spoiled by a splash of white dots, caused by motor-car ignition systems.   There is another kind of noise of a somewhat different nature, often called "cross-talk," which can arise on faulty telephone lines, resulting in a third voice's breaking in upon the conversation.   In a sense, conversation with a friend at a noisy party provides an example of a speech channel subjected to disturbance by the cross-talk of other people's speech.   Cross-talk is one type of noise of particular importance; it may be specified statistically by a set of parameters in a manner similar to that for a wanted speech source.

But there is one other class of noise of outstanding interest, which has received great attention from mathematicians and physicians, often called *Gaussian noise*; it is produced by the random superposition of a great number of independent causes.   Historically, the first random source of this kind to be studied was the so-called "Brownian motion."   In 1827 Robert Brown,[76] an English botanist, saw through his microscope the rapid and apparently random motions of minute colloidal particles suspended in a liquid—haphazard movements due to chance collisions with the liquid molecules.   Figure 5.9 illustrates a part of a typical path taken by one particle, a path such as Brown himself and others since have tried to trace.

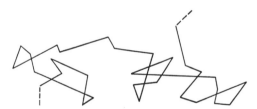

Fig. 5.9.   "Brownian" (random) motion.

If such a path be observed for a long time (i.e., many collisions), it is found that *all* directions are equally probable.   We cannot predict and control such movements in detail, mainly because we can never know the exact positions, directions, and speeds of all the molecules at any instant of time— for there are far too many. But, fortunately, it is possible to describe and predict the motions statistically—that is, on a long-term average.[133,360] The appropriate mathematical method to be applied to such problems, involving enormous numbers of variables which can never be known in detail (microscopically) but only statistically (macroscopically), is not simple mechanics but statistical mechanics.[B]

Similar random motions arise among the electrons in all electrical conductors, in telephones, in radio receivers, and in all telecommunication apparatus, and give rise to the phenomenon of random Gaussian noise. Such random disturbing signals always exist, in varying degrees of magnitude, and are microscopically unpredictable and so cannot be allowed for nor annulled.   Such noise is the ultimate limiter of the fineness with which wave-form ordinates may be effectively quantized, Δs, and is the ultimate limiter of the information capacity of a telecommunication channel—the ultimate limit set by Nature.

A source of such Gaussian noise may be observed and its statistical parameters specified, like any other source of noise, or source of information. The noise disturbing a wanted source of information may either depend upon this source itself or not.   Thus, statistical dependency might be the consequence of some physical control exerted by the signal transmitter upon the source of noise.   The theory of communication has so far been applied, almost entirely, to cases in which the information source and the noise source are completely independent, and the source signals and noise are simply added; any knowledge of the information source, or signals received from it, can give no information about the moment-by-moment noise values.   However, communication theory demonstrates the surprising fact that, solely from knowledge of the statistical parameters of the noise source, the *average* rate of loss of information may be determined.[D]

Figure 5.10 illustrates a source of information selecting messages, which are encoded and transmitted as physical signals, perhaps as wave forms. To these signals noise disturbances are directly added, before they reach the receiver.   The receiver has no means of knowing by how much the true

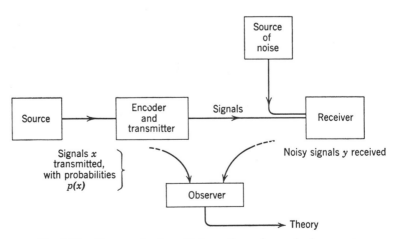

Fig. 5.10.   Communication of information, when noise is present.

signals are perturbed, moment by moment, by this noise. The received noisy signals will consist then of two parts: first, that part representing the (wanted) *yes, no* instructions from the selective actions of the message source; and, second, that part embodying *bogus* instructions from the noise source which is making its own selections from its ensemble of random functions. These bogus instructions interfere with those from the message source and destroy information at a definite rate. The noise source thus *increases* the receiver's doubt, and we may regard it as possessing a certain rate of destruction of information ("negative information").

But we have not, as yet, considered how to specify the information rate of a continuous source; let us do this now and show that, if noise be included, this rate cannot be infinite as seemed to be the case from our earlier arguments (Section 5).

6.2 THE WEIGHING OF EVIDENCE AND FORMATION OF VERDICTS

When noise disturbs the signals, the instructions which they embody to the receiver, to select messages from his ensemble, are not complete, perfect, or definite. The situation is then not one of precise cause and effect, but rather one of effect and *probable* cause. The received noisy signals do not completely represent the messages from the source but constitute only evidence of those messages. The receiver can, at best, weigh this evidence in the light of all the past (*a priori*) knowledge he possesses and make a verdict—his verdict or *decision* being the "best guess" about the transmitted message. And, as with all verdicts based upon limited evidence, this "guess" may be wrong.

That is the logic of the situation, and it may be described mathematically. The process of communication in the presence of noise is essentially one of inference and the appropriate description of the situation is given by Bayes's theorem, which we briefly discussed earlier.*

Call the transmitted signal x and the corresponding received signal y. Then y differs from x, for it has noise in addition, or in combination in some way. The receiver's problem is to extract, from his received signal y, all the possible information about the transmitted signal x (and hence about the message represented by x), and to reject the inherent "bogus information" about the noise source.

Imagine y to be some noisy signal, received on some one specific occasion. Before that moment the receiver's doubt about what signal *might* be sent depends upon the transmitter ensemble probabilities $p(x)$ (so-called *a priori* probabilities). On receiving y he possesses this as *evidence*

* The suggestion that this approach might be appropriate and useful seems to have been made independently by Woodward and Davies, 1950 (reference 361), and by Cherry, 1950 (reference 59).

concerning the actual transmitted x; his doubt is now represented by a new distribution $p(x/y)$, being the probability that any x was sent, when the particular y is received* (so called *a posteriori* probabilities). Then if $p(x|y)$ can be determined by the receiver, the whole of the information about x, contained in the noisy signal y, will be extracted.†

This process represents the "weighing of the evidence," but does not touch upon the verdict. That is, the process of finding the *a posteriori* distribution $p(x|y)$ does not extract the actual message. The verdict, or "best judgment" as to the actual message, is arrived at after consideration of $p(x|y)$, but, as we shall see later, the receiver does not necessarily choose the maximum value of this function (the most likely message x).

If the logarithmic measure be used, as before, then the gain in information, on receiving y, may be expressed:

$$\left.\begin{array}{c}\text{Information content}\\\text{of a received signal } y\end{array}\right\} = I_y = \log \frac{p(x|y)}{p(x)} \qquad (5.20)$$

The following calculation is carried out in the meta-language of our *external* observer (Fig. 5.10) and not in that of a human transmitter or receiver (participant). Let $p(x, y)$ be the probability (or density if x and y are continuous) of the joint event: x transmitted, y received. From the product law:

$$p(x, y) = p(x)p(y|x) = p(y)p(x|y) \qquad (5.21)$$

so that the required distribution:

$$p(x|y) = \frac{p(x)}{p(y)} \cdot p(y|x) \qquad (5.22)$$

However, since y is some one definite received signal, $p(y)$ is known numerically, as a constant $1/K$, which is given by the condition that $\sum_x p(x|y) = 1$ as we shall see by example. Then

$$p(x|y) = K \cdot p(x) \cdot p(y|x) \qquad (5.23)$$

* We use a different notation now for conditional probability because $p_y(x)$, etc., was used before for the special case of *transition* probabilities.

† See Chapter 6 of reference 136, on rational decisions, for general mathematical treatment of Bayes's theorem and of its use for the weighing of evidence. Dr. Good discusses the general problem in a way immediately interpretable in terms of our message extraction problem here.

The reader may ask: "How does the receiver assess the transmitter ensemble probabilities $p(x)$ if he never has (noise-free) access to the transmitter? Surely, his prior doubt can depend only upon the probabilities of his own received message ensemble as gathered from his own past experience and decisions concerning the messages?" The answer is that the theory is expressed in the meta-language of an external observer [Fig. 3.2(*a*)], and it assumes the ensemble at both ends to be known.

As a simple illustration, there is no better example than that given by Woodward.* Suppose it rains four days out of seven and that, when it rains, the barometer is low three times out of four whilst, when it is fine, the barometer is high two times in three. One day the barometer is high; what will the weather be?

Here the barometer is giving *evidence* of the weather, not an absolute indication. If F = Fine, R = Rain, whilst H = High, L = Low, we may represent the problem as a set of equally likely possibilities, thus:

$$\begin{cases} R\ R\ R\ R\ F\ F\ F \\ L\ L\ \underbrace{L{\downarrow}H\ H\ H}{\downarrow}L \end{cases} \quad \begin{array}{l} [p(R) = \tfrac{4}{7}; p(F) = \tfrac{3}{7}] \\ [p(L|R) = \tfrac{3}{4}; p(H|F) = \tfrac{2}{3}] \end{array} \quad (5.24)$$

From inspection we see that $p(F|H) = \tfrac{2}{3}$, $p(R|H) = \tfrac{1}{3}$ is the required answer—the chances of fine or rainy weather when the barometer is high.

This method of enumeration is a much more self-evident demonstration of inverse probability than is direct appeal to the Eq. 5.23. However, we might instead have substituted there, giving:

$$\begin{aligned} p(R|H) &= K{\cdot}p(R){\cdot}p(H|R) = K{\cdot}\tfrac{4}{7}{\cdot}\tfrac{1}{4} \\ p(F|H) &= K{\cdot}p(F){\cdot}p(H|F) = K{\cdot}\tfrac{3}{7}{\cdot}\tfrac{2}{3} \end{aligned} \Bigg\} \quad (5.25)$$

where $K = 1/p(H)$ and is given by the condition $p(R|H) + p(F|H) = 1$, so that $K = \tfrac{7}{3}$, which is obvious also from inspection of Eq. 5.24.

This simple example illustrates one further important point, namely that $p(y|x)$ is not really a probability density (or relative frequency) at all, because the y is one received signal (or evidence) on this one particular occasion. It has a definite value. In our example the barometer was reading high (H) on that occasion. Then $p(H|F)$ and $p(H|R)$ are really *likelihoods* of fine or rain on that specific occasion. Then, in general, $p(y|x)$ is a likelihood function of x, written $L(x)$:

$$p(y|x) = L(x) \quad \text{a likelihood function} \quad (5.26)$$

The method of enumeration, represented by Eq. 5.24, clearly shows the relations between the *a priori* probabilities $p(x)$, the *a posteriori* probabilities $p(x|y)$, and the likelihood function $L(x)$, as in Eq. 5.23. In words, we may describe these functions thus:

$p(x)$ is the probability of message x being sent, assessed from past observations of the transmitter in operation.

$p(x|y)$ is the probability of an x being sent, on those occasions when y is received.

$L(x)$ is the likelihood that, if any particular x *had* been sent, the specific y would be received.

* By kind permission. See page 167 of reference 167.

Then Eq. 5.23 expresses the fact that the probability that a message x has been sent, in the face of some received signal evidence y, is proportional to the likelihood of x, weighted by its prior probability.

6.3. THE AVERAGE INFORMATION RATE OF A CONTINUOUS SOURCE, WHEN NOISE IS PRESENT

So much for the "information content" of a particular received signal y. Let us now consider the regular flow of signals between a transmitter and receiver and, furthermore, go straight to the case of *continuous* signals, having any continuous but bounded range of values.

For example, the signals might be transmitted and received wave forms, having a continuous range of amplitudes between zero and some peak value. The reader will recall that such continuous cases previously led us into difficulties (Section 5), for we saw that if the $\sum$ expression for the rate of information of a discrete source be interpreted as an integral, for a continuous source, the answer was infinity. But we have now included noise, and two statistical sources are at work, one supplying information to the receiver, one destroying it, at different rates.

Rather than write $p(y) = 1/K$, we shall now retain it as $p(y)$ because *all possible* received signal y values must now be considered; it will also be appropriate to retain the form $p(y|x)$ rather than $L(x)$. Putting Equation 5.22 in logarithmic form:[136]

$$- \log p(x) + \log p(x|y) = -\log p(y) + \log p(y|x) \qquad (5.27)$$

Equation 5.22 has expressed the information content of one particular received noisy signal y; to determine the mean rate of information, we must average over all possible x and y. To do this, multiply by the joint-probability density $p(x, y)\, dx\, dy$ and integrate* over the ranges of x and y values.

$$- \int \int p(x, y) \log p(x)\, dx\, dy + \int \int p(x, y) \log p(x|y)\, dx\, dy$$

$$= - \int \int p(x, y) \log p(y)\, dx\, dy + \int \int p(x, y) \log p(y|x)\, dx\, dy \qquad (5.28)$$

Using the product rules, Eq. 5.21, this equation simplifies; thus we may rewrite the different terms in Eq. 5.28 as follows:

$$(a) \qquad - \int \int p(x, y) \log p(x)\, dx\, dy = - \int p(y|x) \int p(x) \log p(x)\, dx\, dy$$

$$= - \int p(x) \log p(x)\, dx = H(x)$$

* For note on this averaging process, see footnote on p. 179.

the information rate of the *ideal*, noiseless source.   This information rate can never be realized through our practical noisy channel; for notice the second term in Eq. 5.28:

(b) $$+ \int \int p(x, y) \log p(x|y) \, dx \, dy = -H(x|y)$$

which represents the average ambiguity, produced by the noise source, in the received signals y; that is, the average rate of production of doubt ("negative information") about what actual x values are transmitted, even when the received signals y are known.

We may write the left-hand side of Equation 5.28 now:

$$H(x) - H(x|y) = R \tag{5.29}$$

the true rate of transmission of information over the noisy channel.   It is the difference of two rates: $H(x)$ is the rate of production of information at the source itself, all of which is not accessible to the receiver because of the inherent effects of noise; it represents the receiver's *a priori* (average) doubt.   Even after receiving the signals y, the *a posteriori* doubt $H(x|y)$ remains, because the noise renders the signals ambiguous.   Thus $H(x|y)$ represents a rate of loss of information, caused by the noise, and it has been termed the channel *equivocation* by Shannon.[D]   Notice that it is distinct from $H(y|x)$, which represents the rate of production of "bogus information" by the noise source as will be shown now.

All these rates have the units of bits per degree of freedom (as was the case for discrete sources), for we may regard the continuous signals as being defined by the values of $2F$ sample ordinates per second.   Thus $2FR$ represents the channel rate, in bits per second.   Once again, this measure of information rate is equivalent to a specification of the minimum number of *yes, no* instructions *about the source* messages conveyed by the noisy signals.

Take now the right-hand side of Equation 5.28.

(c) $$- \int \int p(x, y) \log p(y) \, dx \, dy = - \int p(x|y) \int p(y) \log p(y) \, dx \, dy$$

$$= - \int p(y) \log p(y) \, dy = H(y)$$

which, by analogy with $H(x)$, represents the "information rate" of the received signals y.   But some of this is *bogus* (information about the noise source itself).   The rate of bogus information is:

(d) $$+ \int \int p(x, y) \log p(y|x) \, dx \, dy = -H(y|x)$$

representing, on an average, the doubt about what y will be received, even if the transmitted signals are known anyway. It should be remembered that it is the external observer who assesses these quantities, not the receiver himself.

We have now another, and alternative, expression for the true rate of information:

$$H(y) - H(y|x) = R \tag{5.30}$$

which is similar to Equation 5.29, but with x and y reversed. Again this is the difference of two rates; the rate corresponding to the received signals y, less the "negative" or bogus information rate of the noise source.

The true information rate R is thus, in both forms, given by the *difference* of two integral expressions. It is this fact which renders R finite, although each of the integrals might become infinite. We have not in fact proved here that this difference is finite, but would refer the reader to the original work,[D,*] because our purpose is not to present a condensed version of the theory, but rather to survey and discuss its basis, its objects, and its restrictions.

7. THE ULTIMATE CAPACITY OF A NOISY CHANNEL

Shannon's most important contribution to statistical communication theory is undoubtedly his Capacity Theorem;[D,328] this gives a result which would certainly not be suspected intuitively. It is this: *It is possible to encode a source of messages, having an information rate H, so that information can be transmitted through a noisy channel with an arbitrarily small frequency of errors, up to a certain limiting rate C, called the limiting capacity,* which depends upon the channel constraints (e.g., bandwidth, power restrictions, noise statistics, etc.), provided that $H \leqslant C$.

It might at first be thought that, since noise is present, errors are inevitable; or that perhaps redundancy could be added so as to combat the noise to some extent, but never to remove errors entirely, for this implies that information would be sent with absolute *certainty*, in spite of the unpredictable noise! In fact, any attempt to transmit at a higher rate than C must cause errors; but at any rate below C the errors can be made, in theory, vanishingly few. It is emphasized: *in theory.* For the practical accomplishment of such ideal codes has proved to be of extraordinary

---

* See also reference 133 for a very full discussion of this question. The basic reason why R is finite is that, although both $H(x)$ and $H(x|y)$ have magnitudes which depend upon the co-ordinates of x and y, their *difference* R is invariant under a transformation of these co-ordinates.

difficulty,[D,131,142,328,381,387]* and is somewhat discouraged by the fact that the types of modulation and coding which have been invented already by telecommunication engineers have proved to be remarkably efficient.[252,296]† But the fact that the engineer has "got there first" does not detract one iota from the value of this theorem. Practical accomplishment so frequently precedes theory. The value here lies in the establishment of a *limit* to the capacity; anyone who tries to beat this limit is wasting his time! In this light, the Capacity Theorem is similar to the concept of Absolute Zero of Temperature.

7.1. RECEIVED INFORMATION AND THE EXTRACTION OF MESSAGES

One most significant point about the formulae for the rate of transmission of true information through noisy channels (Eqs. 5.29 and 5.30) is that they are expressed entirely in terms of probability distributions, $\log p(x)$, $\log p(y|x)$, et cetera, or their ensemble averages. The information content of a received signal y has been regarded as the logarithm of the ratio of the posterior to the prior probabilities (Eq. 5.20) of the different possible transmitted signals $x_1 x_2 \cdots x_n \cdots$. But, in practice, communication cannot be said to be established, between a transmitter and a receiver, if the receiver gets nothing but probabilities! A Teletype machine prints definite letters, not probability functions. Nevertheless the production of the posterior function $p(x|y)$ represents the extraction of the information content of the noisy signal y; but, at some stage, one definite value of x must be selected, based on the $p(x|y)$ evidence, as the "best choice" determining the received message.

Curiously enough, the "best choice" need not be the most probable value of x, although in fact it usually is. As I. J. Good has emphasized,‡ this choice may depend upon the future consequences or upon the purposes of the message; more generally, to borrow a term from the economists, the choice depends upon the *utilities* or costs involved.§ Good quotes a most convincing example, drawn from radar (a form of telecommunication very thoroughly treated, from the present point of view, by Woodward[360,362] and by Davies[78]), illustrated by Fig. 5.11. Suppose a radar station is given advance information whenever an enemy aircraft is approaching at a range lying between 100 and 400 miles. The radar receiver problem is to determine the correct range as accurately as possible. The various "possible ranges" now represent messages, x. Before a radar signal is

---

* See also Laemmel in reference 166 and Shannon in reference 167.

† See also Jelonek in reference 166.

‡ See discussion by Good, p. 180 of reference 166.

§ *Utility* is defined as "reasonable measure of value" (e.g., of money). The concept goes back to Bernoulli, in the early history of probability theory and its application to gambling. See p. 52 of reference 136. The word *cost* is also used today.

received, the prior range probability $p(x)$ is assumed uniform between the 100 and 400 mile limits.   Now suppose a noisy radar signal y is received and the complete posterior probability $p(x|y)$ determined, having the form shown in the figure, with a maximum value at range $x = 270$ miles but with a smaller peak at $x = 150$ miles.   The radar operator might nevertheless decide to take action on the basis of the smaller peak at 150 miles, because this represents a more immediate danger.   The rules whereby such *decision criteria* are chosen may be very varied, but, in general, they are all decided upon by quite practical judgments or common sense.   With regard to the practical application of this mathematical Decision Theory, the trouble is often that we cannot attach any numerical values to the various costs (penalties/rewards).   For analytical purposes, we can symbolise them as C_1, C_2, $\cdots$, et cetera, though we cannot necessarily say what are their values.

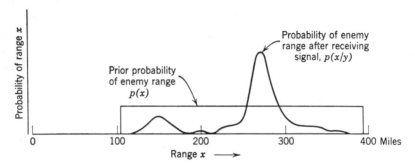

Fig. 5.11.   Measurement of a target range by radar.

The *whole* of the posterior distribution $p(x|y)$ represents information; it represents the receiver's "degree of belief" that any particular range x is the true one.   If one point be chosen as the assumed "true signal x" and the remainder of the curve rejected, then information is thrown away.*   This may be illustrated by the following argument.   Suppose the choice be deferred and a second signal received, for example in this radar case.   Then $p(x|y)$ now becomes the *prior* probability of x, for this second observation.   Suppose the process is continued and a series of consecutive signals are received, $y_1 y_2 \cdots y_r \cdots$, so rapidly that the true x

* This whole question of the determination of the "best" signal x, when noisy signals are received, may be regarded as the testing of statistical hypotheses.   The alternative "hypotheses" are the possible ranges $x_1 x_2 \cdots x_r \cdots$ and the choice of any one carries with it some probability of error.   For discussion of the various types of test, in relation to this problem of signal detection, see Middleton in reference 166.   See also reference 78.

(enemy range) remains substantially constant. Then, from Eqs. 5.23 and 5.26:

After 1st observation $\qquad p(x|y_1) = K_1 p(x) L_1(x)$

After 2nd observation $\qquad p(x|y_1 y_2) = K_2 p(x) L_1(x) L_2(x) \qquad$ (5.31)

After 3rd observation $\qquad p(x|y_1 y_2 y_3) = K_3 p(x) L_1(x) L_2(x) L_3(x)$

and so on.

It will normally happen that the probability curve will become sharper and sharper, centered upon the true x, though this is not inevitable,[360] because the successive true signals will be related whilst the successive noise contributions will be random.

This is similar to adding redundancy at the source by simple repetition of x. However, a radar target is an example of a particularly *unco-operative* source; the enemy does not obligingly code his radar echoes, adding redundancy as required, so as to overcome the noise disturbing the receiver!

In more usual, friendly, telecommunication systems, the transmitter and receiver co-operate. Coding may be designed to include redundancy in the best possible way (as limited in practice by ingenuity and economy) so as to overcome the noise and make easier the receiver's final selection of the "assumed correct signals x" from the posterior distribution $p(x|y)$, and his chances of error fewer. Clearly, then, if ideal coding could be found, it should be such as to reduce $p(x|y)$ to a very sharp, single peak. The selection of the "assumed correct x" would then throw away no information; the signal would be received correctly, with certainty and with no chance of error, in spite of the noise. More specifically, it is the ensemble average of log $p(x|y)$, namely $H(x|y)$ or the equivocation, given by Eq. 5.29, which would be reduced to an arbitrarily small value by ideal coding.[D]

Such ideal coding methods have not been designed and, in practice, they would be unusable, because they would require an indefinitely long postponement of the final identification of the "correct signal." Coding which involves indefinitely long delay is impracticable, and some compromise must be sought.

7.2. STATISTICAL MATCHING OF A SOURCE TO A NOISY CHANNEL

We have already made some preliminary discussion of *statistical matching* of a source to a channel of transmission, in Section 5.1. A channel, such as a telephone or telegraph channel, for example, exerts certain constraints upon the signals it transmits; in particular it restricts the electrical power available, and the bandwidth. In Section 5.1 we referred to the problem of coding the messages from the source in the best way, for transmission, subject to these constraints, where "best way" implied transmission of information at the maximum possible rate.   However, we abandoned our discussion there, when it became clear that factors other than available bandwidth and power determine this maximum rate.   We now see that this new factor is the noise.   The noise also exerts a constraint upon the channel, and the manner of adding redundancy to the, source messages, so as to change their statistical structure in the "best way," depends upon the structure of the noise.

The problem of statistical matching is to find a suitable code for the source such that the ensemble of transmitted signals is given a statistical structure which maximizes R, the rate of transmission of information through the noisy channel.   From Eq. 5.29 and the integral expressions given there for $H(x)$ and $H(x|y)$, this ultimate capacity of a noisy channel, attained by such statistical matching, may be expressed thus:[D]

$$C = \lim_{T \to \infty} \left[\max_{p(x)} \frac{1}{T} \int \int p(x, y) \log \frac{p(x, y)}{p(x)p(y)} \, dx \, dy \right] \text{ bits per sec} \quad (5.32)$$

When we speak of transmitted signals x, these may be taken to be wave forms of duration T and bandwidth F; consequently, such signals are specified by the value $x_1 x_2 \cdots x_{2FT}$ at $2FT$ equi-spaced instants, so that the transmitted ensemble probability distribution has a finite dimensionality $2FT$.   That is $p(x) = p(x_1 x_2 \cdots x_{2FT})$.   This problem of maximizing the rate of information, as the integral expression, Eq. 5.32, over all possible ensembles $p(x)$ and subject to fixed power, bandwidth, and possibly other constraints, is an exercise in the calculus of variations.[D,133,*]

Repetitive redundancy, to which we referred in the last section, is the simplest way of combating noise and reducing the equivocation at the receiver.   It involves prior agreement between the communicating parties that each transmitted sign (letter; binary-code 1, 0; wave-form ordinate, etc.) shall be repeated n times.   The receiver then has a better chance of assessing the signs correctly, but the price he pays is a delay in the process; he must wait until the end of each sequence before making his decision. The same price is always paid; statistical coding involves delay, and this delay becomes longer and longer as better coding is employed, for transmission and errorless reception, at a rate approaching the ultimate capacity C of the channel.   This rate can then in practice never be attained, but only approached asymptotically.   We may infer that this is so from our earlier argument in Section 4.   All forms of redundancy operate by calling upon past experience; perhaps by the inclusion of known digram, or trigram, constraints; perhaps by including the statistical influence of signs

* See also Jelonek in reference 166.   These authors have calculated a number of channel capacities for different signaling systems and noise conditions.

extending even farther back into the past. But to extract the ultimate information out of any sign, we should require to know all the statistical constraints upon it, involving knowledge of the preceding signs extending indefinitely far back into the past. Ideal coding involves taking into account, in the transmitter, indefinitely long blocks, or run-lengths of messages.

8. MANDELBROT'S EXPLICATION OF ZIPF'S LAW —CONTINUED

We are now able to take up again the threads of an earlier discussion (Chapter 3, Section 5.2) concerning Zipf's experimental "law," illustrated by Fig. 3.5, and Mandelbrot's theoretical treatment of this.* In this earlier chapter we were discussing within the field of linguistics; let us now treat messages strictly as sequences of words, each a sequence of letters,† and regard written language as a "code." Difficulties concerning "the word" as a linguistic concept will not be raised again here.

In our earlier section, we referred to Mandelbrot's concept of the "cost" of letters and words (signs). Let c_n represent the cost of a word (assumed to be given) of rank order‡ n in the language, and let p_n be its frequency of occurrence (Fig. 3.5). Then the average cost of messages per word will be:

$$\text{Average cost per word} = \sum_n p_n c_n \qquad (5.33)$$

Mandelbrot proceeds first to minimize this average cost, by carrying out a variation of the distribution of p_n over the different words; that is, he finds the optimum, "cheapest" word ensemble. This minimization process is carried out with the information rate (per word, average) held invariant; but the term "information rate" as used here needs a little clarification.

Shannon has shown that messages may be coded most efficiently if the process is carried out over long blocks of words, although such coding inevitably requires correspondingly long time delays.[D] But Mandelbrot points out that his own problem is different, since human language is uttered or written under conditions which cannot permit such very long time delays. Shannon's ideal coding would be very *efficient* (in information per sign) but not very *practical*. Mandelbrot makes the assumption of a constraint upon the tolerable delay, equal to the word length; that is, *words* are considered to be coded one at a time. Again, every word is considered to end with a certain sign, "space," which never occurs inside

---

* See Chapter 3, Section 5.2 for references.

† Or similarly with phonemes and transcribed texts.

‡ See footnote, p. 102.

a word. If the maximum message information rate be taken as Shannon's H_n, we have

$$H_n = -\sum_n p_n \log p_n \text{ bits per word} \qquad [(5.6)](5.34)$$

with coding carried out using very long blocks. With this rate held invariant, the "cheapest" ensemble of words is shown to have the distribution:

$$p_n = Q\epsilon^{-Kc_n} \qquad (5.35)$$

where Q and K are constants.

This result accords more or less with intuition, since it requires the most frequent words to be the cheapest. (We have already observed that Morse's code was based upon a similar assumption, applied to letters whilst Fano's code represents a more formalized version,[C,D,]* if in both cases we take the length of the code sequences as a measure of their "cost.")

Notice that Eq. 5.35 implies that the rank order of the words is the same, whether quoted with respect to increasing cost c_n or decreasing probability p_n, since the exponential function is monotonic.

Another step in the theory leads to a relation between the cost of a word and its rank order. Mandelbrot considers words, in a first approximation, as random sequence of letters and spaces, and all conceivable sequences of letters of the alphabet are admitted as possible "words." The question, how to assign costs to the various letters of the alphabet, is answered by assuming, initially, that all letters are equally costly; subsequently it is shown that *any* distribution of costs will suffice, for, surprisingly, the choice makes no appreciable difference to the main conclusions. (From Eq. 5.35 we see that assignment of equal costs to letters implies also that all the letters, but not spaces, are equally probable.) Thus the cost of a word is equal to the sum of the costs of its letters, so that if letters be assumed to be equally costly, the cost of a word is proportional to its length. Further, the longer any sequence of letters, the more different words that may be constructed having this length. Then, in an alphabet of M letters:

> There are M possible, equally probable, equally costly 1-letter words.
> There are M^2 possible, equally probable, equally costly 2-letter words.
> There are M^3 possible, equally probable, equally costly 3-letter words.
> $\ldots\ldots\ldots\ldots$, etc.
> There are M^l possible, equally probable, equally costly l-letter words.

In this table the word groups are ranked from top to bottom, as $1\cdots l\cdots M$-letter sequences. They are therefore ranked in groups of increasing cost, on a linear scale, so that from Eq. 5.35 they are also ranked in groups of decreasing probability.

* See also Huffman in reference 166. See our Fig. 5.5(b).

The various l-letter words, within any one group, may be regarded as ranked in arbitrary order. But by rank order, in Zipf's law, it is the order of every *word*, not word group, in the language which is meant. Thus we can say that, approximately, the rank order of any *word* of length l letters is n_l, being equal to the sum of all words of length equal to, or less than, l:

$$\left. \begin{aligned} n_l &\simeq 1 + \sum_{\lambda=1} M^{\lambda} \\ &= M^l \cdot \frac{M}{M-1} - \frac{1}{M-1} \end{aligned} \right\} \tag{5.36}$$

If now we write $M/(M-1)$ as M^{-l_0}, then:

$$M^{l-l_0} = n_l + \frac{1}{M-1}$$

or

$$l = l_0 + \log_M\left(n_l + \frac{1}{M-1}\right) \tag{5.37}$$

This shows that, to a first approximation, the length of any word is proportional to the logarithm of its rank order, with a correction which is serious only when $n_l \ll 1/(M-1)$. But, cost being proportional to word length, we may rewrite Eq. 5.37, dropping the subscript l, as:

$$c_n \simeq c_0 + \log_M n \tag{5.38}$$

and substituting this in Eq. 5.35 eliminates the costs c_n:

$$p_n = Pn^{-B}$$

where P and B are constants that depend upon the K and Q in Eq. 5.35 and, through K and Q, upon the information which we wish to transmit per word, or upon the average cost of transmission per word.

This, of course, is Zipf's law.[367] But in this form, we see the role played by the index B as a measure of the *variety* of our available vocabulary. The smaller B is, the greater the variety.

As illustrated here, Mandelbrot's arguments have been reduced to their simplest terms. He has shown, however, by slightly more involved reasoning, that the relationship in Eq. 5.37 still holds, if *any* costs be assigned to the various letters of the alphabet—or even if the cost of any letter in a word depends upon the preceding letter*—so that this work may bear more relation to real-life printed language (and perhaps other human social constructs) than at first appears to be the case, with this simplest model discussed here.

* See Mandelbrot in references 26, 41.

Mandelbrot proceeds to develop analogous relations between his whole theory and certain result of thermodynamics, and we should refer the reader to his original texts. This question of the relationship between statistical communication theory and statistical thermodynamics has been deliberately avoided in this chapter, until now, for it is the writer's opinion that there is little necessity to make such comparisons; the newer theory may well stand upon its own rights. However, this has frequently been done, especially invoking the concept of entropy so a few words on the subject may not be out of place at this point.

9. COMMENTS UPON INFORMATION INTERPRETED AS ENTROPY

Communication provides an example of a process which we regard as proceeding from the past into the future; time, we say, "has a direction." Phonograph records played backward sound as senseless gibberish. A movie, in reverse. produces comic results—a diver rising from the water, landing on tiptoe; torn scrap paper coming together into folded news sheets; a drinker regurgitating a pint of beer into a glass. The world, run backward, looks ludicrous.

Yet Newton's laws of motion—the backbone of physical science—are reversible; time can have a positive or negative sign. We appear then to regard time in two distinct ways, reversibly and irreversibly. On one hand, if we study, say, the properties of some simple frictionless machine containing relatively few moving parts, we can calculate its precise motions, in detail; we may learn all about it and predict its future behavior with accuracy. In the equations of such mechanical motions, the sign of time may everywhere be reversed, with complete consistency. On the other hand there are whole realms wherein the "direction" of time is of major importance—in studies of life processes, of meteorology, of thermodynamics or again in philosophical questions concerning "creative thinking," "intelligent beings," and many others.[36,289]

This concept of the apparent irreversibility of time has received its most elaborate mathematical formulation in thermodynamics, and is expressed in terms of the so-called Second Law, which holds that a certain quantity called *entropy* can never decrease. Thermodynamics was originally concerned with the properties of gases—that is, enormous assemblies of particles in violent motion. Of such assemblies we can have only partial knowledge; although Newton's laws apply to every individual particle, we cannot observe them all, nor distinguish one from another. Their properties cannot be calculated precisely, like those of a simple machine, but may be discussed only in terms of probabilities, stochastically. We may measure and so learn about their macroscopic properties—their number of degrees of freedom, or dimensionality; their pressures, volumes, temperature, energies.   We may represent certain properties by statistical distributions, such as the particle velocities for example.   We may, with great difficulty, observe some microscopic motions, but we can never have *complete* knowledge of every particle of the system.

Likewise with other systems, of which communication is an important example; it is not surprising that the same mathematical methods should be considered as applicable.   We can have only partial knowledge of a communication source.   We may know the ensemble properties, the coding system, and various constraints upon the messages or the signals; but we (as recipient or participant-observer) cannot know, *a priori*, the moment-by-moment states of the source, the exact messages it will give out next, in microscopic detail, or we should have foreknowledge and receive no information from the signals.

But it was the later formulation of the laws of thermodynamics in terms of probabilities, in the classic work of Boltzmann and Gibbs in particular,[B] as a statistical-mechanical interpretation of the properties of gases which showed the great generality of the laws and concepts.   The existence of a relationship between "entropy" and "information" is, in fact, inherently shown in their work, though the explicit relation was first shown, it appears, by Szilard, in a discussion upon the old problem of "Maxwell's demon."[318,*] This problem, and the entropy-information relation, has subsequently been discussed by Wiener,[349] and by Brillouin in particular.[35-37]

Entropy, in statistical thermodynamics, is a function of the probabilities of the states of the particles comprising a gas; information rate, in statistical communication theory, is a similar function of the probabilities of the states of a source.   In both cases we have an *ensemble*—in the case of the gas, an enormous collection of particles, the states of which (i.e., the energies) are distributed according to some probability function; in the communication problem, a collection of messages, or states of a source, again described by a probability function.

The relationship between information and entropy is brought out most objectively by the Wiener-Shannon formula, Eq. 5.8:

$$H(i) = -\sum p_i \log p_i \qquad [(5.8)]$$

which (with a positive sign) bears resemblance to Boltzmann's formula for the entropy of a perfect gas.   Now, when such an important relationship between two branches of science has been exhibited, there are two ways in which it may become exploited; precisely and mathematically, taking due

---

* The paper by the same author, quoted by Weaver (see reference B, p. 95), appears to be a wrong reference.

care about the validity of applying the methods; or vaguely and descriptively. Since this relationship has been pointed out, we have heard of "entropies" of languages, social systems, and economic systems and of its use in various method-starved studies. It is the kind of sweeping generality which people will clutch like a straw. Some part of these interpretations has indeed been valid and useful, but the concept of entropy is one of considerable difficulty and of a deceptively apparent simplicity. It is essentially a mathematical concept and the rules of its application are clearly laid down.

In a descriptive sense, entropy is often referred to as a "measure of disorder" and the Second Law of thermodynamics as stating that "systems can only proceed to a state of increased disorder"; as time passes, "entropy can never decrease." The properties of a gas can change only in such a way that our knowledge of the positions and energies of the particles lessens; randomness always increases. In a similar descriptive way, information is contrasted, as bringing increasing order out of chaos. Information, then is said to be "like" negative entropy. But any likeness that exists, exists between the mathematical descriptions which have been set up; between formulae and method.

Shannon refers to $H(i)$, as given by Eq. 5.8 above, as the "entropy" of a discrete source of information, having a finite number of states with known probabilities $p_1 p_2 \cdots p_n$. Wiener, earlier, has referred to "negative entropy" in a similar context, and there is a certain difference of point of view. Both physical entropy and information can be only relative, never absolute; we can only have changes. The reader will remember this point was brought out earlier, since the corresponding $H(x)$ for a *continuous* noiseless source appeared to be infinity (Section 6.3). In this case $H(x)$ becomes:

$$H(x) = -\int p(x) \log p(x) \, dx \qquad (5.39)$$

This represents the receiver's prior average doubt, or uncertainty; that is, it represents the "entropy" of the source ensemble. If a signal y is received from this source, perturbed by noise (the noise source itself having a certain "entropy"), the receiver's uncertainty concerning the message state of the source becomes changed—usually lessened—by the quantity I_y, given by Eq. 5.20, the information content of that signal y. If now signals are steadily received, the receiver's uncertainty reduces at an average rate R, given by the averaged contents of all the received signals, which was ex-expressed by Eq. 5.29. This rate R is then the rate of received information, or the *negative* "entropy" (per sign, per degree of freedom, or per second, as required).

This aspect of communication is one special view of a general situation in physics—that of an observer "receiving information" from a physical system under observation. Physical (thermodynamic) entropy is defined for a *closed* system, a system which is considered utterly isolated and incapable of exchanging energy in any way with its surroundings. Again, the term is usually applied to systems which are in a state of near-randomness, and which consist of *truly enormous* systems or assemblies of elements.

In Szilard's discussion of the Maxwell demon problem, the demon was regarded as "receiving information" about the particle motions of a gas, this information enabling him to operate a heat engine and set up a *perpetuum mobile*; the demon was making use of his information, not simply receiving it and passing it into storage. This suggests a violation of the Second Law. But the demon is essentially a participant-observer and must receive energy, in order to make his observations, and so he himself must be regarded as part of the system.[35] As Szilard had shown, in his 1929 paper, the selective action represented by the demon's observations must give rise to an increase of entropy *at least* equal to the reduction he can effect by virtue of this information. The system and the demon exchange entropy, but no overall reduction is necessitated.

But these more general questions take us off our track. Questions of extracting information from Nature and of using this information to change our models or representations lie outside communication theory— for an observer looking down a microscope, or reading instruments, is not to be equated with a listener on a telephone receiving spoken messages. Mother Nature does not communicate to us with signs or language. A *communication channel* should be distinguished from a *channel of observation* and, without wishing to seem too assertive, the writer would suggest that in true communication problems the concept of entropy need not be evoked at all. And again, physical entropy is capable of a number of interpretations, albeit related, and its similarity with (selective, syntactic) information is not as straightforward as the simplicity and apparent similarity of the formulae suggests. This wider field, which has been studied in particular by MacKay,[218] Gabor,[123] and Brillouin,[35] as an aspect of scientific method, is referred to, at least in Britain, as *information theory*, a term which is unfortunately used elsewhere synonymously with communication theory. Again, the French sometimes refer to communication theory as *cybernetics*.[40] It is all very confusing!

BIBLIOGRAPHY

A. Hartley, R. V. L., "Transmission of Information," *Bell System Tech. J.*, 7, 1928, p. 535.
B. Tolman, R. C., *Principles of Statistical Mechanics*, Clarendon Press, Oxford, 1938.

C. Fano, R. M., "The Transmission of Information," *M.I.T., Research Lab. Electronics Tech. Rept., 65,* 1949.

D. Shannon, C. E., and W. Weaver, *The Mathematical Theory of Communication,* University of Illinois Press, Urbana, 1949.

E. Feller, W., *An Introduction to Probability Theory and its Applications,* Vol. I., John Wiley & Sons, Inc., New York, 1950.

F. Woodward, P. M., *Probability and Information Theory, with Applications to Radar,* Pergamon Press, Ltd., London, 1953.

On the Logic of Communication (Syntactics, Semantics, and Pragmatics)

> *He was . . . 40 years old before he looked upon*
> *geometry; which happened accidentally. Being in*
> *a gentleman's library . . . Euclid's* Elements *lay*
> *open and 'twas the 47 El, libri I. He read the*
> *Proposition. "By g*——" say'd he "this is*
> *impossible!" So he reads the demonstration of it,*
> *which referred him back to such a proposition; which*
> *proposition he read. That referred him back to*
> *another, which he also read. Et sic deinceps,*
> *that at last he was demonstratively convinced of*
> *that trueth. This made him in love with geometry.*

* (He would now and then sweare, by way of emphasis.)

John Aubrey (1626–1697), concerning
Thomas Hobbes
Brief Lives, Volume I, 1680

1. "SIGNIFICS"—OR MENTAL HYGIENE

The Honorable Lady Welby, who was Lady-in-Waiting to Queen Victoria, pioneered a movement, at the turn of the century, to tighten discipline of thought and expression in many fields of human interest, in education, in science, in all forms of mental activity, and to examine in the most critical manner concepts such as "meaning," "significance," "truth," "interpretation," and their bearing on what is commonly called the "value" or "import" of any branch of study and enquiry.[A] One most prominent feature has been an increased awareness of the great practical importance of understanding language; how to use it, how to control it; to examine its inadequacies, ambiguities, and sources of error; to check the deceits of idiom, metaphor, and ellipsis. Not only human universal languages, such as English and Spanish, but also other sign systems[B]—the language systems of mathematics, of science, and of logic— are subject to scrutiny. It is only too common for "language" to be considered as though it were one thing, but there are indeed many types of language and language system which are wholly distinct. We have already found it necessary to distinguish, for example, between *object-language* and *meta-language*, when discussing linguistics; again we made reference to the distinction between scientific language and aesthetic language (Chapter 3).

The infant *signifcs* does not rest within the nursery of philosophy; his cries, if not his name, are heard in the outside world of practical affairs. We are all of us affected, in our daily lives, by misunderstandings, verbal and mental confusions, with engrained habits of speech and thought, deceiving ourselves as much as others.

"Mere language reform," Lady Welby suggested, "is not enough"; we need at the same time to understand the processes involved in its use, to examine our methods of reasoning and, in particular, to be critical of the manner of language growth and change.

It may well be that the whole study of communication (or, more generally the theory of information) will make a certain contribution to such a discipline, inasmuch as it clarifies some different aspects of the multi-faceted term *information*.* One side, at least, has been polished with mathematics, whilst other sides (semantic and pragmatic aspects) are beginning to show up, though these other aspects are not, as yet, truly distinct and clear. The formal statistical theory of communication has certainly shown, both as regards its theorems and its measure of "selective information rate," some promise of use and interpretation in those various different sciences which concern, in some way, the idea of "information"; nevertheless caution is needed in extending this existing theory outside its legitimate, and clearly defined, sphere. Information, *of some kind or other*, certainly appears to be a concept of value in many fields, but this is not to say that the one mathematical theory and one measure have indiscriminate application.

* A conference was held in August 1953 at Amersfoort, Netherlands, organized by the International Society for Significs; this conference was concerned with "Semantic and Signific Aspects of Modern Theories of Communication." See reference 301.

Bar-Hillel, in particular, has been loud in his warnings:[c] "Unfortunately, however, it often turned out that impatient scientists in various fields applied the terminology and the theorems of the statistical (communication) theory to fields in which the term *information* was used, pre-systematically, in a semantic sense . . . or even in a pragmatic sense. . . ." The Wiener-Shannon measure of selective information rate has been set up for a specific purpose; it concerns the statistical rarity of signals. What these signals "signify" or "mean," or what their value or truth is, simply cannot be discussed in the language of this statistical communication theory.

1.1. SEMIOTIC,* OR THE THEORY OF SIGNS[B,243,244,]†

All communication proceeds by means of *signs*, with which one organism affects the behavior of another (or, more generally, as we shall argue later, the *state* of another). In certain cases it is meaningful also to speak of communication between one machine and another as, for example, the control signals which pass between a guided missile and a ground radar. But we shall confine our attention mainly to human communication.

There is here immediately a difficulty of definition. How can we distinguish between communication proper, by the use of spoken language or similar empirical signs, and other forms of causation? For instance, if I tell someone to go and jump in the lake and, in fear, he does so, then I have communicated with him; but if I push him in, his final state may appear similar, but I can scarcely be said to have communicated with him! What is the difference, then, between my spoken message and my push?

It is indeed difficult to draw a sharp and clear distinction. Rather we see a gradual change as we shift our gaze from the lowest creatures, through higher forms of animal life, to Man. The various signs used by animals, acting as releaser mechanisms—cries, movements, shapes, postures, patches of color—call for a response of a semi-automatic, involuntary kind.[209, 324] But such responses are not quite as inevitable and automatic as direct forms of causation, such as a push; and the distinction becomes greater as learning ability increases. The learning faculty enables signs to be used in a more flexible manner; standard situations no longer elicit standard responses, inevitably. And at the level of Man, with his most flexible system of signs

* Originally spelled semeiotic, after John Locke's Σημιωτιχή which he used for the "doctrine of signs" (*Essay Concerning Human Understanding*, 1689, Book IV, Chapter XXI).

† The foundations of a theory of signs and of systematic enquiry into their "meaning" were laid by Charles S. Peirce during the last and the early present century; see reference 258. He was followed by William James (see reference 391).

(language), the distinction from direct causation becomes extreme. If I push a man into the lake, he inevitably goes in; if I tell him to jump in, he may do one of a thousand things.*

There is another way of regarding the distinction, which is illustrated by our diagram of an observer watching a communication taking place (Fig. 3.2). The observer in the top diagram (a) is watching the two communicants, as through a peephole, and takes no part in the phenomenon himself. He observes only physical signs (sounds, gestures, etc.) and responses (people's behavior). To such an observer, the distinction between direct causation (e.g., a push) and communication (e.g., a spoken command) is that the first is a simple, inevitable, cause-effect relation, whilst the second is only a probabilistic cause-effect relation. The observer can estimate probabilities of the various signs (as in the theory of communication, which is expressed in the meta-language of such a detached, outside observer) and probabilities of different responses.

But the lower Fig. 3.2(b) shows a situation of a different kind. Here the observer is himself one of the communicants and, to him, the distinction between communication and direct causation is very, very marked. Here the observer forms a major part of the phenomenon he is observing (very frequently linguists and psychologists are in exactly this situation); either he is a source of signs, or he responds to them. He can speak of communication in terms of volition. A remark was made a few paragraphs back, that if I tell someone to jump in the lake, and he does so, or if instead I push him in, his final state is the same. This, however, is true only to the outside observer (a). To the man who is in the lake it is manifestly untrue; his *state of mind* will be very different; so, correspondingly, will be his responses to subsequent signs!† Later in this chapter, we shall be looking at the communication process from the point of view of observer (b) in Fig. 3.2; we shall refer to "subjective probabilities," "degrees of belief," "states of mind."

Charles Peirce[129, 258] distinguished between a sign and other forms of causation by the requirement that a sign must be capable of evoking responses which themselves must be capable of acting as signs for the same (object) designatum. Note: "must be *capable* of . . . ." Signs evoke signs, and so on, in a *potentially* endless sequence. Consequently a sign does not evoke one definite response sign (interpretant), but there can be an indefinite variety of response signs. We shall be making further reference to Peirce's pragmatic philosophy of sign theory and communication in Chapter 7.

---

* See page 136 of reference 129.

† This "state of mind" factor is referred to in a definition of *meaning* given in the Appendix.

Man is a user of signs in great variety: the spoken sounds of speech, written or printed letters and numerals, diagrams, pictures, sketches, money, highway signs, club badges and uniforms, gestures and facial expressions, an endless list of empirical signs, icons, tokens, whereby he achieves some measure of co-ordination and concerted action with his fellows.[380, 399] Again, he has evolved systems of logic and mathematics, using symbols and rules of varied kinds.

The study of the whole broad field is called *semiotic*, and includes the most important domain of human language. Semiotic is studied at three different levels, representing different types of abstracting:[B] *syntactics* (the study of signs and of the relations between signs), *semantics* (study of the relations between signs and designata), *pragmatics* (study of signs in relation to their users). These three have not the nature of separate compartments, but overlap one another, just as chemistry overlaps geology or physics. We might define the three in this way:

Syntactics: signs and their relations to other signs
Semantics: signs and their relations to "outside world" (designation)—a rather questionable notion.
Pragmatics: signs and their relations to users (psychology)

All three levels concern signs and relations, or *rules*. But, as we have already stressed several times, the user of signs does not need to know the rules; we can read, speak, or write effectively, and we can laugh at jokes with little or no knowledge of rules. The rules are not "inherent in the language" but are inherent in the analysis of language. Rules are expressed in meta-language. Pragmatics is the most general, inclusive level of study and includes all personal, psychological factors which distinguish one communication event from another, all questions of purpose, practical results, and value to sign users. It is the "real-life" level. Semantics purports to abstract from all specific communication events and concerns only signs and their designata; it is a less personal and, in a sense, an artificial level of description. Syntactics abstracts still further and concerns signs only; it treats language as a calculus. Figure 6.1 represents these successive abstractions, schematically.

The signs and rules of a language, as set out in meta-language, represent an abstraction from real-life situations. Books of grammar, for example, are not confused with literature; they are anatomy, not the living language. A great deal is necessarily omitted when a language is described as a finite set of signs and rules, and this extracted set, as expressed in meta-language, is called a *language system*.

Logicians work with language systems, frequently with freely invented or set-up systems of signs and rules (*pure* systems); and a competent logician does not confuse logic with life.   Again, linguists work with the language systems which they have extracted from patient observation of historical, human object-languages (*descriptive* systems).   The distinction between the *descriptive* and *pure* systems is important.[D]

Logicians are concerned especially with the syntactic and semantic levels of semiotic, and commonly their pure systems of syntactical and semantical rules appear to have little or nothing to do with everyday human converse and social intercourse.   But just as the linguist's studies

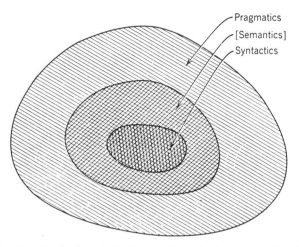

Pragmatics
[Semantics]
Syntactics

Fig. 6.1.   The three levels of semiotic (shown schematically as successive abstractions).

of ordinary (descriptive) language systems help to discipline our writing, thinking, and expression, so the logician seeks to go further still and tighten such discipline upon our use of language for scientific work, for serious debate, for reasoning, to expose fallacious arguments, ambiguities, and inconsistencies, to root out the deceits of language.   Syntactics and semantics concern rules which are abstracted from all specific users of signs and all environmental factors or real-life situations.   Syntactics is a study directed to the signs themselves and their orderings; it aims at the purely *formal* aspects of language.   Descriptive semantics concerns not only these same formal rules but also rules of application to the "real" (extra-linguistic) world.*   In the case of descriptive systems, both these studies represent idealizations, for the collections of signs and rules are gathered only by patient talking to and questioning of individual sign *users*.   A linguist compiles his vocabulary and describes the syntax of a language after interviewing many different natives, and by watching how they live and work

* Poincaré distinguished syntactic (logical) and semantic rules.

with their language. All linguistics involves this pragmatic level, when the rules are first formulated and recorded.[D, 47]

Pure syntax, on the other hand, is to a major extent the interest of logicians, who may invent rules for combining signs to form sentences, together with rules for making subsequent deductions. It is like a calculus. "Pure semantics," too, is entirely analytic and makes no reference to real personal experience or real facts about the world. For instance, a logician might employ the sentence, "The moon is made of green cheese," perhaps as a proposition or to illustrate some point of method in argument; but he need not come into conflict with astronomers! He is free to invent his own worlds, and he is not concerned with emotions.

"Syntactical truth" should be distinguished from experiential, factual, "plain truth." A logician may set up formal rules for combining words, or other signs, into sentences and rules by which deductions, consequences, or implications may be drawn. The "truth" of any such conclusions can then be stated only with reference to this particular syntactical system ("true" in such-and-such a system). Sentences based upon such invented, pure systems need have no factual, experiential truth; and deductions drawn from initial premises do not provide any information about facts.[6, 47, 356]

Carnap has defined as *logical syntax* all the purely formal aspects of the syntax of a language; that is, anything concerning signs and their orderings, but having no reference to designata, real or imagined. He has considered whether it be possible to define too, within syntax (i.e., formally), terms which correspond to semantical terms, as used in pure semantic systems. He points out that modern symbolic logic has developed syntax in just this way, so that pure semantics becomes (largely) mirrored within syntactics.[47] This is the opinion of a logician, dealing with pure language systems; but linguists, seeking to describe real historical languages solely as syntactical systems, entirely in terms of formal rules, may find their problem is not so clearly resolvable.[11]

There are several schools of opinion concerning semantics; at one extreme, there are some who would describe language as a purely syntactic system, avoiding questions of "meaning" and "truth" as they would avoid the plague; at another, there are some who insist that descriptive linguistics cannot ignore semantic considerations. But if the term "semantics" be interpreted simply as the "theory of meaning," the whole place and purpose of it becomes very vague for, as we illustrated in Chapter 3, "meaning" is such an overworked word. At the semantic level, two distinct fields of "meaning" have been distinguished by Quine: first, theory of meaning, and second, theory of reference; the first concerns, for example, whether a statement is logically true or whether two statements are logically equivalent, or two expressions synonymous ("mean" the same thing); the second field concerns extra-linguistic truthfulness and reference, whether a statement is true "in fact" and experience.   As an illustration, we might say that the word "brine" can be substituted for "salt water" in the sentence, "Salt water is a good emetic," obtaining a sentence of similar construction in English (a syntactical fact); then the observation that they are also *synonymous* in that context is a semantical fact ("mean" the same thing).   On the other hand, whether or not the statement is experientially true can be tested only by drinking a glass of the stuff.*

It can well be argued that semantics, in this sense of signs and their relations to designata, being abstracted from pragmatics and therefore from all real-life communicative situations, has little to do with human communication; that its correct place is within the field of logic, and that much human thought and speech, in daily life, have little or nothing to do with logic.   To a major extent the author would incline to this view.   The rules of syntax and of semantics which have been abstracted by patient observation of some human language, like English, are set out in the meta-language, and they constitute a language system.   The modern studies of semantics and of the language of logic will go far to straighten ideas and expressions formulated in the public (abstracted) language of science; but most human utterances are not disciplined by logical rules.   Such rules may, by their very abstraction, ignore a great number of important factors which affect communication and meaning of utterances, by virtue of environmental or pragmatic conditions.   For simple illustration, the sentence, "The King is dead, long live the King!" may seem self-contradictory, nonsensical, and meaningless in a logical, semantic sense; yet in its correct usage, at the correct time and place, such a proclamation is highly significant.

Thus "meaning" and "truth" may be considered at the syntactic and semantic levels, within the discipline of logic; but again, both may be discussed at the pragmatic level, in relation to real-life, everyday, man-to-man communication—the chatter and gossip, the courtesies and remarks which make up the bulk of effective human utterances—meaning *to* somebody, on a certain occasion; truth *about* some reality or experience when a whole range of conditions, education, and history are taken into account. Pilate did not jest about *syntactical* truth.†

* There is controversy as to whether questions of meaning (semantics) can be replaced by structural and distributional procedures in linguistics, that is, whether language can be *presented* purely as a syntactical system.   See discussions by Bar-Hillel, reference 11, and Harris, reference 144, to grasp the nature of such problems.   It is not our purpose to enter such controversy, nor are we competent.

† Concerning the pragmatic value of truth, William James argued that "truth comes very near" [to being] "what we *ought* to believe."

Pragmatic questions cannot be discussed in terms of syntactics or semantics. As a very simple example, the following message might appear in the sports column of a newspaper:

SUNDOWN PARK. 3:30, TISHY, 4 LENGTHS (TOTE 7/1).

Such a message could be regarded syntactically, as a set of signs, or semantically, where the signs denote places, things, events, et cetera. But the pragmatic aspects of the message depend upon each and every different reader of the newspaper. The consequences of the message to you, for instance, depend upon who "you" are and whether you have any money on the horse. The pragmatic properties of any message depend upon the past experiences of the sender or the recipient, upon their present circumstances, their states of mind, and upon all matters personal to them as individuals. Into this level we may enter all psychological aspects of the communication process; such, for instance, as the problems of perception, recognition, or interpretation of messages; studies of verbal or visual memory, of effects of environment upon the recipient; and all those aspects which serve to distinguish one communication *event* from any other where the sign *types* may be the same. In other words, though many different pairs of people may say "the same thing" (linguistically) on different occasions in conversation, each occasion, as an event, is observably different in many aspects from the others; such differences depend upon people's accents, their past experiences, their present states of mind, the environment, the future consequences of interpreting the message, knowledge of each other, and many other factors.

The distinction between an *event* and a *type* is important. In this book we use the terms *sign-events*, *word-events*, *tokens*, *signals* to denote physical transmissions on specific occasions; actual printer's ink or spoken sounds. But we speak of *sign-types* and *word-types* to denote linguistic concepts— the signs "in the language," "in the dictionary," and so on. This distinction appears in various texts under a variety of names,* and corresponds to the difference between a "particular" and a "class"; if the various printed signs on the page you are now reading (as word-events) are *things*, then the corresponding word-types are *classes* of such things.

The Wiener-Shannon statistical theory of communication, as discussed in Chapter 5, concerns only signs. It therefore lies at the syntactic level, if it be considered as a contribution to semiotic. In this field it is essentially a syntactical theory but, from the relationships suggested (Fig. 6.1), it therefore seems basic to any study of semantical or pragmatical aspects

* Other terms are used; e.g., Carnap employs *sign design*. Peirce's original terms were *sinsign* (the particular) and *legisign* (the class). See Appendix.

of information.   True, the signs may in certain cases be actual things or people—but they would nevertheless be serving as signs.   But the statistical theory does not concern "meaning" in any sense, nor questions of truth, value, practical use, et cetera, to specific individuals; no semantic or pragmatic considerations enter into that theory.

1.2. Some different views of "information"

The word "information" is used, in everyday speech, in different ways. We speak of *useful* information, of *valuable* information, of *factual* information, of *reliable* information, of *precise* information, of *true* information.   But none of these expressions occurs in statistical communication theory, which describes information solely as the statistical rarity of signals from an observed source.   Let us now look at some of these more popular aspects of information but without attempting any formal theorizing; for the time being, we shall *not* confine the word "information" to its technical Wiener-Shannon usage.

It may be helpful to refer to three levels of information, corresponding to the three levels of semiotic—the syntactic, semantic, and pragmatic levels.[B]   We may confine the Wiener-Shannon statistical theory to the syntactic level, since it essentially concerns signs and statistical relations between signs.   But "information," in its popular use, is regarded as information *about* something other than the signs themselves; it is considered to refer to designata (objects, people, times, places, events, relationships, etc., in the outside world); and it also involves users (informants, advisers, reference book compilers, etc., as well as those who act on the information).   These popular interpretations are essentially semantic and pragmatic.   Again at semantic level, it may be possible to infer one piece of "information" from another. ("This shop is closed only on Sundays" implies "This shop is open on weekdays," in common English.)

We have stressed that statistical communication theory abstracts from the semantic and pragmatic aspects of the set of signs used.   Similarly it is possible to discuss *semantic information*, regarded as abstracted from pragmatics—information conveyed by sentences "in the language," not information for, or to, any particular person.   (In Section 3.3 we shall refer to one mathematical theory of semantic information.)   Clearly, the adjectives *useful, useless, valuable*, and the like, applied to "information," suggest some definite user (useful or valuable to whom?) whereas *factual* or *precise* do not.   As a simple illustration of such distinction between the pragmatic and semantic levels of information, the sentence, "A train will leave from somewhere, for elsewhere, soon," contains less information—is less precise—than "A train will leave from London, for Edinburgh, today." And this is even less precise than "A non-stop train will leave from King's

Cross Station, for Edinburgh, at 10:00 a.m. today." These three sentences convey increasingly precise information to anybody (at least to anybody who understands English). But whether the information is useful, or valuable, depends upon a person's needs or circumstances. Whether it is *reliable* depends upon personal experience of that particular source of information (the informant, timetable, information booth, etc.).

The first statement here contains less semantic information (about trains, etc.) than the last, because it can logically be deduced from the last, but not vice versa. The statements are rank-ordered here in increasing precision; such semantic precision, or "information," is correlated with precision of potential action on the part of any (English-speaking) recipient. But clearly, such discussion of "information" has little or no connection with the aspect we considered in Chapter 5.

Such examples illustrate one of the principal ways in which we daily seek, or offer, information, by successive subdivision of some whole field of inquiry into smaller and smaller regions of uncertainty. Countless illustrations might be cited. A postal address seeks out one specific person by locating first *country*, then *town*, *street*, *number*; again the whole animal kingdom is classified successively into *classes*, *orders*, *families*, *genera*, *species*, et cetera; bibliographical references are given by *journal*, *volume*, *number*, *month*, *page*, or the like; times are quoted (in reverse), such as *8:00 p.m.*, *18 September 1955* A.D. And so on. Such taxonomical interpretation of "information" as "successive selection" is natural and widespread. Figure 6.2 represents such a form of classification or sorting topologically—like a stream breaking into tributaries. Diagram (*a*) shows successive breaking down of a field of inquiry into smaller and smaller regions of uncertainty, in an empirical manner; diagram (*b*) shows a dichotomous subdivision.

The reader will appreciate that such successive selections are similar to those employed in defining "selective-information content" of signals in the statistical theory of communication, but there is here an essential difference. Again such diagrams might be replaced by the multi-dimensional cube representation, such as we have used before (see Fig. 3.1). But the difference is now that designata are involved; the "field of inquiry" concerns outside (extra-linguistic) things or events, and the successive subdivisions specify these more and more precisely. Usually empirical names or signs are used to correspond to each successive region of uncertainty (e.g., *classes*, *orders*, *families*, in the example above); however, we can denote these regions by signs, according to some rule. Thus in diagram (*b*), Fig. 6.2, binary signs *0*, *1* are used, and the region marked with an asterisk is denoted by 1001. Again diagram (*a*) employs capital and lower-case letters in alphabetic order, so that the region marked by an asterisk is denoted by *ChF*.

Sorting is the chief function of descriptive words in language. Words like "blue," "square," "big," "old," and "flat" serve to sort, or discriminate; by continuing description, we can achieve greater and greater precision of sorting.

There have been many attempts in historical times to classify human knowledge in this logical manner; perhaps the most noteworthy are those of Francis Bacon, George Dalgarno, Herbert Spencer, and André Ampère.

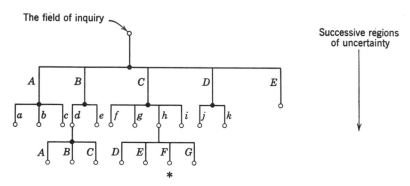

(a) Subdivision of a "field of enquiry" into successive "regions of uncertainty"

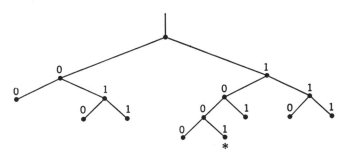

(b) Dichotomous subdivision (an example)

Fig. 6.2.   Semantic information interpreted as "successive selection" or "classifications."

We have already made some reference to this subject in the historical essay of Chapter 2, and the reader is referred again to the special system of George Dalgarno (Chapter 2, Section 1). Both Ampère and Jeremy Bentham[A] evolved systems based upon successive *dichotomies*.

Such classification is performed by a language system with simple and precise syntactical rules. Yet, ordinary language is frequently employed for conveying information in a similar, though less highly formalized, manner, as was illustrated at the commencement of this Section by sentences about trains leaving stations, et cetera.   Although the syntactical structures of such sentences are relatively complex, the narrowing down of uncertainty, at semantic level, rests upon there being a kind of syntactical hierarchy amongst words or phrases denoting classes, things, events, et cetera, about which information is sought.   If we use these same sentence examples again, the word "somewhere" may be substituted, in simple direct statements, for the word "station," but the converse does not always hold; again "station" may be substituted for "King's Cross Station," but not necessarily conversely.

2. ARE DIFFERENT MEASURES OF "INFORMATION" NEEDED?

It could be argued that although *information* is a many-sided concept, the Wiener-Shannon measure of the selective information rate of signals in terms of their statistical rarity is all that is needed; that to refer to semantics and pragmatics is to introduce red herrings.   Such an argument might be based, for instance, upon the assumption that the frequency with which a statement is uttered (e.g., "I missed the train") equals the frequency with which the event or experience actually occurs.

But such a view would be demonstrably false and would rest upon a misunderstanding of the term "semantic information."   It is true, of course, that the Wiener-Shannon measure may be applied not only to signals, to ensembles of letters, words, phrases, or to any segments, but also to ensembles of specified things, events, et cetera, or even to ensembles of reactions of the recipient of the signals.[9,*]   It might be possible to go further; perhaps most generally a complete ensemble might be conceived, representing the statistical properties of a source, consisting not only of signals with known *n*-gram probabilities but taken together with their designata; in order to include the semantic, "meaningful" aspect as far as possible, account might be taken of the recipient's interpretations or reactions, by associating these with the signals through a set of conditional probabilities.   Such would be a purely objective use of the Wiener-Shannon measure, merely by interpreting the term *ensemble* in a broader sense than they do; but it rather misses the point.   Let us look further.

The Wiener-Shannon measure applies to a statistically stationary source of signals (or observed events).   Suppose that by immense effort and patience we observe these signals (but not any actual person uttering them)

* G. A. Barnard suggests a general abstract theory, in which the elements in the *ensemble* alternatively represent (*a*) "signs," as in the theory of communication; (*b*) "propositions," in the theory of probability; or (*c*) "problems," in the theory of computation.   See reference 14.

for long enough to gather many samples or segments, which we compare and analyze; we might, too, make good estimates of the various *n*-gram probabilities. From examination of this mass of signal data we might, in principle, formulate the syntactic rules of the source language (but without reference to designata). Such rules might tell us how sentences are constructed, but the sentences would be utterly void of "meaning" to us the observers; they would be mere chains or signal elements and spaces. (The fact that we might make prudent guesses, by comparison to known language habits, is immaterial.) We should not be able to draw any logical conclusions from these sentences enabling us, for example, to take action with regard to their designata; they would tell us nothing about the outside world from which we, as detached observers of the source, could draw conclusions. For example, we might observe both the signals "This shop is open only on weekdays" and "This shop is closed on Sundays" with certain probabilities, but there would be no means of ascertaining their semantic identity—because the mutual exclusiveness of open/closed and weekdays/Sundays would not be evident. Naturally we might be able to guess, or infer, a great deal more about this source language than its syntactical structure, as we do when learning a foreign language or when breaking a cryptogram; but this would be cheating, from our present point of view, since it would require us to go beyond mere observation of physical signals. Being human, by the use of judicious guessing we might infer much of the semantic structure of the source language.

"Semantic information" cannot then be interpreted solely at syntactic level. But it undoubtedly depends in part upon the syntax of the language, upon the rules for the construction of sentences and upon rules whereby other sentences may be constructed from these sentences.

So far, everyday human languages have proved impossibly complex for any precise measure to be applied to their "semantic content." We have made some examination of their extraordinary flexibility, in Chapter 3, and of how they attain their purpose in ways which are so frequently not in the least logical. But everyday languages are not the only systems of signs. A great deal of scientific language is highly disciplined, especially that which is set down as mathematical theory. Such language systems, having more truly logical structures, provide material more amenable to semantic-information measurement.

Pure mathematics is a "language" possessing a logical syntax, a system of signs, and rules for relating signs. Regarded as a pure syntactical system, there can be no designata for the signs, in contrast to *applied* mathematics in which the signs denote magnitudes, numbers of things, and other properties of the outside world.[266] Given a set of algebraic equations, we can deduce their solution by acting upon the syntactical rules. It is frequently stated that this solution, being implicit in, and deduced from, the set of equations, contains "no more information" than they do. In what sense can the term "information" be taken here? Clearly not in the Wiener-Shannon sense, but at best in some rather vague logical sense again not in any semantical sense, for the system is one of pure syntax. G. A. Barnard has pointed out that this conclusion does not imply that mathematicians do no useful work! Rather than speak of information, he suggests that a number may be attached to any computational problem as a measure of its *difficulty*.[14]

In regard to deduction in logic (rather than in pure mathematics), it was John Stuart Mill who, a hundred years ago, observed that induction and not deduction is the only road to new knowledge.[A] He argued that, from the famed syllogism "All men are mortal; Socrates is a man; therefore Socrates is mortal," we do not infer a new truth. Rather the step to novelty comes from formulating the initial premise, "All men are mortal," for this itself is either an induction from particular observations ("Tom, Dick and Harry are men") or the class "all men" presupposes the conclusion: "Socrates is a man."

It is the writer's opinion that, as yet, it is too soon to pronounce judgment as to whether there is any value in setting up different measures of information. Here, we merely introduce the reader to some of the theoretical studies and arguments in this new field. We shall be returning to this general question in Section 4, but let us now glance at one particular mathematical treatment of information at the semantic level.

3. ABOUT "SEMANTIC INFORMATION"

The only investigation, of which your author is aware, into the possibilities of actually applying a measure to semantic information is that done by Bar-Hillel, being based upon Carnap's theory of inductive probability.[49,*]

We shall argue later that *semantics* is the one aspect of semiotic which is of less interest in the mathematical or physical study of human communication; it really falls between the two stools of *syntactics* and *pragmatics*. Both these latter concern more objective aspects of the study. Syntactics concerns the physical signs themselves, abstracted from their users, and it is in this field that Shannon's theory lies. Pragmatics concerns specific users and their responses to signs; it is the psychological side.

It will be remembered that the semantic side of the Ogden and Richards triangle (Fig. 3.6) was shown dotted, representing an imputed relationship;

---

* For those readers to whom such matters are new, an elementary introduction will be found in reference 52.

the true relationship between the symbol and the referent is via the other two sides of the triangle (symbol-thought, thought-referent), as these authors point out.[E]   For a discussion of "meaning," in a human communication situation (see Chapter 3, Section 6.2), it is necessary to bring in the specific users of the signs, those in whom the referent and the sign are associated in thought—an association dependent upon their individual past experiences (meaning *to* somebody).   That is, the discussion cannot lie wholly within the abstracted semantic level but must include pragmatic considerations.

Bar-Hillel and Carnap, to whose theory of semantic information we shall refer in Section 3.2, declare in fact that they are not concerned with human communication at all, or indeed with ordinary, historical languages. Their theory relates to *language systems*, and sets up a measure of the *semantic-information content* of simple statements or propositions; but the process of communication is not referred to.

In spite of this lack of relevance to our main study here, the writer feels it advisable to give some sketch of the basic idea in order to see better their relationship with other aspects of our subject.   First it will be necessary to glance again at two distinct concepts of probability.

3.1. STATISTICAL PROBABILITY AND INDUCTIVE PROBABILITY

The term *probability* is ambiguous.   Broadly speaking, it is used for two distinct concepts.   The simpler of these, statistical probability,[G] deals with the outcome of physical or conceptual experiments, such as the probability of having twins or the probability of living to be a hundred or, to use an example in communication theory, as when we say the probability of the letter N in printed English in 0.08.   In practice, such figures are *estimates* of probabilities, being based upon a finite, though no doubt large, frequency count.   The statistical probability itself is a limit toward which we assume our estimate converges, as we perform longer and longer counts. As with all mathematics, there is no need of definition of the basic concepts, but only of the formulation of rules for using them.   We do not need to know what probabilities "are," but rather how to combine them.[G]   But, nevertheless, it helps most people to have intuitive notions of the basic concepts, though such notions can become a hindrance to the expert.

Historically speaking, probability theory first emerged from a correspondence between Pascal and Fermat, in connection with betting and games of chance, at the middle of the seventeenth century.[76]   This original interest is somewhat in contrast with the modern emphasis on statistical, or direct, probability, since it is concerned with the making of judgments and with inductive reasoning.   When a racegoer places a bet on a horse, he is expressing his confidence in a hypothesis—that the horse will ("probably") win. Such an *inductive probability* cannot be interpreted as a frequency, because there is here only one event (one race, one win). His estimate of the chance will usually be based upon knowledge of this horse's past performances, and of those of the others.

So, too, with the scientist. His laboratory observations provide him with *evidence*, which enables him to place "odds" upon different explanatory hypotheses. Further experiments may confirm some hypotheses, weaken others, and so change the odds. The process of human communication is equally based upon such inference. The signals constitute no more than evidence of the speaker's messages; the listener is in effect continually forming hypotheses, at many different levels—about the speaker's language, his subject matter, his interests, purpose, and argument. In the study of human communication both statistical and inductive probabilities are relevant—but they should be carefully distinguished.

A statistical probability applies to classes of things, or to a system; but an inductive probability applies to pairs of statements, the "hypothesis" and the "evidence." For example, the probability of letter E in English, of someone's being left-handed in London, of a "wrong number" telephone call, are all estimated relative frequencies; they are on a level with physical properties of the systems referred to. But on the other hand, the "probability" of a horse's winning a race is different—it depends upon the evidence expressing, say, the bettor's knowledge. If our bettor is a complete novice, then there will be no reason to attach a higher probability to one horse than to any other; as with tossing a coin, we assume *a priori* that the two sides are so physically alike that the odds are 50-50.* Such assumption would be a consequence of the *principle of indifference* or of *insufficient* reason (or again, of *cogent* reason[F]). However, if our bettor is an old hand at race going, and studies form, then relative to his knowledge as evidence, there is reason to place far higher odds on the success of one horse than on that of the others; again, when tossing a coin a gambler may be a cheat who knows the coin to be loaded.† Inductive probability is then not a physical property of a thing or a system but is a relation between a hypothesis and some evidence, the latter usually expressing someone's knowledge.

In his *Logical Foundations of Probability*, Carnap sets out to sharpen the theory of inductive probability into as precise a tool of research as that of statistical probability. He approaches this task through consideration of *statements* and their logical form, and makes extensive use of symbolic logic; in particular, he is concerned with the question of the *a priori* probabilities

---

* In fact, the two sides of a coin are not *exactly* alike in all physical respects, or they would be indistinguishable.

† However, if the user performs the experiment of tossing the coin thousands of times, he may estimate the *statistical probability* of heads or tails.

of statements and of how measures may be attached to these. Here, we shall do no more than distinguish between two different measures and give some slight indication of their relevance to the semantic information content of statements, as expressed in Bar-Hillel's theory.

It is of course only the question of the *a priori* probabilities of hypotheses which presents any difficulties or matters of controversy; only the question of assigning or distributing a probability measure over a number of alternative hypotheses, in the first place, in the absence of evidence or with limited evidence. The actual process of applying Bayes's theorem to the calculation of a posterior probability, as a likelihood function, on the basis of some evidence, is quite straightforward and is as precise and logical as a calculation in statistical probability.*   Intuition and judgment are not involved; it is over Bayes's axiom, which assigns equal *a priori* probabilities to alternative hypotheses in the absence of initial evidence, that discussion may arise.

3.2. A priori probabilities and the principle of indifference— Carnap's two methods

For a simple example of two different methods of assigning *a priori* probabilities to hypotheses, as suggested by Carnap,[52] let us suppose we have access to a library which we understand may contain both English books and Translations—though we have no idea of their relative proportion. We enter the library and take a book at random; what is the probability of its being English? From the Principle of Indifference we should assign probability 1/2. Then we take a second, a third, and, say, a fourth book. How should we readjust the probabilities, each time, of the last one's being English, and can allowance be made for learning from the accumulating evidence of successive books?

Let us imagine four books to have been taken; Fig. 6.3 shows the sixteen possible alternative sequences. From the Principle of Indifference we might assign prior probability 1/16 to each alternative. Now suppose we have drawn the first three, thereby identifying one particular sequence. Then the probability of the fourth's being English is still 1/2, as the reader may test for himself. Of course, such a principle of distributing the prior probabilities equally among all possible alternative *sequences* takes no account of accumulating evidence.

Instead, Carnap suggests assigning equal prior probabilities to the different combinations. In Fig. 6.3, the 16 alternative sequences are grouped together in groups having equal proportions of like to unlike members; there are 5 groups and equal prior probabilities 1/5 attached to each. But the groups must be of different sizes, consisting of the various

* See Chapter 2, Section 4, and Chapter 5, Section 6.2.

alternative sequences; then the group probability 1/5 is divided equally, again from the Principle of Indifference, amongst these alternative sequences within the group.   This determines the prior probability of every possible sequence of four, as listed in the last column (individual distribution); these are now not all equal.

		Possible Sequences				Method I — A Priori Probability	Method II — A Priori Probabilities of	
							Groups	Sequences
1	1	●	●	●	●	$\frac{1}{16}$	$\frac{1}{5}$ {	$\frac{12}{60}$
2	2	●	●	●	○	$\frac{1}{16}$		$\frac{3}{60}$
	3	●	●	○	●	$\frac{1}{16}$		$\frac{3}{60}$
	4	●	○	●	●	$\frac{1}{16}$	$\frac{1}{5}$	$\frac{3}{60}$
	5	○	●	●	●	$\frac{1}{16}$		$\frac{3}{60}$
3	6	●	●	○	○	$\frac{1}{16}$		$\frac{2}{60}$
	7	●	○	●	○	$\frac{1}{16}$		$\frac{2}{60}$
	8	●	○	○	●	$\frac{1}{16}$	$\frac{1}{5}$	$\frac{2}{60}$
	9	○	●	●	○	$\frac{1}{16}$		$\frac{2}{60}$
	10	○	●	○	●	$\frac{1}{16}$		$\frac{2}{60}$
	11	○	○	●	●	$\frac{1}{16}$		$\frac{2}{60}$
4	12	●	○	○	○	$\frac{1}{16}$		$\frac{3}{60}$
	13	○	●	○	○	$\frac{1}{16}$		$\frac{3}{60}$
	14	○	○	●	○	$\frac{1}{16}$	$\frac{1}{5}$	$\frac{3}{60}$
	15	○	○	○	●	$\frac{1}{16}$		$\frac{3}{60}$
5	16	○	○	○	○	$\frac{1}{16}$	$\frac{1}{5}$ {	$\frac{12}{60}$

Fig. 6.3.   The Principle of Indifference.   A priori attachment of probabilities to the drawing of books from a library, containing English ● and translated ○ books in unknown proportions (after Carnap, with grateful acknowledgment).

Such a method of employing the Principle of Indifference, says Carnap, takes account of learning by experience.   For example, suppose an actual drawing of three resulted in the sequence: English-English-Translation (numbers 3 or 6 in the figure); such evidence suggests a preponderance of

English books over Translations. As we see, the chance of the fourth's being English is in fact 3/60 as against 2/60 for Translation. The ratio is three to two, which gives the odds in favor of English.

3.3. A MEASURE OF SEMANTIC-INFORMATION CONTENT, BASED UPON CARNAP'S "LOGICAL PROBABILITIES"

The concepts used in this theory are expressly framed for discussion of semantic content, as opposed to those of Shannon's selective-information theory which are deliberately abstracted from such content.[13] Nevertheless, this semantic theory is likewise restricted to a right and proper sphere of application. It is concerned only with the *semantic-information content* of simple "declarative sentences" ("statements" or "propositions") and does not touch upon the pragmatical aspect of language; that is, it does not concern specific users of the statements, or involve the consequences or the value of the information to any one person.[C, D] The theory is in no way concerned with distinction between the "meaning of a sentence to a recipient" and the "intended meaning of a speaker," which Weaver refers to as "the semantic problem of communication."* In fact, we should warn the reader, the theory is not concerned with *communication* at all—only with the semantic information "contained in" statements. Care must therefore be taken to guard against temptation to use this theory, and the information measure it sets up, in relation to experimental psychological work. The theory relates only to the semantic and syntactic aspects of *language systems* and abstracts from pragmatics. Although, in the study of human language, these three divisions—syntactics, semantics, and pragmatics—cannot be completely isolated, but are to some extent mutually dependent, it is more readily possible to keep them distinct in the setting up of language systems.

A pure *language system* is an artificial ("synthetic," "constructed," "set-up") language with clearly defined syntax and rules. The language system concerned here is used for making simple statements about *individuals* (things, people, events, situations, etc.) having certain *attributes* or properties. The words or symbols denoting such attributes are termed *predicates*. Statements are then formed with the aid of the *logical connectives* (*not* $\sim$; *and* & ; *or* $\vee$; *if . . . then . . .* $\supset$; *if and only if* $\equiv$). To take a most simple example, we may set up a language system for describing the books in a library (*individuals* denoted by $a_1 \, a_2 \cdots a_n$) which are either Fiction or non-Fiction (*predicates*, F or $\sim$F) and written in English or in some foreign language (*predicates*, E, $\sim$E). With such a language system we are restricted to a "universe of discourse" concerning books, fiction-or-not, in English-or-not; we can discuss nothing else—not, for instance, the political

* See Chapter 3, Section 6.2, and footnote on p. 114.

situation in Bulgaria, nor the weather, nor the declining morals of our young—we are simply outside ordinary language.

With this system, there are four *strongest factual* statements which can be made about any one individual (book a)*: (*a*) Fa & Ea; (*b*) Fa & ~Ea; (*c*) ~Fa & Ea; (*d*) ~Fa & ~Ea.   Other statements are (*e*) Fa ∨ ~Fa, which is a tautology, or (*f*) Fa & ~Fa, which is a contradiction.

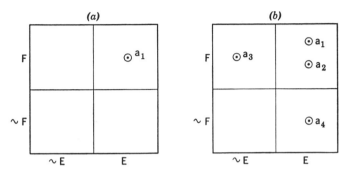

Fig. 6.4.   Simple attribute space of two predicates and their negations, showing (*a*) one individual system point a_1 corresponding to the statement: "Fa_1 & Ea_1," and (*b*) one state-description of four individuals Fa_1 & Ea_1 & Fa_2 & Ea_2 & Fa_3 & ~ Ea_3 & ~ Fa_4 & Ea_4.

We have selected here a very simple language system, but it will serve our purpose, which is not to give an exposition of one theory of semantic information (so adequately presented elsewhere)[c] but to introduce it and to set it in relation to the whole study we are attempting in this book. Such a language system is another instance of a *system*, to which some of the concepts of statistical mechanics are relevant, in a manner which is somewhat analogous to their use in statistical communication theory (see Chapter 5).   Boltzmann's system of description for a "perfect gas" has been found to be of extraordinary generality and applicability, as Wiener has observed.[349]   Language systems are as distinct from real historical languages as "perfect gases" are from the gases in Nature; both are artificial, ideal constructs.   But just as "perfect gases" have proved to be of the greatest value in physics, so language-system study may eventually prove to be of value in the understanding of historical human language, and hence of communication.

The diagram in Fig. 6.4 represents the "universe of discourse" for our present example—the discussion of library books (F, ~F; E, ~E)—as a two-dimensional attribute space, quantized into four cells.   The predicates (denoting attributes) are binary in this example, and the diagram may be

* In this notation Fa reads "the book 'a' is Fiction" . . . etc.

compared to that of Fig. 3.1(b).   In the general case, n pairs of attributes are used and the space becomes an n-attribute space, quantized into 2^n cells; it then simulates a special analogy to Boltzmann's quantized phase space.

Any statement, such as Fa_1 & Ea_1 (read "Book a_1 is Fiction and English"), is represented by placing a *system point* inside the appropriate cell, as shown by the point a_1 in the diagram; if points $a_2 a_3 \cdots a_n$ are inserted in turn, according to the statements made about these individuals, then we have a whole distribution of identified system points in the attribute space.   Then, to continue the statistical-mechanical analogy, the *structure-description* of this semantical system (Boltzmann's "macrostate") tells *how many* individuals occupy each cell; but a *state-description* tells *which* individuals occupy them (Boltzmann's "microstate").   All this of course accepts that the various "states of the system" are deductively independent—that is, statements about any one individual cannot be deduced from statements about any others.

Any statement of the type Fa_1 ("Book a_1 is Fiction") is called an *atomic statement*, and does not wholly locate a system point within one cell; then from the accepted independence of states, just referred to, we may say:

$Fa_1 \equiv Fa_1 +$ any state of the remaining $(n - 1)$ individuals
Hence

$$
\left.
\begin{aligned}
Fa_1 \equiv \ & (Fa_1 \text{ & } Ea_1 \text{ & } Fa_2 \text{ & } Ea_2 \text{ & } \cdots \text{ & } Fa_n \text{ & } Ea_n) \\
\vee \ & (Fa_1 \text{ & } Ea_1 \text{ & } Fa_2 \text{ & } Ea_2 \text{ & } \cdots \text{ & } Fa_n \text{ & } \sim Ea_n) \\
\vee \ & (Fa_1 \text{ & } Ea_1 \text{ & } Fa_2 \text{ & } Ea_2 \text{ & } \cdots \text{ & } \sim Fa_n \text{ & } \sim Ea_n) \\
\vee \ & \ldots \text{. etc.} \\
\vee \ & (Fa_1 \text{ & } \sim Ea_1 \text{ & } \sim Fa_2 \text{ & } \sim Ea_2 \text{ & } \cdots \text{ & } \sim Fa_n \text{ & } \sim Ea_n)
\end{aligned}
\right\}
\begin{aligned}
& z_1 \\
& z_2 \\
& z_3 \\
& \vdots \\
& z_2 2^{n-1}
\end{aligned}
$$
(6.1)

(braced group labelled: Exclusive State-Descriptions*)*

That is to say, any such statement is logically equivalent to a *disjunction* of many state-descriptions.   Notice that a state-description represents a "strongest" factual statement which can be made, within a given universe of discourse; it uniquely places the complete set of system points within the cells of attribute space.   Figure 6.4(b) illustrates one state-description corresponding to the simple case of four individuals and two pairs of properties (attributes).

Now, given such a language system, what measure may be applied to the "semantic-information content" [cont (i)] of an atomic statement, such as Fa_1 for example?   The measure which has been suggested is a function of the *logical probability*[49] $P(i)$ of the statement.   If i and j are two statements, and if

$$P(i) > P(j)$$

Then

$$\text{cont } (i) < \text{cont } (j)$$

Here P is not a relative frequency, but is a logical probability—a term which will require clarification.

One would like to have:

$$\text{cont } (i \,\&\, j) = \text{cont } (i) + \text{cont } (j) \tag{6.2}$$

in the case that i and j are logically independent. However, "logical independence" may be interpreted in two ways. First, it may imply that i and j are content exclusive (contain no factual consequences in common); second, that i and j are inductively independent. Roughly, inductively independent means that $P_j(i) = P(i)$. For example, the two statements Fa_1 and $\sim Ea_1$ are independent in the second sense, but not in the first, since their contents are not exclusive. Bar-Hillel observes that these two interpretations of "logical independence" appear to be in conflict, suggesting that, dependent upon the specification of "logically independent," there are two concepts of "amount of information" contained in a statement. We refer here to one only.

In order to clarify the term "logical probability," let us return to equation 6.1 above, relating an atomic statement Fa_1 to a disjunction of exclusive state-descriptions $z_1 z_2 \cdots z_2 2^{n-1}$. Can we assign a measure M to each state-description, such that $\sum_r M(z_r) = 1$? Then the M-value of the statement Fa_1 is equal to the sum of all the M-values of the state-descriptions to the disjunction of which Fa_1 is logically equivalent. It might seem simplest to assign *a priori* equal measures to each state-description (by the Principle of Indifference)—but there are many M-functions which could be chosen.

As an alternative, there is another approach (referred to by Carnap [49] as "not inadequate"), which is to assign equal measure-values M to each *structure*-description. [13] Now a given structure-description may be represented as a disjunction of a number S_r of different state-descriptions (by permuting the individuals); but the number S_r depends upon the particular structure-description r. Thus it is clear that the various state-descriptions cannot all receive the same measure-value, if each is assigned $1/S_r$th of that assigned to each structure-description. It is this measure-function M which is termed a "logical probability."

We have already illustrated the difference between assigning equal measure-values to the structure-descriptions and to the state-descriptions, in the preceding Section 3.2, by a most simple example of two predicates (statements: "This book is English," "This book is not English," denoted by ● and ○ in Fig. 6.3). In Fig. 6.3 the five *groups* (structure-descriptions) of four individuals are shown to include the alternative combinations (state-descriptions); then the final column shows the logical probabilities.

As we illustrated Carnap's argument before, using this simple example, such logical probabilities take account of our intuitive notions about learning from experience.   If $a_1\ a_2\ a_3\ a_4$ represent the sequence of individuals, then

$$P(Ea_4|Ea_3 \ \& \ Ea_2 \ \& \ Ea_1) > P(Ea_3|Ea_2 \ \& \ Ea_1) > P(Ea_2|Ea_1) > P(Ea_1)$$

(where $>$ means "is greater than"), as the reader may check for himself by calculating the values of these probabilities.   Such a method of assigning *a priori* probabilities then, it is argued, accords with our notions about confirmation of hypotheses by accumulating evidence.

Bar-Hillel and Carnap have developed a number of theorems concerning the content of a statement [cont (i)] including those for disjunctions and conjunctions of different statements.[13]   In many ways their theory conceptually parallels the statistical theory of communication of Shannon, though of course it is concerned essentially with the semantic level of language and not purely with the syntactic or signal level.   Again it is based upon inductive logic (as Shannon's theory concerns inductive or "inverse" probability), and presents theorems about conditional statements such as, for example, cont $(j|i)$ = cont $(i \ \& \ j)$ − cont (i), which bears superficial resemblance in form to Shannon's theorem $H(x|y) = H(x,y) - H(y)$, though this latter theorem refers to information-rate *averages*.   These authors refer also to semantic *noise* (the cause of wrong interpretation of messages) which bears some analogy[155] to the engineer's "noise" (the cause of wrong reception of signals); and again, they refer to the *efficiency* of a language, in comparison to the efficiency of a signal code.

Information is always a relative matter—an increase or a decrease. The semantic-information content of a statement (which includes all that is logically implicit in that statement) is available only insofar as the rules of the language system are known; similarly, in the Shannon theory, selective information from a source of signals depends upon prior knowledge of the signal probabilities (and, if noise is present, of its statistics too).

Bar-Hillel has suggested that the statistical theory of communication may be mapped, without remainder, on to the semantic theory, but not vice versa. For although it appears that the semantic theory is severely restricted to simple declarative statements (whereas the statistical theory may be set to work upon any *ensemble* of signs), Bar-Hillel and Carnap observe that: "To the expression 'the amount of information conveyed by the symbol s' the expression 'the amount of (semantic) information conveyed by the statement "the symbol s is transmitted"' can be correlated."[13,*] Referring back to Fig. 3.2(a) we may regard the signal ("symbol") s as one of the set employed in the communication channel $A \rightarrow B$, being

* We speak of *sign* or *signal* rather than "symbol," in this book.

watched and described by an external observer; then the statement "The symbol *s* is transmitted" is made by this observer is his meta-language, whereas *s* is in the object-language and its "meaning" is quite irrelevant to the measure of the semantic information content of this statement. It is the semantic theory of this meta-language upon which the statistical theory may be mapped. There is here of course no question of semantics within the object-channel itself; the "meanings" of the transmitted signals (such as *s*) to either communicants *A* or *B* are entirely private to them but do not form any part of either the statistical theory or the semantic theory, as formulated by the external observer.*

4. SYNTACTIC, SEMANTIC, AND PRAGMATIC "INFORMATION"—A RELATIONSHIP

Let us return for a moment to the discussion started in Section 1.2 concerning different aspects of the concept of "information."

We have referred to the division of language study (or semiotic in general) into *syntactics* (signs and relations between signs), *semantics* (relations between signs and their designata) and *pragmatics* (aspects which involve sign users). This is a convenient classification only; such divisions do not form distinct, self-contained studies.[B]

Weaver[297] has classified the whole problem of communication into three parts: (*a*) the *technical* problem (signals and their correct transmission), (*b*) the *semantic* problem, and (*c*) the *effectiveness* problem (effect of signals upon behavior of recipient).

At this point we should be careful, or we may be tempted to identify (*a*), (*b*), and (*c*) here to the three levels of semiotic—syntactics, semantics, and pragmatics. However, we should note that these three levels, each concerning rules (relationships), are relevant to analysis of language as expressed in meta-language, not to object-language itself. We have sought to avoid confusion on this point by use of Fig. 3.2 and by drawing a distinction between an external observer and a participant-observer (though both of course report their findings in a meta-language). At the moment, it is the term *semantics* which appears ambiguous. For instance, as used by logicians (e.g., in the Carnap and Bar-Hillel theory), *semantics* refers to theory expressed in meta-language, abstracted from all specific human sign users, and concerns rules relating signs and designata. But semantics is also a term frequently employed by others to denote "theories of meaning," discussed in relation to specific sign users in specific environments;

* See MacKay's remarks in discussion following Bar-Hillel and Carnap's paper in reference 166.

such a view of semantics is more closely related to study of communication, and it is this which Weaver presumably has in mind.

We have so far discussed two concepts of "probability," in relation to the syntactic and semantic levels. Let us summarize these before looking at the pragmatic level:

(a) The Shannon theory of communication describes "information rate" objectively, entirely in terms of signs and of statistical relations between signs. It may thus be regarded as a syntactical theory (though concerned only with a part of syntax, namely with the rules of *formation*) and, as such, lies at the most *basic* level of the whole concept. The probabilities concerned are relative frequencies of signs—or their estimates (*statistical probabilities*). The theory is wholly expressed in the meta-language of an outside observer [(a) in Fig. 3.2].

(b) The Bar-Hillel and Carnap theory is essentially a semantic theory but, as such, includes elements of syntactics also. It is a synthetic, rather than analytic, approach, having as its purpose the measurement of the semantic-information content of simple declarative sentences (statements, propositions) formed in a defined language system. It makes no reference to *communication* between persons per se, or to natural historical languages. The measure is set up in terms of Carnap's *logical probabilities*, and again the theory may be regarded as expressed in the meta-language of an external observer.

Now what of "pragmatic information"? At present, no mathematical theory has been published, corresponding in any way to extensions of the existing theories. It is at this level that the true process of human communication can be considered—the use of signs by people in specific circumstances and environments, the whole "effectiveness" problem of Weaver. To the pragmatic level we must relegate all questions of value or usefulness of messages, all questions of sign recognition and interpretation, and all other aspects which we would regard as psychological in character. Again, the concepts of meaning *to* specific people reaches this level; associations of signs and designata in the mind of someone, in some specific situation, are semantic-pragmatic questions.

While discussing this more full-blooded problem of human communication, it may be helpful to make reference to several ideas from which the existing mathematical theories necessarily abstract; but we are forced, from this point on, to be speculative.

Thus it may be illuminating to consider some of the pragmatic aspects of communication from the point of view of one of the participants, in terms of subjective probabilities[190] interpreted as *degrees of belief*; we shall be referring to this, shortly.

"Information" in most, if not all, of its connotations seems to rest upon the notion of *selection power*. The Shannon theory regards the information source, in emitting the signals (signs), as exerting a selective power upon an ensemble of messages.* In the Carnap-Bar-Hillel semantic theory,

* See Weaver's section of reference 297.

the information content of statements relates to the selective power they exert upon ensembles of states. Again, at its pragmatic level, in true communicative situations (and speaking only descriptively now) a source of information has a certain value to a recipient, where "value" may be regarded as a "selection power." Gabor,[125] for example, observes that what people value in a source of information (i.e., what they are prepared to pay for) depends upon its *exclusiveness* and *prediction* power; he cites instances of a newspaper editor hoping for a "scoop" and a racegoer receiving information from a tipster. "Exclusiveness" here implies the selecting of that one particular recipient out of the population, while the "prediction" value of information rests upon the power it gives to the recipient to select his future action, out of a whole range of prior uncertainty as to what action to take. Again, signs have the power to select responses in people, such responses depending upon a totality of conditions. Human communication channels consist of individuals in conversation, or in various forms of social intercourse. Each individual and each conversation is unique; different people react to signs in different ways, depending each upon their own past experiences and upon the environment at the time. It is such variations, such differences, which give rise to the principal problems in the study of human communication.

4.1. The subjective and objective worlds—the Cartesian dualism

The "external observer" is limited in what he can report upon. Thus he can observe the transmission of signs between the communicants, and assess their probabilities objectively, as frequencies; he can observe the overt reactions set up by these signs in their users. In principle, and if instruments were available, he might look inside the heads of those he is observing, and note physiological processes at work. But on no account can he observe the thoughts of these people. Thoughts, beliefs, judgments, emotions are all private; they cannot be observed* and described in an external observer's meta-language.

We have inherited a philosophical theory, which perhaps originates from Descartes, that there are two distinct worlds; an external or "real" world, and an internal or "mental" world. · This dualism achieved its most distinct form as the machinist-vitalist schism, and it has colored our thinking to this day. We speak of the body *and* the mind, the first being material, subject to the laws of mechanics, the second non-material; the mind "controls" the body.[284] Again, we have come to regard the "external real world" as sending signs or stimuli to our eyes, ears, and skin; we see

---

* The fact that we cannot observe what goes on in another person's mind must not lead us to assume that we necessarily do know what goes on in our own (see Chapter 7, Section 2).

or hear this world "through" our eyes and ears, as though "we" were all little creatures sitting inside skulls, looking and listening through eye and ear windows and keyholes.   To refer to an earlier metaphor, we sometimes speak of "ultimate reality" as though it were a kind of loom, behind which we can never pass and the true workings of which we can never see; we must remain content to watch the patterns it weaves.

With the growth of the modern interest in cybernetics and in the development of calculating machines with amazing potential, questions such as "Can a machine think?" have been raised from their seventeenth- and eighteenth-century interment.   Such questions are now passing out of fashion again and losing their popular appeal, as it is realized that a string of words with a query mark at the end need not be a question.   Such pseudo-questions can be formed by taking terms from the two sides of this Cartesian dualism—words like *machine* come from an external-world language, proper for the discussion of overt behavior, physics, physiology, et cetera; and words like *think* are proper to discussion of cognitive matters. Rather than speak of two worlds, it helps clarify the issue to speak of two languages.   Sometimes it is convenient to formulate propositions in one language and sometimes in another.[244]   This is not to say that distinguishing between two types of language (overt and cognitive) *solves* philosophical problems necessarily;* rather it helps to clarify argument and avoid pseudo-questions.   The pragmatist William James, referred to "dispute that is purely verbal" as being the source of the materialist-theist dualism.[391]

Though there are some who would seek a purely behavioristic description of human communication, such an approach puts a severe restriction upon the aspects of the phenomena which may be examined.   While there remain so many obscure aspects, understanding may come more readily if we use all the tools at our disposal.   It is, of course, important to *distinguish* between the objective and subjective views, but we cannot pretend the latter are of no concern.   Dismissal of subjective matters as being scientifically indecent springs from an excessive zeal for detachment, from the view that an observer is a kind of inanimate transducer of the raw data of Nature, which reaches his senses, is coded there into meta-language, and is finally given out to the publisher to appear in printed papers (these are usually written in the third person, which adds to the illusion of impersonality).   But it must never be forgotten that the observer, too, is one of God's creatures—he experiences emotions and desires, he has prejudices and beliefs.   The "observations" he makes are nothing but his own hypotheses, which he frames as best he can in the light of his personal experience.

As with other dualisms in science, there can be advantages in referring to both sides of the picture, as long as we do not always insist on seeing

* For example, Popper (see reference 267) stoutly maintains it does not.

both sides at once. The objective view, which is predominant in the physical sciences and in strict behaviorist psychology, comes from regarding the observer as being "in" the real world, which is "out there," around him; he can stretch out his hand and touch it, or he can see it "through" his eyes. The subjective view comes from regarding the world as being in the mind of the observer, reality as mental experience.

The necessary distinction between "objectivity" and "subjectivity," in the study of communication, may be brought out by distinguishing between the two kinds of observer [Fig. 3.2(a) and (b)]. Thus the observer type (a) is external to the observed phenomenon; he can observe and report upon signals and overt behavior—but he can make no observations upon thoughts other than his own. Although the observer is himself a human being, it can readily be arranged that his own behavior does not reflect back upon, and disturb, the object-channel. But if one of the communicants acts also as an observer, as in (b), and gives his account of the phenomenon of which he himself forms an integral part, with his thoughts and beliefs, then the situation is very different.

4.2. SUBJECTIVE PROBABILITIES AND "DEGREES OF BELIEF"

Putting yourself in the position of observer-communicant B in Fig. 3.2(b), you might speak of the probabilities of sign-events *to* you. From past experience you have built up degrees of belief, concerning which signs arrive more often than others. Though you may be unable to attach numerical frequencies to the signs, such beliefs may extend to *rank-ordering* them. You may believe that the letter T occurs more often than Z, or that some words or phrases are more frequent than others;* you have an immense store of beliefs, gathered from experience, concerning the probabilities of events of all kinds. Good[F] speaks of *intensities* of beliefs; "my belief that it will rain tomorrow is more intense than my belief that the roof above me will collapse."† Of all the immense mental store of data you possess, gathered from experience and contributing to your beliefs, none are more important to communication than those concerning language; beliefs about words and people's habits of speech, about standard phrases, about clichés and the situations in which they are used. On any particular occasion, when communicating, your beliefs concerning what your partner says will, in Good's words, depend upon who *you* are and upon your "state of mind" at the time—that is, upon that particular accumulation of past experiences represented by the word "you."

* The extent of our knowledge, concerning probability rankings and statistical data of our language, is well illustrated by "guessing games" such as described by Shannon, to which we have referred in Chapter 3, Section 6.3.

† With kind permission of the author and of the publisher, Charles Griffen & Co., Ltd.

"Beliefs" and "degrees of belief" are terms we are asked to accept intuitively. But this is no new situation in mathematics (including probability theory) which deals with *relations* between terms leaving an ultimate undefined residue. Mathematics does not enter into what these basic terms "mean," but concerns only relations between them; thus geometry does not depend for its development upon any preconceived ideas as to what "straight lines" *are*, though we may comfort ourselves that we have intuitive thoughts about them.

Ordinary logic and pure mathematics are such highly formalized systems that they are usually regarded as quite abstracted from pragmatics; that is, the specific user and his beliefs do not enter into the system. The rules of (established) mathematics are "generally accepted" (though the beliefs of any particular user are involved in this very acceptance). A lesson we have learned from Locke is that beliefs arise more particularly in connection with the initial axioms or assumptions of a descriptive theory; that is, concerning the real world (see Section 5). Of the real world we can have no true undoubted knowledge. Repeated experience may only give us confirmation or denial of our beliefs, may increase or decrease our degree of belief concerning initial axioms or assumptions made, which are subsequently operated upon deductively by mathematical rules.[190]

Good's primary interest, in this connection, lies in the formulation of a theory of probability which may serve as a basis for examining processes involving *judgments*, the weighing of evidence, and the making of *rational decisions*. These occur in everyday life, in business, in politics, in science. Can they be treated mathematically? It is essentially a pragmatical approach, involving the user and his "state of mind," M; if M be interpreted as the user's "accumulation of experiences," then such a theory of probability partly loses its psychological color and becomes "the logic of degrees of belief and of their possible modification in the light of experience."[F]

We may appear to be straying from our subject of "communication"; but this digression is intentional. There are many points in common between the logic of communication and the logic of experiment and scientific method; there are also many points of distinction, on several planes. On the most objective plane, a distinction arises from the "non-co-operative" nature of the source (an observed phenomenon) in the case of a physical experiment. Mother Nature does not speak to us in language (see Chapter 1, Section 5), or vary her "signs" to assist an investigator in interpreting her "message." Various authors have drawn distinctions between the theories of experiment and of communication; in particular MacKay,[218] whose theory of scientific information is based upon different premises and is quite distinct, in application, from Shannon's theory of communication.*

But in this book we are not concerned with general scientific method, only insofar as certain aspects have some relevance to the problems of human communication. When you are in conversation with a friend, you are certainly observing a phenomenon of Nature—but a unique one. In comparison with looking at, say, plankton through a microscope, there are certain obvious distinctions. First and most important, there is the fact that true communication proceeds by signs, most often linguistically; second, you do not usually make conversation with your friend for the *purpose* of describing his observable attributes of behavior in a scientific report (unless you are a linguist, studying the language of a native); third, there is a distinction of psychological attitude or set;[235] fourth, few would deny that distinctions arise at the ethical level.

To recapitulate: terms such as *belief*, *judgment*, et cetera, do not normally come from the lips of an external passive observer [Fig. 3.2(*a*)], although, being human, all his objective reportings, including probabilities, correspond in fact to his personal judgments, and beliefs; but in the situation as illustrated by Fig. 3.2(*b*) the observer-communicant forms part, a very essential part, of the phenomenon he is observing and reporting upon—like the linguist who converses with a native—so that his beliefs and judgments, and his whole conduct, reflect back upon and affect the behavior, linguistic or otherwise, of the partner he observes, and with whom he communicates.[315] Of course, there are countless examples of scientific experiments in which the observer is physically coupled to the phenomenon observed, to various degrees. In astronomy he is probably the most divorced. But the phenomenon of human communication is particularly sensitive to such coupling.

When conversing with a friend upon some topic, you speak to him and, in turn, you hear him. Physical sounds or signs pass to and fro in a closed cyclic manner; the signs of one stimulate response signs in the other. Conversation we have described as a convergent or "goal-seeking" activity.[256] Breaking into this cycle, at some instant, let us assume you are the hearer, receiving a stream of sounds. Just before receiving these sounds you are in a certain state of mind M_1 possessing certain sets of beliefs. Such beliefs may be regarded as forming your prior set of hypotheses, weighted hypotheses, as though you had in your brain a physiological representation of a *likelihood function* in a space of very large dimensionality—representing your expectations regarding words, subject matter, prejudice, etc., such as have been built up from the evidence of the preceding conversation, and

* In Britain, we try to reserve the title "theory of communication" to denote the theory of communication, reserving the title "theory of information" for a broader field of scientific method, including communication.

dependent upon your whole past experience.   You may then be described as being in a certain initial state of preparedness or *prior state of belief*.*

When your friend now starts to speak, the sounds he makes constitute evidence to you concerning his intended messages.   To these intended messages, being in his mind, you have no direct access, no "true knowledge"; as with any experiment, the evidence received can at best alter your state of belief.   This evidence then converts this prior state of belief to what we may call your posterior state of belief, or preparation for response.[308] Such a change we may perhaps interpret as a kind of pragmatic-information content of the signs—though with no pretense of setting up any true theory —the change from a prior to posterior state of belief.   Such information will be positive if your range of beliefs is sharpened by the receipt of the signs; if your range of hypotheses is reduced, your beliefs become more restricted, your uncertainty is made less.   When you eventually make some overt reaction or response sign, such as answering back, this constitutes a selective action exerted upon you, by the signs (a selection, perhaps, corresponding to your "most intense" belief, though not necessarily).

Your hearing of the utterance, as a physical event, has then two results; it has changed your state of belief and it has selected an overt response in you.   This total change of state, mental and physical, we have previously identified with the "meaning of the utterance to the recipient"[B] (Chapter 3, Section 6.2).

Your hearing of your friend's utterance represents a selective action upon your ensemble of hypotheses—strengthening some, weakening others. From that instant on, you are no longer the same person; the experience has changed your "state of preparedness" for other signs.   Overtly speaking, any utterances or gestures evoked in you constitute signs which correspondingly set up changes in your partner's beliefs; and so the cyclic, goal-seeking process continues.   Your "beliefs" here include not only beliefs about syntactics and semantic attributes of the conversation (i.e., about language and topics), and about the whole environment, but, in particular, *beliefs about your friend's beliefs*.†

A conversation, regarded then as a closed-cycle, goal-seeking activity proceeding by a continual modification of the two communicants' "states of belief" is of extraordinary complexity.   The course of such goal-seeking activity depends upon beliefs about past, present, and future events.   In

* In this book we do not touch upon the physiological correlates of mental processes; we shall say nothing about how probabilities are represented in the brain, how inferences are carried out—nothing, in fact, about brain structure or "mechanism." We discuss only *what*, not *how*.

† Under such a heading might be included those subjective factors we term *confidence*, *suspicion*, *respect*, and many others, which play so important a part in personal communication.

overt terms, behavioral responses are *definite* actions, definite selections from a range of alternatives. A response sign, an utterance or gesture, may be delayed until more evidence is gathered from the partner's speech or action, but it must be made at *some* time.[137]

It is not suggested that a listener's overt response to a sign is a "verdict," arrived at rationally by conscious logical methods, after weighing the "evidence" he has heard. A great deal of our responses in conversation, our interjections, gestures, clichés, are selected in us largely involuntarily; the words are out before we know it—and we may sometimes wish to bite our tongues. Instead, we describe the process *as though* it were of this nature. It is rather the physiological correlates of our "beliefs," "decisions," et cetera, which could be discussed in terms of objective probabilities and logic*—not the (we) mental side, but the (brain) physical side of the dualism. On the mental (we) side then, probabilities are discussible as beliefs, nonnumerical but partially rank-ordered; on the physical (brain) side, probabilities could be considered to be represented as physical matrices, and logical procedures discussed. But "we" do not know what logical processes are executed in the mechanisms of our brains.

There have been many attempts made at descriptions of brain processes according to known physical principles, to set up constructs or artifacts, the properties of which may be compared with those of the brain. Such comparison may lead to suggestions for tests, to find out points of incompleteness in the constructs which may, in turn, be improved. Such a conceptual model building[5, 329, 349] is a principal part of physical science,[162] part of the normal inductive-deductive procedure. And, as such, this type of brain-machine comparison is likely to be of far greater value than making naive comparison between brains and *existing* digital computing machines (let us leave talk of "electronic brains" to newspaper reporters). As models of the brain, these present-day computers fail in many respects[216, 217]—they have never been intended to serve as such, and their designers are justifiably irritated by such comparison. Calculating machines are designed to take over some of the more laborious tasks of human computers, counting, adding, et cetera, . . . extensive arithmetical work, as the spade and lathe take over manual tasks; it is not so much that these machines serve certain brain-like functions, but rather that the human brain is frequently employed on machine-like functions.†

---

* See von Neumann in reference 178.

† Turing (1936) has discussed the possible mechanization of certain procedures in formal logic, with the suggestion that such a machine forms an abstract model of (certain attributes of) a human being. His machine has a finite number of physical "states," which are compared to "states of mind"—or to the physiological correlates of states of mind. See reference 329.

But to return to our theme. A conversation is like a game; and the theory of games has undoubted relevance to the theory of communication.[247] But a game like, say, chess has highly formalized signs and rules; the "language" of chess may be exhaustively described by logical syntax, without the fluidity and uncertainty of human language. So such games form an oversimplified analogy to human conversation.* Before your partner makes a move, you have a prior set of beliefs concerning his strategy (and about his own beliefs, toward the game of chess and toward you). When he makes his move, your beliefs concerning his strategy change; you alter your weighting of alternative hypotheses concerning his play, and you yourself make a move. Such a move is your "verdict," a decisive action, based upon one or more of these hypotheses. Such a decision may be logical and rational on your part, because the rules of chess are so clear-cut and definite. Persons conversant with the rules of chess may proceed rationally and logically—but persons engaged in conversation have no such precise rules to guide them. You don't converse with your wife much in logic unless she too happens to be a logician (in which case, heaven help the children!) The well-defined rules of chess do lend themselves to mechanization, and a great deal of thought has been put into such possibilities; but the development of more complex artifacts, possessing a more flexible and human-like behavior, with ability to overcome errors and to learn by experience, may be long delayed, not, it has been suggested, on the grounds solely of increased complexity but because of the lack of an adequate and suitable theory of logic.†

5. LANGUAGE, LOGIC, AND EXPERIMENT

What has all this talk of mathematics and logic to do with our theme, human communication? Linguists frequently stress that logical implication and inference have little to do, directly, with language as it is actually used in everyday human intercourse. It is, however, not the object-language itself which is necessarily logically structured, but rather the (scientific) meta-language in which the linguist makes statements and propositions about the object-language he is observing.

Intellectual effort and conscious reasoning form a relatively small part of our mental activity. When I am engaged in the to-and-fro cross fire of casual conversation, I do not reason out every word before I speak it, or deliberately structure my phrases in any determined logical way. I do not have to reflect upon the laws of grammar—the words simply tumble out. Just as when I walk along the pavement, I do not reason out every

* See also Ross's remarks after Mandelbrot in reference 166.
† See again von-Neumann in reference 178.

step. Again, when I first learned to drive a car, I needed to "think out" which was the clutch, brake, and accelerator and use them according to rules; but now the habits of driving have become engrained. No; the act of speaking is not to be confused with its description. The great majority of people speak and chatter without one moment's reflection upon the rules of syntax, or logic.

We have already considered poetic language and scientific language (to which we may perhaps add the language of statutes and legal agreements) as polar extremes of the world of language. Scientific language forms but a small part of human verbal expression, though in our present context a rather important part. It is perhaps worth noting, at this point, that when science emerged from the Medieval world at, let us say, the time of Bacon, only ordinary human languages existed; scientific language has had perforce to evolve from this (e.g., Latin, English), and it may not be particularly suited to the new modes of thought. It is at best an adaptation. Using its severely disciplined vocabulary and syntax, the scientist-observer makes public his theories and laws relating to his observations; let us glance at a few elementary points of scientific language, because in a sense it is the simplest kind.

At the heading of this chapter is quoted the story of Thomas Hobbes's coming one day by accident upon a copy of the first Book of Euclid, in the library of a gentleman; he read it from the *end* to the *beginning*. So thunderstruck was he that logical deductive argument was possible (for he was educated in the classical tradition) that he is said to have exclaimed "By God; this is impossible!" Those of us who have received scientific or mathematical training may wonder sometimes how those who have not can argue and arrive at sound conclusions—as they undoubtedly can do, very frequently. But we should not pride ourselves that we are always so logical about everyday affairs outside the laboratory or study! Scientific thinking is a special way of thinking; but it is not the only way. Logic may sometimes stultify imagination. Minds can become logic-bound, as bowels can be muscle-bound, and horses hidebound.

To the Greeks, logic was a mental exercise and discipline, part of an attempt to comprehend the natural world from within the mind, without appeal to observation and experiment. The strictly ordered relations between the terms in a syllogistic argument, for example, were not always correlated with similar strict relations between observed things and events in the outside world. Since Aristotle's day, logicians have been concerned with deduction, as the study of relations between signs in a language; with the axiomatic system as a system of closely knit signs and operations which lead to further sets of signs—that is, with syntax. But it is a mistake to assume that good sound argument did not exist before Aristotle's day; he did not invent reasoning—rather he was among the first to formulate a description of it.

Leibnitz was deeply impressed with the idea of mathematics as a logical language so structured that, if a given set of "ideas" be denoted by mathematical symbols, all the consequences could be deduced from the symbols alone, by obeying accepted rules.   Mathematics, in such a view, becomes a "machine" operating deterministically; if premises (judgments) are fed into the machine, they are "processed" and delivered out as conclusions (obligatory judgments).[135]

It may be of interest to remark that, though Leibnitz may have dreamed of constructing actual logical machines, in the metal, these have been realized only in the past century.*   Such interpretation of mathematics has been greatly extended since Leibnitz's day, in the form of symbolic logic and, in Carnap's hands, has been molded into the form of "logical syntax."[47,50]

Scientific theory rests upon statements, upon sets of axioms.   These statements present relations between various terms; to the syntactical relations between these terms is correlated, we imagine, relations between things and events in the real world.   But science is not concerned with the "meanings" of the various terms, only with their relations; this is true of both the exact sciences and the inexact (e.g., sociology[84,256]).   For example, when we say in mechanics: "Force is rate of change of momentum," we are not saying what force *is* or what momentum *is*.   Nevertheless, experience and custom instill in each of us certain feelings and thoughts about force and momentum, just as we have ways of imagining Euclidean lines and planes pictorially—though such imagery is not necessary.   At the basis of all scientific statements lie terms which are "taken for granted," which are intuitive and indispensable, "transmitted to us when we were children . . . without which the Axioms of Euclid or of Hilbert would be of little use to us."[57]   Indeed not only science but the whole process of human communication rests upon certain "ultimate presumptions without which no system of symbols, no science, not even logic, could develop."[E] Language continually chases its tail; terms can only be defined by other terms and, however we transform statements, we can but follow a perpetual circle; there must remain an ultimate intuitive residue which the rules of syntax cannot give us.

Apart from the words or mathematical symbols which denote things or events, the various logical terms—*is, is not, and, or, if,* et cetera—and their rules of use have become deeply engrained upon our minds, by custom.

* A machine for testing a syllogism was constructed in 1885 (reference 19), and more complex logical problems have been tackled by machines recently; e.g., see reference 329.

So accustomed are we to their use that we can readily carry out deductive argument using nonsense terms, which do not denote anything in particular; for instance, the syllogism;

All hoodles are snurds.
This gabooge is a hoodle.
Therefore it is a snurd.

is as "comprehensible" as an algebraic solution, where the x and y symbols do not denote specific things; yet hoodles and snurds are not within our experience.   As it has evolved, science has generally become more and more *formal*—that is, concerned with expression of ideas in language and signs; the realization has gradually grown that all communicable ideas must be conveyed in signs and syntax.   Such apparent "reduction" of experience to a calculus seems cold and empty to many people; like Hamlet, we read only "words, words, words."   As a reaction to this emptiness, we build models and make analogies, but whereas conceptual model building was feasible and helpful at earlier stages of physics, especially by the use of mechanics, the growth of quantum theory, relativity, wave mechanics, and the whole move toward greater abstraction forces the scientist back toward formal expression.[162]   Philosophy has always, to a great extent, been concerned with language, and today it is a principal interest.

There is a belief amongst laymen that science purports to represent a system of absolute truth, which is furthermore wholly independent of language; that the world behaves in such and such a way according to "blind immutable laws"—forgetting that such laws are man-made and expressed in human language.   It is *we* who (agree to) accept the laws of nature—not nature itself.   They are not, said William James, "decipherment . . . [of] the eternal thoughts of the Almighty."*   Scientific laws are not a set of rules which Nature must obey; if they are considered laws or *rules* at all, they are rules which we ourselves must accept, if we are to communicate with one another in scientific discussion.   In other terms, a scientific law does not "explain" any part of Nature; a cricket ball does not execute a parabolic flight "because" of Newton's law of motion.   "Evolution," said T. H. Huxley, "is not an explanation of the cosmic process but a generalised statement . . . of the results of that process."*†   Scientific laws are generalizations, inferred from individual statements or recordings of observations and representing assumptions as to the best description of what is believed will happen in *future*.ᴴ   By accepting such laws, we agree with one another and adapt ourselves the better to Nature.[266]

The great philosopher John Locke (1632–1704), whose nature set him so opposed to dogma and authoritarianism, found the deductive, rational

* *Pragmatism*, Meridian Books, 1955, p. 49.
† Romanes Lectures, 1894.

approach to understanding of the physical world, by itself, incomplete and unsatisfactory.   To him a pure rational science, based upon abstract *a priori* reasoning, was unacceptable, because the initial thoughts or ideas about the world, upon which we set our mental, reasoning processes to work are not inborn; they are gained through experience, through sense impressions. Understanding of the world, Locke stresses, can come only from the experience of our senses, operated upon by our reason, and essentially in a spirit of free inquiry and of rational criticism.

The ideas of each one of us concerning the various attributes of Nature can only be based upon use of our eyes, ears, touch; from repeated experience we build up sets of similar ideas and, through their association, arrive at general abstractions or universals.   From the constant handling of square things I build up the idea of "squareness"; from continually seeing red things, "redness"—and so with all those general concepts about which we talk and write.   In science today, we speak of "electricity," "gravitation," "light," when we have observed only a finite number of physical events. In linguistics, we have the idea of "words," though we have heard nothing but specific word-events, in many different accents and contexts.   In everyday speech we are continually using terms to signify general properties held in common by members of a class, though we have never seen "the class," but only its members.

To Locke, knowledge consisted in perceptions of relations between ideas; true knowledge lay only "in the agreement or disagreement of ideas." But as regards the external world itself, he taught that we can have no true knowledge; all that we can affirm or deny about it is a matter of probability —an act of "presumptive trust."   His insistence that all knowledge of the external world is probabilistic is one of Locke's greatest contributions to scientific method.

The statement, "This book weighs two pounds," cannot, by itself, be regarded as "true" or "false."   It expresses a relation between two ideas, a belief referring to two attributes of the external world—a book and its weight.   The making of such a statement does not imply that an observer "knows" the true relation between the book and its weight.   He can but *verify* the statement, perhaps changing his beliefs, by performing successive experimental weighings of the book and expressing his results in other statements; and, by comparing all the statements, he may arrive at a probable weight for the book.

It was David Hume who, following after Locke, searched more deeply into the basis of the inductive method.   The extrapolation from limited experience to general conclusions, from present knowledge of the world to a belief concerning future events, all the gradual growth and extension of our knowledge, was to be explained only by *custom*—no deeper explanation is open to us; it is all that we have. "Custom and custom alone." The "association of ideas" and the inference from particular to general is a method which essentially contains within itself a source of possible error, since we can never be in a state of absolute certainty. Yet it is the only method available. A poor thing maybe, but our own.

BIBLIOGRAPHY

A. *Encyclopædia Britannica*, Cambridge University Press, London, 11th Ed., 1911.

B. Morris, C. W., "Foundations of the Theory of Signs," *International Encyclopædia of Unified Science Series*, Vol. I, No. 2, University of Chicago Press, Chicago, 1938.

C. Carnap, R., and Y. Bar-Hillel, "An Outline of a Theory of Semantic Information," *M.I.T., Research Lab. Electronics, Tech. Rept., 247*, 1953.

D. Carnap, R., *Introduction to Semantics*, Harvard University Press, Cambridge, Mass., 1946.

E. Ogden, C. K., and I. A. Richards, *The Meaning of Meaning*, Routledge & Kegan Paul, Ltd., London, 1949 Ed.

F. Good, I. J., *Probability and the Weighing of Evidence*, Charles Griffen & Co., Ltd., London, 1950.

G. Feller, W., *An Introduction to Probability Theory and Its Applications*, John Wiley & Sons, Inc., New York, 1950.

H. Ayer, A. J., *Language, Truth and Logic*, Victor Gollancz, Ltd., London, 1936.

CHAPTER SEVEN

On Cognition and Recognition

It is the common wonder of all men, how among so many millions of faces, there should be none alike.
Sir Thomas Browne (1605–1682)
Religio Medici

Cognition is "knowing"; recognition is "knowing again." In this chapter we shall solve no problems, but remain content to discuss some of the great difficulties behind these apparently simple statements.

We are performing acts of recognition every instant of our waking lives. We recognize the objects around us—doors, chairs, lamp posts—and we move and act in relation to them. We can spot a friend in a crowd, recognize what he says; we can read handwriting; we distinguish smiles from gestures of anger. Social life is rendered possible. How is it that these objects and signs can set up distinct responses in us? How do the keys find the right locks?

1. RECOGNITION AS OUR SELECTIVE FACULTY

What do we mean when we say we "know" somebody? Possibly one of several things; for instance:

(1) That we can name him on sight.
(2) That we have heard his name before, or learned about his activities, though possibly we have never met him. That is, we "know him by name."
(3) That we can pick him out in a crowd.
(4) That we know "him" in the sense of his personality, understanding his peculiar habits, weaknesses, interests.

258

All knowings of this kind are selective; selective of a name, of a particular set of experiences which to us represents that individual, of a face or bodily appearance, of one personality from among all those with which we are personally acquainted. A question asked by a friend, "Do you know so-and-so?" or a face spotted in the street has selected in us a particular mental response, and perhaps some overt response; some personal encounter, some sight or sign, has tapped our memories and we react to certain *habits*; the key has found the lock.

The analogy with a lock and key is too simple, for several reasons. A lock cannot be said to "recognize" its key. Again, a pinprick selects a definite overt response in us—a yelp and a leap—but we should not say, at that very instant, that the yelp and leap signify a "recognition" of the pinprick. A flower turns toward the sunlight; a stoat stands stock-still at the appearance of a gull; in such cases, rather than speak of "recognition," we would say the signs *cause* the responses. Recognition implies cognition; these are terms referring to the mental experience of the recipient of the signs, expressed overtly by his behavior. Other terms, such as "knowing," "intention," "thinking," are cognitive terms and similarly restricted. The recipient's overt response is itself a *sign* of his recognition—a sign to an observer. At the physical and physiological level, the "problem of recognition" is the problem of the functioning of the neural mechanisms whereby the response signs are selected by the stimulus signs.

To an external observer, the phenomenon of recognition of, say, some simple shape such as a square is observed from the overt behavior of the subject who is shown the square. The stimulus sign (a square card) sets up a response sign; the subject may run his finger round the square, or draw it on paper, or name it as a "square card." But study of overt responses alone cannot give the whole story. For the subject who sees the card, and recognizes it as square, has taken part in a communication event and from that time forth is no longer the same person. His mental state has undergone a change; his subsequent responses have partly been determined by this event. For example, he may recognize a second card more quickly, or he may respond by saying: "It's like the one before." But, without using cognitive terms, we can say that the communication event alters the subject's nervous system in some way, setting him into a different state of preparation for receipt of subsequent stimuli.

A key may fit a lock when it is slightly worn, but it will not do so if broken or bent. Fortunately for us humans we are vastly more tolerant of signs. We can understand the speech of all our friends, with their varied accents, and with a background of street noises or of chatter; we may read their handwritings, though copperplate or scribble; we recognize their faces, in many positions and in various lights. There are no mathematically exact, standard signs, no standard keys to fit standard locks. We can even read the handwriting of a stranger, though we have never seen it before; we understand his speech on immediate first hearing.

Walking in my garden I spot a weed, recognizing it as a buttercup—as a member of the species *ranunculus bulbosa*. What kind of lock or template could there be in my brain, to be opened by any one of the myriad forms of this flower? Tuning my radio, I hear swift snatches of speech and recognize the accents of France or Germany. These are examples of allocating a particular sign-event to a general class, the faculty of *classification* or discrimination between classes, without which we could not communicate one with another, or perform the simplest willful action. We hear a spoken utterance, and class it with an ensemble of similar utterances already experienced, and respond to it as a "word"—according to the habits acquired from that past experience. As a simple illustration, Fig. 7.1 shows a number of letters taken from newspaper advertisements; all are readily recognizable, though some you have never seen before. Nevertheless you respond to them, and they call upon your habits, each in its own selective way.

Fig. 7.1. Various printed letter signs.

Sir Richard Paget[254] tells of a toy celluloid dog, which would jump out of his kennel (propelled by a spring) when he called him "Rex," the toy being fitted with an acoustic resonator which responded to the [e] vowel sound of his name. But this animal would also respond to some other sounds, including certain notes struck on the piano!

Recently, a more sophisticated device has been described* which discriminates between the spoken numerals (zero, one, two . . ., nine. This instrument uses electric wave filters for detecting the two lower speech formants, or vocal concentrations (see Chapter 4, Section 3.4), subsequently comparing the result in a certain way with a set of ten standards and selecting the one of closest fit.   Still, unlike a brain, this device operates successfully only with a single speaker.   If someone else is to operate it, the controlling parameters of the device must be changed accordingly.

All the examples which we have cited, of familiar daily acts of recognition, may suggest that the function is not affected by the *whole* of the sights or sounds constituting the physical stimuli but that it depends upon certain properties or attributes only, and even then only by virtue of the fact that, under all the various distortions, transformations, and disturbances of the stimuli which the brain so readily tolerates, certain invariants remain.   For instance, that the voices of all English-speaking people form a class, having certain acoustic properties in common; that handwritings, though all differing, have properties of shape in common.   Such assumed basic residua or invariants have been called "information-bearing elements." But this view, in the writer's opinion, is mistakenly simple.   For one thing, it suggests that much of a physical stimulus could be pared off, and that these information-bearing elements or residua constitute the "true signs," the perfect keys.   This view is no doubt admirable as a basis for many technological devices† designed to carry out certain brain-like functions, such as the spoken-numeral-operated device just cited, for to imitate the brain itself would be excessively expensive!   But again, it suggests that a *single* fixed set of attributes suffices, whereas there is no reason to suppose that human recognition of a sign depends upon a fixed set of sign attributes, when environmental or other conditions change.   We may recognize the first few words of a stranger's speech in one way, but operate upon a succession of different attributes as he continues to speak, and as we gather more experience of the conversation, bringing in knowledge of syntactic conventions, subject matter, aspects of personality, and a host of varied factors. The process of recognition need not remain stationary as conversation proceeds.   Again, we may recognize a friend from a certain set of attributes of his appearance when met in familiar surroundings, but recognition may depend upon an utterly different set if we encounter him unexpectedly in a

---

* See Davis, Biddulph, and Balashek in reference 166.   The device described may ultimately be developed to enable telephone numbers to be spoken by the subscriber, rather than using the present system of manual dialing though, as we indicate here, there are great difficulties to this.

† Devices such as "automatic stenographers," or reading "machines for the blind," etc., to which we referred in Chapter 4, Section 4.2.

strange place (say a foreign city). We may even fail to recognize him, or we may reject the recognition as an unlikely hypothesis, being "unable to believe our eyes." Being *in* certain familiar surroundings may be one of his essential attributes whereby we recognize him. A sign is not received isolated from an environment; it is part of a whole complex situation.

This is not to say that invariants do not exist among those various sign-events which we class together as one sign-type, for controlled experiments suggest that this may well be the case, but rather that the situation in which a sign-event occurs must be regarded as a whole and that the attributes and their invariant factors, by which we recognize an object or a sign, cannot be laid down in any general and inflexible way. They may differ on different occasions, depending upon the whole environment. Again, it depends upon who "we" are; recognition is the setting-up of a *relationship* between two people, or one person and an object, and the particular relevant attributes, the information-bearing elements, depend upon the individual recognizing the sign. "Information," in this sense, is information *to* someone—to the recognizer, with his own peculiar experience and habits.

2. SOME SIMPLE PHILOSOPHICAL NOTES

In the last pages of his *Essay Concerning Human Understanding*, Locke divided all that falls within the compass of human knowledge into three. The first he called *Physica* ("the knowledge of things as they are in their own proper beings, their constitutions, properties and operations. . . ."). The second, *Practica* ("the skill of right applying our own powers and actions for the attainment of things good and useful. . . ."). And the third, *Semeiotica* ("the doctrine of signs . . . to consider the nature of signs the mind makes use of for the understanding of things, or conveying its knowledge to others. . . .").

2.1. REALITY—TO WHOM?

Physica: "*things as they are. . . .*" But as they are to whom? In everyday life we imagine a world of reality, solid and substantial, which we see, hear, and touch which, like Dr. Johnson's stone, we may kick and stub our toes on. But the physicist has built up another view of the world, based on concepts of electrons, nuclei, and waves. And the artist yet another, in terms of color values, and form.

We do not perceive and know "*things as they are*"; we perceive signs, and from these signs make inferences and build up our mental models of the world; we say we see and hear it; we talk about "real" things.

We do not perceive more than a minute fraction of the sights and sounds that fall upon our sense organs; the great majority pass us by. They may make physical impressions on our retinas or in our ears but seem not to have any effect upon our subsequent perceptions, thoughts, or behavior. When I gaze out of my window I see a tree; I do not perceive every leaf and twig upon it, but merely certain of its attributes, and these stimulate me to see "the tree." I have looked at this tree thousands of times in the past and have acquired habits of perception. The tree has operated upon these habits and caused me to see it; I react toward it as a whole. But turning from the window to look at my clock on the wall, I see it stands at one minute past nine. It must therefore have struck the hour a moment ago; I just had not noticed.

A man blind from birth who has his sight restored by an operation might be expected to gaze with wonder upon a world so long hidden from him. ("So *that* is what it looks like!") But he does nothing of the kind. He finds a bizarre patchwork of meaningless shapes and colors, having nothing whatever to do with the real world. He shuts his eyes, once again to feel and to hear reality as he knows it.[C, 280, 291, 364] It may take years of patient training before he learns to see well, before he acquires habits which can be operated upon by visual signs, so that sights become part of his "real" world.

The schizophrenic has his own world, the dipsomaniac his nightmare; it is conceivable that a butterfly, with organs of smell in its feet, has a world of smells possessing shapes. We each of us have our own models of reality.

To take up a thread from an earlier section (Chapter 6, Section 4.1), there is the notion which forms part of the everyday thinking of most people—the notion that is exhibited by our way of speaking about two distinct worlds; the external, solid, "reality" and the world within us, our mental experience, the evidence of our sense impressions. On the one hand, we speak of physical actions and laws; we do laboratory experiments and observe overt behavior; a cranium may be opened and brains examined, their anatomy and physiology discussed. This is the world of physics and physical experiment. On the other hand, when speaking of mental experience, we use words such as *know, feel, imagine, aware,* and many other cognitive words. It is sometimes convenient to set up propositions in the "external," physical language and on other occasions in the "internal," cognitive language—but we should be careful when mixing the two.

The terms "real" and "reality" are commonly used to mean "nonmental." We speak of the "real world" as being "outside us," a curious phrase—outside *what* exactly? Strictly, this is putting the cart before the horse, for if anything is "real" to each one of us, it is our experiences, our sensations. Is a rainbow real? Mind, sensation, mentation are real; the material world, matter, externals are all inference. All we have directly is mental experience—mind. Volumes have been written upon the eternal question of the mind-body relationship; of how it is that mice and men are conscious, thinking creatures showing purposeful behavior, whereas sticks and stones are otherwise. What differences are there in their material compositions? Or in their structure? Or do we need concepts and language beyond those of physics for distinguishing one from the other? Many views have been expressed, countless arguments made, and different schools have arisen. And through much of this debate one senses a reverence for mind, often with a too-ready contempt for "mere matter." But it is our mental experience which to each of us constitutes reality; it is mind which is "real"; but matter is also a mystery.

The distinction between objective and subjective terms should of course be kept clear, but this is not the point at issue. A source of confusion and error arises from thinking of two worlds—the "external" and the "internal" —we might well ask ourselves: external to *what*? It has led us to infer that the two worlds are correlated with two "things," bodies and minds. A man, people often say, possesses both a body and a mind. They regard bodies as spatial-temporal things (one body can causally affect another); on the other hand minds, though nobody would think of them as substantial, material things, are nevertheless often spoken of as though they were things, unsubstantial "things," existing in time and requiring a location. We regard the mind ("it") as being in the head, rather as Descartes found the soul situated in the pineal gland. Strange to say, though we speak of the heart as the seat of love, this deceives no one! The idea that a man possesses a body *and* a mind has, as Professor Ryle expresses it, the nature of a category mistake. Minds are not things, to be possessed. I can say that I am "in a certain state of mind," but not that I possess a mind, as I possess whiskers and pants.

From this bifurcation of a man, into a body and a mind, a further inference inevitably follows. This is the view we have of "ourselves" as being locked in "our" bodies, in lifelong solitary confinement; shut in our prison cells, catching nostalgic glimpses of one another through the window bars. We can shout and gesticulate at one another but can never have real knowledge of one another's true selves. Minds cannot have direct contact with minds. We can but frame our thoughts into signs and communicate with these; a poor thing, hopelessly inadequate, but all we can do.

Such a view may be satisfactory and adequate for many purposes, for study of communication as a physical or a social phenomenon, for example. But in relation to psychological problems, it can be a snare, because we can be led to draw two further inferences. The first is that the sights and sounds we receive, the signs, (casually) affect our minds and, subsequently, our minds cause our bodies to move and react. (*Our* minds, *our* bodies— with the possessive pronoun.)   The mind is imagined as a kind of operator who sits in our heads, like a telephone operator receiving incoming calls and routing them through to outgoing lines.   Psychologists are constantly fighting against such animism,[c] against the "Ghost in the Machine."[A] But a second conclusion may perhaps be drawn, even more delusive; namely that though we can never have direct contact with other people's minds, we think we know what goes on in our own—not fully, we may be prepared to admit, for Freud has brought to light many strange things from the darker corners of our mental prison cells, but to a large extent we are led to believe that we know our own minds.   In our silent soliloquy, in sorting out the sights and sounds around us, in argument or discussion with friends and in all our communicative actions, we may think we know what processes are going on—how we build arguments, reach conclusions, and what is the content of our minds which we seem to see so clearly and which we frame into speech, so as to share it with others.   The first really forthright attack on this classic view was made by Charles Peirce,[B] and his ideas upon communication and the true functioning of signs are fundamental to our study.

2.2. PEIRCE AND HIS PRAGMATIC THEORY OF SIGNS[B,*]

In his philosophy, called pragmatism, Peirce made a stout denial of the classical, Cartesian theory of knowledge and of its communication, which rested upon "intuitions."

Intuitions were held to be our ultimate, rock-bottom knowings, un-explainable and impervious to analysis.   From these, our beliefs are built up, ideas and theories formed, arguments and reasonings produced.   Our mental experience springs from this basic content of our minds; such was the classical view.

Peirce asserted that, in believing we have such basic intuitions, we deceive ourselves, and that, just as we can have no precise knowledge of other people's thought, we can have no precise knowledge of our own.   We use signs when communicating with others, and we can but observe our own signs.   Thinking to oneself is, in this view, a soliloquy carried on in signs, mostly in language.   "We" can argue with "ourselves," or with our "consciences"; "we" can search "our hearts."   Such arguings and searchings have the nature of dialogue, expressed in signs, just as though we were holding an internal conversation.

* Charles Sanders Peirce (1839–1914).   His publications, extensively scattered, have been collected into six volumes (see reference 258).   For our purpose here the reader is referred to the short and most readable account prepared by *Gallie*, reference B.

In formal sign systems, such as mathematics, it is widely and readily accepted that we do not need to know what the fundamental concepts "are"—only how they are related, as we have discussed before (Chapter 6, Section 5). In Euclid, we do not know what are "straight lines," "infinity," et cetera, we need only know the rules of the system and can build up all the theorems. We may think we have intuitive knowledge about these basic concepts, but whether or not we have is immaterial to Euclid; the system is self-contained and complete. So too in mechanics, we know how to relate forces, masses, et cetera, but never need to consider, say, *force* by itself, in a void—only in relation to *mass* or *acceleration*. Peirce asserted that all sign usage, in human communication, is similar in nature, though language is not a highly regular system like mathematics. Signs are only used in relation to one another, in a working system of signs, but never in isolation. Every sign requires another "to interpret it."

Another cornerstone of Peirce's theory is his insistence on the essentially triadic nature of every sign situation (sign-designatum-user). A sign cannot be said simply to signify something, but only to signify something to somebody. The user is essentially involved. Signs are used for indicating, informing, for arguing, and they can only indicate *to* someone, or inform someone or persuade someone. Ogden and Richards[250] recognize this pragmatic, three-cornered nature of sign situations, in their discussion of "meaning" [Fig. 3.6(a)]. From this point of view, "the meaning" of a sign can be discussed only with reference to some specific user; the same sign may mean different things to (set up different reactions in) different people, because every individual has a different background, different communicative experiences, and every sign-event occurs in a certain environment and in a certain temporal relationship to other sign-events. By analogy, economic "value" involves a person and his condition.* A beefsteak may be priced $1, but it can only be said to be *worth* $1 *to* someone; to a dyspeptic it may not be worth a cent, but to a hungry man a fortune.

It is generally agreed that the "state" of an individual, at any time in his life, depends upon (1) inborn, inherited, factors, (2) environmental influences; but for our present purpose we may lump these together and consider any individual as a specific ensemble of experiences, that is, of communicative experiences, communicated to him at birth by his parents and ancestors, or gathered during his lifetime. In Peirce's terms, "a man's essential life is made up of his communings."[B] The interpretation of a sign, the reaction set up in some individual, then, depends upon the particular accumulation of experiences which that individual comprises.

---

* Bernoulli's measure of money value was given as $u \propto \log{(c + m)}/c$ where $c =$ money already possessed, $m =$ money received.

As we have presented our argument here, a sign sets up two kinds of reaction in a recipient—overt responses and other internal changes in the state of his nervous system correlating with a changed "state of mind" [Fig. 3.6 (b)]. The receipt of the sign causes him to make some overt response and at the same time adds to his accumulation of experiences; from that instant he is no longer the same man.

Now Peirce puts a requirement upon the stimulus and response, if these are to be regarded as signs, which at first seems rather strange but which is really implicit in his insistence that a sign cannot exist in a vacuum, but only in association with other signs in a *working* system. A sign must be associated with other signs, statements, questions, remarks may be built up, and these must require expansion, answerings, retorts. Signs must admit of *development*.[B] Roughly expressed, Peirce's requirement of a sign is that it should stimulate its recipient into making some response which itself may be capable of acting as a sign for the same object signified. More precisely, a sign is such that it stands in triadic relation to an object ("designatum") by stimulating the recipient into making a response which itself *is capable of* standing in the same triadic relation to the same object. In everyday terms, the first sign (say, a remark) calls up a second sign (reply) in the recipient. This second sign, in turn, calls up a third, and so on in a potentially endless chain. Note the italics here: *is capable of*. Conversations, arguments, and speeches do end at some time, fortunately; but signs of language have the *potentiality* for continuing the process indefinitely. It is always possible to add some further *relevant* remark. Signs set up a working system by virtue of their potentiality for calling up other sign responses, and Peirce's stipulation, that an initial sign and its response sign shall stand in similar triadic relation to the same object, satisfies the requirement that conversations, arguments, speeches, and other social communications must have continuity, keeping on a track or "line of thought," to perform their goal-seeking task.

A first (stimulus) sign calls up a second (response) sign which depends upon the particular recipient, according to the habits he has acquired from his past communicative experiences. Different individuals respond differently, and their response to a sign may vary with the context in which this sign appears and, in fact, with the whole environment. A sign has an unlimited variety of possible *interpretants* (response signs). Kenneth Pike* tells a story which illustrates vividly one difficulty of a linguist making his first approach to natives, in order to gather even the simplest expressions for objects. He plays a game with them, not unlike the familiar pastime called "Twenty Questions"; but since he is unable to frame his questions in their language, which is unknown to him, he can only gesture, or touch

* In private correspondence.

objects, in the hope of eliciting interpretable responses.   But, as you may imagine, there exists an extensive semantic ambiguity.   For example, if the linguist hits a table, the natives standing by may answer with half a dozen words, which subsequently turn out to signify "slap," "table," "hand," "noise," "anger,"—so that he can only assume one of these, as a working hypotheses, and proceed to make further gestures, in the hope of obtaining confirmatory evidence and so gradually build up his model of their language. For example, the word "kangaroo" means "I don't know" in Aborigine, the response made to Captain Cook when he pointed out one of the animals to a native.*

Communication, then, cannot be a determinate process.   An individual's knowledge of signs cannot be perfect and absolute, nor can his knowledge of things signified or, at longer range, of any subject.   He has always something to learn by further communings.

It is a widely held belief that our minds are reasoning engines; that our thinking is a rational process, conforming to logical principles and so raising us above the brutes.   To some extent this may be true, as when we do mathematics or physics, or when we are engaged in constructed debate. In such activities we are being deliberate and critical; we start from premises, follow certain principles, and arrive at conclusions; we correct errors, change our minds.   But such "reasonings" constitute a small part of the entire contents of our minds.   The history of invention, for example, shows countless cases of brilliant ideas and discoveries, got by flashes of insight— but by what logical or reasoned steps the inventor had no notion.   Nor need he know its scientific basis, or principles of operation and, in many cases, years may pass before adequate theories are formulated.

Peirce stressed the limited use of reasoning[B] and made a further classification.   A great deal of our activity is not set by us to conform to any particular rules or logical principles; it is not deliberately constructed and involves no criticism.   When engaged in casual conversation, I do not act upon rules of grammar or logic.   The words, idioms, clichés and phrases come pouring out.   Of what mental processes are involved, I have no notion. When someone tells me a joke I may laugh, without knowing any theory or laws of humor.   Even more removed from reasoning are our moment-by-moment recognitions, as of the shape, position, color of all the familiar objects around us, or of a friend's voice on the telephone.   Such perceptual judgments are, in Peirce's terms,[B] "forced upon us," involving no reasoning, but setting us into habitual response.   For instance, there is at the moment a teacup standing beside me on my desk, which I see to be blue; *after* glancing at it, I may argue with myself that I am deceived by some trick of the light, and that it is "really" green.   But, during my glance I *see* it as

* Or so the story goes!

blue and am incapable of seeing it as any other color.   If I look at a rose-bush and recognize it as a rosebush, I cannot un-recognize it and see it as a railroad train, however hard I try.   These are uncritical perceptual judgments, or habits of inference, which the perceiver himself executes without logical analysis.   He cannot *un-perceive* a color or a shape, as he can argue against, and reverse, a false conclusion in debate, though he may *subsequently* infer a misjudgment.

This returns us to an earlier point; namely, that we must distinguish between a *description* of a phenomenon, made by an external observer, and the phenomenon itself; this is particularly true of human communication phenomena.   We have already made such a distinction, at the linguistic level [see Fig. 3.2(a)], and it is equally important at this psychological level.   An external observer may attempt some kind of analysis of the perceptual phenomena he sees taking place—of people's reactions to sights and sounds, shapes and colors; he may form hypotheses and test these experimentally, form new theories, correct earlier ones, guided by certain logical principles.   But such an analysis by an observer is not to be confused with the perceptual phenomena themselves.   A perceiver may not reason out what, why, or how he has perceived, any more than he can give much account of other of his thought processes.

2.3. SOME DIFFERENT CLASSES OF RECOGNITION

One of the difficulties which beset us, in discussion of recognition, is that the word is used in several senses; recognition, "knowing-again," is a general term given to several classes of phenomena which should be distinguished.   Charles Peirce's classification, to which we have just referred, makes certain distinctions clear.   For example, we "recognize" square cards, faces, flowers, bowler hats, et cetera, the objects around us, their properties and qualities.   But we speak also of "recognizing" an old argument, or a fallacy, a solution to a problem, or an error.   We speak too of *following* an argument or *seeing* reason; but we can do both with our eyes shut, sitting in a chair.   Such words are borrowed from the vocabulary relevant to physical observation.   But the two classes of recognition are surely not to be equated, and we should not assume that their physiological basis are necessarily the same.

3. RECOGNITION OF UNIVERSALS

Looking around my room, I see a number of objects which seem to have a certain property in common; to this property I give the name "squareness." For example, I see a square window, a square picture frame, a square sheet of paper, et cetera; that is, I see a number of square things.   Yet I have never seen "squareness."   It could be said that I have the *concept* of squareness, together with that of "straightness," "angle," and many others which we handle with such familiarity when doing geometrical problems. Again, on my desk I see a red box, a red book, and a red pencil, but I have never seen "redness," only red things.   In yet another way, we refer to "words," like the English word-types "book," "box," "pencil," yet all we ever see or hear are specific word-events—printed signs in varied characters, or spoken sounds in different accents.

3.1. Universals as habits of inference

The most direct way of interpreting such *universals*, as "squareness," "redness," "straightness," et cetera, is to speak of them as invariant, or common, properties of the objects.   But such an interpretation relates to the objects only, and leaves out the person recognizing the squareness or straightness.   A *concept*, such as that of squareness, cannot be said to be solely a property of a thing, but concerns also the conceiver.   As remarked earlier, a great deal of useful work has been done in searching for invariant properties of speech stimuli, with different accents or distortions—the "information-bearing elements"—but such invariants are not to be identified with the word-concepts.   They rather define common properties of the physical stimuli, as measured by an outside observer; but the word-concepts involve a conceiver, or someone to respond to the stimuli as though the common property was recognized.   And the response made will depend upon the individual; that is, upon his particular experiences, and upon the particular habits of inference which he has acquired.

By "word-concept" here is meant not individual word-events, spoken with varied accents and tones, but the universal, the class into which an ensemble of words-events is grouped.   For instance, the English word-type "man" is a universal; it is a class comprising a host of varied utterances made by different people, all different in physical characteristics yet, in spite of this, having the remarkable property of leaving the communication process largely unimpaired.   This universality is indeed remarkable, yet so commonplace an idea that we take it for granted.   For universality implies more than mere grouping, or associating, of different sign-events into a class; it refers to all three levels of language—the syntactic, semantic, and pragmatic—and it is our extraordinary ability to handle abstract concepts, facilitated by this fluidity or universality of language, which makes human communication so successful.

Charles Morris refers to word-universals as "laws, or habits of use," [244] as opposed to specific "replicas, or word-tokens" (word-events).   A word-event is one of a class of objects, all subject to the same linguistic rules and usages.   In the meta-language, word universality implies a plurality of situations for a word; different sentences may be formed using it (syntactic universality); different things may be denoted by it (semantic universality), as, for instance, the word "man" may refer to the human race, to the male state, to a personal friend, et cetera; different people may respond similarly to the word when spoken in different accents (pragmatic universality). Under all these changes, of context, of designata, of user, there is a certain invariance and communication is established. Universals, as concepts, are indeed "signs pointing to invariant relations."[66] There is great difference between *recognition*—the knowing again of something, real or abstract, which has already fallen within our experience—and the *perception* of some radically new concept. Recognition implies a classification of the recognized object into an existing class; but the setting-up of a new class is a creative act. Helen Keller, the girl who became blind and deaf whilst still a baby, could recognize by touch the faces of those around her, and chairs, doorknobs, and other objects; she even developed speech play by sensing with her hand the motions of her nurse's mouth and the vibrations of her throat. But it was some years before the idea came to her that everything had its name, suddenly, in a flash of insight. She had perceived the universal—the concept of "name," as applying to an infinite variety of situations—and she responded by running around and learning the names of hosts of already familiar objects (see also Chapter 3, Section 2.1).[186]

Man has developed a remarkable power of handling concepts, facilitated by that most wonderful of all faculties, human language. The life of the lower animals, the birds and insects, must largely be a here-now existence, and their "languages" refer only to their present and future "intentions." But man can talk of things in their absence; he can talk about classes of things; he can, above all, use his language to refer to the past. And all these abstractions and generalities and the whole compass of time—past, present, and future—may be expressed in language.

4. THE IMPORTANCE OF PAST EXPERIENCE: REALITY AND NIGHTMARE

Man's outstanding communicative and organizing powers depend upon his capacity for storing past experiences, not only in memory, as individuals, but collectively through writing and other inventive genius by which continued records may be made. Those simplest creatures, having powers of learning only through trial and error, live in their here-now world; higher up the scale of evolution, where learning faculties are more developed, creatures benefit from their past experiences to various extents. But a man's life is a continuity; his succession of experiences are not isolated here-now events, but become accumulated. He has evolved the ability to handle and relate many abstract concepts, to see generalities from experience of specific events, and to form and name new classes.   He can "think up" universals and give them names ("square," "red," "six," and so on). Memory and abstraction are the two fundamental properties of the human brain.[2]

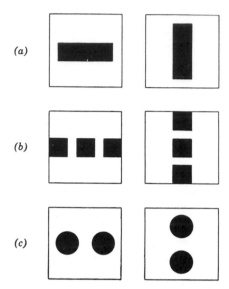

Fig. 7.2.   Recognition of the universals "horizontal" and "vertical," by rats (after D. O. Hebb, *The Organization of Behavior*, 1949, with very kind permission from the author and John Wiley & Sons, Inc.).

The inferential act of recognizing a universal, whether it be the result of conscious reasoning (as in scientific work) or whether it be at the other extreme of making the simplest perceptual judgments (such as recognizing the grass as green—an unreasoned judgment, in Peirce's words, "forced upon us"), calls upon a man's innate reflexes and upon learned responses dependent on his whole past experience.   But every individual has different past experiences, and the response of any one, to some sign or stimulus, will depend upon the individual.   Whereas the innate "releaser mechanisms" of birds and animals give fairly definite, regular, automatic responses to certain simple signs, it is far less certain what a man will do when you address him, challenge him, or question him.

Of course we should not attribute powers of abstraction solely to man. If an animal has been trained to respond to, say, a square card irrespective of orientation, or over a certain range of size, it should be credited with recognition of the universal.   Hebb[c], for instance, has shown that rats trained to distinguish between a vertical and a horizontal bar sign [Fig. 7.2

(a)] can subsequently be tested with (b) broken rectangles or (c) circles lying above one another and side by side, and still show similar discriminating powers. The universals "horizontal" and "vertical" are distinguished, at least within this rather limited range of forms. But it is the remarkable extension and development of these abilities that gives us our own great communicative powers. For animals are more readily "caught out" than we. It is a question of degree; animals may have certain powers of abstraction, and may be trained to improve them, whilst man has such powers extensively. He can abstract and form concepts; he can abstract further and form more general concepts. Again, he can relate concepts and form larger classes, of classes. His concepts and his language seem potentially capable of unlimited development.[B]

4.1. Past experience facilitates inference

As I glance around my room I see a number of square objects—a window, a writing pad, some books—and in spite of the fact that these are different in size, color, and orientation, and appear against different backgrounds, I am prepared to place them in the same class, to which I give the name "square." Further than this, if I hold a book in front of me, and turn it away from me horizontally, the retinal image produced is not square, but lozenge-shaped; yet the same inference is still executed, and the abstraction, the universal, of "squareness" is recognized.[250] I see it as square and call it "square." Had I been living in ancient Egypt, I might have drawn it or painted it square,* because the lozenge shape of the two-dimensional optical image and the laws of perspective would have been beyond my ken. I would have *known* it to be square, in accord with experience.

Now square things do not occur commonly in nature, and it is difficult to believe that the concept of squareness is inborn in us. But during life we encounter a multitude of square objects, in the man-made world. The square (or rectangular) shape is of particular significance. If we were to live in a world in which the lozenge shape was more common and important than the rectangle, then some chance rectangular retinal image might lead us to see a lozenge. We respond to our acquired habits.

The recognition of faces, of friends or foes, is of great social importance to us, and we have developed this faculty to a remarkable degree. At a glance you can usually identify one face out of thousands, in a great number of positions, smiling, frowning, or roaring with laughter. You recognize a sketch or a photograph. But in spite of these remarkable powers, you will have some immediate difficulty in recognizing even your own mother from a photograph presented to you upside down, because this view has not been part of experience.

---

* See *Egyptian methods*, in Gombrich's index, reference 134.

When I look at someone standing in the corner of the room, the vertical line of the walls is broken by his figure.   Yet I do not see it as a broken line, interrupted by patches of color corresponding to his face, hands, and clothes—I see someone standing in the corner of the room.   Walls are customarily vertical and continuous, and any other possibility is not given a moment's thought; the broken nature of the line is overlooked.   We have a great knowledge of visual forms, of the shapes and outline curves of the objects of our common experience.   We learn and subsequently expect those forms which do occur, out of the myriad shapes which could occur.[34] Most readers will have seen those puzzle pictures given to children, showing two drawings in one.   If a card, previously cut with a number of parallel slits to resemble a cage, be placed upon the picture, we see perhaps a tiger, safely behind the cage; if the card be slid sideways, by the width of the bars, another animal is exposed, perhaps a monkey.   But, each time, only half the picture is exposed to view.   An analogous, but quantitative, experiment has been carried out with speech, in which spoken recorded messages are periodically interrupted, on and off, at a varied rate; the ear is remarkably resistant to such disruption.[238]   We have a vast statistical knowledge concerning the sounds of our speech, and of syllable sequences, out of all the possible sounds and their permutations which *could* be produced by the human mouth.[237]

Again, we have a great store of experience of printed letter sequences and readily recognize that "nidificate" is a typically English word, though we may not know it, whereas "gelijkwaardig" is not.   We know to a great extent the probable letter sequences, out of all the possible permutations of twenty-six letters.

The signs used in communication and the sights and sounds of the world around us represent, within our experience, but a small part of all the phantasmagoria that could conceivably be constructed out of the same materials, or component parts.   From experience we learn these forms as they occur, and see in them order, rule, and law.   We know our reality from our nightmare.

In an earlier section we have discussed the concept of *redundancy* of signals.   Redundancy is the property which our experience and knowledge endow upon signals, when we know that only certain patterns of component parts (e.g., letters, syllables, continuous lines) are used, out of all possible arrangements.   The signs of communication, or other sights and sounds around us, are never entirely and utterly new to us, but to some greater or lesser extent contain elements within our past experience.   We have discussed redundancy already, from several points of view, and in Chapter 5, Section 4, we have referred to its quantitative measurement, in the theory of communication, later we shall refer again to quantitative estimates of redundancy, in psychological experiments.

These few examples illustrate the evident fact that recognition, interpreted as response according to habits, depends upon the past experience from which an individual acquires his particular habits. These long-term experiences are, broadly speaking, common to people in similar circumstances; we all learn certain similar types of response. But to a major extent, the response set up on any occasion will depend also upon the *immediate* past experience of the perceiver and upon the environment at that time. Let us now look at a few examples of the way in which this shorter-term experience so largely determines the character of each communication event.

4.2. A PRIORI KNOWLEDGE: PSYCHOLOGICAL EXPECTANCY, OR "SET"

As I walk along the street a stranger approaches me, raises his hat, and opens his mouth to ask me the way somewhere. Being in London, I expect him to speak in English, and I am prepared with my English speech habits. But, to my surprise, he addresses me in French. Immediately I have perceived this, my state of preparation is changed. I pack away my English speech habits and call up what French ones I possess.

We might *describe* such a change by saying that, before the stranger spoke, my expectancy was represented by a number of hypotheses concerning his language—English, French, Italian, et cetera—and that the whole environment and circumstances placed a heavy *a priori* weighting upon the first of these hypotheses; and that his speech subsequently caused these weightings to be changed. Broadly, the perception of signs confirms or denies hypotheses,[B] thereby changing the perceiver's state of expectancy or "set" toward the communication event. His beliefs, represented by a relative weighting of a range of hypotheses, are converted from an initial to a final set.

A person's psychological "set" toward some task, situation, or communication event depends upon his past experience, upon a host of preceding events which have led up to that moment. Such a "set" is considered to influence his formation of associations, by bringing to bear certain "determining tendencies," and hence influencing his way of organizing or executing the task,[235] or affecting the degree to which he recognizes signs, or forms perceptions, in a communication event. "Set" depends upon his past experience, and upon his predictions or anticipations about the likely consequences or requirements of future tasks, which he is led to make by virtue of this past experience.

For this reason, the results of recall or memory tests,[185] of visual or aural recognition tests, of word association tests, and of many direct psychological experiments may depend markedly upon the way in which the instructions are presented to the subject beforehand.[269, 366]

Such a point of view might, at casual glance, suggest a parallelism with statistical communication theory; but we must be most careful, because the present problems are psychological and lie at the pragmatic level, not the syntactic. In Chapter 5, "communication" was interpreted as the conversion of a prior probability distribution to a posterior distribution, measured logarithmically. But communication theory is strictly a mathematical theory; the alphabet of signs is assumed given, and the probabilities are relative frequencies, or density functions. If this is not the case, we are not entitled to speak of information numerically, in binary digits, or *bits*. On the other hand, in the psychological problem we are speaking of probabilities as *beliefs*, at present non-numerically, and no fixed and closed alphabet of signs has been defined. However, there are two directions in which the mathematical concept of (syntactical) information has shown some promise of application to problems of perception. The first points to experiments carried out with *defined* sets of sign stimuli, together with numerical, statistical assessment of responses. Secondly, the binary measure of information has found some application to the study of the structure and physiology of the nervous system, to the neural channels and nets, and to their capacities for storing binary units of information. We shall return to these points later.

At present, the only relation between our psychological problems and communication theory, of which we are taking note, arises from the essentially inferential basis of both. In communication theory, we regard the receipt of noisy signals as providing *evidence* of the messages selected at the transmitter, such evidence converting the receiver's hypotheses concerning the possible messages from a prior set [probabilities of messages $p(x)$] to a posterior set [probabilities $p(x/y)$], from which the receiver can make some "best" guess, with a chance of error. The mathematical basis to such an inference process we saw to be given by Bayes's theorem (Chapter 5, Section 6). Analogously, in performing an act of recognition, the received signals may be said to constitute evidence, converting the perceiver's beliefs, or "hypotheses," from a prior to a posterior set. He may receive only slight evidence, snatches of speech sounds heard in a crowd, or a few lines and squiggles sketched on paper; then he may infer spoken words, or recognize the drawing of a well-known face. In both the communication problem, and the psychological problem, the *prior* hypotheses and their weightings (probabilities, or beliefs) are of major importance. But apart from the inferential nature of both, we should not draw too close a parallel between the syntactic and the pragmatic problems.

Inference is essentially fallible—but it is the only way of increasing knowledge.[B, 105] Statistical communication theory shows how syntactical errors occur in a noisy communication channel—with the surprising proviso, given by Shannon's Capacity Theorem,[297] that these errors can in principle be reduced to zero, within specified limiting conditions, by suitably encoding the source of messages. Analogously, perceptual errors frequently occur; for example, a bank of clouds, low on the horizon, may readily deceive the sharpest-eyed observer and be taken for a range of hills.

Having mentioned errors in relation to perception, perhaps we should refer back for a moment to Peirce's view that a direct perceptual judgment cannot, from its nature, be something that is "right" or "wrong."[B] When the clouds were seen, they were perceived *as* hills; they were responded to as such, perhaps by evoking the response (in soliloquy or aloud): "Look at the snow on those hills!" Subsequently an error might be inferred, perhaps on the receipt of fresh evidence after a second glance, and this perception of an error be shown by a response such as: "I thought for one moment those clouds were snow!" But in such a case there are *two* perceptions; first the clouds were perceived as snow and second the error was perceived.*

It can scarcely be repeated too often that the giving of a certain logical form (such as inference) to *description* of a psychological process does not imply that logical argument or reasoning goes on in the head. When you see a bank of clouds as a range of hills, you may no more be aware of the thought sequences and processes which produced this illusion than you know the anatomy and physiological actions going on in your brain. The description provides a specification of the apparent *functions* executed by the brain; it does not specify the brain *mechanism*, or specify thoughts. Thus, we should not dare to say that "perceptive activity involves the perceiver in such and such a mental procedure"; rather, we might say that "perceptive activity proceeds *as though* the perceiver's brain operates upon such-and-such general principles." Referring back to an earlier example, when I see a book lying on the table, I see it as a book, square, or rectangular; I do not see a lozenge-shaped patch of color and subsequently reason out that it must be a book. But the end result could be described in terms of certain logical procedures.

It is in this sense that the word "hypotheses" is used when we say that initial (*a priori*) beliefs have the nature of hypotheses; the immediate environment and a person's past experience, then, determine an ensemble of weighted hypotheses representing a psychological "set" toward a communication event about to take place. When a friend rings me up on the telephone, and gives his name, immediately a whole collection of habits of association are evoked and I am put into a certain "state of expectancy." As the conversation unfolds, my accumulating experience modifies this state, as items of news, the names of places or of acquaintances, or other material operate upon my associative habits.[235, 366]

* See William James footnote on page 226.

D. B. Fry* has given a remarkable demonstration of the way in which *a priori* knowledge bears upon recognition.   He has made a gramophone recording of two men holding a conversation, but with their speech so artificially distorted that not a word can be recognized.   After one playing of the record, the listener is informed that the speakers are discussing the subject of "buying a new suit"; they refer to their tailors, the price of clothes, styles, et cetera.   The record is then played a second time, and most listeners are able to follow the whole conversation.   The words "jump out" at one.   Now we could interpret this result by saying that, in the absence of any prior hints about subject matter, the listener could form

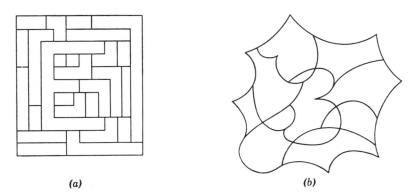

(a)   (b)

Fig. 7.3.   Two well-known signs, submerged in "noise."

hypotheses which range over the whole of human speech—all words and topics are possible—whereas after the clue word "tailor," the listener is given a certain psychological "set"; his hypotheses become more restricted, to cover only words and phrases which past experience causes him, habitu- ally, to associate with tailors.   "Speech is no more than a series of rough hints which the hearer must interpret. . . ."[255]   Any additional hints facilitate this interpretation.   In this experiment, by virtue of the hint "tailor," the range of possible messages becomes reduced.

An analogous visual example may be given to the reader.   Figure 7.3(a) shows a pattern of rectangular tiles, among which some have been arranged to form a certain well-known sign.   You may have difficulty in identifying it—but now, if I tell you it is an English capital letter, you may quickly spot it.†   Again Fig. 7.3(b) shows another well-known sign submerged amongst a number of curved lines; but the prior information that it is a

* See Fry in reference 336.
† It is an E.

numeral should enable you to spot it.*   One is perhaps reminded, by these illustrations, of the Ishihara tests for color blindness; but the case is really quite different.   In those tests, the subject is presented with cards covered by an irregular mass of vari-colored spots, but so colored that only those who are color blind can recognize numerals formed by the lie of some of the spots.[165]   But this result does not depend at all upon prior knowledge of the possible range of messages, or upon the subjects's psychological "set," or prior hypotheses; it depends upon the physical properties of the (human) channel.   No amount of experience and learning will help a person who has no color blindness.

Communication proceeds in the face of a number of uncertainties and has the character of, or may be described as consisting of, numerous inductive inferences being carried out concurrently.   The number and variety of these uncertainties is particularly apparent in the case of speech. For instance:

   (1) Uncertainties of speech sounds, or acoustic patterning.   Accents, tones, loudness may be varied; speakers may shout, sing, whisper, or talk with their mouths full.
   (2) Uncertainties of language and syntax.   Sentence constructions differ; conversational language may be bound by few rules of syntax.   Vocabularies vary; words have many near-synonyms, popular usages, special usages, et cetera.
   (3) Environmental uncertainties.   Conversations are disturbed by street noises, by telephone bells, and background chatter.
   (4) Recognition uncertainties.   Recognition depends upon the peculiar past experiences of the listener, upon his familiarity with the speaker's speech habits, knowledge of language, subject matter, et cetera.

There are many sources of uncertainty, yet speech communication works. It is so structured as to possess redundancy at a variety of levels, to assist in overcoming these uncertainties.   Only at the acoustic level is it a simple one-dimensional flow; but in its production and in its recognition, speech is a manifold, a number of concurrent activities, as we shall argue later.

4.3. "THE COCKTAIL PARTY PROBLEM"

These examples are but a few that come to mind, to illustrate our extraordinary powers of perception and recognition.   From the flimsiest evidence we make general inferences and are triggered into response, or at least our actions may be so described.   The more prior relevant experience, the sharper the "set" and the more ready the response.   The human nervous system is a "machine" of such a nature that it can successfully operate with a minute fraction of the controls normally available; it has an immense safety factor.   It is unlike any machine constructed by

* It is a 3.

engineers, partly for that very reason.   The "machine" can work in this way only by virtue of the astronomical scale of the memory store, a store of response habits.   Our lives are a continuity of experiences, accumulating and building up this immense store of habits, by virtue of which we are enabled to respond to the slightest shreds of signals.

One of our most important faculties is the ability to listen to, and follow, one speaker in the presence of others.[377, 371]   This is such a common experience that we may take it for granted; we may call it "the cocktail party problem."   No machine has yet been constructed to do just this, to filter out one conversation from a number jumbled together (as electric wave filters separate various telephone messages), and the reason is not far to seek; given a store with a suitably immense capacity, we might achieve at least partial success!   Your author has had some interest in this problem and has carried out the following experiment, as one of a series.[61]   A tape recording is made of a reading from a book (message A) and then, superimposed upon this, a second recording is made (message B) of a reading by the same speaker, using a different text.   The result is a complete babel, but it is presented to a listener who does not know either message, with instructions to separate A from B.   He may play the record over and over again, under his own control, listening on headphones; he is not allowed to write but dictates bits and pieces of phrases as he identifies them, and they are recorded for him.   The remarkable thing is that over very wide ranges of texts, he is successful, though finds great difficulty.   Because the same speaker reads both messages, no clues are provided by different qualities of voice, which may help in real-life cocktail party conversation.   Again, since the messages are recorded and heard through headphones, all binaural directivity aids are removed.   The only remaining control is provided by the different syntactic structures of the two message texts and by our myriad store of speech habits—our knowledge of syllables and their preferred sequences, of acoustic patterning, of phrases, of clichés, of word sequences, et cetera.   Such habits are deeply engrained in us and play a major role in our recognition of speech.   Speech played backward does not just sound like bad speech; it sounds quite unlike speech.   Speech interfered with, in its *temporal* patterning (by various technical means), is strikingly different to the ear.

An illustration of the mastery these habits exercise over us is provided by the result of this same experiment, when carried out with an *English* speaker reading the superposed messages A and B, whilst an *American* listener separates them.   Though English and American are similar languages, they are not identical; it turns out that the American listener, identifying and reading bits and pieces of phrases, unwittingly falls prey to his American speech habits.   He uses, for example, words like "gotten" (got), "railroad" (railway), "airplane" (aeroplane), "ash can" (ash bin), which are not used by English speakers.*

We have stressed the importance of our ingrained speech habits at the acoustic, syllabic, or syntactic levels—our habits of making certain sounds and sound sequences—but we have made less reference to sequences or association of ideas, or of our knowledge of subject matter, that is, to the semantic level. It might be argued that the two superposed messages *A* and *B* were separated by the listener by virtue of their distinct subject matters. Somewhat analogously, it has been shown easier to memorize and recall long sentences of "meaningful" text than similar chains of random words.[239] But your author would place more stress upon our syntactical habits; upon our knowledge of sounds and their sequences, of syllabic patterning and word sequences.

Another simple experiment that highlights our acquired habits of uttering preferred syllable, word, and phrase sequences is the following.[61] A tape recording is made of a reading from a passage of prose and played through headphones to a listener; the listener is instructed to repeat what he hears concurrently, in a subdued or whispered voice. He is then listening and speaking at the same time, but this is found to be an extremely simple task.† His spoken repetition tends to be in irregular detached phrases and, with most people and most texts, is given in a singularly emotionless voice as though intoning. It seems as though he is unable to copy the emotional content of the words he hears and, since he is following so close upon the heels of these words, he is unable to see far enough ahead to create his own emotional content. He mouths the words like an automaton and extracts little semantic content, if any. If questioned subsequently, he can say little about the text, especially if it is at all "deep" or difficult. He cannot, for example, act upon a complicated set of instructions if he receives them under such conditions. He is almost in the situation of a parrot which has been taught to speak and can say "Wipe your feet!" or "Go to hell!" without having thoughts of dirty shoes or of damnation.

Our powers of concentrating upon one speaker's voice when another conversation is interrupting are remarkable. We can separate the totality of sounds falling upon our ears into two groups, by inference. There is no doubt that the possession of two good ears greatly facilitates this inference, for the sounds reaching each ear differ somewhat and the brain makes use

---

* See reference 45 for an excellent American-English dictionary of words, phrases, and grammatical constructions. This is most useful for constructing experimental stimulus texts.

† Stutterers can also do this readily. The writer and colleagues gave a preliminary account of the clinical use of this technique in *Nature*, Nov. 5, 1955, and a more complete account later.[378]

of this difference when analysing the complex of simultaneous voices.[377, 379] It may be argued that the whole connected sentences of the one speaker to whom we are listening have "meaning" or semantic content, that these sentences conjure up connected thoughts and images. It can also be argued that connected sentences have a certain statistical structure, that sounds follow one another in certain sequences and rhythms, and that we have acquired extensive knowledge of speech sound transitions (as preferences or rankings, beliefs or subjective probabilities). We have acquired these transitions as an essential part of our speech habits. Perhaps both aspects play a part, but the author inclines toward stressing the latter.

5. THE INTAKE OF INFORMATION BY THE SENSES: SOME QUANTITATIVE EXPERIMENTS

Passing reference has been made already to the intake of "information" by the human senses, and to the use of this term in a loose, descriptive manner, as contrasted with the use of the mathematical measure of information in controlled psychological experiments. We shall describe briefly one or two such experiments now, in order to illustrate useful and strictly correct applications of the mathematical measure.[371, 407, 397]

5.1. TACHISTOSCOPIC EXPERIMENTS: RECOGNITION FROM VERY BRIEF GLIMPSES

With an instrument known as a *tachistoscope*,* photographs, printed letters and words, diagrams, and drawings may be flashed upon a screen for very short intervals of time which may be controlled precisely. The instrument resembles a lantern projector or *epidiascope*, fitted with a camera shutter. With such an instrument, experiments upon visual recognition may be made with a deliberate restriction of the duration of exposure. In an early set of experiments, Miller, Bruner, and Postman[236, †] have measured the degree of correct recognition of printed sequences of letters ("words") in such a way as to show, numerically, the ease of recognition afforded by familiarity with the sequences. In a flash lasting, say, 100 milliseconds, only a few letters of a random sequence may be identified correctly, whereas a familiar word of the same length will readily be spotted. But "familiar" may perhaps be regarded as a vague psychological term; these experimenters have wisely sought to avoid this objection by using not dictionary words but letter sequences constructed to have the zero-order, monogram, digram, etc., statistical structure of printed English. List A, below, shows some dummy words; such sequences may be made either with the assistance of

* J. McK. Cattell, 1885 (see references 236, 268).
† See also reference 159 for some earlier experiments.

tables of letter frequencies or, more simply, by using the Miller-Shannon guessing technique which was described in Chapter 3, Section 6.3. The results of such experiments must be interpreted statistically, not as the responses of one person, to one or a few such stimuli, but in *averages*, over a

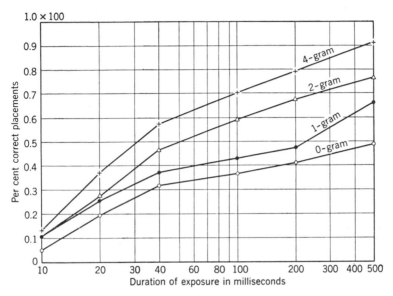

Fig. 7.4.   Average placement scores plotted against duration of exposure, for dummy "words" at four orders of approximation to English (after Miller, Bruner, and Postman).

number of people and long lists of stimulus "words." Figure 7.4 gives a plot of some results,* showing the percentage of letters identified in their correct places (placement score) as a function of the time of exposure. Clearly the "words" having correct quadrigram structure are recognized with far greater facility than are the random sequences.

It is the corollary to this experiment which is so interesting. Miller, Bruner, and Postman have shown that although such dummy "words" are recognized more readily as the approximation to English spelling is improved, the intake of information is nearly constant (for any one exposure). In the case of zero-order (0-gram) sequences, no statistical constraints exist between successive letters, so that each letter represents one equally likely selection out of 26, requiring, on an average, $\log_2 26 = 4.71$ bits per letter. Hence, if at some given exposure S per cent are correctly recognized and placed, the response may be reckoned as $4.71 (S/100)$ bits per exposure. In

* For precise conditions of the experiment, see the original paper, reference 236. Figures 7.4, 7.5, and List A are reproduced here with very kind permission of the Journal Press, Provincetown, Mass.

the case of the sequences of 1-gram, 2-gram, 4-gram structure sequences, the per cent of redundancy may be estimated fairly accurately;[236, 294] the figures are given in List A. Calling this redundancy R_n, for an n-gram structure, we find the information carried by S per cent correctly recognized letters is reduced from 4.71 ($S/100$) to 4.71 ($S.R_n/100$) bits per exposure. Applying such corrections for redundancy to the results already cited, we obtain the graphs of Fig. 7.5, which lie quite closely together.

LIST A

Some of the eight-letter dummy "words," forming different orders of approximation to English, as used by Miller, Bruner, and Postman

0-gram (Zero redundancy)	1-gram (15% redundancy)	2-gram (15% redundancy)	4-gram (43% redundancy)
YRULPZOC	STANUGOP	WALLYLOF	RICANING
OZHGPMTJ	VTYEHULO	THERARES	VERNALIT
DLEGQMNW	EINOAASE	CHEVADNE	MOSSIANT
CFUJXZAQ	IYDEWAKN	NERMBLIM	POKERSON
etc.	etc.	etc.	etc.

Notice that we cannot make time averages here, and we quote the information rate in bits per second; if the exposure time is long enough, every letter of a sequence can be identified correctly and *all* the information content extracted. Since the process is non-stationary, information has been averaged over the *ensemble* of people under test, with the assumption that their experiences of English texts have been roughly similar.

A person's psychological "set" toward some communication event which is about to take place has been interpreted in terms of expectancies or "hypotheses," having various prior weightings; when the event takes place, the perceived signs confirm or deny these hypotheses. Wilkins,[351] for example, has reported that nonsense words cunningly constructed to resemble familiar words, for use in tachistoscopic tests, may operate upon engrained habits of response; thus *talder powcum* would be read as *talcum powder*, being a more likely hypothesis. Any sequence of letters might be flashed upon the screen, but their possibilities are weighted according to the observer's experience of texts. Again, Siipola[302] has shown that subjects fail to perceive errors deliberately introduced in familiar words, under conditions of tachistoscopic presentation; also that identification depends in part upon expectancies which have been established in the mind of the subject during the experiments. We all often overlook printer's errors.

In controlled experiments of the kind just described, the prior weightings become numerical probabilities, and the information content of the perceived signs may be measured.   But such numerical interpretation makes sense only if we average over an *ensemble* of sign recipients (subjects).

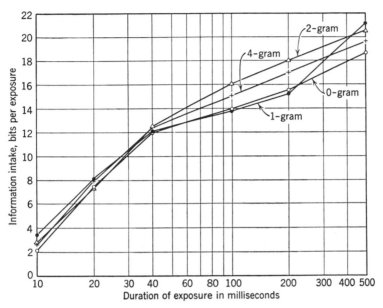

Fig. 7.5.   Intake of visual (letter sequence) information plotted against duration of exposure; results of Fig. 7.4 corrected for per cent redundancy (after Miller, Bruner, and Postman).

5.2. CONTROL OF "MEANINGFULNESS" OF TEST MATERIAL

Turning now to spoken rather than written texts, we may see the same kind of influence exerted by contextual constraints; for instance, upon ease of memory or recall,[239, 251] or again, upon ease and accuracy of recognition of words or sentences against a noisy background.   It may be demonstrated that "meaningful" sentences are far easier to remember with accuracy than is gibberish;[251] they are also easier to recognize under noisy conditions.[237]   But "meaningfulness" raises personal questions once more. As with the visual experiments, it is possible to overcome this objection and to set up texts which have an assigned value of sense or nonsense. There are several ways in which this can be done.   It would be possible to list all the syllabic sounds of, say, English and to construct different sequences of dummy "words" having the digram, trigram, ···, *n*-gram structure of the language.   Such texts would be rubbish, but pronounceable rubbish.   Alternatively, the commoner English dictionary words may be taken[320] and set into sequences making such successive approximations to English. The results of such tests show once again that the important factor controlling success in response is not the long-range semantic associations evoked by the stimulus, but merely the short-term statistical dependences of the language.[235,239] This is not to say that these dummy-"word" stimuli do not set up thoughts or semantic associations[132,161,*] in the mind of the recipient. No; the conclusion is rather that the technique of constructing stimuli having n-gram statistical structure of a language, and of averaging the responses over an ensemble of recipients, provides an objective way of controlling the relative degree of "meaningfulness." Verbal behavior is one of our most important activities and a most fruitful source for psychological study; it is essentially patterned behavior and the patterning needs a quantitative measure.[161,235]

Statistical communication theory showed early promise for psychological experiments, but it has not subsequently been maintained. It has found application to all kinds of articulation test, and tests of visual acuity, in which people are required to distinguish between, and respond to, one sign out of a set constrained in some prearranged contextual way.[†] Experiments suggest that the organism has a definite limit for information which is a minute fraction of the content of the physical signals that reach the eyes, ears, and epidermis; and further, that this limit is measurable as tens or at most hundreds of bits per second, not hundreds of thousands or millions such as are contained in the physical signals themselves reaching the sense organs. The redundancy is enormous.

5.3. CHOICE REACTION-TIME EXPERIMENTS

Choice reaction-time experiments provide another field to which the information measure has shown some relevance. Briefly, a choice reaction time is the minimum time required for a recipient to respond, by some simple voluntary movement, to one of a number of alternative signals. Hick[‡] has observed that if the signals are drawn at random from a prearranged set of n (such as a number of lamps arranged in a small circle), and the reaction is made by touching the appropriate one of n corresponding push buttons, then the choice reaction time increases with the logarithm of n. This may be taken to suggest a constant *rate* of intake of information, measured as simple selections or bits per second, on an average. He has also investigated the "overloading" of the capacity of the human channel, by speeding up the test until mistakes occur in the choice reactions.[153]

* See Hilgard in reference 315.

† See Swets, reference 408, for examples of relevance of Decision Theory to psychological work.

‡ See Hick in reference 167.

As a variant of this experiment, the touching of a button may automatically light the next lamp at random, thereby allowing the subject to proceed as fast as his reaction times allow him.[191]

The diagram shown at the side of this page represents a simple means of demonstrating this.* Strips of such a kind are prepared (larger in size), and the task is to touch each black square with a finger tip, consecutively, starting from the top end and proceeding downward. The black squares have been selected "out of a hat." It is found that, over wide variations of square size, roughly the same reaction time is taken by any one individually, and this time increases with the logarithm of the number of alternatives in the row (eight here). In this case, the eye can see a *little* way ahead, so providing a slight redundancy. Such choice reaction-time experiments reduce the basic perceptive action of *discriminating*, or making selections, almost to its simplest proportions.

We could add to such a list of experiments. But it may be fair to say that information theory has been a better stimulant to new experiments than it has been an interpretant.[407]

5.4. SACCADIC MOVEMENTS OF THE EYES: FEEDBACK

When reading, we do not scan our eyes smoothly along the printed line, but in an irregular sequence of rapid jerks. Figure 7.6 illustrates the motion.† At each *point of fixation*, the eyeball is (almost, not absolutely) stationary for an interval of approximately one-quarter second for adults; the saccades, or jerks, from one point to another are rapid, and the eye spends 90 per cent of the time fixated. A reader is not aware of this irregularity of motion, and the *time* taken over any one saccadic leap is not under his control.

The question may well be asked: Why does the center of vision choose to rest upon these particular points of the printed lines? Experiment shows that the eyes do not fixate upon every letter, nor every word, for whole phrases to be perceived by the reader. Again, no preference is shown for fixating any particular part of a letter, or of a word. But there seems to be some evidence to suggest a relation between the numbers of fixation pauses per line and the reader's familiarity with the text—a point we shall take up again.

* First demonstrated to me by J. C. R. Licklider.

† The data given here upon the subject of saccadic movements are drawn entirely from Carmichael and Dearborn, reference 46. These authors describe several techniques for measuring the movements of the eyes.

When we look at scenes around us, we have the impression that our whole field of vision is very sharp; yet if the eyes are rested for a moment on one spot, it will be realized that only a minute area of the visual field is at all acute, whilst the rest is a blur. The *fovea centralis*, the center of sharp vision, covers an angle of less than one degree[214] (the reader may test this by looking fixedly with one eye shut at one letter on this page, and without moving his gaze, sense the blur round about this one letter). As the eyes scan a scene with leaping, saccadic movements, the succession of fleeting images, sharp only over this minute region, are associated and we imagine that we are seeing the scene and seeing it whole.*

An experimental tachistoscopic exposure corresponds to one period of fixation, but with a controlled duration; from such experiments the minimum times of perception of letters or words can be found, and the results suggest that visual perception, during reading, takes place almost entirely during the times of fixation. Though the eyes see a sharp letter only at the point of fixation, there is little doubt that it receives clues as to the general shape or contour of words in the neighborhood—including words *ahead*, giving the reader some visual aid to prediction (added to his knowledge of statistical context constraints). Such *peripheral* vision is important and may provide clues which partly determine the point of location of the next fixation.

It would seem that the intake of visual information is controlled by a *feedback* action, and that we have, in these instrumental means of measuring points of fixation, an ideal way of exploring this intake of information, though the writer knows of no such experiments having been made. If the points fixated on the printed text be regarded as giving a succession of input signals, and the perception regarded as an output response, then the points of fixation and lengths of saccades may depend upon this output; that is to say, the point to which the vision is shifted, in any one saccade, may be the result of a prediction based upon preceding perceptions. This control might be explored quantitatively, by constructing texts having known monogram, digram, $\cdots$, n-gram structure, as used for example by Miller† and others for aural experiments, and observing the points of fixation and their distribution, whilst the texts are read aloud.

There is some qualitative evidence that the number of points of fixation depends upon the "familiarity" of this text, but once again this statistical method of constructing texts of measurable familiarity may find a useful application. Carmichael and Dearborn find that proper names and titles

* See reference 34 for eye movements, observed by corneal reflections, when reading, watching advertisements, geometrical figures, drawings and, paintings; numerous examples and illustrations are given.

† For references, see Section 5.2.

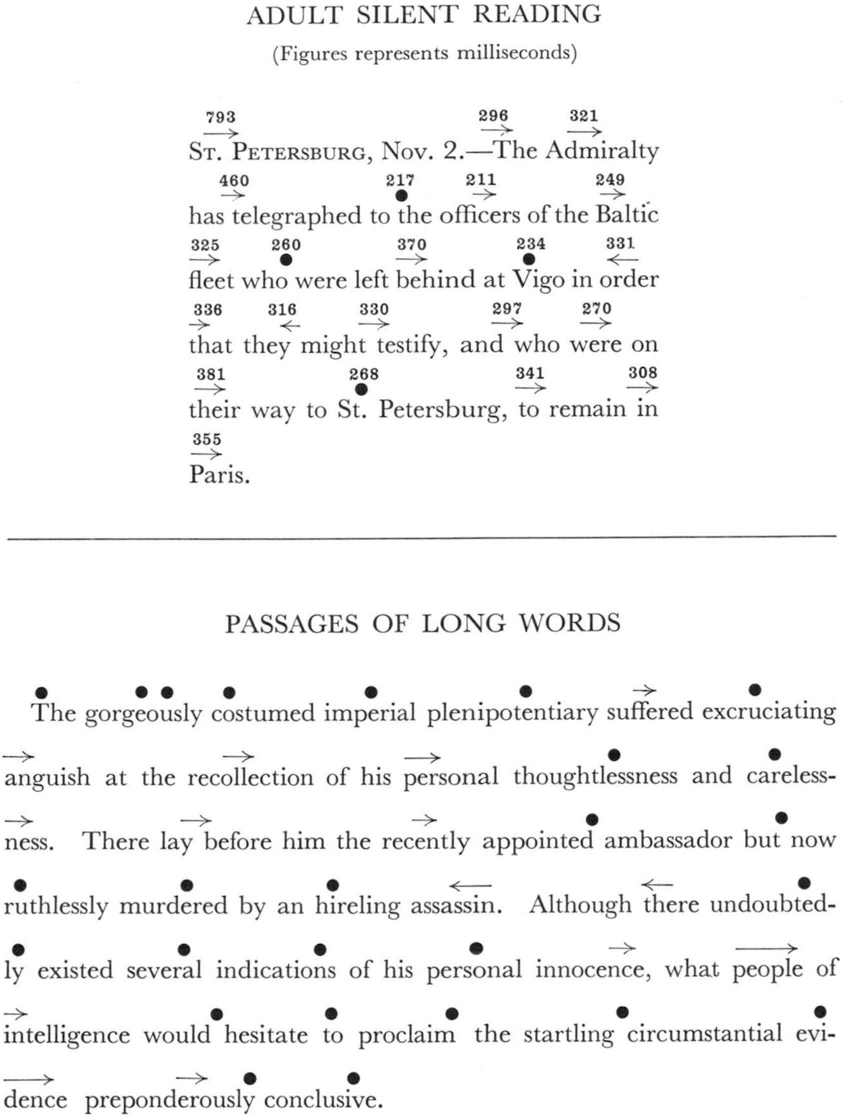

ADULT SILENT READING

(Figures represents milliseconds)

793
→
St. Petersburg, Nov. 2.—The Admiralty
296   321
→   →

460   217   211   249
→   •   →   →
has telegraphed to the officers of the Baltic

325   260   370   234   331
→   •   →   ←
fleet who were left behind at Vigo in order

336   316   330   297   270
→   ←   →   →   →
that they might testify, and who were on

381   268   341   308
→   •   →   →
their way to St. Petersburg, to remain in

355
→
Paris.

PASSAGES OF LONG WORDS

•   • •   •   •   •   →   •
The gorgeously costumed imperial plenipotentiary suffered excruciating

→   →   →   •   •
anguish at the recollection of his personal thoughtlessness and careless-

→   →   →   •   •
ness. There lay before him the recently appointed ambassador but now

•   •   •   ←   ←   •
ruthlessly murdered by an hireling assassin. Although there undoubted-

•   •   •   •   →   ⟶
ly existed several indications of his personal innocence, what people of

→   •   •   •   •   •
intelligence would hesitate to proclaim the startling circumstantial evi-

⟶   →   •   •
dence preponderously conclusive.

Fig. 7.6.   Fixation points of the eyes whilst reading.   Early measurements by Professor W. F. Dearborne (reproduced with his very kind permission).   The dots show sharp fixation points; the arrows indicate by their length and direction possible small movements of the eyes whilst fixated.   Modern measurements show that such *tremors* are in fact negligibly small.*

* H. B. Barlow (*J. Physiol.*, *116*, 28 March 1952) shows that the rms deviation, over 4 seconds fixation, is only 0.25 minute arc.

require a greater number of fixation pauses, and that common phrases require fewer or are overstepped by saccadic leaps; words like "in," "at," "to," are overstepped in the examples of Fig. 7.6. Such findings could be made quantitative. One interesting statistical result is given by Buswell;[43,46] the number of fixation pauses, averaged per line, decreases smoothly with the age of the reader; so too does the average duration of the pause, up to the age of ten years, whilst the number of regressions or backward saccades owing to failure to comprehend the text continues to decrease with age and experience.

5.5. Sense intake and perceptual intake of information

Perhaps it would be well here to distinguish two ways in which the "information capacity" of an organism has been discussed. There is, first, the capacity of the physical sense organs (receptors) themselves, estimated in thousands or millions of bits per second; secondly, there is the perceptual rate of information intake, dependent upon the rate at which discriminatory actions can actually be performed, and measured more nearly in tens of bits per second. Grey Walter, for example, has remarked upon the fact that although the nervous system, with its 10,000 million neuron "relays," has presumably a capacity for a similar astronomically large number of bits, the total number of degrees of freedom of the body (the "number of things it can do") is of the order of five hundred.[340] The enormous ratio here is our safety factor.

We may illustrate this with the example of reading of texts. There is, first, the information rate of the text itself, considered as a sequence of letters having known relative frequencies. Shannon's estimate for the information rate of printed English tends toward 1.5 bits per letter, if long-range statistical dependencies are considered[294] (Chapter 5, Section 4.1). If there are 70 letters per line, and the reader absorbs 1 line in 2 seconds average, we might conclude that he takes in $(1.5 \times 35) = 52.5$ bits per second; this figure, however, gives the information rate of the text (the *signs*) and makes no correction for the fact that printed lines are not only chains of letters, but have outlines and form, nor for the dynamic, saccadic actions of the eyes of a reader. The retina receives a rapid sequence of optical images, and its information capacity shows a very different figure. Jacobson, for example, has estimated the information capacity of the human eye[169] at about 4.3 million bits per second by regarding the field as a mosaic of elements having areas subtending the angle of acuity at the eye (due account being taken of change of acuity in peripheral vision). Incidentally, a television receiver carries signals of no more than 100 million bits per second. The exact figures do not matter; they are in millions, not dozens, and represent the eye's capacity for optical stimuli. Although we can in principle, and given time, detect the presence or absence of optical energy in any one mosaic element (logon, cell, etc.) under suitable conditions, we cannot react at this rate. Printed letters differ one from another by vastly more than one such mosaic element and this, together with their preferred sequences, gives them an enormous redundancy. Shannon's figure comes much nearer to the perceptual capacity of the reader, although he does not consider the saccadic movements in reading. His estimates of printed-text information rate are based upon human prediction of letter sequences;[294] but in these observations his human subjects had ample time to make such predictions, or guesses, and were not required to carry them out at the speeds required when reading. However, this low figure of about 50 bits per second suggests that the eye saccadic movements provide an efficient intake of information.

Similarly with hearing. The informational capacity of the ear itself too may be measurable in tens of thousand of bits per second.[168,*] But this does not mean that we can react at this rate, for most of these bits represent redundancy. Speech is so structured, and our prior knowledge of sounds and their sequences so extensive, that we "take in" or react, at far slower rates—again, nearer to dozens, than thousands of bits per second.

The organism reacts to signs with remarkable accuracy and success; communication is established and maintained in spite of a hundred and one reasons against it. The receptor organs have the necessary capacity for accepting the generous supply of signal information, and the nervous system is such that it takes full advantage of the redundancy. It is this which safeguards the organism and ensures its communicative success, when all hazards seem to be against it.[411]

6. THE SEARCH FOR INVARIANTS, IN PATTERN RECOGNITION

In this section a few comments will be passed upon the assumption that because visual, aural, and other patterns are recognizable under a great variety of transformations, distortions, and presentation, they necessarily retain some common properties (invariants) under all these changes. A triangle is recognized as a triangle in all positions, forms, and sizes; the face of a friend is well known in a variety of expressions; speech is recognized, with most accents and in spite of extreme distortion. That certain invariant properties exist will not be denied here; we only comment upon some difficulties of this problem.

* For example, good-quality telephone speech, quantized into 128 levels, and transmitted in a frequency band of 5000 cycles per second, conveys $2 \times 5000 \log_2 128 = 70,000$ bits per second.

"Pattern recognition" implies a relationship between a pattern and an individual; and the individual, with his own peculiar experiences, should not be too lightly dismissed, as is sometimes the case. Recognition is not explicable in terms of properties of the patterns, or signs, alone. It is conceivable, for instance, that you and I would recognize the face of a third person, from quite different feature characteristics. This is conceivable, though perhaps unlikely. Even if we use the same set of features, we may weight them differently.[c]

6.1. IN RECOGNITION OF GEOMETRIC FIGURES

Figure 7.7 shows three caricatures of a well-known British statesman, drawn by the artist David Low for the *Manchester Guardian*. Few readers will have difficulty in recognizing the subject. Yet these drawings appear to be quite different in detail; the facial expressions, the head positions are dissimilar. What can there be in common among these drawings that leads us to associate them all with the same personality?*

The problem of visual recognition is frequently reduced to its simplest dimensions by discussing geometrical figures—squares and triangles. We say "simplest" guardedly. But if recognition of simple geometrical figures could be explained, it would carry us a long way toward understanding recognition of more complex figures—of faces, of scents, or of speech, for example.[2] Assuming that we carry, within our heads, replicas or representations of those features of the physical world which matter to us, which we have learned, and which are brought into some kind of correspondence when we recognize objects, or voices, or scents, what particular features are singled out for building into these representations? And how is the nervous system organized into such representation?

In the case of recognizing a triangular or a square card, the most obvious invariant features among cards of different sizes and orientation are the numbers of corners. To refer again to the case of a blind man who has been operated upon and given his sight, whilst he is still in the early stages of learning to make some kind of sense out of the jazz of colored patches he sees, he may slowly and laboriously count the corners. He may then identify the card as a square or triangle, though see little purpose in this exercise; how much easier to pass his hands over it and get back again into the feel-world where he has the right habits![364] But we who have sight are stimulated at once into response by the card, without conscious counting, though we may have done this as children, and may still have to do it to recognize, say, a ten- from a twelve-sized figure. What kinds of representations have our brains organized from our many experiences of squares, triangles, and other shapes, which give us such habitual and ready response?

* See reference 194 for a discussion of caricature drawings and their recognition.

Fig. 7.7. Caricatures of the late Sir Winston Churchill, by David Low (with very kind permission of the artist).

In the case of spacial shapes or forms, the importance of outline and the existence of mathematical invariants have frequently been stressed. For example, a pencil point moved around the boundary of a triangle, a circle, or other shape, is undergoing a sequence of motions which is characteristic of the shape and independent of the size, the orientation, and of any co-ordinate system. A boundary curve may be described as a sequence of radii of curvature, and other differential forms; a pattern of lines, areas, and boundaries has connectivity and other topological properties, independent of precise geometrical form.*

Recognition involves motor response, or preparation for motor response. At least in early stages of learning to recognize shapes, the eye or the finger may explore, and it is conceivable that exploration of contours and boundaries could generate sequences of neural signals characteristic of the shape explored; the representations set up and stored in the brain might be representations of characteristic differential forms, natural equations, or topological invariants. There is, however, a complication to this simple kinematic theory, because the eye does not trace around outlines smoothly, at uniform speed, but rather samples it in a few saccadic leaps.† It is difficult then to imagine how such mathematical properties and invariants can be abstracted from these jerks. A deal of experimental work is at present under way, to observe how the eye moves when viewing and recognizing geometrical shapes, and the results of this work are likely to cast light upon the problems of recognition.[34] How does the eye move around boundaries? Where are the points of fixation? How do these factors vary with familiarity with the shape? Or when counting patterned groups of dots? Or when driving a car? The eyes do not scan shapes, faces, and scenes in a predetermined manner, like television scanning, but in ways which depend upon the forms under view and, equally important, upon the particular habits of the individual, dependent upon his particular past experiences of these forms. Once geometric shapes (e.g., printed letters) have been learned, the eyes do not need to move, for recognition, as the tachistoscopic experiments show. Simple shapes are recognized in a flash—even peripherally.‡

Television scanning has been mentioned. There is one further point, suggested by study of different forms of scanning, which may have some slight relevance to visual recognition. With geometrical figures or black-and-white drawings, or restricting the argument to *outlines*, only two kinds of element exist—boundary lines and flat empty areas. In systems of television scanning employing the "stopped spot" principle, the scanning spot wastes no time over the empty areas but passes over them rapidly, coming to a temporary halt when it meets a boundary line.§ By various methods, the positions of the boundary lines are coded for transmission, the advantages of such systems being that the signal redundancy is reduced, because the "boundary-line signals" and "empty-area signals" have been coded so as to acquire more nearly equal probabilities (see Chapter 5,

---

* See discussion after Loeb's in reference 166.
† See footnote, p. 286.
‡ See Section 5.1 for references.
§ See (*a*) Loeb and (*b*) Cherry and Gouriet in reference 166.

Section 4.1). There is a possibility that the eye provides a similar economy by virtue of its saccadic movements, leaping from boundary to boundary but wasting little time on the empty areas between.[340] Further experiments upon occular saccadic behavior are needed.

6.2. IN RECOGNITION OF SPEECH

We can usually recognize what someone is saying, whether they whisper, shout, or sing; whether they have a cold or whether they have their mouths full. What is invariant here? Surely, it is the same set of vocal organs being used. When searching for the acoustic invariants in speech sounds, we should not be guided by mathematical simplicity or nicety alone, but we should look for properties of the sounds which are special to speech sounds. For speech sounds form a class on their own and are distinct from sounds of motor horns, bells ringing, bird song, frying bacon, and all the sounds of daily life. Since birth we have been learning both to hear speech and to produce it; it represents a very great and important part of our experience. A child learns to imitate the speech sounds of its mother; it does not learn to make sounds like bells or frying bacon. It would appear then that the production of speech and the perception of speech are, at the least, related phenomena, for a normal individual learns them together. And such sounds represent, to we who both hear and make them, a distinct and special class.

It may be possible to take this point further and to argue that speech perception and production are one and the same phenomenon, in normal individuals; that when we listen to someone speaking, we are also preparing to move our own vocal organs in sympathy—not necessarily effecting motor responses, but subthreshold—and that our imitative instincts of childhood never leave us. Paget, for instance, comments upon our instinctive recognition of mouth position when hearing speech.[254] It is extraordinarily easy to copy another person's speech, while they are speaking[61] and, in fact, many people mumble when you address them or even, more annoyingly, put words "into your mouth." Children mumble whilst reading (hearing themselves in silent soliloquy?) and silent reading was rare in the Middle Ages.[A] It is also easy, for most people, to sing in tune with others, but it is infernally difficult to sing an harmonically unrelated tune, or to sing deliberately flat or sharp. Imitation of the sounds, or the movements, of others lies very near the surface in human as well as animal behavior.* Mimicry is a basic human and animal faculty.

Although not bearing directly upon this question, one experiment should be mentioned which illustrates the integration of speech production

---

* Haldane has remarked upon the ease of such imitative behavior, in analogy to animal ritual and intention movements. See Chapter 1, Section 5, and reference 139.

and perception, in a striking manner; this is sometimes referred to as "delayed playback speech." In this experiment[107,148,197] a subject, wearing a well-fitting pair of headphones, is asked to describe a scene or a picture, whilst his voice is recorded by microphone and magnetic tape, delayed by about a fourth of a second, and played back into his headphones. In this way the acoustic environment is changed in a way wholly unnatural, for throughout our lives we learn our speech habits in a certain time relationship to hearing and perception of our own speech sounds. This relationship is destroyed by such artificial means and the result is violent stuttering and drawling, reminiscent of drunken speech.

Whether or not speech perception and (preparation for) production are closely related, or are even to be equated, can only be proved physiologically, and we shall not carry this point further here, except to stress that the "representations" we carry in our heads, of speech sounds, are likely to be formed of data concerning vocal organ configurations, the cavity resonances (formants), the larynx frequencies, et cetera. Again experiments by Lawrence and others at Edinburgh,* suggest that such data need be relatively few and simple. Regarded this way, speech is gesture communication.

Speech is a manifold operation; we do a number of things concurrently with our lips, tongue, larynx, and the other organs, resulting in the one-dimension speech sound wave. In the light of our previous argument, it seems reasonable that recognition of speech is similarly a manifold operation; that we recognize positions of lips, tongue, larynx, et cetera, and their dynamic changes. It is from this point of view that the writer finds the "distinctive feature" specification of speech, of Roman Jakobson and his colleagues, singularly attractive[174] (Chapter 3, Sections 3 and 4). They suggest the breaking down of speech into a number of concurrent "features," each determined by some characteristic vocal action. Such features represent, however, the dimensions of a quantized attribute space for a *language*, not for acoustic speech signals.

There are two points about this "feature" theory which should be stressed, now that we are discussing recognition of speech, and not language. First, recognition is a problem concerning the relationship between some specific individual and some specific stimulus; Jakobson's theory is a *linguistic* theory, abstracted from specific individuals and utterances. Secondly, it is not the particular features, chosen by Jakobson and his colleagues, which we suggest utilizing here; it is only the idea that speech is a number of concurrent activities; and that not only is this multi-dimensional "feature" description applicable at the production end, but similarly at the recognition end. Since we are discussing the psychological question of recognition,

* See Lawrence in reference 166; see also Chapter 4, Section 3.4.

and not linguistics, we shall need a somewhat different approach. Jakobson's theory, being a linguistic theory and abstracted from individuals, treats phonemes as bundles (dimensions) of features, each quantized into one of two values (±). We shall need to replace these quantal values by probabilities, and phonemes need not be mentioned. But, we repeat, this is not extending or modifying the distinctive-feature theory—because we are not now discussing linguistics.

The suggestion made, then, is that recognition of speech may perhaps involve principles and physiological processes which differ from those used in recognition of non-vocal sounds. This point of view distinguishes two classes of experiment: (1) those carried out with spoken stimuli, and (2) those using pure tones, clicks, and other non-vocal stimuli. Extensive studies of aural stimuli have been made, and of their effects—masking, fatigue, pitch and intensity discrimination, beats, aural harmonics, and so on.[D] But all such effects concern people's *sensations* and involve the relationship between physical stimulus and a listener; they are not physical attributes of the sounds themselves. These effects may vary between individuals but, although subjective, may be measured fairly objectively (Chapter 4, Section 1). Such experiments, using pure tones or clicks, relate to the properties of the ear and to our powers of aural perception, but not specifically to speech or to the particular ways in which these abilities are organized for the recognition of speech.

6.3. RECOGNITION OF DISTORTED SPEECH

Speech is surprisingly resistant to certain distortions. The fact that spoken words are quite recognizable, under all kinds of distortion produced artificially (e.g., electronically) might at first appear to contradict the thesis that recognition depends upon the "natural" attributes of vocal organ configuration. However, closer examination strengthens this view.

A speech wave form, like any other, may be regarded as a carrier wave modulated simultaneously in amplitude and phase.[38,*] If this is the case, then it appears that the phase modulation is vastly more important than the envelope, or variations in amplitude. Numerous experiments have been performed which suggest that the amplitude fluctuations of speech are relatively unimportant, but may be stripped off, electronically; it is the wave alternations (phase modulation) which carries the bulk of the intelligibility.

Speech wave forms may be subjected to destructive or to non-destructive transformations; it is the retention of high intelligibility under certain types of destructive transformation which is indeed so surprising. Non-

---

* There is no *unique* pair of amplitude and phase modulation functions, mathematically speaking, but there are preferred choices. See reference 339.

destructive transformations, such as simple differentiation or integration of the wave form, are reversible and merely represent a tilting or other "boosting" of the voice spectrum; speech will tolerate several successive differentiations, and perhaps one integration.

This high intelligibility of speech remaining after removal of the envelope may most strikingly be illustrated from an experiment by Licklider and others at Harvard,[D, 204, 205] showing the high intelligibility of "infinitely clipped speech," a process which has been illustrated by Fig. 4.1 (c). Such a destructive transformation results from amplifying the speech wave and severely limiting it in amplitude, electronically, so that all that is left consists of an irregular rectangular wave, constant in amplitude, the vertical edges of which cross the time axis at points corresponding to the crossover points of the original speech wave.* This is indeed a destructive transformation! Virtually the *whole* of the wave form is thrown away, yet the intelligibility is retained by nothing more than a distribution of points along the time axis. The result sounds like a speaker with a sore throat, but the ear is tolerant of this.

These experiments have been extended in the writer's own laboratory,[112] where the "clipped-speech" wave has been reduced to a distribution of *identical* impulses along the time axis, whilst room noises and the speaker's breath sounds, between words and at their onset, have been removed. If these impulses be modulated in amplitude by the envelope of the original speech wave (extracted from this wave, using a time constant of 20 milliseconds) the intelligibility is not noticeably improved—again illustrating the secondary value of this amplitude variation in speech.

What can be the invariants under such transformations? Clipped speech has a constant amplitude, unchanged whether the speaker whispers, speaks, or shouts; the whispering, speaking, or shouting is evident to a listener. What characteristic changes of spectral form show up under these changes? What are the invariants of the clipping process itself— what is there in common between the speaker's true voice spectrum and that of the clipped signal? Evidence is scanty on these points at present, but the few measurements which have as yet been made support the view that we must not infer, from the fact that signals are recognizable under certain destructive transformations, that the spectra are unaltered to any major extent. It would seem that those invariants which do exist are distributed among certain speech sounds, although other speech sounds may be largely destroyed. Again, both theoretically and experimentally there is good reason to believe that the highest-energy voice formant is retained when speech is infinitely clipped.[112] Perhaps we need not expect

---

* The limiting is carried out to 45–50 decibels. The transformation may be represented by $f^{\sqrt{n}}(t)$ as $n \to \infty$.

invariants to be many and major, for the brain gets along with the slenderest of clues. But one invariant clearly remains under this extreme distortion of "clipping," namely the temporal pattern of the wave pressure fronts and so, also, of the syllables. The ear is very intolerant of any interference with temporal patterning.

6.4. A Comment upon the purpose of searching for invariants

It should not be assumed that the writer is denying the existence of information-bearing elements, or invariants, among our various sense data which lead to recognition. Rather the question is asked whether the evidence of our senses may not, in fact, frequently be microscopic and, further, that the information-bearing elements need not be unique, but differ with different people and on different occasions. For human recognition is a psycho-physiological problem, involving a *relationship* between a person and a physical stimulus; it is a phenomenon which can scarcely be explained solely in terms of properties of the object or pattern alone. For when a person perceives or recognizes an object, a spoken phrase, a face, or any pattern, he is making an inductive inference, and associating that perception with some general concept, class, or universal; and part of the clues upon which that individual operates may be private to him and depend upon his own past experiences.

It might be argued against me here that an artist, especially a caricaturist, has the peculiar skill of picking out those information-bearing elements which are recognized by all of us in common, for we recognize caricatures of, say, a well-known personality from the few lines drawn by the artist.* But in this case we are not recognizing the man himself, but rather drawings made in certain styles which we may see regularly in newspapers; and different artists use different styles, emphasizing different physical features. For instance, most people will recognize the personality in the drawings by Mr. Low (Fig. 7.7), even though they have never seen the man himself. The artist certainly has the skill to abstract *some* set of features which facilitate recognition by a wide public.

The face of someone you know well is, to you, an ensemble of past impressions; so with spoken words, or flowers, or the feel of a matchbox in the hand. And the brain, as a "machine," has a property possessed by no present man-made machine—a storage capacity of astronomical scale. That a person who knows a language possesses an immense storage of its statistics (represented by habits) has already been illustrated by different guessing tests; so too with all the sights and sounds and feels of our everyday experience, to which we habitually respond.

* See reference 194 for a discussion of caricature recognition.

Perhaps we may conjecture that we store representations of universals as sets of statistical populations; perhaps the bulk of our knowledge is of such a kind. Recognition then would not be a question of a standard key's fitting a lock, in our brains; it is a question of estimating the relative odds that received sense data are to be associated with one or another of a set of statistical populations. Our various concepts, universals, or hypotheses (however we like to refer to them) may perhaps be represented by such sets of populations; and the problem of recognition regarded as one of inferring to which set our received sense data should be associated, a problem of discriminating not between individuals but between populations.

The search for invariants amongst members of a universal is of particular interest in two fields, in psycho-physiology and in technology, and it seems to the writer that these are sometimes in danger of being confused. The search for real invariants, as attributes only of a pattern and abstracted from all specific people, is of great value in the technical field; operation based upon a set of comparatively simple invariants must necessarily be the principle of any machine designed to recognize drawings, or printed words—at least of practical machines, as they are understood at present. And such machines will be very prone to error. As machines are conceived at the present day, they cannot have the flexibility and resistance to distortion shown by our brains, compared to which their storage of experiences is like a drop in the ocean.

7. ON THE BRAIN AS A "MACHINE"

When we see a familiar face, or smell a rose, or hear a boy whistle a tune, what actions are carried out in the brain? What are the physiological correlates of mental experience? What representations of the world do we carry in our heads? What is the nature of this "machine"—or do we require more than the language and concepts of physics and chemistry to pin-point the unique properties of the brain? Is mind merely a by-product of living matter—only "a necessary result of the organization of the human machine"?*

Is the mind-brain relationship solely a question of words, of distinguishing between cognitive language and external language? Surely not; the distinction between the two languages may help to avoid false arguments, but it cannot solve the problem.[267]

The mind-body question arose as soon as man became a self-conscious creature and began his self-inquiry. It has been discussed for centuries,

* Julien de la Mettrie, 1740.

giving ground for free speculation among philosophers, physiologists, psychologists, and the laity; and it continues to do so. But although the problem remains with us, there are signs today that at least it is becoming better formulated.

Our position is like that of a puppy who sees himself in a mirror; after sniffing at his reflection he walks behind—and sees only strips of wood and tacks. So, being nonplused, he starts to tear the mirror apart in his search. We too tend to see one side or the other of our problem: the physiological and behavioral side on one hand and on the other the side of experience and sensations. Our difficulty is to see the problem and to see it whole, to see both the mirror and our reflection, and to understand their unity.

At a more physical level, another duality arouses controversy; this is the relationship between behavior and neurophysiology. The earlier behaviorists put themselves under a severe discipline which, in its more tolerant form today, sets out to create a pure stimulus-response psychology, having no need of cognitive language. On the other hand the physiologist examines the "mechanism" itself; the properties of sense organs, the physical and chemical bases of motor action, the neural pathways. Clerk Maxwell once drew analogy to the inaccessible and unobservable aspects of nature by imagining a complex mechanism, hidden in a room, to which strings were attached, leading through holes in the floor; we pull one rope and find that the others are set in motion, so without going into the room, what can be discovered about the nature of the mechanism?* The analogy might be applied to psychology today; the ropes are like stimuli and responses, the hidden mechanism like the quality we call "mind." Physiologists too are pulling ropes, but they cannot break into the room.

About 10 years ago the brain was commonly compared to a computing machine, especially to the new high-speed electronic machines—a comparison happily now passing out of fashion. For the brain is like nothing of the kind. This analogy has been prompted partly by the binary-impulse character of neural transmission and partly by the fact that certain central processes of the brain are concerned with discriminating, sorting, abstracting and correlating. But the brain bears little comparison with *existing* computing machines.[38c] Such machines spend their whole time making determinate and absolutely error-free calculations. They mostly work with low redundancy codes, whilst in contrast the organism depends upon the enormous redundancy of its sensory data, for communication and survival.[411] In fact, calculating machines have as their purpose, the execution of tasks not lightly undertaken by brains. That is why they are built!

* Sir James Jeans, *Electricity and Magnetism*, Cambridge University Press, Cambridge, 5th Ed., 1948, p. 486.

A more relevant analogy, perhaps no more than metaphor, might be to compare the brain to a gigantic totalizator, at a race track, which accepts the tokens (money) from the outside world (bettors), calculates the odds on various hypotheses (horses) to give the greatest expectation of goal attainment (profit) according to assumed standards of utility.

A more old-fashioned idea is comparison of the brain to a telephone exchange. "Messages" are received at the eyes, ears, skin, nose, tongue, and routed through to the various muscles, organs, and glands; basically this is a pure Cartesian model, for it suggests a little demon (Mind) in our heads who acts as a telephone operator, receiving incoming calls and routing them through. Nowadays we have automatic exchanges of course, and these too have been taken as models; certainly these may be regarded as *self*-routing, sorting, and organizing devices, but the analogy fails in other respects. Recently models of radically new types, employing feedback, and showing self-organizing action and "adaptive behavior," have been considered. In particular we may mention the early work of Ashby, who gave a simple mathematical account of the dynamical theory which might find application to the study of organisms and their "adaptive behavior," by which he meant maintenance of their essential variables within physiological limits, under environmental changes. He has described a practical model (his Homeostat), which is a feedback mechanism able to throw itself into a succession of random states, an action which continues until it reaches dynamical stability, within some threshold. The behavior of this mechanism is compared to that of the simpler organisms, being a process which is *selective* toward different conditions of stability or instability; it is able continually to steer itself away from critical, unstable states—and so maintain "ultra-stability."

If such analogies do nothing more, they serve the purpose of pin-pointing the seat of the main problem. It is not so much the receptors and the afferent nervous system (with their function of coding the received data, filtering and sorting) or the efferent system which present the greatest mystery, but rather it is the central processes of transmission between them. Perhaps a few illustrations of the brain's remarkable features as a "machine" may show the limitations of any naive telephone-exchange theory.

There is, first, the remarkable fact that large portions of the cortex may be cut away (except the speech areas), often with little or no effect upon memory, personality, or intelligence.[C, E] But in telephone exchanges each wire has a unique function, and destruction of any part has a permanent and serious result. To take another simile, if we imagine a great library containing books which have a vast number of cross references one to another, then should one whole shelf be burned, it might be possible to reconstruct the lost books—but somewhat less perfectly than at first. There would be great structural redundancy; and the brain appears to possess such safety factors to an immense degree.   There is secondly a property of the nervous system which has been called *plasticity*.   When we learn to perform some task, we appear to learn the means of approaching the end result, or of seeking the goal, but without being restricted to a unique set of muscles;[E] Bates, for example, remarks that having learned to write your name with the right hand, you can make a good shot at writing it with your nose!*

A simple object held in the hand, such as a matchbox, is recognized by its feel most readily, not by holding it in a predetermined, standard position, but by passing the fingers over it, moving it about.   Further than this, the nerve endings branch out near the skin to cover a small area.   How then can the matchbox "message" be set up in any unique manner?   Again, in recognizing an object visually, we may make a series of rapid saccadic movements; and only the central cones have one-to-one connections with the brain, whilst over the main area of the retina the rods are bunched together in hundreds for connection to single nerve fibers.   There is similar dynamic action, and neural "diffusiveness," with the tongue and nose. What kind of "telephone exchange" is this, in which wires do not connect the same subscribers from one instant to another?†

Two particular trends away from the simple switchboard analogy should be mentioned.   More recent studies of neural structure show the importance of *time* coincidence of neural impulses; a single impulse cannot normally cross a synapse—two or more must arrive simultaneously from different fibres—so that the whole activity depends not only upon a spacial pattern of connections, but upon a temporal distribution too.[C,]‡   Another significant movement today is away from the notion of fixed point-to-point switchboard-type connections, to regarding the central processes of the brain as processes of self-organization from initially random states; toward analysis of permutation and combination of immense populations of neural elements and study of interaction between populations, regarding them as nets.[29,337,338]   Such work is receiving considerable impetus from communication theory and has to some extent had common origin, namely Boolean algebra and application of this calculus to nets of bi-stable elements (relays, neurons).[178]   Pitts and McCulloch, in particular, have studied the properties of such networks.[228,264]   This modern trend may eventually reconcile the switchboard theories and the field theories.

---

* J. A. V. Bates in reference 167.

† It is the Gestalt psychologists who stress in particular the fact that the same set of cells need not be excited to set up some specific perception (e.g., Lashby, Köhler), but rather that the *pattern* of excitation should have a major degree of invariance.   See reference C for additional sources.

‡ See McCulloch in reference 178.

As we survey the various stages of evolution, from the simplest one-cell creatures up to man, we see a steady improvement in the methods of learning and adaptation to a hostile world. Each step in learning ability gives better adaptation and greater chance of survival. We are carried a long way up the scale by innate reflexes and rudimentary muscular learning faculties. Habits indeed, not rational thought, assist us to surmount most of life's obstacles.

Most, but by no means all; for learning in the high mammals exhibits the unexplained phenomenon of "insight," which shows itself by sudden changes in behavior in learning situations—in sudden departures from one method of organizing a task, or solving a problem, to another.[c] Insight, expectancy, set, are the essentially "mind-like" attributes of communication, and it is these, together with the representation of concepts, which require physiological explanation.

At the higher end of the scale of evolution this quality we call "mind" appears more and more prominently, but it is at our own level that learning of a radically new type has developed—through our powers of organizing thoughts, comparing and setting them into relationship, especially with the use of language. We have a remarkable faculty of forming generalizations, of recognizing universals, of associating and developing them. It is our multitude of general concepts, and our powers of organizing them with the aid of language in varied ways, which forms the backbone of human communication, and which distinguishes us from the animals.

BIBLIOGRAPHY

A. Ryle, G., *The Concept of Mind*, Hutchinson's University Library, London, 1949.
B. Gallie, W. B., *Peirce and Pragmatism*, Pelican Books, Ltd., Harmondsworth, England, 1952. A condensed and most readable account of Peirce's scattered works.
C. Hebb, D. O., *The Organization of Behavior*, John Wiley & Sons, Inc., New York, 1949.
D. Stevens, S. S., Editor, *Handbook of Experimental Psychology*, John Wiley & Sons, Inc., New York, 1951.
E. Adrian, E. D., *The Physical Background of Perception*, The Waynflete Lectures, Clarendon Press, Oxford, 1946.

Appendix[*]

Definitions and Explications of some of the terms used in this book. Where different *schools of thought* or *shades of opinion* are of serious consequence, this is indicated.

ALPHABET. A set of distinct SIGN-TYPES from which MESSAGES may be generated by selection.

ATTRIBUTE. Any property of a phenomenon, thing, event . . . assumed, by the observer to be of significance.

ATTRIBUTE SPACE. The (mathematical) hyperspace, the co-ordinates of which represent the ATTRIBUTES of some phenomenon. Also called SYSTEM SPACE, PHASE SPACE, in certain cases.

BANDWIDTH (of signals). The maximum (sinusoidal, Fourier component) frequency which the SIGNALS are considered to contain. (A term in telecommunication; measured in cycles per second.)

BINARY DIGIT (see BIT). Broadly: one digit of a scale-of-two notation.

BIT (abbreviation of BINARY DIGIT). The unit measurement of quantities of SELECTIVE INFORMATION as used in communication theory.

BINARY CODE. A code which employs two distinguishable signs only (BINARY DIGITS).

CAPACITY (of an INFORMATION store). The maximum number of independent BINARY DIGITS which may be stored unambiguously. See LIMITING CAPACITY.

CODE. An agreed TRANSFORMATION, or set of unambiguous rules, whereby MESSAGES are converted from one representation to another.

COMMUNICATION. Broadly: The establishment of a social unit from individuals, by the use of language or signs. The sharing of common sets of rules, for various goal-seeking activities. (There are many *shades of opinion*.)

COMMUTATION (in linguistic analysis). The substitution of one SEGMENT for another, in a context.

CONTEXT (of a word or other linguistic SEGMENT). The linguistic environment. (Broadly: the words or other segments which precede or follow a particular word or segment and which bear upon the meaning.)

[*] Attention is called to a very full glossary of terms used in information theory, by D. M. MacKay under reference 167.

DENOTATION. The imputed non-causal relationship between a SIGN and its REFERENT, especially when the latter is a physical thing, event, or property (a "denotatum").

DESCRIPTIVE SYNTAX. The SYNTAX of historical, ordinary, languages. In contrast to *Pure Syntax.*

DESIGNATUM (of a sign). "That which is referred to." Any ATTRIBUTE of the outside (non-linguistic) world with which a SIGN-EVENT is associated in thought. (There are many *shades of opinion.*)

DISJUNCTION (in logic). An alternative (thus "*a* or *b*" is a disjunction of *a*, *b*).

DISTINCTIVE FEATURES (in linguistic analysis). A minimal set of binary ATTRIBUTES (oppositions) by superposition of which PHONEMES may be represented. The attributes may be defined by spectral or articulatory criteria (after Jakobson).

ENCODE. To transform a message from one representation into another, by operation of CODE rules.

ENSEMBLE. A collection (e.g., of possible signs, signals, messages, from a specified SOURCE, with a set of estimated probabilities of occurrence).

ENTROPY (in statistical thermodynamics). The expected log probability of the states of a thermodynamic SYSTEM. The term is used, by analogy, in communication theory, to refer to the INFORMATION RATE of a SOURCE of MESSAGES, though we deprecate its unqualified usage, in this book.

ENVIRONMENT. The totality of conditions which affect the behavior of an organism. (There are several usages of this term; e.g., (1) only the immediate physical surroundings, (2) all conditions including past experiences, anticipations, etc.) In this book the word *environment* is qualified whenever used.

EPOCH. An instant in time.

EQUIVOCATION (of a NOISY communication channel). As used in communication theory: the rate of loss of SELECTIVE INFORMATION at the receiver's end of a channel, due to the NOISE (measured in BITS per second or per sign as stated). Broadly, the receiver's average doubt about the transmitted signals.

ERGODIC (SOURCE, sequence, etc.). A statistically STATIONARY SOURCE, sequence, etc. which has statistical influences extending over finite sequences only.

GAUSSIAN (probability distribution). A very common probability distribution in physical random processes. It is defined in equation 5.16. Sometimes called *normal density function.*

ICON (—SIGN). A sign which is considered to bear some analogy or resemblance to the form of its DESIGNATUM (e.g., a picture).

INDIVIDUAL (as used in logic). Any single element, item, or unit falling within a specific "universe of discourse."

INDUCTIVE PROBABILITY (of a hypothesis). A logical relationship between a hypothesis and some evidence (after Carnap).

INFORMATION (see SELECTIVE INFORMATION).

LANGUAGE SYSTEM. A set of SIGNS and rules representing, in the META-LANGUAGE, a description of an OBJECT-LANGUAGE (we again distinguish *pure* and *descriptive* systems, as for SYNTAX).

LIKELIHOOD (of one *specific* event). An "inverse probability," as opposed to a direct (frequency) probability in an ensemble of past events. (Broadly: the chances of predicting the occurrence of some specific event correctly, as inferred from past frequency of that occurrence by inductive inference.) See INDUCTIVE PROBABILITY.

LIMITING CAPACITY (of a communication channel). The upper limiting rate at which (selective) INFORMATION may be communicated by a specific channel, with any arbitrarily small frequency of errors. It may depend upon SIGNAL power, NOISE power, and other physical properties of the channel.

LOGICAL CONNECTIVES (in symbolic logic). For example, the signs of *negation* $\sim$ (not), of *conjunction* & (and), of *equivalence* $\equiv$ (if and only if), of *disjunction* $\vee$ (or), etc.

LOGICAL PROBABILITY (in logic). A measure-function distributed uniformly over STRUCTURE-DESCRIPTIONS (after Carnap).

LOGICAL SYNTAX. The purely *formal* parts of SYNTAX (after Carnap).

LOGON. The shortest distinguishable SIGNAL element which may be received through a specified channel (after Gabor). A dimension or degree of freedom of signal space.

MACROSCOPIC ASPECTS (of a SYSTEM or ENSEMBLE). Statistical aspects, not concerning specific individuals, elements, members. Concerning "how many" rather than "which" (in contrast to MICROSCOPIC ASPECTS).

MARKOFF (MARKOV) PROCESS. Originally any process generating a stochastic series, the *adjacent* terms of which are related by given transition probabilities. Now extended to include stochastic series, having statistical influence extending over *any* finite-length sequences.

MEANING. This word is ambiguous; it is used for: (1) Translation ("What does the Latin *amo* mean?") (2) Near-synonyms, as in dictionaries ("Hit" means "strike.") (3) Significance ("What does £ mean?") (4) Value ("Life has little meaning for me now.")

In its interpretive usage, the meaning of an utterance, to some specific person (perceiver) in some specific context and environment is the total change of state of that person (overt and mental) on receipt of that utterance. It is thus a relationship.

The meanings to the utterer and to the perceiver, in general, are different; that to the utterer is the *intended* change of state of the perceiver. The mental change is important, because this conditions the meaning of the subsequent utterance; all utterances are in contexts which, in principle, may continue indefinitely.[258,129] (There are various schools of thought; the above definition aims to be pragmatic.)

MESSAGE. An ordered selection from an agreed set of SIGNS (ALPHABET) intended to communicate information.

META-LANGUAGE (observer's language). The language used by an observer for describing an observed OBJECT-LANGUAGE. Language used for expressing rules, laws, relationships.

MICROSCOPIC ASPECTS (of a SYSTEM or ENSEMBLE). Detailed aspects, concerning specific individuals, elements, members. Concerning "which," not merely "how many" (in contrast to MACROSCOPIC ASPECTS).

NOISE (in telecommunication). Disturbances which do not represent any part of the MESSAGES from a specified SOURCE.

OBJECT-LANGUAGE. A language under observation and study (not to be confused with META-LANGUAGE). The language of communication events.

OBSERVER. (We distinguish between EXTERNAL OBSERVER and PARTICIPANT OBSERVER.) The former is quite detached from the communication event he is observing; his reportings are entirely objective. The latter reports upon communication events, in which he is one partner; he may use cognitive terms. Both observers report in a META-LANGUAGE.

PHASE SPACE. A hyperspace, in which the STATES of a SYSTEM may be represented, the axes of which represent a specific set of independent ATTRIBUTES (variables). Originally used in statistical mechanics.

PHONEMES. There are several *schools of thought*. We distinguish here: (1) a minimal set of shortest SEGMENTS of a language which, if substituted one for another, convert one word (or "meaningful segment") to another; (2) sets of DISTINCTIVE FEATURES (after Jakobson); (3) the quantal cells of a language ATTRIBUTE SPACE, the axes of which represent distinctive features. Phonemes are essentially abstracted, linguistic elements, not physical utterances.

PRAGMATICS. That branch of SEMIOTIC (or of linguistics) which specifically concerns the *user* of signs.

PURE SYNTAX. The SYNTAX of a SYNTACTICAL SYSTEM or calculus.

QUANTUM, QUANTUM CELL. An interval on a scale of measurement, fractions of which are considered to be of no significance.

REDUNDANCY (of a SOURCE). Unity minus the ratio of the INFORMATION RATE of the source to its hypothetical maximum rate, when encoded with the same set of signs. Broadly, a property given to a source by virtue of an excess of rules (syntax) whereby it becomes increasingly likely that mistakes in reception will be avoided.

REFERENT. That which a SIGN "refers to," or "stands for," or denotes, more especially when this is a physical or imagined thing, event, quality, et cetera. The term DESIGNATUM is used more generally.

SAMPLING (of wave forms). Specification of wave forms by values of their amplitudes at agreed successive instants of time (usually equally spaced at intervals of $1/2F$ seconds, where F is the BANDWIDTH).

SEGMENT (of text or utterance). Any continuous part of a text or utterance. See QUANTUM.

SELECTIVE-INFORMATION CONTENT (in communication theory). The least number of BINARY DIGITS (*yes*, *no*) required to ENCODE some particular message (or alternatively to specify its selection from an alphabet). See ENTROPY for definition of *average* rates.

SELECTIVE-INFORMATION RATE, of a SOURCE (in communication theory). The minimum average number of BINARY DIGITS required to encode (represent, specify) the source MESSAGES—per second, or per sign, as stated. This refers to SELECTIVE INFORMATION as opposed to SEMANTIC INFORMATION.

SEMANTICS. There are different *schools of thought*. We refer to (1) the branch of SEMIOTIC (sign theory, linguistics) concerned with "meaning" of signs. (2) study of the non-causal, imputed relations (rules) between SIGNS and their DESIGNATA. We distinguish DESCRIPTIVE SEMANTICS (study of semantic features of historical languages) and PURE SEMANTICS (analysis of semantic rules of freely invented or set-up systems). After Carnap.

SEMIOTIC. The theory of signs (i.e., of linguistics, logic, mathematics, rhetoric, etc.) Subdivided into SYNTACTICS, SEMANTICS, PRAGMATICS (after Charles Peirce and C. W. Morris).

SET (in psychology). Mental expectancy corresponding to preformed hypotheses concerning a future event. (There are different *shades of opinion*.)

SIGN (we distinguish SIGN-TYPES and SIGN-TOKENS). A transmission, or construct, by which one organism affects the behavior or state of another, in a communication situation.

SIGNAL. The physical embodiment of a message (an utterance, a transmission, an exhibition of SIGN-EVENTS). A sign-event or a sequence of sign-events.

SIGN-EVENT. (See SIGN-TOKEN).

SIGNIFICS. Inquiry into questions of meaning, expression, interpretation, and of the influence of language upon thought.

SIGN-TOKEN. A physical sign-event; a written, spoken, gestured sign. The physical embodiment of a selected SIGN-TYPE on some one specific occasion. Also called *sinsign, sign-event*.

SIGN-TYPE. (A universal; not a physical event.) A sign as it is listed in an ALPHABET, dictionary, et cetera. Also called *legisign, sign-design*.

SOCIETY. People in communication.

SOURCE (of MESSAGE-SIGNALS). That part of a communication channel where MESSAGES are assumed to originate (where selective action is exerted upon an ensemble of SIGNS).

STATE (of a SYSTEM). Some specific set of values of all the ATTRIBUTE variables of a SYSTEM. (Broadly: a specific configuration of a system capable of many configurations.)

STATE-DESCRIPTION (in logic). A statement which connects every individual to a specific predicate or its negation.

STATIONARY SOURCE. A source of MESSAGES (or signals) the statistical properties of which are invariant under a shift of the time origin.

STOCHASTIC PROCESS. Any process which may be described in terms of probabilities.

STRUCTURE-DESCRIPTION (in logic). The disjunction of all possible, mutually exclusive, STATE-DESCRIPTIONS.

SYMBOL. "(Sign) regarded by general consent as naturally typifying or representing or recalling something by possession of analogous qualities or by association in fact or thought" (*Oxford English Dictionary*). We avoid the term *symbol* as far as possible in this book and use the more general term, SIGN.

SYNTACTICS (a branch of SEMIOTIC). The study of SYNTAX; of the SIGNS and rules relating signs.

SYNTACTICAL SYSTEM (in logic). A calculus, consisting of rules of formation and rules of deduction (transformation), formulated or freely invented (after Carnap).

SYNTAX. The formal aspect of a language. (We distinguish DESCRIPTIVE SYNTAX and PURE SYNTAX.)

SYSTEM. A whole which is compounded of many parts. An ensemble of ATTRIBUTES. (Broadly: any phenomenon describable in terms of a large number of variables.)

SYSTEM POINT. The point in ATTRIBUTE SPACE which defines the values of the attribute variables of a SYSTEM in some specific STATE.

TOKEN. (See WORD-TOKEN and SIGN-TOKEN).

TRANSITION PROBABILITY (of a term in a series). The probability of a term following (or preceding, as stated) a prescribed term of set of terms.

UNIVERSAL. "General notion, or idea, a thing that by its nature may be predicated of many" (*Oxford English Dictionary*). An inferred general property or class—in contrast to a *particular* thing, event, et cetera.

WORD-TOKEN. A physical utterance; the physical embodiment of a WORD-TYPE. See SIGN-TOKEN.

WORD-TYPE. (A universal, a linguistic concept.) A word of the language. A word as listed in a dictionary.

References

1. Adrian, E. D., *The Physical Background of Perception*, The Waynflete Lectures, Clarendon Press, Oxford, 1946.
2. Adrian, E. D., *Sensory Integration*, The Sherrington Lectures, I, University Press of Liverpool, England, 1949.
3. Allen, W. S., *Phonetics in Ancient India*, Oxford University Press, London, 1953.
4. Allport, G. W., and L. Postman, *The Psychology of Rumor*, Henry Holt & Co., Inc., New York, 1947.
5. Ashby, W. Ross, *Design for a Brain*, John Wiley & Sons, Inc., New York (Chapman & Hall, Ltd., London), 1952.
6. Ayer, A. J., *Language, Truth and Logic*, Victor Gollancz, Ltd., London, 1936.
7. Babbage, H. P., *Babbage's Calculating Engines*, Spon, Ltd., London, 1889.
8. Bar-Hillel, Y., "Can Translation be Mechanized?" *Am. Scientist*, *42*, April 1954, pp. 248–260.
9. Bar-Hillel, Y., "An Examination of Information Theory," *Philosophy of Science*, *22*, No. 2, April 1955, pp. 86–105.
10. Bar-Hillel, Y., "Linguistic Problems Connected with Machine Translation," *Brit. J. Phil. Sci.*, *20*, No. 3, July 1953, pp. 217–225.
11. Bar-Hillel, Y., "Logical Syntax and Semantics," *Language*, *30*, No. 2, April–June 1954, pp. 230–237.
12. Bar-Hillel, Y., "The Present State of Research on Mechanical Translation," *Am. Doc.*, *II*, No. 4, 1952.
13. Bar-Hillel, Y., and R. Carnap, "Semantic Information," paper appearing in *Proceedings of a Symposium on Applications of Communication Theory*, Butterworth Scientific Publications, London, 1953; also published in *Brit. J. Phil. Sci.*, *4*, Aug. 1953, pp. 147–157.
14. Barnard, G. A., "The Theory of Information," *J. Roy. Statist. Soc.* (Series B), *XIII*, No. 1, 1951.
15. Bartlett, Sir F. C., *Remembering: a Study in Experimental and Social Psychology*, Cambridge University Press, London, 1932.
16. Baudouin, R., *Elements de Cryptographie*, Editions Pedone, Paris, 1946.
17. Bavelas, A., "Communication Patterns in Task Oriented Groups," *J. Acoust. Soc. Am.*, *22*, Nov. 1950, pp. 725–730.
18. Bavelas, A., "A Mathematical Model for Group Structures," *Appl. Anthrop.*, Summer 1948.
19. Baxendall, D., *Calculating Machines and Instruments*, Catalogue of the Collections

in the Science Museum, London, Her Majesty's Stationery Office, 1926. An historical account.

20. Bayes, T., "An Essay Towards Solving a Problem in the Doctrine of Chances," *Phil. Trans. Roy. Soc., I*, iii, 1763, p. 370.

21. Bell, A. G., *Mechanisms of Speech*, Funk & Wagnalls, Ltd., New York and London, 1914. Includes essay on "Vowel Theories."

22. Bell, A. M., *English Visible Speech for the Million*, N. Truebner & Co., London and New York, 1867.

23. Bell, A. M., *Visible Speech; the Science of Universal Alphabetics*, Simpkin, Marshall & Co., London, 1867.

24. Bell, D. A., *Information Theory, and its Engineering Applications*, Sir Isaac Pitman & Sons, London, 1953.

25. Berkeley, E. C., *Giant Brains, or Machines That Think*, John Wiley & Sons, Inc., New York, 1949.

26. Berkeley Symposium, "On Statistical Methods in Communication Engineering," *Trans. I.R.E. Prof. Group on Information Theory*, March 1954.

27. Berry, J., Studies carried out at the Post Office Research Station, as yet unpublished except in the form of an internal report (British Post Office, Dollis Hill, London N.W.2). See also Berry under *Jackson*, Symposium 1952.

28. von Bertalanffy, L., "An Outline of General System Theory," *Brit. J. Phil. Sci., I*, Aug. 1950 (Thomas Nelson & Sons, Edinburgh).

29. Beurle, R. L., (a) "Activity in a Block of Cells Capable of Regenerating Pulses"; (b) "Properties of a Block of Cells Capable of Regenerating Pulses"; *Radar Research Establishment Memoranda, 1042* and *1043*, 1954 (Great Malvern, England).

30. Bloch, B., and G. L. Trager, *Outline of Linguistic Analysis*, Linguistic Society of America, Waverley Press, Baltimore, 1942.

31. Bloomfield, L., *Language*, Henry Holt & Co., Inc., New York, 1933.

32. Bodmer, F., *The Loom of Language*, W. W. Norton & Co., Inc., New York (George Allen & Unwin, Ltd., London), 1944.

33. Bowden, B. V., Editor, *Faster than Thought; a Symposium on Digital Computing Machines*, Sir Isaac Pitman & Sons, London, 1953.

34. Brandt, H. F., *The Psychology of Seeing*, The Philosophical Library, New York, 1945.

35. Brillouin, L., (a) "Information and Entropy I," *J. Appl. Phys., 22*, No. 3, 1951, p. 334; (b) "Physical Entropy and Information II," *J. Appl. Phys., 22*, No. 3, 1951, p. 338.

36. Brillouin, L., "Life, Thermodynamics and Cybernetics," *Am. Scientist, 37*, 1949, p. 554.

37. Brillouin, L., "Thermodynamics and Information Theory," *Am. Scientist, 38*, 1950, p. 549.

38. British Association, "Symposium on Cybernetics," three papers: (a) E. C. Cherry, "Organisms and Mechanisms"; (b) W. E. Hick, "The Impact of Information Theory on Psychology"; (c) D. M. MacKay, "On Comparing the Brain with Machines"; *Advancement of Sci., 40*, March 1954.

39. British Post Office, (a) J. Swaffield and R. H. de Wardt, "A Reference Telephone System for Articulation Tests," *Post Office Elec. Engrs. J., 43*, April 1950; (b) R. H. de Wardt, "The Conduct of Articulation Measurements," *Post Office Elec. Engrs. J., 44*, Jan. 1952.

40. de Broglie, L., "La Cybernétique," report of Conference in Paris, 1951, published by *Rev. opt.* (165 rue de Sèvres, Paris).

41. Third Symposium on Information Networks, Proceedings of the Polytechnic Institute of Brooklyn, New York, 1955.

42. Bürck, W., P. Kotowski, and H. Lichte, (a) "Development of Pitch Sensations," *Elek. Nachr-Tech.*, *12*, 1935, p. 326; (b) "Audibility of Delays," *Elek. Nachr-Tech.*, *12*, 1935, p. 355.

43. Buswell, G. T., "Fundamental Reading Habits; a Study of Their Development," *Suppl. Educ. Monographs*, *21*, 1922.

44. Cambridge University, *Report of a Conference on High Speed Automatic Calculating Machines*, University Mathematical Laboratory, Ministry of Supply, 1950. This report has an extensive bibliography.

45. Carey, G. V., *American into English*, Wm. Heinemann, Ltd., London, 1953. A comparison of these languages; contains an American-English glossary.

46. Carmichael, L., and W. F. Dearborn, *Reading and Visual Fatigue*, George G. Harrap & Co., Ltd., London, 1948.

47. Carnap, R., "Foundations of Logic and Mathematics," *International Encyclopaedia of United Science Series*, Vol. I, No. 3, University of Chicago Press, Chicago, 1939. Quite "popular" reading.

48. Carnap, R., *Introduction to Semantics*, Harvard University Press, Cambridge, Mass., 1946.

49. Carnap, R., *Logical Foundations of Probability*, University of Chicago Press, Chicago, 1950.

50. Carnap, R., *The Logical Syntax of Language*, Kegan Paul, Trench, Trubner & Co., Ltd., London, 1937.

51. Carnap, R., *Meaning and Necessity*, University of Chicago Press, Chicago, 1947. A study in semantics and modal logic.

52. Carnap, R., "What Is Probability?" *Sci. American*, *189*, Sept. 1953, pp. 128–136. An elementary introduction to his theory of inductive probability.

53. Carnap, R., and Y. Bar-Hillel, "An Outline of a Theory of Semantic Information," *M.I.T., Research Lab. Electronics, Tech. Rept.*, *247*, 1953.

54. Carrington, J. F., *The Drum Language of the Lokele Tribe*, African Studies, Witwatersrand University Press, Witwatersrand, 1944.

55. Carrington, J. F., *The Talking Drums of Africa*, Carey Kingsgate Press, 6 Southampton Row, London, 1949.

56. Carson, J. R., "Notes on the Theory of Modulation," *Proc. I.R.E.*, *10*, 1922, p. 57.

57. Ceccato, S., "Contra Dingler, Pro Dingler," *Methodos*, *IV*, 15–16, 1952, pp. 266–290 (Milan). In English also.

58. Chang, S. H., G. E. Pihl, and J. Wiren, "The Intervalgram as a Visual Representation of Speech Sounds," *J. Acoust. Soc. Am.*, *23*, No. 6 Nov. 1951, pp. 675–679.

59. Cherry, E. C., "The Communication of Information (an Historical Review)," *Am. Scientist*, *40*, No. 4, Oct. 1952, pp. 640–663. First published in *Proceedings of a Symposium on Information Theory*, under auspices of the Royal Society, 1950; see under Jackson.

60. Cherry, E. C., "'Communication Theory'—and Human Behaviour," an essay appearing in a book published by Martin Secker & Warburg, Ltd., London, 1955; see under University College.

61. Cherry, E. C., "On the Recognition of Speech with One, and with Two Ears," *J. Acoust. Soc. Am.*, *25*, No. 5, Sept. 1953, p. 975.

62. Cherry, E. C., M. Halle, and R. Jakobson, "Toward a Logical Description of Languages in Their Phonemic Aspects," *Language*, *29*, No. 1, Jan.–March 1953, pp. 34–46.

63. Cherry, E. C., and W. K. Taylor, "Some Further Experiments upon the Recog-

nition of Speech with One, and with Two Ears," *J. Acoust. Soc. Am.*, *26*, No. 4, July 1954, pp. 554–559.

64. Chiba, T., and M. Kajiyama, *The Vowel—Its Nature and Structure*, Tokyo-Kaiseikan Publishing Co., Ltd., Tokyo, 1941.

65. Christie, L. S., R. D. Luce, and J. Macy, "Communication and Learning in Task-Oriented Groups," *M.I.T.*, *Research Lab. Electronics, Tech. Rept.*, *231*, May 1952.

66. Cohen, M. R., *A Preface to Logic*, George Routledge & Sons, Ltd., London, 1946.

67. Cooke, D., Z. Jelonek, A. J. Oxford, and E. Fitch, "Pulse Communication," *J. Inst. Elec. Engrs. (London)*, *94*, Part IIIA, 1947, p. 83.

68. Cooper, F. S., P. C. Delattre, A. M. Liberman, J. M. Borst, and L. J. Gerstman, "Some Experiments on the Perception of Synthetic Speech Sounds," *J. Acoust. Soc. Am.*, *24*, Nov. 1952, pp. 597–606.

69. Cooper, F. S., A. M. Liberman, and J. M. Borst, "Interconversion of Audible and Visible Patterns as a Basis for Research in the Perception of Speech," *Proc. Nat. Acad. Sci.*, *37*, May 1951, p. 318.

70. Crandall, I. R., "The Sounds of Speech," *Bell System Tech. J.*, *4*, 1925, p. 586.

71. Cranston, M., "Freedom: A New Analysis," Longmans, Green & Co., London, 1953. Applies the techniques of linguistic analysis to some words in our political vocabulary.

72. Crossman, E. R. F. W., "Entropy and Choice Time: the Effect of Frequency Unbalance on Choice Response," *Quart. J. Exp. Psychol.*, *V*, Part 2, June 1953.

73. D'Agapayeff, A., *Codes and Ciphers*, Oxford University Press, London, 1939. Historical reference.

74. Dale, E., *Bibliography of Vocabulary Studies*, Bureau of Educational Research, Ohio State University, Columbus, 1949.

75. Dalgarno, G., *Didascalocophus or the Deaf and Dumb Man's Tutor—a discourse of the nature and number of double consonants*, British Museum Shelf Mark 1041. C. 25, 1680.

76. Dampier, Sir W. Cecil, *A History of Science*, Cambridge University Press, London, 1st Ed., 1929, 4th Ed., 1948.

77. Davenport, W. B., "Probability Distributions of Spoken Sounds," *J. Acoust. Soc. Am.*, *24*, 1952, pp. 390–399. Long-term statistics.

78. Davies, I. L., "On Determining the Presence of Signals in Noise," *Proc. Inst. Elec. Eng. (London)*, *99*, Part III, March 1952, p. 45.

79. Davis, R. C., "On the Theory of Prediction of Non-Stationary Stochastic Processes," *J. Appl. Phys.*, *23*, Sept. 1952, pp. 1047–1053.

80. Dearborn, W. F., "The Psychology of Reading," *Arch. of Phil., Psychol. and Sci. Method (New York)*, 1906 (British Museum Shelf Mark pp. 1247 ga.).

81. Delattre, P., "The Physiological Interpretation of Sound Spectrograms," *Publ. Modern Lang. Assoc. Am.*, *LXVI*, No. 5, Sept. 1951, p. 864.

82. Deloraine, E. M., "Pulse Modulation," *Proc. Inst. Rad. Engrs.*, *37*, 1949, p. 702.

83. Descartes, René, *A Discourse on Method (and other Philosophic Essays)*, 1637. Mainly of historical interest.

84. Deutsch, K., "On Communication Models in the Social Sciences," *Public Opinion Quart.*, *16*, 1952, pp. 356–380.

85. Dewey, G., *Relative Frequencies of English Speech Sounds*, Harvard University Press, Cambridge, Mass., 1923. Frequencies of words.

86. Diringer, D., *The Alphabet*, Hutchinson & Co., Ltd., London, 1948.

87. Dreyfus-Graf, J., "Sonograph and Sound Mechanics," *J. Acoust. Soc. Am.*, *22*, Nov. 1950, p. 731 (Speech Conference Report).

88. Dudley, H., "The Carrier Nature of Speech," *Bell System Tech. J.*, *19*, Oct. 1940, p. 495.

89. Dudley, H., "Remaking Speech," *J. Acoust. Soc. Am.*, *2*, 1939, p. 165.

90. Dudley, H., R. R. Riesz, and S. S. A. Watkins, "A Synthetic Speaker," *J. Franklin Inst.*, *227*, 1939, p. 739.

91. Dudley, H., and T. Tarnoczy, "The Speaking Machine of Wolfgang von Kempelen," *J. Acoust. Soc. Am.*, *22*, 1950, p. 151.

92. Dunn, H. K., "The Calculation of Vowel Resonances and an Electrical Vocal Tract," *J. Acoust. Soc. Am.*, *22*, Nov. 1950, p. 740 (with erratum, March 1951, p. 234).

93. Dunn, H. K., and S. D. White, "Statistical Measurements on Conversational Speech," *J. Acoust. Soc. Am.*, *11*, 1940, p. 278.

94. Egan, J. P., "Articulation Testing Methods," *Laryngoscope*, *58*, Sept. 1948, p. 955.

95. Einstein, A., *A Theory of Brownian Movement*, Methuen & Co., Ltd., London, 1926.

96. Eldridge, R. C., *Six Thousand Common English Words*, The Clement Press, Buffalo, New York, 1911.

97. *Encyclopædia Britannica*, 14th Ed., 1929.

98. Fairthorne, R. A., "Automata and Information," *J. of Doc. (London)*, *8*, No. 3, p. 164.

99. Fairthorne, R. A., "Information Theory and Clerical Systems," *J. of Doc. (London)*, *9*, No. 2, June 1953, pp. 101–116.

100. Fano, R. M., "Short Term Autocorrelation Functions and Their Power Spectra," *J. Acoust. Soc. Am.*, *22*, 1950, p. 546.

101. Fano, R. M., "The Transmission of Information," *M.I.T.*, *Research Lab. Electronics, Tech. Rept.*, *65*, 1949.   See also reference 381.

102. Fant, C. G. M., "Transmission Properties of the Vocal Tract," *M.I.T.*, *Acoust. Lab. Rept.*, *12*, 1952.

103. Farnsworth, D. W., "High Speed Motion Pictures of the Human Vocal Chords," *Bell Labs. Record*, *18*, 1940, p. 203.

104. Feller, W., *An Introduction to Probability Theory and Its Applications*, Vol. I, John Wiley & Sons, Inc., New York, 1950.

105. Fisher, Sir Ronald, *The Design of Experiments*, Oliver & Boyd, Ltd., London, 1935,

106. Fisher, Sir Ronald, *Statistical Methods for Research Workers*, Oliver & Boyd, Ltd., London, 1925.

107. Flanagan, J. L., "Effect of Delay Distortion upon the Intelligibility of Speech," *J. Acoust. Soc. Am.*, *23*, 1951, p. 303.

108. Fletcher, H., *Speech and Hearing*, D. van Nostrand Co., Inc., New York, 1929 (later edition 1953; earlier version preferred).

109. Fletcher, H., and R. H. Galt, "The Perception of Speech and its Relation to Telephony," *J. Acoust. Soc. Am.*, *22*, March 1950, p. 89.   Contains bibliography of articulation testing methods.

110. Fletcher, H., and J. C. Steinberg, "Articulation Testing Methods," *Bell System Tech. J.*, *8*, Oct. 1929, pp. 806–854.

111. Forsyth, E., and L. Katz, "A Matrix Approach to the Analysis of Sociometric Data," *Sociometry*, *9*, 1946, p. 340.

112. Fourcin, A. J., London University Ph.D. Thesis, "An Investigation into the Possibility of Bandwidth Reduction in Speech."   Studies of "clipped speech," statistical properties, et cetera.

113. Fowler, H. W., and F. G. Fowler, *The King's English*, Clarendon Press, Oxford, 3rd Ed., 1931.

114. French, N. R., C. W. Carter, and W. Koenig, "The Words and Sounds of Telephone Conversations," *Bell System Tech. J.*, *9*, 1930, pp. 290–324.

115. French, N. R., and J. C. Steinberg, "Principles of the Articulatory Index," *J. Acoust. Soc. Am.*, *19*, 1947, p. 90.

116. Frick, C. F., and G. A. Miller, "A Statistical Description of Operant Conditioning," *Am. J. Psychol.*, *LXIV*, Jan. 1951, pp. 20–36.

117. Fries, C., *The Structure of English*, University of Michigan Press, Ann Arbor, 1952. Significance of function words and class words.

118. Frisch, Karl von, *Bees: Their Vision, Chemical Senses and Language*, Cornell University Press, Ithaca, 1950.

119. Fucks, W., "On Mathematical Analysis of Style," *Biometrika*, *39*, 1952, p. 122.

120. Fürth, R., "Physics of Social Equilibrium," *Advancement of Sci. (London)*, *8*, March 1952, pp. 429–434.

121. Gabor, D., "Acoustical Quanta and the Theory of Hearing," *Nature*, *159*, 1947, pp. 591–594.

122. Gabor, D., "Communication Theory and Cybernetics," Milan Symposium paper published in *Trans. I.R.E. Prof. Group on Non-Linear Circuits*, Dec. 1954.

123. Gabor, D., "Communication Theory and Physics," *Phil. Mag.*, *41*, 1950, p. 1161.

124. Gabor, D., "Investigations in Communication Theory," *Union Radio Sci. Intern.*, *6*, 1950.

125. Gabor, D., *Lectures on Communication Theory*, published by M.I.T., Cambridge, Mass., 1951.

126. Gabor, D., "New Possibilities in Speech Transmission," *J. Inst. Elec. Engrs. (London)*, *94*, Part III, 1947, p. 369; and *95*, Part III, 1948, pp. 39 and 412.

127. Gabor, D., "Theory of Communication," *J. Inst. Elec. Engrs. (London)*, *93*, Part III, 1946, p. 429.

128. Gallard, J. S., "An Historical and Analytical Bibliography of the Literature of Cryptology," *Northw. Univ. Stud. in the Humanities*, *10*, 1945 (Evanston, Ill.).

129. Gallie, W. B., *Peirce and Pragmatism*, Pelican Books, Ltd., Harmondsworth, England, 1952. An outline of Peirce's scattered work.

130. Gardiner, A., "The Definition of the Word and the Sentence," *Brit. J. Psychol.*, *XII*, Part iv, 1921–1922, pp. 352–361.

131. Gilbert, E. N., "A Comparison of Signalling Alphabets," *Bell System Tech. J.*, *31*, May 1952, p. 504.

132. Glaze, J. A., "The Association Value of Nonsense Syllables," *J. Genet. Psychol.*, *35*, 1928, p. 255. See also Hull.

133. Goldman, S., *Information Theory*, Constable & Co., Ltd., London, 1953.

134. Gombrich, E. H., *The Story of Art*, Phaidon Press, Ltd., London, 1950.

135. Good, I. J., "The Appropriate Mathematical Tools for Describing and Analysing Uncertainty," paper before British Association, 8 Sept. 1953. Also forms Chap. III, pp. 19–34 of *Uncertainty & Business Decisions* (C. F. Carter, G. P. Meredith, and G. L. S. Shackle, Editors) Liverpool University Press, Liverpool, England, 1954.

136. Good, I. J., *Probability and the Weighing of Evidence*, Charles Griffen & Co., Ltd., London, 1950.

137. Good, I. J., "Rational Decisions," *J. Roy. Statist. Soc. (Series B)*, *XIV*, No. 1, 1952, pp. 107–114.

138. Gowers, Sir Ernest, *ABC of Plain Words*, Her Majesty's Stationery Office, London, 1951. A criticism of "business and official" English.

139. Haldane, J. B. S., "Animal Ritual and Human Language," *Diogenes*, *4*, 1953, pp. 3–15.

140. Halle, M., "The Strategy of Phonemics," *Word, 10,* Aug.–Dec. 1954, pp. 197–209.
141. Halsey, R. J., and J. Swaffield, "Analysis-Synthesis Telephony, with Special Reference to the Vocoder," *J. Inst. Elec. Engrs. (London), 95,* Part III, 1948, p. 391.
142. Hamming, R. W., "Error-Detecting and Error-Correcting Codes," *Bell System Tech. J., 29,* 1950, p. 147.
143. Harris, C. M., "A Study of Building Blocks in Speech," *J. Acoust. Soc. Am., 25,* Sept. 1953, p. 962; also "A Speech Synthesiser," p. 970.
144. Harris, Zellig S., *Methods in Structural Linguistics,* University of Chicago Press, Chicago, 1951. See also reviews of this in *Language, 29,* No. 1, Jan.–March 1953.
145. Hartley, R. V. L., "Transmission of Information," *Bell System Tech. J., 7,* 1928, p. 535.
146. Hartree, D. R., *Calculating Instruments and Machines,* University of Illinois Press, Urbana, 1949.
147. Harvard University, "Proceedings of a Symposium on Large-Scale Digital Calculating Machinery," *Ann. Comput. Lab. Harv., 16,* 1948 (Oxford University Press, London). A second symposium was held in 1949, reported in the same *Annals, 26,* 1950.
148. Hass, H., "Über den Einfluss eines Einfachechos auf die Hörsamkeit von Sprache," *Acustica, 1,* 1951, p. 49.
149. Hebb, D. O., *The Organization of Behavior,* John Wiley & Sons, Inc., New York (Chapman & Hall, Ltd., London), 1949.
150. Heise, G. A., and G. A. Miller, "Problem Solving by Small Groups Using Various Communication Nets," *J. Abnormal and Social Psychol., 46,* July 1951, pp. 327–335.
151. Helmholtz, H. L. F., *On the Sensation of Tone* (English translation by A. J. Ellis), Longmans, Green & Co., London and New York, 1875.
152. Herzog, G., "Drum Signalling in a West African Tribe," *Word, I,* No. 3, Dec. 1945, p. 217.
153. Hick, W. E., "On the Rate of Gain of Information," *Quart. J. Exp. Psychol., IV,* 1952, pp. 11–26.
154. Hirsh, I. J., H. Davis, *et al.,* "Development of Material for Speech Audiometry," *J. Speech and Hearing Disorders, 17,* No. 3, Sept. 1952, pp. 321–337.
155. Hockett, C. F., "An Approach to the Quantification of Semantic Noise," *Phil. Sci., 19,* 1952, pp. 257–260.
156. Hogben, L., "Astraglossa," *J. Brit. Interplanetary Soc., 11,* No. 6, Nov. 1952, pp. 258–274.
157. Holbrook, R. T., and F. J. Carmody, "X-ray Studies of Speech Articulations," *Univ. Calif. Publs. in Modern Philology, 20,* No. 4, 1937, p. 230. X-rays for several languages.
158. Horn, W., *Sprachkörper und Sprachfunktion,* Mayer & Muller, Berlin, 1921.
159. Howes, D. H., and R. L. Solomon, "Visual Duration Threshold as a Function of Word Probability," *J. Exp. Psychol., 41,* 1951, pp. 401–410.
160. Huggins, W. H., "System Function Analysis of Speech Sounds," *J. Acoust. Soc. Am., 22,* Nov. 1950, p. 765 (Speech Conference Report).
161. Hull, C. L., "The Meaningfulness of 320 Selected Nonsense Syllables," *Am. J. Psychol., 45,* 1933, pp. 730–734.
162. Hutten, E. H., "The Rôle of Models in Physics," *Brit. J. Phil. Sci., IV,* No. 16, 1954, pp. 284–301.
163. Huxley, J., "Essays of a Biologist," Chatto & Windus, London, 1923 (also Pelican Books, Ltd., Harmondsworth, England).
164. International Phonetic Association, *The Principles of the International Phonetic*

Association, Department of Phonetics, University College, London, 1949. Description of the International Phonetic Alphabet, and of its use.

165. Ishihara, S., *Tests for Colour Blindness*, Karehara, Tokyo, 6th Ed., 1932, H. K. Lewis & Co., Ltd., London, 9th Ed., 1948.

166. Jackson, Willis, Editor, *Proceedings of a Symposium on Applications of Communication Theory*, London, 1952, published by Butterworth Scientific Publications, London, 1953.

167. Jackson, Willis, Editor, *Proceedings of a Symposium on Information Theory*, Royal Society, London, 1950, published by Ministry of Supply, and subsequently by the American Institute of Radio Engineers, Feb. 1953.

168. Jacobson, H., "Information and the Human Ear," *J. Acoust. Soc. Am.*, *23*, July 1951, pp. 463–471.

169. Jacobson, H., "The Informational Capacity of the Human Eye," *Science*, *113*, March 16, 1951, pp. 292–293.

170. Jakobson, R., "Kindersprache, Aphasie und Allgemeine Lautgesetze," *Sprakvetenskapliga Sällskapets i Uppsala Förhandl.*, 1940–1942.

171. Jakobson, R., "Notes on the Correct Presentation of Phonemic Problems," *Symposium*, *V*, No. 2, Nov. 1951 (Department of Romance Languages, Syracuse University, Syracuse, New York).

172. Jakobson, R., "On the Identification of Phonemic Entities," *Trav. cercle linguistique de Copenhague*, *5*, 1949, pp. 205–213.

173. Jakobson, R., *Sound and Meaning*, to be published in this series.

174. Jakobson, R., G. Fant, and M. Halle, "Preliminaries to Speech Analysis," *M.I.T.*, *Acoust. Lab. Rept.*, *13*, 1952.

175. James, H. M., N. B. Nicolls, and R. S. Phillips, *Theory of Servomechanisms*, McGraw-Hill Book Co., Inc., New York, 1947 (Rad. Lab. Series, Vol. 25).

176. James, William, *Principles of Psychology*, 2 Vols., Macmillan & Co., Ltd., London, 1890.

177. Jeans, J., *Science and Music*, Cambridge University Press, London, 1937.

178. Jeffress, L. A., Editor, *Cerebral Mechanisms in Behavior*, The Hixon Symposium, John Wiley & Sons, Inc., New York (Chapman & Hall, Ltd., London), 1951.

179. Jones, D., *An Outline of English Phonetics*, W. Heffer & Sons, Ltd., Cambridge, 1950.

180. Jones, D., *The Phoneme: Its Nature and Use*, W. Heffer & Sons, Ltd., Cambridge, England, 1950.

181. Jones, D., *The Pronunciation of English*, Cambridge University Press, London, 3rd Ed., 1950.

182. Joos, M., "Acoustic Phonetics," Supplement to *Language* (Monograph No. 23), *24*, No. 2, April–June 1948.

183. Joos, M., "Description of Language Design," *J. Acoust. Soc. Am.*, *22*, No. 6, 1950, pp. 701–709 (Proceedings of the Speech Conference at M.I.T.).

184. Kaeding, F. W., *Häufigkeitswörterbuch der Deutschen Sprache*, Berlin, 1898. Statistical count involving eleven million running words of German.

185. Kay, H., and E. C. Poulton, "Anticipation in Memorizing," *Brit. J. Psychol.* (*Genet. Sect.*), *42*, Parts 1 and 2, March, May 1951, pp. 34–41.

186. Keller, H., *The Story of My Life*, Hodder & Stoughton, London, reprinted 1945.

187. von Kempelen, Baron Wolfgang, *Mechanism de la parole suivit d'une description de la machine parlante* 1791 (British Museum Shelf Mark 7610 b. 32). Simultaneously published in German. For modern account of this historic work, see under Dudley and Tarnoczy. See also Philips, *Tech. Rev.*, *25*, 1963/4, page 48.

188. Kendall, M. G., *The Source and Nature of the Statistics of the United Kingdom*, Royal Statistical Society, Oliver & Boyd, Ltd., London, 1952.

189. Keynes, J. M., *A General Theory of Employment, Interest and Money*, Harcourt, Brace & Co., Inc., New York, 1936, 1949.

190. Keynes, J. M., *A Treatise on Probability*, Macmillan & Co., Ltd., London, 1921.

191. Klemmer, E. T., and P. F. Muller, Jr., "The Rate of Handling Information— Key-Pressing Responses to Light Patterns," *Human Factors Oper. Research Lab. Memo Report, 34*, March 1953, unclassified (Air Research and Development Commission, Bolling Air Force Base, Washington 25, D. C.).

192. Koenig, W., H. K. Dunn, and L. Y. Lacy, "The Sound Spectrograph," *J. Acoust. Soc. Am., 18, 19*, July 1946.

193. Kolmogoroff, A., "Interpolation und Extrapolation von stationärem zufälligen Folgen," *Bull. acad. sci. U. S. S. R. ser. math., 5*, 1942, pp. 3–14.

194. Kris, E., *Psychoanalytic Explorations in Art*, International Universities Press, Inc., New York, 1952. See Chapter 7, "The Principles of Caricature."

195. Küpfmüller, K., "Über Einschwingvorgänge in Wellenfiltern," *Elek. Nachr-Tech., 1*, 1924, p. 141. The bandwidth × time uncertainty.

196. Lazarsfeld, P. F., "Communication Research and the Social Psychologist," in *Current Trends in Social Psychology*, W. Dennis, Editor, University of Pittsburgh Press, Pittsburgh, 1948.

197. Lee, B. S., "Effects of Delayed Speech Feedback," *J. Acoust. Soc. Am., 22*, No. 6, Nov. 1950, pp. 824–826; see also earlier paper in *22*, No. 5, 1950, p. 639.

198. Lévi-Strauss, C., "Language and the Analysis of Social Laws," *Am. Anthrop., 53*, No. 2, April–June 1951.

199. Lévi-Strauss, C., *Race and History*, Unesco, Paris, 1952.

200. Lévi-Strauss, C., "Social Structure," in *Anthropology Today*, A. L. Kroeber, Editor, University of Chicago Press, Chicago, 1952.

201. Lewin, K., *Principles of Topological Psychology*, McGraw-Hill Book Co., Inc., New York, 1936.

202. Liberman, A. M., P. Delattre, and F. S. Cooper, "The Role of the Selected Stimulus Variables in the Perception of the Unvoiced Stop Consonants," *Am. J. Psychol., 65*, 1952, pp. 497–516.

203. Licklider, J. C. R., "Basic Correlates of the Auditory Stimulus," in *Handbook of Experimental Psychology*, S. S. Stevens, Editor, John Wiley & Sons, Inc., New York, 1951.

204. Licklider, J. C. R., "The Intelligibility of Amplitude-Dichotomized, Time-Quantized Speech Waves," *J. Acoust. Soc. Am., 22*, Nov. 1950, pp. 820–823.

205. Licklider, J. C. R., D. Bindra, and I. Pollack, "The Intelligibility of Rectangular Speech Waves, *Am. J. Psychol., 61*, No. 1, Jan. 1948, pp. 1–20.

206. Littlewood, J. E., *A Mathematician's Miscellany*, Methuen & Co., Ltd., London, 1953.

207. Locke, John, *An Essay Concerning Human Understanding*, 1689. Numerous editions; e.g., Ward, Locke and Bowden, Ltd., London.

208. Locke, W. N., and A. D. Booth, *Machine Translation of Language*, The Technology Press, M.I.T., and John Wiley & Sons, Inc., New York, 1955.

209. Lorenz, K. Z., *King Solomon's Ring*, Methuen & Co., Ltd., London, 1952. A delightful "popular" study of animal behavior.

210. Lorge, I., *The English Semantic Count*, New York Institute of Psychological Research, Teachers College, Columbia University Press, New York, 1949.

211. Luce, R. D., "Connectivity and Generalised Cliques in Sociometric Group Structures," *Psychometrika, 15*, No. 2, June 1950.

212. Luce, R. D., "A Survey of the Theory of Selective Information and Some of its Behavioural Applications," *Bur. Appl. Social Research Tech. Rept., 8,* p. 140 (Columbia University, New York).

213. Luce, R. D., and A. D. Perry, "A Method of Matrix Analysis of Group Structure," *Psychometrika, 14,* No. 1, March 1949, pp. 95–116.

214. Luckiesh, M., and F. K. Moss, *The Science of Seeing,* D. van Nostrand Co., Inc., New York, 1937.

215. Macdonald, D. K. C., "Information Theory and its Application to Taxonomy," *J. Appl. Phys., 23,* May 1952, p. 529.

216. MacKay, D. M., "Mentality in Machines," *Proc. Aristotelian Soc. Suppl.,* 1952, p. 61.

217. MacKay, D. M., "Mind-like Behaviour in Artefacts," *Brit. J. Phil. Sci., II,* No. 6, 1951, pp. 105–121.

218. MacKay, D. M., "Quantal Aspects of Scientific Information," *Phil. Mag., 41,* 1950, p. 289.

219. MacKay, D. M., "Operational Aspects of some Fundamental Concepts of Human Communication," *Synthese, IX,* Issue 3, Nos. 3–5, pp. 182–198 (F. G. Kroonder, Bussum, Netherlands).

220. Macmillan, R. H., *An Introduction to the Theory of Control,* Cambridge University Press, London, 1951.

221. Mandelbrot, B., "Contribution à la théorie mathématique des jeux de communication," *Publ. Inst. Statist., 2,* 1953, p. 1 (University of Paris).

222. Mandelbrot, B., "An Informational Theory of the Structure of Language Based upon the Theory of the Statistical Matching of Messages and Coding," Proceedings of the London Symposium, 1952; see also in reference 166.

223. Mandelbrot, B., "Statistical Mechanics and the Theory of Information" (in French), *Compt. Rend., 232,* 1951, pp. 1638 and 2003.

224. Mandelbrot, B., "Structure formelle des textes et communication," *Word, 10,* No. 1, April 1954, pp. 1–27.

225. Markoff, A. A., "Essai d'une recherche statistique sur le texte du roman 'Eugene Onegin' . . . ," *Bull. Acad. Imper. Sci. St. Petersbourg, VII,* 1913.

226. Martin, W. H., "Rating the Transmission Performance of Telephone Circuits," *Bell System Tech. J., 10,* 1931, pp. 116–131.

227. McCallum, D. M., and J. B. Smith, "Mechanised Reasoning: Logical Computors and Their Design," *Electronic Eng.,* April 1951.

228. McCulloch, W. S., "The Brain as a Computing Machine," *Electronic Eng.,* June 1949.

229. McCulloch, W. S., and W. Pitts, "A Logical Calculus of the Ideas Immanent in Nervous Activity," *Bull. Math. Biophys., 5,* 1943, p. 115, and *9,* 1947, p. 127; also in Warren S. McCulloch, *Embodiments of Mind,* M.I.T. Press, Cambridge, Mass., 1965, p. 19.

230. McDougall, W., *The Group Mind,* Cambridge University Press, London, 1927.

231. McDougall, W., *An Introduction to Social Psychology,* Methuen & Co., Ltd., London, 1st Ed., 1908.

232. McKown, F. W., and J. W. Emling, "A System of Effective Transmission Data for Rating Telephone Circuits," *Bell System Tech. J., 12,* 1933, pp. 331–346.

233. McMillan, B., "The Basic Theorems of Information Theory," *Ann. Math. Statist., 24,* No. 2, June 1953.

234. Mertz, P., and F. Gray, "A Theory of Scanning and its Relation to the Characteristics of the Transmitted Signal in Telephotography and Television," *Bell System Tech. J., 13,* July 1934, pp. 464–515.

235. Miller, G. A., *Language and Communication*, McGraw-Hill Book Co., Inc., New York, 1951.

236. Miller, G. A., J. S. Bruner, and L. Postman, "Familiarity of Letter Sequences and Tachistoscopic Identification," *J. Genet. Psychol.*, *50*, 1954, pp. 129–139.

237. Miller, G. A., G. A. Heise, and W. Lichten, "Intelligibility of Speech as a Function of the Context of the Test Materials," *J. Exp. Psychol.*, *41*, No. 5, May 1951, pp. 329–335.

238. Miller, G. A., and J. C. R. Licklider, "The Intelligibility of Interrupted Speech," *J. Acoust. Soc. Am.*, *22*, 1950, pp. 167–173.   Includes a good list of references.

239. Miller, G. A., and J. A. Selfridge, "Verbal Context and the Recall of Meaningful Material," *Am. J. Psychol.*, *63*, April 1950, pp. 176–185.

240. Miller, N. E., and J. Dollard, *Social Learning and Imitation*, Institute of Human Relations, Yale University, New Haven, 1941.   See especially Appendix 2.

241. Monboddo, Lord (James Burnett), *Of the Origin and Progress of Language*, 6 Vols., Edinburgh, 1773–1792.   Of historical interest.

242. Moore, P., "Motion Picture Studies of the Vocal Folds and Vocal Attack," *J. Speech Disorders*, *3*, 1938, p. 235.

243. Morris, C. W., "Foundations of the Theory of Signs," *International Encyclopedia of Unified Science Series*, Vol. I, No. 2, University of Chicago Press, Chicago, 1938. A brief introduction.

244. Morris, C. W., "*Signs, Language and Behavior*," Prentice-Hall, Inc., New York, 1946.

245. Morse, P. M., and G. E. Kimball, *Methods of Operations Research*, John Wiley & Sons, Inc., New York, 1951.

246. Mumford, Lewis, *Technics and Civilisation*, George Routledge & Sons, Ltd., London, 1946.

247. von Neumann, J., and O. Morgenstern, *Theory of Games and Economic Behavior*, Princeton University Press, Princeton, 1947.

248. Nyquist, H., "Certain Factors Affecting Telegraph Speed," *Bell System Tech. J.*, *3*, 1924, p. 324.

249. Ogden, C. K., *The System of Basic English*, Harcourt, Brace & Co., Inc., New York, 1934.

250. Ogden, C. K., and I. A. Richards, *The Meaning of Meaning*, Routledge & Kegan Paul, Ltd., London, 1949 (1st Ed., 1923).

251. Oldfield, R. C., and O. L. Zangwill, "The Acquisition of Verbal Repetition Habits," *Brit. J. Psychol.* (*Genet. Sect.*), *29*, Part 1, July 1938, pp. 12–26.

252. Oliver, B. M., J. R. Pierce, and C. E. Shannon, "The Philosophy of P.C.M.," *Proc. I.R.E.*, *36*, 1948, pp. 1324–1331.

253. Oswald, V. A., and S. L. Fletcher, "Proposals for the Mechanical Resolution of German Syntax Patterns," *Modern Lang. Forum* (*U.S.A.*), *36*, Nos. 3–4, 1951.

254. Paget, Sir Richard, *Human Speech*, Kegan Paul, Trench, Trubner, & Co., Ltd., London, 1930.

255. Palmer, L. R., *Introduction to Modern Linguistics*, Macmillan & Co., Ltd., London, 1936.

256. Parsons, T., and E. A. Shils, Editors, *Toward a General Theory of Action*, Harvard University Press, Cambridge, Mass., 1951.   See Article by R. C. Sheldon, "Some Observations on Theory in Social Science," p. 30.

257. Partridge, E., *A Dictionary of Clichés*, Routledge & Kegan Paul, Ltd., London, 4th Ed., 1948.

258. Peirce, C. S., *Collec ed Papers of Charles Sanders Peirce*, 6 Vols., C. Hartshorne and P. Weiss, Editors Harvard University Press, Cambridge, Mass., 1931–1935.

Peirce's works are extensive and the reader is referred to an excellent review and account, in one most readable volume, by W. B. Gallie.

259. Penrose, L. S., *On the Objective Study of Crowd Behaviour*, H. K. Lewis & Co., Ltd., London, 1952.

260. Pike, K. L., *Intonation of American English*, University of Michigan Press, Ann Arbor, 1947.

261. Pike, K. L., *Language*, Part 1, Summer Institute of Linguistics, Glendale, California, 1954.

262. Pike, K. L., *Phonemics*, University of Michigan Press, Ann Arbor, 1947.

263. Pike, K. L., *Phonetics*, University of Michigan Press, Ann Arbor (Oxford University Press, London), 1943.

264. Pitts, W., and W. S. McCulloch, "How We Know Universals, the Perception of Auditory and Visual Form," *Bull. Math. Biophys.*, 9, 1947, p. 127.

265. Pledge, H. T., *Science Since 1500*, Her Majesty's Stationery Office, London, 1939.

266. Poincaré, Henri, *Science and Hypothesis* (in English), The Walter Scott Publishing Co., Ltd., London and New York, 1905.

267. Popper, K. R., *Language and the Body-Mind Problem*, Proceedings of the XIth International Congress Philosophy, North-Holland Publishing Co., Amsterdam, 1953.

268. Postman, L., J. S. Bruner, and R. D. Walk, "The Perception of Error," *Brit. J. Psychol.* (*Genet. Sect.*), 42, Parts 1 and 2, March, May 1951, pp. 1–10.

269. Postman, L., and W. O. Jenkins, "An Experimental Analysis of Set in Rote Learning: the Interaction of Learning Instruction and Retention Performance," *J. Exp. Psychol.*, 38, 1948, pp. 683–689.

270. Potter, R. K., "Objectives for Sound Portrayal," *J. Acoust. Soc. Am.*, 21, Jan. 1949, p. 1.

271. Potter, R. K., G. A. Kopp, and H. C. Green, *Visible Speech*, D. van Nostrand Co., Inc., New York, 1947.

272. Potter, R. K., and J. C. Steinberg, "Toward the Specification of Speech," *J. Acoust. Soc. Am.*, 22, No. 6, 1950, pp. 807–820.

273. Pratt, F., *Secret and Urgent*, The Bobbs-Merrill Co., Indianapolis, Ind., 1939 (Blue Ribbon Books). Frequencies of letters, digrams, trigrams.

274. Rattray, R. S., *Ashanti*, Oxford University Press, London, 1923. For Congo drum language.

275. Rayleigh, Lord, *Theory of Sound*, Macmillan & Co., Ltd., London, 1896.

276. Rees, M., "Digital Computors—their Nature and Use," *Am. Scientist*, 40, No. 2, April 1952.

277. Rice, S. O., "Communication in the Presence of Noise—Probability of Error for Two Encoding Schemes," *Bell System Tech. J.*, 29, 1950, p. 60.

278. Rice, S. O., "Mathematical Analysis of Random Noise," *Bell System Tech. J.*, 23, 1944, p. 282, and 24, 1945, p. 46.

279. Richards, I. A., "Toward a Theory of Translating" (an essay in the volume *Studies in Chinese Thought*, A. F. Wright, Editor), *Am. Anthrop. Assoc.*, 55, Memoir 75, Dec. 1953.

280. Riesen, A. H., "The Development of Visual Perception in Man and Chimpanzee," *Science*, 106, 1947, p. 107.

281. Rignano, E., *Man Not a Machine*, Paul, Trench & Trubner Co., Ltd., London, 1926.

282. Russell, G. O., *Speech and Voice*, The Macmillan Co., New York, 1931. X-ray pictures of vowel formation; diagrams of oral musculature.

283. Russell, G. O., *The Vowel*, Ohio State University Press, Columbus, 1928. X-ray pictures of vowel formation.

322 REFERENCES

284. Ryle, G., *The Concept of Mind*, Hutchinson's University Library, London, 1949.
285. Sapir, E., *Language*, Harcourt, Brace & Co., Inc., New York, 1939.
286. de Saussure, F., *Cours de linguistique générale*, published by C. Bally and A. Sachehaye, with collaboration of de A. Reidlinger, Paris, 1949.
287. Schatz, C. D., "The Role of Context in the Perception of Stops," *Language, 30*, No. 1, Part 1, Jan.–March 1954, p. 47.
288. Schott, L. O., "A Playback for Visible Speech," *Bell Labs. Record, 26*, Aug. 1948, pp. 333–339.
289. Schrödinger, E., *What Is Life?* Cambridge University Press, London, 1944.
290. Scripture, E. W., *Experimental Phonetics*, Charles Scribner's Sons, New York, 1902. Excellent historical survey of work up to 1902.
291. Senden, M. von, *Raum- und Gestaltauffassung bei operierten Blindgeborenen vor und nach der Operation*, Barth, Leipzig, 1932. An account of a series of case histories.
292. Shannon, C. E., "Communication in the Presence of Noise," *Proc. I.R.E., 37*, 1949. p. 10.
293. Shannon, C. E., "Communication Theory of Secrecy Systems," *Bell System Tech. J., 28*, 1949, p. 656.
294. Shannon, C. E., "Prediction and Entropy of Printed English," *Bell System Tech. J., 30*, 1951, pp. 50–64.
295. Shannon, C. E., "Programming a Computor for Playing Chess," *Phil. Mag., 41*, 1950, p. 256.
296. Shannon, C. E., "Recent Developments in Communication Theory," *Electronics, 23*, April 1950, pp. 80–84.
297. Shannon, C. E., and W. Weaver, *The Mathematical Theory of Communication*, University of Illinois Press, Urbana, 1949; published earlier in *Bell System Tech. J., 27*, 1948, pp. 379 and 623.
298. Shaw, A. G., *The Purpose and Practice of Motion Study*, Harlequin Press Co., Ltd., Manchester, England, 1952.
299. Shortley, G., Editor, *J. Oper. Research Soc. Am.* (Operations Research Office, 7100 Connecticut Avenue, Chevy Chase, Maryland).
300. Shower, E. G., and R. Biddulph, "Differential Pitch Sensitivity of the Ear," *J. Acoust. Soc. Am., 3*, 1931, p. 275.
301. Significs Conference (Amersfoort, Holland, 1953), Symposium on "Semantic and Signific Aspects of Modern Theories of Communication," papers published in *Synthese, IX*, Issue 3, Nos. 3–5 (F. G. Kroonder, Bussum, Netherlands).
302. Siipola, E. M., "A Group Study of Some Effects of Preparatory Set," *Psychol. Monographs, 46*, No. 6, 1935.
303. Simon, H. A., *Administrative Behavior: A Study of Decision-Making Processes in Administrative Organization*, The Macmillan Co., New York, 1947.
304. Skinner, B. F., *The Behaviour of Organisms*, Appleton-Century Co., London, New York, 1938 (Century Psychological Series).
305. Slattery, T. G., "The Detection of a Sine Wave in the Presence of Noise by the Use of Non-Linear Filter," *Proc. I.R.E., 40*, Oct. 1952, pp. 1232–1236.
306. Speech Spectrographs, collection of papers in *J. Acoust. Soc. Am., 18*, July–Oct. 1946.
307. Spencer, Herbert, *The Principles of Sociology*, Vol. I, Part II, Williams & Norgate, Ltd., London, 1877. Mainly of historical interest.
308. Sperry, R. W., "Neurology and the Mind-Brain Problem," *Am. Scientist, 40*, No. 2, April 1952, pp. 291–312.
309. Stebbing, Susan, *Thinking to Some Purpose*, Pelican Books, Ltd., Harmondsworth, England, and New York, 1941.

310. Stetson, R. H., *Motor Phonetics*, North-Holland Publishing Co., Amsterdam, 2nd Ed., 1951.

311. Stevens, K. N., F. Kasowski, and G. M. Fant, "An Electrical Analogue of the Vocal Tract, *J. Acoust. Soc. Am.*, *25*, July 1953, pp. 734–742.

312. Stevens, S. S., "Articulation Testing Methods," *O. S. R. D. Rept.*, *383*, 1942 (Psycho-Acoustics Laboratory, Harvard University, Cambridge, Mass.); *U.S. Dept. of Commerce Publ. Board Rept., 22916.*

313. Stevens, S. S., "Introduction: A Definition of Communication" (in Proceedings of the Speech Communication Conference at M.I.T.), *J. Acoust. Soc. Am.*, *22*, No. 6, Nov. 1950, pp. 689–690.

314. Stevens, S. S., "Psychology and the Science of Science," *Pyschol. Bull.*, *36*, April 1939.

315. Stevens, S. S., Editor, *Handbook of Experimental Psychology*, John Wiley & Sons, Inc., New York, 1951.

316. Stevens, S. S., and H. Davis, *Hearing—Its Psychology and Physiology*, John Wiley & Sons, Inc., New York, 1938.

317. Straus, O., "Relation of Phonetics and Linguistics to Communication Theory," *J. Acoust. Soc. Am.*, *22*, No. 6, Nov. 1950, pp. 709–711.

318. Szilard, L., "Über die Entropieverminderung in einem Thermodynamischen System bei Eingriffen Intelligenter Wesen," *Z. Physik*, *53*, 1929, p. 840.

319. Thompson, D'Arcy, *On Growth and Form*, Cambridge University Press, London (1917), 1942. Mathematical study of form of organisms.

320. Thorndike, E. L., and I. Lorge, *The Teacher's Word Book of 30,000 Words*, Bureau of Publications, Columbia University Press, New York, 1944. Frequencies of English lexical units.

321. Thouless, R. H., *Straight and Crooked Thinking*, Hodder & Stoughton, Ltd., London, 1930; also Pan Books, Ltd., London, 1953. "A practical book for the man in the street."

322. Tinbergen, J., *Business Cycles in the United Kingdom, 1870–1914*, North-Holland Publishing Co., Amsterdam, 1951. For graphs of "business cycles."

323. Tinbergen, J., and J. J. Polak, *The Dynamics of Business Cycles*, Routledge & Kegan Paul, Ltd., London, 1950.

324. Tinbergen, N., *Social Behaviour in Animals*, Methuen & Co., Ltd., London, 1953 (Methuen Biological Monographs).

325. Tolman, R. C., *Principles of Statistical Mechanics*, Clarendon Press, Oxford, 1938.

326. Toynbee, A. J., *A Study of History*, Oxford University Press, London, 1946.

327. Trubetzkoy, N. S., *Principes de Phonologie*, Paris, 1949 (University of Algiers).

328. Tuller, W. G., "Theoretical Limits on the Rate of Transmission of Information," *Proc. I.R.E.*, *37*, 1949, p. 468.

329. Turing, A. M., "Computing Machinery and Intelligence," *Mind*, *59*, 1950, p. 433.

330. Turing, A. M., "On Computable Numbers, with an Application to the Entscheidungs Problem," *Proc. London Math. Soc.* (Series 2), *24*, 1936, pp. 230–265.

331. Tustin, A., "Do Modern Mechanisms Help Us to Understand the Mind?" *Brit. J. Psychol. (Genet. Sect.)*, *XLIV*, Part I, Feb. 1953.

332. Tustin, A., *The Mechanism of Economics*, Wm. Heinemann, Ltd., London, 1954.

333. Tustin, A., "A Method of Analysing the Behaviour of Linear Systems in Terms of Time-Series," *J. Inst. Elec. Engrs. (London)*, *94*, 1947, Part II, A, p. 130.

334. Tustin, A., Editor, *Department of Scientific & Industrial Research, Cranfield Conference on Automatic Control, Proceedings*, published by Butterworth Scientific Publications, London, 1951.

335. Twaddell, W. F., "On Defining the Phoneme," *Lang. Monographs, 16,* 1935 (Linguistic Society of America, Baltimore).

336. University College (London), Communication Research Centre, *Studies in Communication,* Martin Secker & Warburg, Ltd., London, 1955. This volume covers a wide range of communication topics. See reference 60.

337. Uttley, A. M., "The Classification of Signals in the Nervous System," *Radar Research Establishment Memorandum, 1047* (Great Malvern, England); also published in *Elec. Enceph. J., 6,* 1954, p. 479.

338. Uttley, A. M., "The Probability of Neural Connections," *Radar Research Establishment Memorandum, 1048,* 1954 (Great Malvern, England).

339. Ville, J. A., "Théorie et applications de la notion de signal analytique," *Câbles et Transmission, 2,* 1948, p. 61.

340. Walter, G., "The Functions of Electrical Rhythms in the Brain," *J. Mental Sci., 96,* 1950, p. 1 (24th Maudsley Lecture).

341. Walter, G., *The Living Brain,* Gerald Duckworth & Co., Ltd., London, 1953.

342. Wegel, R. L., "Theory of Vibration of the Larynx," *Bell System Tech. J., IX,* Jan. 1930, pp. 209–227. With excellent picture of larynx, windpipe, and vocal folds.

343. Weston, J. D., "A Note on the Theory of Communication," *Phil. Mag., 40,* 1949, p. 449.

344. Whatmough, J., An extensive critical bibliography of language studies, including many statistical analyses, published by Comité International Permanent de Linguistes, Harvard University Press, Cambridge, Mass., 1954.

345. Wheatstone, C., "Talking Machines, etc.," *London & Westminster Rev., 28,* Oct. 1837, p. 27, British Museum Shelf Mark RPP59871. A review article of the following papers: (1) R. Willis, "On the Vowel Sounds, and on Reed Organ Pipes" (1829); (2) M. de Kempelen, "Le Méchanisme de la Parole, suivi de la Description d'une Machine Parlante" (1791); and (3) G. G. Kratzenstein, "Tentamen Coronatum de Voce" (1780). This forms a review of talking machines from the Greek Oracles to the nineteenth century.

346. Whitehead, A. N., *Science and the Modern World,* Lowell Lectures, Cambridge, 1952; also published by Pelican Books, Ltd., Harmondsworth, England.

347. Whittaker, J. M., *Interpolatory Function Theory,* Cambridge University Press, London, 1915 (Cambridge Mathematical Monographs).

348. Whyte, L. L., Editor, *Aspects of Form,* A Symposium on Form in Nature and Art, Percy Lund Humphries & Co., Ltd., London, 1951. A series of illustrated papers, discussing various interpretations of the concept of *form* in both science and art. With very extensive bibliography.

349. Wiener, N., *Cybernetics,* The Technology Press of M.I.T. and John Wiley & Sons, Inc., New York, 1948. 2nd Ed., M.I.T. Press, Cambridge, Mass., 1961.

350. Wiener, N., *The Extrapolation, Interpolation, and Smoothing of Stationary Time Series,* The Technology Press of M.I.T. and John Wiley & Sons., Inc., New York, 1949.

351. Wilkins, M. C., "A Tachistoscopic Experiment in Reading," Master's Thesis, Columbia University, New York, 1917.

352. Williams, C. B., "The Statistical Outlook in Relation to Ecology," *J. Ecology, 42,* No. 1, Jan. 1954. Includes long list of other studies of the "logarithmic law" of biology—including language statistics.

353. Williams, C. B., "A Note on the Statistical Analysis of Sentence-Length as a Criterion of Literary Style," *Biometrika, XXXI,* Parts III and IV, March 1940.

354. Williams, J. D., *The Compleat Strategyst,* McGraw-Hill Book Co., Inc., New York, 1954.

355. Wittgenstein, L., *Philosophical Investigations*, The Macmillan Co., New York (Basil Blackwell & Mott, Ltd., Oxford), 1953.

356. Wittgenstein, L., *Tractatus Logico-Philosophicus*, Kegan Paul, Ltd., London, 1922.

357. Wolfe, J. M., *A First Course in Cryptanalysis*, Brooklyn College Press, New York, 1943.

358. Wood, A., *Acoustics*, Blackie & Son, Ltd., London, 1940.

359. Wood, A. B., *A Textbook of Sound*, George Bell & Sons, Ltd., London, 1930.

360. Woodward, P. M., *Probability and Information Theory, with Applications to Radar*, Pergamon Press, Ltd., London, 1953.

361. Woodward, P. M., and I. L. Davies, "Information Theory and Inverse Probability in Telecommunication," *Proc. Inst. Elec. Engrs. (London) 99*, Part III, March 1952, p. 37.

362. Woodward, P. M., and I. L. Davies, "A Theory of Radar Information," *Phil. Mag. (Series 7)*, xli, Oct. 1950, p. 1001.

363. Yngve, V. H., "The Machine and the Man," *Mech. Translation, 1*, Aug. 1954, pp. 20–22 (M.I.T., Cambridge, Mass.).

364. Young, J. Z., *Doubt and Certainty in Science*, Reith Lectures, Oxford University Press, London, 1951.

365. Yule, G. U., *The Statistical Study of Literary Vocabulary*, Cambridge University Press, London, 1944.

366. Zangwill, O. L., "A Study of the Significance of Attitude in Recognition," *Brit. J. Psychol., 28*, 1937, pp. 12–17.

367. Zipf, G. K., *Human Behavior and the Principle of Least Effort*, Addison-Wesley Publishing Co., Inc., Cambridge, Mass., 1949. Includes a good bibliography of statistical data.

ADDITIONAL REFERENCES FOR SECOND EDITION.

368. Acoustics. The International Congress on Acoustics, which meets every 3 years, is sponsored by the International Union of Pure and Applied Physics, which itself comes under Unesco. The papers from the First Congress, held in Delft, The Netherlands, in 1953, were published in *Acustica, 4*, Part 1, 1954; for the Second Congress in Cambridge, Mass., 1956, in *J. Acoust. Soc. Am.* during 1957; for the Third Congress in Stuttgart, Germany, 1959, in book form, by Elsevir, the Netherlands, 1961; for the Fourth Congress, in Copenhagen, Denmark, in 1962, in 2 vols., by the Technical University of Denmark.

369. Bailey, D., *Essays in Rhetoric*, Oxford University Press, London, 1965. This includes examples from Aristotle, Socrates, Plato, Cicero, Richards, Lewis, and others, to modern times.

370. Brillouin, L., *Science and Information Theory*, Academic Press, Inc., New York, 1956.

371. Broadbent, D. E., *Perception and Communication*, Pergamon Press, London and New York, 1958.

372. Chapuis, R., "Work of the Plan Committee in the Intercontinental Sphere," Rome, December 1963, *Telecommunication Journal 31*, No. 4, April 1964, p. 98.

373. Cherrill, F. R., *The Fingerprint System at Scotland Yard*, Her Majesty's Stationery Office, London, 1954.

374. Cherry, Colin, Ed., *Information Theory: Proceedings of the 3rd London Symposium*, Butterworths, London, 1955. (See also references 166 and 167.)

375. Cherry, Colin, Ed., *Information Theory: Proceedings of the 4th London Symposium*, Butterworths, London, 1961. (See also references 166 and 167.)

376. Cherry, Colin, "On Communication before the Days of Radio," *Proc. Inst. Radio Engrs., Jubilee Issue, 50*, March 1962, p. 1143.

377. Cherry, Colin, "The Cocktail Party Problem," *Discovery*, March 1962, p. 32 (a popular exposition).

378. Cherry, Colin, and B. Mc. A. Sayers, "Experiments upon the Total Inhibition of Stammering by External Control and Some Clinical Results," *J. Psychosomatic Res. 1*, 1956, p. 233.

379. Cherry, Colin, and B. Mc. A. Sayers, "On the Mechanism of Binaural Fusion," *J. Acoust. Soc. Am. 31*, April 1959, p. 535.

380. Davitz, J. R., Ed., *The Communication of Emotional Meaning*, McGraw-Hill, New York and London, 1964. (Facial expressions, personality, metaphor, ear/eye substitutes for the blind, etc.)

381. Fano, R. M., *Transmission of Information*, M.I.T. Press and John Wiley & Sons, Inc., New York and London, 1961.

382. Fant, G., *Acoustic Theory of Speech Production*, Mouton, Netherlands, 1960.

383. Fant, G., "Acoustic Analysis and Synthesis of Speech with Applications to Swedish," *Ericsson Technics*, No. 1, 1959. This contains an extensive bibliography on artificial vocal tract studies.

384. Flanagan, J. L., *Speech Analysis, Synthesis and Perception*, Springer-Verlag, Berlin, 1965.

385. Freudental, H., *LINCOS: Design of a Language for Cosmic Intercourse*, North-Holland Publishing Co., Amsterdam, 1960.

386. Gabor, Dennis, *Inventing the Future*, Secker and Warburg, London 1963.

387. Gallager, R. G., *Low-Density Parity-Check Codes*, M.I.T. Press, Cambridge, Mass., 1963.

388. Gombrich, E. H., *Meditations on a Hobby Horse—and Other Essays on the Theory of Art*, Phaidon Press, London, 1963.

389. Good, I. J., Ed., *The Scientist Speculates—an Anthology of Partly-baked Ideas*, Heinemann, London, 1962.

390. Goodman, R., Ed., *Annual Review in Automatic Programming*, Pergamon Press, Oxford and New York, annual vols. from 1960. These reviews are prepared at the Brighton College of Technology, U.K., and cover all forms of computer "language."

391. James, William, *Pragmatism*, Meridian Books, World Publishing Co., Cleveland and New York, 1955. This is a reprint of James' 1907 lectures together with four essays from *The Meaning of Truth*, 1909.

392. Koch, S., Ed., *Psychology: a Study of a Science*, McGraw-Hill, New York, 1959.

393. Langer, Suzanne K., *Philosophy in a New Key: a Study in the Symbolism of Reason, Rite, and Art*, 3rd Ed., Harvard University Press, Cambridge, Mass, 1957.

394. Miller, G. A., "Computers, Communication, and Cognition," *The Brit. Assoc. Adv. Sci., 21*, No. 93, January 1965, p. 417.

395. Minski, M., "A Selector Descriptor: Indexed Bibliography to the Literature on Artificial Intelligence," *I.R.E. Transactions on Human Factors in Electronics*, 1961, p. 39. (A list of 600 references concerning computers, "cybernetics," nervous system studies, automata, behavior studies, etc.).

396. Mumford, Sir Albert, "Communications in the Public Service of the United Kingdom," *J. Inst. Elec. Engrs. (London), 9*, November 1963, p. 460.

397. Quastler, H., *Information Theory in Psychology*, The Free Press, Glencoe, Ill., 1955. (The Proceedings of the Monticello Conference, July 1954.)

398. Quine, W. van O., *Word and Object*, M.I.T. Press and John Wiley & Sons, Inc., New York and London, 1960.

399. Reusch, J., and W. Kees, *Non-Verbal Communication*, University of California Press, Berkeley and Los Angeles, 1964.

400. Rosenblith, W. A., Ed., *Sensory Communication: Symposium on Principles of Sensory Communication*, Endicott House, Mass. Inst. Tech., 1959, M.I.T. Press and John Wiley & Sons, Inc., New York and London, 1961.

401. Sapir, E., "Communication," *Encyclopædia of the Social Sciences*, Macmillan Co., New York, 1933, Vol. 4.

402. Schrödinger, Erwin, *My View of the World*, Cambridge University Press, London, 1964.

403. Sheastley, P. B., and J. J. Feldman, "The Assassination of President Kennedy," *Public Opinion Quarterly, 28*, No. 2, Summer 1964, p. 189.

404. Sondel, Bess, *The Humanity of Words*, World Publishing Co., Cleveland and New York, 1958.

405. Stathan, Commander E. P., "*Wireless Telegraphy on Board the Europa*," *The Navy and Army Illustrated*, August 26, 1899, London.

406. *Speech Communication Seminar*, Royal Inst. of Tech., Stockholm, 1962.

407. Swets, J. A., Ed., *Signal Detection and Recognition by Human Observers*, John Wiley & Sons, Inc., New York and London, 1964.

408. Uttley, A. M., "The Conditional Probability of Signals in the Nervous System," *Radar Research Establishment Memo. No. 1109*, Great Malvern, Britain, 1955.

409. Whatmough, J., *Language: a Modern Synthesis*, Secker and Warburg, London, 1956.

410. Winograd, S., and J. D. Cowan, *Reliable Communication in the Presence of Noise*, M.I.T. Press, Cambridge, Mass., 1963. (Automata theory.)

411. Youden, W. W., Ed., *Computer Literature Bibliography: 1946–63*, U.S. Department of Commerce, Nat. Bureau Stand. Misc. Pub. 266, March 31, 1965. (An exhaustive bibliography of 6100 references covering all aspects of computer work.)

Index

329